Minnesota Mediterran… European
Monographs

PERMANENT REVOLUTION

A Study of the Early Soviet State

Elizabeth A. Harry

A *Modern Greek Studies Yearbook* Supplement

UNIVERSITY OF MINNESOTA

MINNEAPOLIS, MINNESOTA

Number 22 2018

Minnesota Mediterranean and East European Monographs (MMEEM)

The objective of the MMEEM is the dissemination of scholarly information about the Mediterranean and East European region. The field is broadly defined to include the social sciences and the humanities. Even though the emphasis of the series is on the Greek and Slavic worlds, there are no thematic, geographical, or chronological limitations. Through the series we hope to encourage research in a variety of contemporary problems in their historical context. In this regard, special efforts will be made to accommodate proceedings from scholarly conferences as well as monographic studies with a diachronic approach.

Monographs in the MMEEM series are published by the Modern Greek Studies Program at the University of Minnesota as supplements to the *Modern Greek Studies Yearbook*. *Permanent Revolution: A Study of the Early Soviet State* by Elizabeth A. Harry is number 22 in the series. Its publication has been made possible by subvention from the Modern Greek Studies Program at the University of Minnesota.

The price for this volume is $30.00, paperback. Make checks payable to:

Modern Greek Studies
327 Social Science Building
UNIVERSITY OF MINNESOTA
267—19th Avenue South
Minneapolis, MN 55455
Telephone: (612) 624-4526

Library of Congress Control Number: 2018905010
ISSN: 1057-3941
ISBN–13: 978-0-9791218-8-3
ISBN–10: 0-9791218-8-4

Cover: The first state emblem (1923–1936) of the Soviet Union, with the legend in the languages referred to in Art. 34 of the Constitution of the USSR:
"Workers of all countries, unite!"

The UNIVERSITY OF MINNESOTA is an equal-opportunity employer.
Printed in the United States of America on acid-free paper

For Genny

Die Liebe hoeret nimmer auf

CONTENTS

CHRONOLOGY

1861—Defeat in the Crimean War prompts Tsar Alexander II to enact the Great Reforms, in an attempt to modernize Russia; the Emancipation Edict ends serfdom but forces the peasants to compensate the aristocracy through "redemption payments" for the land; rapid industrialization leads to the growth of a small working class and the spread of revolutionary ideas.

1897—The Marxist Russian Social Democratic Labor Party is founded; in 1903 it splits into the Menshevik and Bolshevik (Marxist) factions.

1904–5—Russian expansion in Manchuria leads to war with Japan; Russian defeat leads to the 1905 revolution, which forces Tsar Nicholas II to grant a constitution and establish a parliament, the Duma.

1914–18—Russian-Austrian rivalry in the Balkans contributes to outbreak of World War I, in which Russia is allied with Britain and France against the Central Powers; on 1 August (19 July) 1914, Germany declares war on Russia; on 18 (31) August 1914, St. Petersburg is renamed Petrograd.

1917

February Revolution: 8–16 March (23 February – 3 March)—War weariness and food scarcity cause riots and strikes to erupt in Petrograd; mutinies in the armed forces and street disturbances in major cities result in the abolition of the monarchy in Russia; Liberal leaders force Tsar Nicholas to abdicate, and a series of provisional governments seek to continue the war against Germany, despite a disintegrating military and chronic unrest at home.

April—Vladimir Lenin returns from exile, traveling to Petrograd in a sealed train from Switzerland via Germany and Finland.

July Days: 16–20 (3–7) July—Spontaneous armed anti-government demonstrations of industrial workers and soldiers begin in Petrograd; Socialist Revolutionary Alexander Kerensky takes over the Provisional Government and crushes the demonstrations; Lenin goes into hiding.

Kornilov affair: 9 September (22–27 August)—A coup by General Lavr Kornilov, commander of the Russian army, fails, after he orders troops to Petrograd to counter the Bolshevik threat; the failure of the coup secures power for the Bolsheviks among Petrograd's workers and soldiers and destroys the credibility of the coalition government between socialists and liberals implicated in the affair.

October Revolution: 7–8 November (25–26 October)—The Bolsheviks seize control of Petrograd and overthrow the Provisional Government; the Decrees on Land (proclaiming the abolition of private property and the redistribution of the land among the peasantry) and Peace (proposing the immediate withdrawal of Russia from World War I) are issued by the new Bolshevik government; subsequent workers' decrees outline measures for an eight-hour workday, a minimum wage, and workers' control of the factories; the death penalty is abolished.

9 November (27 October)—The Decree on the Press abolishes the free press.

25 (12) November—Elections to the Constituent Assembly are held; the Socialist Revolutionaries win the most seats, while the Bolsheviks win less than one quarter of the vote.

15 (2) December—An armistice between Russia and the Central Powers is signed.

1918

18–19 (5–6) January—The Constituent Assembly meets but is dissolved by the Bolsheviks.

28 (15) January—The Council of People's Commissars (Sovnarkom) issues a decree forming the Workers' and Peasants' Red Army.

14 February—Russia adopts the Western (Gregorian) calendar.

Brest-Litovsk Treaty: 3 March—The Treaty of Brest-Litovsk ends Russia's participation in World War I; Bolshevik Russia forfeits to Germany a third of the old empire's population, a third of its railway network, half its industry, three quarters of its supplies of iron ore, nine tenths of its coal resources, and much of its food supplies.

8 March—At the Seventh Russian Social Democratic Labor Party Congress, the Bolsheviks change the name of their party to the Russian Communist Party; the Russian capital is also moved from Petrograd to Moscow.

Civil War: 1918–22—The Bolsheviks win the civil war against the White Russians, who are aided by Britain, France, Japan, and the United States; defeat in war with Poland ends Soviet expansion west until World War II.

10 July—The first constitution of the Russian Socialist Federated Soviet Republic grants equal rights to men and women.

16–17 July—Tsar Nicholas II and his family are executed by the Bolsheviks in Ekaterinburg, Siberia.

30 August—An assassination attempt by Socialist Revolutionary Fanny Kaplan leaves Lenin seriously wounded and sparks mass arrests and executions.

March 1919—The Comintern (Third Socialist International) is formed in Moscow.

November 1920—The Red Army invades and occupies Crimea, and the White Army is forced to withdraw.

March 1921—The Kronstadt mutiny, an unsuccessful uprising against the Bolsheviks, takes place; the Tenth Party Congress shuts down party factionalism and introduces the New Economic Policy (NEP).

1922

April—Lenin appoints Joseph Stalin as General Secretary of the Communist Party.
May—Lenin suffers a stroke, following surgery to remove a bullet left from the assassination attempt in 1918.
December—Lenin suffers a second stroke that leaves him paralyzed on his right side; Lev Kamenev becomes chair of the Politburo and the effective leader of the party and government.
29 December—The Bolsheviks reorganize remnants of the Russian Empire as the Union of Soviet Socialist Republics (USSR), comprised of the Russian Socialist Federated Soviet Republic, the Ukrainian Soviet Socialist Republic, the Transcaucasian Socialist Federated Soviet Republic, and the Belorussian Soviet Socialist Republic.

1923

January—Lenin completes his Testament, with proposed changes to the structure of communism and his thoughts on his possible successors; he indicates that he is uncomfortable with Joseph Stalin and suggests that he be replaced as General Secretary.
March—Lenin suffers a third stroke that leaves him totally paralyzed and unable to speak; a power struggle among the party leadership emerges between the Triumvirate (Stalin allied with Grigory Zinoviev and Lev Kamenev) and the Left Opposition, headed by Leon Trotsky.
April—Lenin's wife Nadezhda Krupskaia keeps his Testament secret in the hope that Lenin would recover and be able to deliver it himself.
October—The Declaration of the Forty-Six, written by left-wing communists, expresses concern about the lack of democracy in the party; the Scissors Crisis, a gap between low agricultural and high industrial prices, peaks.

1924

January—The Thirteenth Party Congress orders a recruitment drive to bring workers into the Communist Party subsequently known as the Lenin Enrollment or Lenin Levy and carried out by Stalin as General Secretary.
21 January—Vladimir Lenin dies; Petrograd is renamed Leningrad.
March—The new gold ruble, equivalent to 50,000 old rubles, is introduced to stop inflation.
May—Nadezhda Krupskaia hands over Lenin's Testament to be read at the Thirteenth Party Congress, but it is largely ignored.

1925—Stalin introduces his theory of "Socialism in One Country," splitting the Triumvirate; Stalin allies himself with Nikolai Bukharin and removes Trotsky from the government and his position as head of the Red Army.

December—At the Fourteenth Party Congress, Zinoviev and Kamenev oppose NEP and socialism in one country and advocate large-scale industrialization and world socialism; they are opposed by Stalin and Bukharin and are removed from the Politburo.

1926—In the so-called "Kulak Grain Strike," peasants profiting from NEP stop selling their grain against insufficient and expensive industrial commodities, and grain prices begin to rise; the "regime of economy" austerity campaign is launched by the government to cut production costs, causing industrial cutbacks and layoffs.

1927—As a result of the Kulak Grain Strike, grain prices rise alarmingly; Zinoviev and Kamenev in alliance with Trotsky form the United Opposition and argue for a change in government policy; grain procurement levels are about half those of 1926.

May—The Conservative government in Britain expels the Soviet ambassador and breaks diplomatic relations with the Soviet Union; the resulting "War Scare" increases fears of war between capitalist powers and the Soviet Union.

June—The Soviet ambassador to Poland, Petr Voikov, is assasinated.

July—News reaches Russia that Chinese Nationalist leader Jiang Jieshi had ordered the massacre of Chinese Communists in Shanghai in April.

1928—Stalin splits with Bukharin and reverses government policy.

January—Stalin visits the agricultural regions of Siberia and the Urals and imposes grain requisitioning quotas; peasants respond by decreasing grain production; Trotsky is exiled to Kazakhstan.

February—Stalin begins removing Bukharin's followers and supporters from the party.

October—Stalin introduces the first Five-Year Plan to increase the pace of industrialization.

1929

February—Trotsky is convicted of counterrevolution and banished from the Soviet Union.

October—The Wall Street Crash begins the Great Depression.

November—Stalin publishes his "Year of the Great Turn," signaling the end of NEP and outlining the move toward greater industrialization and collectivization of agriculture; the Central Committee decides to send 25,000 industrial workers, known as the twenty-five thousanders, into the countryside to help impose collectivization.

December—Forced collectivization begins; on his fiftieth birthday, Stalin makes a speech highlighting Lenin's mistakes.

1930—Lenin's mausoleum is unveiled.

PREFACE

THE present work originated in graduate research on the interwar period in Germany and Russia. It has been revised and reconsidered, especially the central question it raises, namely, the nature of the connection between leader and led and how it shapes politics and history in the modern world. In 2018 America and the world this question continues to be relevant, regardless of government systems and, given the present political culture, a discussion of it more timely than ever.

The purpose of this study is to determine how early Soviet society—party members, communist sympathizers, and nonparty citizens—perceived inequality, and how this perception contributed to the formation of the world's first communist state. The objective is to look at social tensions and underlying motivations, to remove the "ism" from historical study by examining the language, metaphors, and messages in letters from the populace to the party leadership in the mid-1920s, when Stalinism was formed. In these letters, definitions of terms like "Leninism," "Marxism," and "Stalinism" were so varied, idiosyncratic, and even apolitical, that a discussion of ideology becomes almost meaningless. There were, rather, many bolshevisms, socialisms, communisms, leninisms, and stalinisms, as well as many private agendas and values attached to each of these terms.

Several studies on 1920s Russia have exposed numerous areas of conflict and tension—an abiding, angry resentment among the lower social orders—that exploded at the end of the decade in the "Great Turn" under Stalin. These studies, however, have only suggested the underlying meanings of the verbal or physical expressions of rage and animosity. The main focus of this work is thus to explore and decode those meanings through an examination of the voluminous letters and appeals written to the Communist Party leadership during that period. It aims to shed light on how discontent and militancy may have contributed to the development of Stalinism in the mid-1920s during the struggle for power and direction among top party leaders. Put in the old idiom of Soviet historiography, this study deals with class struggle in NEP Russia. It suggests that a pervasive leveling impulse, redoubled by individual social and material aspirations, helped shape a constituency and political base for the evolution of Stalinism.

The critical question of how the aspirations of average people connect with the agendas and actions of political leaders and movements is highly complex under any form of government, particularly a dictatorship. The purpose here is to consider popular desires and agendas that later became policies of the Soviet government, to survey the messages to Stalin before Stalinism—that is, to establish the common junctures between popular grievances and the system that developed.

A primary form of communication was the tradition of supplication, a conduit from people to their leaders. This medium was used throughout Russian history, beginning with Ivan the Terrible. But in the Soviet period, it facilitated "the only form of spontaneous activity on the part of the ordinary citizen to receive official approval and even encouragement in the USSR."[1] The nature of petitions to the center changed over time and reflected the evolution of political participation by the Russian people.[2] As the tsarist autocracy progressively crumbled under the forces of modernity, petitions became more political and more militant.

After the October Revolution, the communist leadership encouraged petition as a vehicle for keeping in touch with and gauging the mood of the masses. The new communist state decreed the right of all citizens to petition and lodge complaints as early as November 1918. In the eyes of the party leadership and Lenin in particular, citizens' participation in and control of the state and its authorities were "welded together." Through petitions, complaints, and appeals, the people were to act as watchdogs of those in power and of society, and thus contribute to the political process. This vigilance included the right and the responsibility to denounce oppositionists to communist power and the state.[3]

Until the 1990s, research in the social history of the NEP period was hampered by the inaccessibility of material in the Soviet archives. Gauging the sympathies and aspirations of average communists and nonparty citizens required an unofficial, unsolicited, and uncensored source of opinion. Letters and petitions to central party leaders fulfilled these requirements and, with the opening of the archives, have become the focus of much scholarly interest. Using these and related sources, scholars already have produced several studies on public opinion, focusing mainly on the 1930s.[4]

The main source for this study consists of letters written primarily to Stalin but also other leaders from 1923 to 1927,[5] years that saw the rise and decline of the New Economic Policy. These letters, located in the confidential files of the archive of the Party Secretariat, the central organ of party control that Stalin headed beginning in 1922, concern a variety of personal and general subjects. They contain appeals for help, advice and warnings to the party leadership, and general musings on the meaning of socialism. Since they came from a variety of citizens, more or less literate, party and nonparty alike, from disparate regions throughout the Soviet Union, these letters express a wide range of views. As a whole, they provide invaluable insight into their authors' views, aspirations, grievances, and concerns. While the language is somewhat qualified in its frankness, the general level of candor, in hindsight, seems surprising. Supplicants often politicized their aspirations and complaints, voicing disappointment and disgruntlement, even toward Stalin.

In chronological terms, the letters present a continuum: those to Lenin end in January 1924, those to Stalin begin in 1923. Some letters were addressed collectively to the Secretariat, the Central Committee, the Central

Control Committee, or other central government or party bodies. Occasionally, letters addressed personally to other party leaders were used, but these were rare in the targeted collections. No attempt was made to examine all, or even to make a statistically valid sampling of letters and appeals to the center during this period, since such a study would be well beyond the scope of this work. The emphasis here is not on a quantitative, but a qualitative study of the language and meaning embedded in the letters and appeals, to allow the messages to speak for themselves. The appeals used were addressed to the party leadership, mostly to Stalin, during NEP. Letters to other leaders or ministries, or to group-specific newspapers (for instance, those catering to professional organizations), might well yield a different perspective.

The authors of letters used tended not to be professionals or members of pre- or postrevolutionary elites, although some appeals emanated from communists or nonparty citizens who clearly were educated. The appeals came from throughout the Soviet Union, including Siberia and many of the constituent republics and autonomous regions; they were not organized in the collections or in this study geographically. A majority came from workers, peasants, and party or Komsomol (Communist Youth League) members who possessed some education and were moderately literate.

Are the letters authentic? They were collected in confidential Secretariat files, sometimes loosely organized by the type of complaint, other times grouped more randomly. In any case, the level of organization is low. Typed copies appear to have been produced for most letters; in a few cases, these copies were filed alongside the originals. Random checks of the typed texts against the originals revealed verbatim reproductions, except for spelling corrections (especially when the level of literacy made the original almost illegible). Rarely, typed copies were translations from Georgian or another national language. In no case did there appear to be any attempt to censor or delete material, even when letters were extremely critical of the regime or threatening in their tone.

As to "social authenticity," the standards employed by Gregory Freeze in his collection of prerevolutionary petitions served as a model.[6] Particularly useful were letters and petitions rich in detail and commentary that articulated sentiments commonly expressed, but in a manner that shed more light on the authors' motivations, conclusions, and suggestions. In this sense, the letters' tone and sense of urgency were at times extremely compelling. In gauging how representative these letters were, special attention was given to appeals of supplicants who claimed the universality of their problems or viewpoints. Finally, regarding the influence of the party press, Freeze maintained that "evidence of external influence is not ipso facto grounds for exclusion—not only because that intrusion is itself an important historical datum."[7] There is no question that the official party press influenced and at times inflamed public opinion on a variety of issues.[8] The importance of such an intrusion lies in the fact that certain party slogans and propaganda were significant, precisely because people responded to them. The challenge lies in determining why.

One last note on the letters and appeals' authenticity is that to readers a hundred years later, and in retrospect, their tone might seem insincere. But we must suspend our cynicism and consider the possibility that a hundred years ago, many people believed that building a new, better, more just world was an attainable goal. We must also remember that people then had no experience of the virtual world that most elite societies seem to inhabit in the twenty-first century. Theirs was rather a world only of hard realities few elites then or now could imagine, with little chance of escape, even in a virtual sense.

Throughout this study there is little evidence of change over time, or that social disgruntlement or grievances were actually mounting during NEP. Indeed, a constant refrain throughout the letters and appeals is that "nothing has changed," meaning that nothing had improved for the supplicants compared to what had been before the Revolution—implying, of course, that their revolutionary expectations had been disappointed. The appeals under consideration end in 1927, about the time when historians have noted a marked increase in militancy, discontent, and protest presaging and precipitating the so-called Cultural Revolution at the end of the decade.[9] Indeed, 1927 seems to have been a watershed year, not only in foreign policy (the threat of war with England and annihilation of the Chinese Communists) but in domestic terms as well: the year marked the tenth anniversary of the October Revolution. Not a few supplicants writing to party leaders in that year made bitter observations that, even ten years later, the revolution had changed nothing.

One final word on methodology is in order. Appeals are not categorized according to social group or class, because the social, physical, and psychological dislocation of the period made social identity and status a slippery business. Indeed, the fluidity of social definitions reflects the intense social upheaval and uncertainty characteristic of postrevolutionary Russia.[10] That this upheaval and uncertainty increased instability and inflamed popular discontent forms one of the main themes of this study. In identifying supplicants, their own descriptions of themselves were used. How they described themselves had as much to do with their self-perceptions and aspirations, as with how they currently or formerly made a living, or their social origin or official class. A similar confusion reigns in regard to the "enemy." Throughout appeals, terms used for the enemy are conflated: nepmen, bourgeoisie, intelligentsia, bourgeois intelligentsia, specialists, and so on; these terms came to be used interchangeably and pejoratively.[11] By examining the context in letters and petitions in which such terms were employed, one gains a sense of the grounds for both conflation and resentment. Clearly, resentment was not exclusively economic, political, or ideological. That all these groups were in some way considered superior—both by themselves and by society—appears to have been a common denominator and a major clue to the basis for popular resentment.

There was a tremendous contrast between the highly complex social order of the tsarist regime and the postrevolutionary structure, composed (at least officially) of relatively few legal definitions of persons. Leopold Haimson discussed the problem of social identity in tsarist Russia, reiterating an observation that scholars had stressed earlier. He emphasized that, in part due to the forces of modernization, Russia already before 1917 "was a society out of joint" and that there existed "glaring . . . contradictions . . . between sosloviia and sostoianiia—the legal statuses assigned . . . by the state—and the nature of the occupations in which [those not in state service] actually engaged."[12] However, the Bolsheviks in postrevolutionary Russia were no more successful than the tsarist government had been in classifying individuals and groups on the basis of social origin in the midst of profound social change. The problem of social identity in the 1920s was thus not new, but persistent.

The chapters here are organized according to the main subjects expressed in letters and petitions.[13] The first chapters focus on popular ideals and expectations of the new socialist society. After an historical overview of NEP society in chapter 1, chapter 2 examines the theme of community and inclusion in a communal organism, subsumed here under the term "collective." This term does not refer to a form of economic or peasant organization, but to an organic community envisioned and demanded by socialism's supporters.

The middle chapters deal with the major sources of discontent in NEP society. Complaints fell mainly into the following categories: disparity and party elitism, bureaucracy and corruption, lack of educational opportunities, and, most frequently, unemployment and hunger. Most complaints could be categorized in more than one area, since, for instance, lack of a job or educational opportunity could be, and often was, attributed to elitism, bureaucracy, or corruption of the party or government. Chapter 3 concerns social and economic disparity, and its material and psychological effects on society, while chapter 4 examines the major cause of disparity—unemployment—and supplicants' unsuccessful efforts to escape it through education. Chapter 5 considers the party and government bureaucracy—its gargantuan scale and causes, and proposals on how to combat its corruption. Chapter 6 explores the issue of party elitism, a source of discontent that was so contradictory to the egalitarian ethos of the revolution. As will become clearer in the course of the discussion, however, all of these problems ultimately were rooted in disparity. Supplicants often recognized this connection, and sought the cause—often, they concluded, an internal or external enemy that threatened and corrupted society.

Thus, the last chapters explore the search for enemies and scapegoats to blame for the failure to establish an organic socialist society. Chapters 7 and 8 examine fears over invasion of the social organism, whether from without or within, or by some combination of both. Both chapters discuss the common—and crucial—conflation of external and internal enemies, and the bases on which this conflation was made. Chapter 9 considers the anti-intelligentsia sentiment that runs throughout many appeals, and why the intelligentsia in particular were blamed for the failure of revolutionary aspirations. Finally, chapter 10 deals with the critical question of how the letters and appeals used here may have influenced the Soviet leadership and the course of events, that is, the relationship between above and below.

I would like to express my gratitude to my graduate advisor, Gregory Freeze, for inspiring and enabling the research that laid the basis for this study, and for his guidance, criticisms, and suggestions that helped me to improve it in many ways; to the late Rudolph Binion, whose brilliant work on Hitler and Nazism in Germany informed my work on Soviet Russia; to Sheila Fitzpatrick, whose seminal work on Soviet social history opened new possibilities for me and countless others; and to Paul Jankowski and Elizabeth Wood, for their assistance and critical observations and insights. I also want to thank Alexis

Pogorelskin, for her scholarship, inspiration, and support. My thanks are due to the History Department and the Graduate School of Brandeis University, for years of financial and academic support. I would also like to thank J. Arch Getty, Leonid Vaintraub, and Elena Drozdova of the Center for the Study of Russia and the Soviet Union and to the program and staff of ACTR/ACCELS, for their scholarly and material assistance connected with my initial research trips to Russia; and to Andrei Sokolov of the Institute of Russian History of the Russian Academy of Sciences in Moscow and the staff of the Russian State Archive of Socio-Political History, for their expertise and gracious assistance in helping me locate the requisite documents.

I am deeply grateful to my colleagues and friends, Theofanis Stavrou, for publishing my work and bringing these documents to light, and Soterios Stavrou, from whom I have learned so much, for his editorial expertise and assistance in improving my work immensely.

Finally, I would like to express my deep love and gratitude to my wonderful friends and families, here and in Russia; my beloved parents, John and Mary Harry; my second parents, Dennis and Sharon Ryan, for being wonderful and supportive in every way; and my dear sisters and brothers, and my husband, Scott Ryan, whose individual and collective brilliance, love, friendship, help, and support have sustained and inspired me and made life worth living.

INTRODUCTION

For What Did We Shed Workers' Blood?
Communist miner, February 1925

THE purpose of all revolution is leveling: political, social, cultural, and especially economic. This study examines the tensions in the early years of communism in Russia caused by continuing economic and social inequality, which contributed, near the end of the 1920s, to the so-called Stalinist revolution—a revival of revolutionary militancy, a renewed attempt to level society.[1] In spite, or perhaps because of the horrors of war and revolution from 1914 to 1921, there were in the early Soviet state great expectations of a new and just society, expectations that were further fueled by communist rhetoric and propaganda. When in 1921, in an attempt to quell popular unrest and economic collapse, the Bolsheviks partially restored a capitalist economy by adopting the New Economic Policy (NEP), those expectations were dashed.[2]

The NEP of the 1920s has been touted as a relatively liberal period in Russia's history, characterized by rapid social change, cultural experimentation, and relative economic freedom. In this optimistic perspective (first adumbrated by Western scholars, later by post-Soviet historians), liberal economic policies of the 1920s offered the possibility for economic growth without coercion and represented the "happy" alternative to later developments under the Stalinist system of the 1930s. Moreover, 1920s Russia witnessed a flowering of cultural production and social experimentation, sparked by revolutionary iconoclasm and enthusiasm over the possibilities the revolution had to offer in building a new society and a new human being.[3] This cultural freedom and social experimentation stood in stark contrast to the cultural conformity and social conservatism that characterized Stalinism.

In spite of the government's efforts, however, the 1920s were also years of political and social chaos, economic disparity, and deep anxiety over the nation's, and the individual's, prospects.[4] A long-standing sense of social injustice pervaded society, and the revolution only fueled growing expectations of change. Instead of social justice, however, the 1920s brought new and widespread suffering—famine, inflation, unemployment. More importantly, deprivation and hardship were not shared equally. On the contrary, the limited economic opportunities afforded by NEP enriched private entrepreneurs, government officials, speculators, and the ubiquitous middlemen who plied trade and plundered state industry. While workers suffered from cutbacks, the nepmen (entrepreneurs) reaped profits, and industrial specialists were paid increasingly higher salaries. Moreover, NEP seemed to favor stronger peasants over poor peasants and workers. In short, NEP brought economic growth and cultural freedom but exacerbated economic and social disparities. In doing so, it violated the egalitarian aspirations of the October Revolution and contributed to the popular perception that the Bolsheviks had abandoned socialism. These policies and developments had grave social and political consequences.

The focus here is the reemergence of intolerance toward social inequality that eventually formed the basis for political action. Such animosities and grievances were not new to postrevolutionary society; they had roots deep in the prerevolutionary period.[5] Indeed, the central dilemma facing the new Bolshevik regime was a deep polarization of society—between the *verkhi* (elites) and *nizy* (lower orders)—that was the driveshaft of politics throughout the revolutionary year of 1917. Leopold Haimson suggested that the dual power arrangement (the Provisional Government on the one hand and the soviets on the other)[6] that emerged immediately after the tsar's abdication in the February Revolution only reflected "the deep divisions that separated the upper and lower strata of urban and rural Russia." This polarization ultimately led to the abandonment of a liberal solution to Russia's social and political problems and the Bolsheviks' ascent to power.[7]

Moreover, this polarization was by no means exclusively economic. Disparity in culture and education were also factors in determining social standing and prestige.[8] Although the economic and cultural elites in Russia were not identical—many members of the intelligentsia were not of the propertied classes, and the professional classes, along with their bids for a voice in a government, had been growing for decades—to the lower orders, peasants and workers, culture and wealth were inextricably intertwined, if not coterminous.[9] Soviet historians generally included the educated and cultural elite of prerevolutionary Russia among the "bourgeoisie,"[10] but this had become a resonant term of disparagement long before the October Revolution.[11] As we shall see, in letters to the party leadership during the 1920s, communists and nonparty citizens alike used "bourgeois" and "intelligent" interchangeably.

Thus, the disparity that prompted the October Revolution was not merely material. The revolutionaries sought both greater material and cultural equity, for privilege and hierarchy persisted in both. Indeed, contradicting Marxist theory, Lenin argued that the proletarian revolution would be easier to realize in Russia than in more advanced Western countries, because the relatively low cultural level of Russian workers would make them easier to direct.[12]

Western historians traditionally have neglected or downplayed the conflicts of the NEP period.[13] Perhaps this was because cataclysmic events, repression, and suffering under Stalin made the NEP years appear as a veritable oasis of stability, normalcy, and freedom in the history of the Soviet Union. Moreover, the Cold War encouraged both Soviet and Western historians to adopt extreme, opposing views of the Soviet state and to credit or blame Stalin for its development. Determining the connection between NEP and high Stalinism was of critical importance.

Thus, post-Stalinist Soviet historiography criticized the Western view that NEP was a "retreat from Marxism" and stressed the continuity between the 1920s and 1930s (and the logic and legitimacy of the party line) without diminishing the enormous importance of what came in the 1930s.[14] The overriding aim was to see the 1920s as a necessary "breathing spell" and basis for the later socialist construction. The "mistakes" of the 1930s were blamed on Stalin himself—notwithstanding some acknowledgment after Khrushchev of Stalin's positive role—while the party and masses were credited for all the positive dimensions. During the height of the Cold War, Western historiography, too, tended to see continuity between the Lenin (hence NEP) and Stalin eras, but chiefly in negative terms. The construction of concentration camps, not socialist planning and economic growth, lay at the center of attention.[15] It hardly needs mentioning that both Soviet and Western historiography during the Cold War was based primarily in ideological agendas.

By the 1970s, Western revisionists began to modify the evil-continuity paradigm, but this revision tended to take two different, even opposing, forms. One was the early NEP idealization school, which admitted not only cultural experimentation during, but also the economic potential of, NEP. This form of revisionism took the Bukharinite view, which blamed Stalin for failing to allow NEP to follow a natural line of development. This position had some roots in Khrushchev destalinization historiography, which blamed Stalin for failing to lay an adequate basis for collectivization.[16]

By the late 1980s, perhaps reflecting both developments in the Cold War and the growing pro-capitalist Zeitgeist, Soviet historians came to adopt this new Western view of NEP, and even to hold it up as a model for current Soviet and Russian economic development.[17] Thus, NEP's character underwent a complete reversal: instead of marking the struggle and ultimate triumph of socialism over capitalism,[18] it came to represent a brief period when sober economic analysis and prospects reigned over party ideology and socialist utopianism.[19] What came before Stalin's ultimate predominance, therefore, loomed in Western historiography, and now in Soviet historiography as well, as the Soviet Union that might have been.[20]

This historiography was rooted not merely in the desire to reveal Russia's lost chances, but also in traditional historians' conception of how history happens, which held that the political, economic, and social transformation of the Soviet Union that began in the late 1920s was a "revolution from above" (an assertion made by Stalin himself). A politicized, "totalitarian" interpretation of the Soviet system of government consistently emphasized ideological, center-based explanations for the development of communism. According to this view, Marx's theories impelled Lenin and a tiny revolutionary intelligentsia to mobilize a proletarian vanguard to lead the working classes first to revolution and then to a dictatorship of (not by) the proletariat once the communists had gained power. The Bolsheviks assumed that the people in a backward, largely agrarian society (especially the peasants) were not ready to govern themselves and to complete this advanced socialist revolution.[21] Traditional, center-based analyses essentially accepted the assumptions and prejudices inherent in Bolshevik ideology—namely, that the broader masses did not create the Soviet system. Thus, studying expressions of mass attitudes was relegated to a position of relatively minor importance, since, according to this interpretation, the party leadership controlled the process that generated the Stalinist system.

A second line of historiography, beginning in the 1980s, challenged center-based interpretations of the Soviet period, or, as Stephen Cohen put it, "explaining complex historical and social developments by high politics."[22] Instead of concentrating on high politics and the struggle for succession to the leadership of the Communist Party, scholars in the West increasingly addressed the everyday life of average citizens, how they viewed and shaped the communist experiment, and how Soviet leaders responded to, and attempted to mold, popular views. Postcommunist studies concentrating on party politics and Soviet society at the grassroots level have shown that in the formative years of the Soviet Union, the division between government and society, leaders and led, was less pronounced than had previously been assumed.

This revisionism turned attention away from politics and economics, and focused more on NEP society and the darker sides of the continuity between the 1920s and the 1930s. It examined the anti-intelligentsia sentiment, social antagonism, worker unrest, and family breakdown of the NEP era. In challenging the traditional model, revisionist historiography suggested a "revolution from below"—a strong mass impetus behind the transformation of Soviet society.[23] By examining the complex and turbulent society of the NEP period, historians exposed multiple areas of conflict and ongoing revolutionary tension endemic to NEP. Social tensions grew from extreme competition among various groups—skilled and unskilled workers, landed and landless peasants, veterans, clerical workers, lower party apparatchiki—for work, position, and a future in the new socialist society. There was high demand for, and low availability of, such opportunities. The intense social conflict, aggravated by superfluity of labor, unemployment, and frustrated revolutionary expectations, exacerbated pervasive radicalism. Many felt that the revolution had failed or was incomplete. Revisionist works on popular participation in collectivization and on the Red Army during NEP testified to the existence of extensive radicalism throughout the military, the party rank and file, and the working class generally. This radicalism generated popular enthusiasm for, and participation in, the dismantling of NEP. These studies also pointed to social and economic disparities as major factors behind the radicalism.[24]

However, despite abundant evidence of widespread social unrest and revolution from below brewing during NEP, a modified revolution from above interpretation has continued to dominate histories of the Soviet period.[25] Admitting the existence of social discontent during NEP, these interpretations nevertheless minimize or attribute it to the party alone, and not to conditions outside party control, or, indeed, to which both party and society were subject. Thus, the party is once again portrayed as totalitarian, all-controlling, standing distinctly apart from, and in opposition to, the masses, except for its cadres, who will thoughtlessly and obediently fulfill future Stalinist directives—not out of personal conviction or political belief, but for the sake of party patronage.

Another, related feature of post-Soviet studies is a tendency to minimize or deny inter- and intraclass conflicts. Peasants especially are viewed as "the peasantry," a monolithic entity devoid of internal tensions except those introduced by the party.[26] In general, the construct of party and society as distinct, opposing entities persists. Communism remains an alien, disruptive force that has little basis and support in society.

Other developments in both Russian and Western post-Soviet scholarship provide alternative directions for research on the Soviet period, away from high politics and mass political phenomena in general to a focus on the individual. In relation to the revolutionary experience, one line of inquiry has centered on the psychopathology of revolution.[27] Partly in reaction to the Soviet emphasis on Marxist paradigms, some Russian historians embraced the Annales-inspired study of mentalité that has long influenced Western historical inquiry.[28] The emphasis thus shifted once again away from politics and toward a cultural history of the Soviet period. And although mentalité describes an aggregate, long-term phenomenon, its construction and study, as one Russian historian maintained, must ultimately be based on individual perceptions and experiences, of which the aggregate experience is comprised.[29]

The study of mentalité also necessarily implies a study of language in order to move beyond Marxist notions of class and causation and to deconstruct individual experience. This methodology has long been employed in other areas of Western historical research. In his studies on the English working class, Gareth Steadman Jones recognized that social historians' notions of class and behavior, intentions, and desires had been predetermined by Marxist paradigms, themselves ironically influenced by mid-nineteenth-century English middle-class judgments and fears of the working classes.[30] It was necessary to study the actual language of historical protagonists, Jones argued, because their beliefs could not "simply be inferred . . . from . . . the material situation of a particular class or social group. Nor is it adequate," he continued, "to treat . . . language as a more or less immediate rendition of experience into words."[31] In her study of the political culture of the French Revolution, Lynn Hunt viewed the connection between language and action as more direct: "values, expectations, and implicit rules that expressed and shaped collective intentions and actions" were encoded into revolutionary language, itself part of a political culture that in turn influenced political action.[32]

One important result of the study of language in Soviet history is that it has not only clarified the perceptions of average people and their roles in the construction of communism and the Soviet state, but also helped to blur the distinction, and opposition, between state/party and society.[33] Language has shown the discourse not only between cultural and material experience, but also between party and people, a discourse that shaped the communist state and society.[34] The present study continues to blur that distinction. Moreover, as this blurring of lines and shared language imply, the authorship of language is also indistinct.[35] Although it was propagated throughout society, official rhetoric was molded by the party to enhance its receptivity, and selectively processed and manipulated by everyone to achieve individual ends.

Another, less helpful outcome of the study of language is a social history of the Soviet period increasingly influenced by postmodernist cultural theory and literary criticism. This trend has induced historians to consider language "not as a reflection of material reality but as a system of signification that creates meaning and shapes people's identities and behaviors."[36] However, as Mark Steinberg observed, cultural forms cannot replace material experience as an explanatory paradigm for mentalité and behavior; rather, there is a discourse between cultural and material experience, and it is this discourse that ultimately produces meaning, for

> Most historians engaged in the cultural study of society have recognized that the ways people use language, symbols, ideas, and other cultural forms are inescapably shaped by the harder surfaces of their lives—material conditions, social location, and relative power—even as these cultural forms influence how these structured experiences are perceived and made meaningful.[37]

Steinberg's qualifier about including material reality in considering the meaning of language implies a real danger inherent in the newer trend of analysis, the danger of losing touch with just how central the "harder surfaces" were in the lives of historical subjects. In treating language as an abstraction, the analysis loses a sense of material reality, itself becoming an abstraction in the process. It is understood that language describes not reality, but perceptions of reality—and, in the case of this study, descriptions that are made for a purpose. At the same time, excessive emphasis on meanings and codes hidden within texts can subjectify that text to the point of losing completely its connection to the often harsh material realities of the lives of those we study. Historians by and large generate historical analysis from a relatively comfortable social and material vantage point that makes it easier to underestimate the primacy of economic and social insecurity as motivating factors throughout history.[38]

With the opening of the archives in the 1990s, post-Soviet Russian scholars have focused on an assessment of both NEP and the Stalinist legacy mainly by publishing documentary collections.[39] Western scholarship on social history and the foundations of the Soviet state has focused primarily on the 1930s, that is, after the Stalinist system was already in place. In contrast, the 1920s—when the Soviet system was being formed—are relatively neglected.[40]

Thus, the present work attempts to fill this gap and deals with the very real economic and social insecurity in the early years of Soviet history. It demonstrates that during NEP, certain impulses within and without the party prompted a fear of capitalism and renewed desire to establish a communist social order. One of these was the extreme need for material security, which many individuals hoped to acquire within a communal social organism. The other was a widespread craving within party and society for social status. Not satisfied during NEP, these needs were usually expressed in the negative. Thus, supplicants to the center commonly lamented of being *zabroshennyi* (abandoned) and *negodnyi* (worthless). The need for security was particularly intense during the 1920s, following a prolonged period of war, revolution, and famine. Coupled with this profound lack of security was the frustration of the dreams of countless citizens, who sought to secure their economic and social position and earn dignity through inclusion in the effort to build socialism. The party's failure to satisfy popular expectations, by reverting to a competitive, exclusive economic and social system, fueled a general cynicism with profound repercussions. People's needs for security and dignity contributed to NEP's demise and became the catalyst for ongoing social revolution.

CHAPTER ONE

Politics and Society between the October Revolution and Stalin's "Great Turn"

THE October Revolution was not a mere coup d'état; it was a popular revolution.[1] The Bolsheviks succeeded in seizing and holding power because they included popular participation in government, and acceded, at least initially, to the demands of peasants, workers, and soldiers: workers' control of the factories, peasants' control of the land, and peace for all. The operative phrase was popular control, which promised not only material but also social betterment for lower-class citizens. As will be shown, workers and peasants sought to invert the economic and social hierarchies, to depose the elites and empower themselves.

During the civil war following October, the Bolsheviks were necessarily concerned less with production than with the distribution of industrial goods, commodities, and especially foodstuffs. Within months of assuming power, however, it became apparent that control over distribution was out of their hands as well. As the economy disintegrated, factories had to shut down, unemployment grew, and local governments struggled to cope with the task of feeding the urban population. The Bolsheviks, therefore, felt compelled to nationalize the factories, taking control from workers and handing it over to the state. The government also initiated a policy of forced grain requisitioning from the peasants. Thus began the period referred to as "War Communism,"[2] the Bolsheviks' attempt to gain control over goods and commodities necessary to win the civil war and save both the revolution and their control over it.

Ultimately, grain requisitioning alienated virtually the entire peasantry. By 1921, economic collapse and massive unrest (among not only peasants, but also workers, soldiers, and sailors) forced the Bolsheviks to adopt the New Economic Policy (NEP).[3] At Vladimir Lenin's behest, they substituted grain seizure with a tax in kind, allowing the peasants to market their surplus. The government also legalized private trade, denationalized and privatized small production (keeping control, however, over the "commanding heights" of the economy, i.e., heavy industry, banking, transport, and foreign trade), and adopted budget austerities that led to a sharp contraction in state services. Although the government enabled a restoration in agriculture and industrial production, its policies appeared to many communists and nonparty citizens to represent the reversion to capitalism, social injustice, and the predominance of the *byvshie* (literally, 'formers'; the old elites).

Thus, NEP violated the egalitarian ideals of the October Revolution and contributed to the popular perception that the Bolsheviks had abandoned socialism. Under the new system, both industries and individual workers were deprived of government assistance; curtailment and abolition of state subsidies caused many plants to cut back production and workforce. Moreover, it seemed to favor the interests of the stronger peasants over those of the poor peasants and workers. While the workers suffered from cutbacks, the nepmen reaped profits, and industrial specialists were paid increasingly higher salaries.

In the end, NEP was unable to resolve the competing interests of industry and agriculture, or of workers and peasants. Nor could it sustain growth; by 1926, economic recovery and expansion had slowed markedly, and the system lacked investment capital and control mechanisms to expand and modernize agriculture. Unemployment grew steadily. Peasant control over agriculture caused severe crises in grain procurement; as a result, the government could neither feed the city nor export grain. Ultimately, confronted by the irreconcilable contradictions of NEP, the Bolsheviks resorted to the "Great Turn" under Stalin: collectivization and industrialization.

1917: Aspirations and Expectations

In February 1917, when tsarism finally failed under the pressures of World War I and the popular revolution it spawned, the Provisional Government that came to power sought to construct a liberal government along Western European lines. The February Revolution failed in its turn, because moderate politicians of the Provisional Government—including only one socialist—represented but a small minority, whose political and economic objectives not only differed from those of the lower orders, but were diametrically opposed to them.[4] Most critically, the government failed to end Russia's involvement in the war. In contrast, the Bolsheviks, who came to power in October, did not make a revolution, but simply bestowed official sanction on a popular revolution that had been raging in rural and urban Russia for months. The workers and peasants had different demands, but both groups wanted not only to better their material situation, but also to gain control over their own affairs. In contrast to the Whites (supporters of tsarism), the Bolsheviks co-opted the lower classes in the construction of the government through the soviets and organizations, such as the Communist Party, Red Army, and Komsomol. As a result, workers, peasants, and soldiers felt that the Soviet government was their government: they had brought it to power, and it belonged to them.[5]

By controlling their own existence, the workers sought not only material betterment but also social power. They generally welcomed their liberation in February 1917 from industrial serfdom in the tsarist factory, where they had no authority over production or their conditions of work or wages.[6] For the masses, the February Revolution provided a clean slate to reconstruct society along egalitarian principles, and to dispense with structures of authority and privilege that prevailed before 1917.[7] In short, workers would gain power by establishing democracy in the factory and restructuring factory administration to include worker deputies to represent their interests.

Moreover, this was to be a workers', not a universal democracy. Its rights were to be conferred only on manual laborers—not owners, management, engineers, or even clerical workers.[8] Determined to secure and enlarge the rights they had gained, the factory committees formed after February fought to extend their control over factory administration and curb the traditional power of owners, administrators, and engineers. Factory activists viewed the building of socialism as a reconstruction not just of economic but also of authority relationships.[9] They sought to reform the economy and their place within it by limiting the power of the producers. So long as war production continued, factory administrators were compelled to bow to worker demands. After the Bolsheviks came to power in October, the workers formally gained control through the promulgation of the Decree on Workers' Control in November 1917.

As for the peasants, the Bolsheviks initially allowed land seizure and redistribution, not because they favored a proliferation of small, inefficient peasant landholders, but because they were not in a position to do otherwise.[10] In the land decree of November 1917 (promulgated as statutory law by the Congress of Soviets in February 1918), the Bolsheviks nationalized the land and acquiesced to peasant actions to seize, redistribute, and use the land as they saw fit. Local committees and soviets were to supervise distribution. In theory, no peasant was to hold more land than he could cultivate, but in fact the Bolsheviks relinquished the power of land distribution to village authorities. Generally, local power continued to reside with the elders, the strongest peasants in the village.[11] This proved crucial in the following years. For their part, the Bolsheviks were concerned exclusively with obtaining sufficient food to feed the army and the cities—a critical need in the early years of the new regime that essentially determined Bolshevik policy toward the countryside.

War Communism

In the first months of power, when they allowed workers to take over the factories and peasants to seize and divide the land, the Bolsheviks did so partly out of revolutionary enthusiasm and partly to gain the upper hand in the struggle for power. But they had seized power on the assumption that imminent worldwide revolution would end World War I (the "imperialist war"), enable the working class to consolidate power in a sea of petit-bourgeois peasantry, and provide economic assistance from other socialist countries to bring Russia back from the brink of ruin. Indeed, the Bolsheviks took charge of society in the midst of its disintegration, a fact that greatly determined their subsequent actions.[12] By spring 1918, the economy—fueled earlier by war production—had virtually collapsed, casting industrial workers into the ranks of the unemployed. Factory employers had tolerated a modicum of worker participation during the war (as part of a patriotic struggle) but resisted militant demands for greater worker control in 1917. By winter 1917, as the economy collapsed, many plants had ceased to function, whether as the result of anti-labor lockouts, shortage of materials and fuel, or lack of demand. Local governments, originally independent of Bolshevik control, quickly became overwhelmed by the task of providing food and other necessities to their populations. Popular unrest and discontent with the government grew in response to food shortages, increasing unemployment, and the general chaos and suffering.[13] As economic collapse accelerated and unemployment increased, Lenin concluded that workers' control of factories could not resolve the industrial crisis and abandoned his earlier support for worker management in the factories.[14] Thus, the Bolsheviks nationalized industry in June 1918, giving factory control to the state.

By that time, the Bolsheviks' hold on power was already threatened by the onset of a civil war that would rage for another three years. Under what was later (and retroactively) called "war communism," the Bolsheviks embarked on a policy of "extreme communization,"[15] expressed first and foremost by the nationalization of industry and trade.[16] The government attempted to bring some order and control to the distribution of goods, even as it waged war in a desperate bid to retain power. Thus, various decrees later construed as a systematic program to communize society were actually efforts to cope with confusion and anarchy and provide the wherewithal to wage war on all fronts.[17]

War Communism was chiefly an attempt to gain control over the output of goods and commodities needed to win the civil war. Initially, the Bolsheviks did not even seize the railroads from the powerful Menshevik-controlled railroad trade union; the Bolsheviks succeeded in bringing the railroads under their control only in March 1918. In November and December 1917, the government seized the State Bank, nationalized private banks, and amalgamated all into the People's Bank of the Russian Republic; in February 1918, it expropriated all bank shareholders and repudiated foreign debts. In December 1917, the government had already established the Supreme Council of the National Economy, or Vesenkha,[18] with orders to organize the national economy and state finance and coordinate central and local regulating agencies. Vesenkha was under the jurisdiction of Sovnarkom (the Council of People's Commissars); its administration included representatives from various commissariats as well as workers. *Sovnarkhozy* (regional economic councils) oversaw the economy on the local level under the supervision of Vesenkha and local soviets and workers' councils. Various departments within Vesenkha called *glavki* were to control the activities of the various branches of industry, such as mining, oil and fuel production, and textiles. The glavki inherited their structure and staff from private business syndicates established before the revolution. In this, they resembled much of the Bolshevik administrative apparatus that, except for a thin layer of professional revolutionaries dedicated to the cause of the revolution, was of necessity composed of prerevolutionary administrative and technical personnel with varying loyalties. The necessity to retain such personnel fueled mounting frustration and resentment among communists and nonparty citizens seeking to create an entirely new society.

During the civil war, industry and production suffered from a constant drain of manpower—the very proletariat that had supported the Bolsheviks—

and from constant struggles of workers against prerevolutionary managers and specialists that the government effectively left in power. To combat this struggle and the resulting economic havoc that threatened military production, the government sought to impose strict labor discipline and outlaw strikes. It also constricted the right of self-management that the workers saw as the very heart of economic reform and productivity.

Like the workers in the factories but with far greater success, the peasants acted to satisfy their age-old aspiration of seizing control over private, state, and church land. But the peasants controlled the supply of food and could withhold grain from the cities, a situation the government could not allow. Like the workers' struggle to control the factories, the peasants' seizure of land had a disruptive effect on production. Through communes, land-hungry peasants repartitioned seized land into small allotments.[19] Rural and urban Russia became increasingly isolated from one another; in response to inflation and a goods shortage, the peasants ceased to trade their produce on the market. Although the peasants initially were willing to sell grain to the government, the situation began to change as the government became more desperate and more authoritarian.[20] In order to gain control over the supply of bread to the urban population, in 1918 the government initiated *prodrazverstka*—the seizure of "surplus" grain and other produce from the peasants. This theoretically came from peasants who had a surplus, namely, the *kulak* (lit. 'fist'; a traditional term denoting stronger peasants); in fact, however, the confiscation struck—and alienated—virtually the entire peasantry.[21] By February 1918, Lenin declared war on the kulaks for allegedly hoarding grain. The peasants, on their part, were attempting to sell their grain for the best price. Under conditions of hyperinflation, government grain prices were well below rising prices for consumer goods in short supply. The peasants thus sold their grain on the black market, which flourished in response to the dearth of goods and general economic chaos and in spite of a draconian ban on speculation.

Like the peasants, and despite a ban on private trade, millions of ordinary citizens ignored official efforts to control the economy and took to the road as bagmen to hawk basic commodities, most of which were no longer produced by state factories or stocked by state stores. The Bolsheviks were frustrated by their inability to stem the economic breakdown, a "petit-bourgeois flood" that stymied efforts at effective economic control. Bolshevik theory considered free trade as "monstrous speculation" and hoarding tantamount to sabotage. The party leadership, and Lenin in particular, became obsessed with controlling trade. Lenin directed the Petrograd Soviet in January 1918 to make mass searches of stores and houses.[22] This obsession, however, was in response to terrible hunger and deprivation in the cities that had already helped to topple two governments and threatened to do the same to the new Bolshevik regime. In the first winter after the revolution, the daily bread ration in Petrograd fell to 50 grams (two ounces) for the most favored stratum of society, the workers. Industrial production was hampered further by a general flight from the cities, as millions returned to the countryside to escape starvation.[23]

Even though hostilities with Poland, the final stage in seven continuous years of war, ended in October 1920, the Bolsheviks did not immediately relax their struggle to control and defend the country and the revolution. The strain caused by responding to the total collapse and chaos of the Russian economy left its mark on Lenin and other top Bolsheviks, who planned to base economic reconstruction on the militarization of labor, included in a resolution in April 1920 at the Ninth Party Congress "On Urgent Tasks of Economic Construction." As early as December 1919, War Commissar Leon Trotsky proposed to create "labor armies" of demobilized soldiers who would work in military-style detachments on public works and industrialization projects. After a winter of general starvation in the face of a food supply insufficient even for the workers, the Bolsheviks called for discipline and sacrifice.[24]

Bolshevik attempts to control the economy only contributed to the chaos, yet continued even after the civil war ended. In November 1920, even small industry was nationalized, and grain requisitioning was "strongly reasserted." Lenin attributed widespread peasant revolts in Tambov province and elsewhere not to government requisitioning, but to a Socialist Revolutionary conspiracy.[25] Ubiquitous discontent among the rural population spread to the armed forces, which had drawn its conscripts mainly from the peasantry. In March 1921, the discontent came to a head with a frightening revolt at the Kronstadt naval base by the very group that had helped to bring the Bolsheviks to power.[26]

The New Economic Policy (NEP)

Faced with an erosion of support among even its most loyal backers, in March 1921 under Lenin's leadership the Bolshevik government adopted a new approach. Their earlier attempts to control the economy were neither successful nor popular, and the country was on the brink of economic collapse, with its resources depleted, industry at a standstill, and food shortages widespread. Most importantly, Bolshevik economic policies were causing general revolt and threatening the regime. In response, Lenin was forced to abandon grain requisitioning and adopt measures that became known as the New Economic Policy, which lasted effectively until the Great Turn of the late 1920s under Stalin. The purpose of NEP was to appease the peasants by allowing free trade of food and other basic commodities. The government introduced a series of measures, including substituting prodrazverstka with a *prodnalog* (tax in kind) considerably lower than the requisitioning targets—and well below the government's actual needs for produce. The prodnalog was first to be paid in kind but later, after the government stabilized the currency in 1924, in money.

After paying the prodnalog, peasants could market their surplus. At first, they could only sell their goods locally, but this restriction was soon abandoned. Because of the need to move food to remote industrial areas, legalization of private trade inevitably soon followed. Even so, many party members, including Lenin himself, were loath to allow free trade. In a speech to the Tenth Party Congress, Lenin observed that "freedom of trade, even if at first it is not linked with the white guards, like Kronstadt was, nonetheless inevitably leads to white-guardism, to the victory of capital, to its full restoration."[27]

In NEP's early years, economic recovery seemed to justify these fears. NEP was not intended as a long-range strategy for implementing socialism, but rather, just as with War Communism, dictated by necessity. Lenin was forced to respond to a state of affairs that threatened the revolution and party control. He hoped that, if it controlled the commanding heights of the economy, the regime could lay the foundation for a socialist society.

Nevertheless, NEP seemed to herald the return of capitalism. It included the introduction of a stable new currency called the *chervonets*, backed by gold, which gradually replaced the *sovznak* that had succeeded the imperial ruble and become virtually worthless. The Bolsheviks also established a State Bank (October 1921) and Narkomfin (the People's Commissariat of Finance). Together, these agencies oversaw the stabilization of the currency and, by 1924, balanced the state budget. By then, the atmosphere had changed completely from the days of War Communism. Instead of the possibility of doing away with money altogether—and thus, it was thought, with economic disparity—the government now concerned itself with sound fiscal management.

Money's growing importance signaled ominous social developments, especially the appearance of a new class that controlled money and trade. "Nepmen" was the name popularly—and pejoratively—used to identify those who engaged in private business during the 1920s.[28] The nepmen were particularly active in retail trade, but some engaged in industrial production as well. They also functioned as middlemen, contractors, and sales agents for state and cooperative enterprises. In addition, the term referred to moneylenders and speculators in currency and scarce commodities.

The great majority of nepmen, however, were in retail trade, serving as the primary link between producer and consumer. This private trade soon ceased to restrict itself, as Lenin had hoped, to the exchange of goods at the local level. By fall 1921, the country was engulfed by what contemporaries termed an "orgy of trade." By the end of 1922, over 400,000 individuals had received trade licenses, accounting for 95 percent of all such licenses, with state and cooperative enterprises accounting for the rest. Most permits were for urban trade, where government surveillance was more effective; the number of traders outside this official net, however, was far greater. Private trade ranged from itinerant peddlers to urban department stores, but most was conducted in the traditional marketplaces and supplied basic consumer goods. By 1923, the private sector controlled over 80 percent of retail trade.[29] Although the regime periodically, or spasmodically, attempted to suppress these capitalists (as in 1925, when it took measures against nepmen), their numbers and presumed wealth seemed to grow inexorably. The number of private traders peaked in 1926, when 600,000 trade permits were granted.

Trade was not the only area opened to private activity. The government recognized that the nationalization of industry during War Communism had been unrealistic. By 1921, many plants were idle for lack of materials and, especially, fuel. In response, the Bolsheviks took measures to restore small manufacturing to private entrepreneurs and cooperatives. Hence, decrees of May-July 1921 denationalized small industry and empowered any citizen to organize and engage in cottage and small-scale industry (defined as any enterprise employing fewer than "ten to twenty" workers).[30] Vesenkha also leased enterprises under its control; by 1922 their number reached 10,000. Fifty percent of lessees were private individuals, some of them former owners.

Although nepmen did engage in industrial production (20 percent of industrial output in 1926), their role here was more modest. Private investment in industry was limited by several factors. Nepmen officially were prohibited from owning enterprises that employed more than twenty workers. Moreover, nepmen could never be certain how long NEP policies would continue and hence were reluctant to invest in large enterprises difficult to liquidate or conceal from state scrutiny. State enterprises were fewer in number, but far larger: in 1923 they accounted for 10 percent of plants but employed 85 percent of all industrial workers. Private producers, however, supplied most of the essential consumer goods sold by private traders.

Early Problems of NEP

NEP returned industry and agriculture to prewar production levels in a few short years, but recovery did not occur before disaster struck. In 1921, due to grain confiscations and a drought in major grain-producing areas, the harvest was less than half of the prewar average. Widespread famine resulted. The government responded by releasing affected areas from tax obligations and organizing emergency relief, but it did not have the resources to extend anything close to the level of relief required. The Bolsheviks had to accept foreign aid, particularly from the American Relief Administration.[31] Despite these efforts, millions of people died, and countless others fled famine areas. The experience left a deep impression on the collective memory of the country.

These years also saw a traumatic crisis in industry. During the civil war, the government attempted to sustain industry with funding based on rough estimates of enterprise needs. Factories received production orders, and whatever raw materials and fuel were available, to meet them. Workers' wages lost all value under hyperinflation, and so the government provided rations and social services, such as public transportation, healthcare, and housing, free of charge. But the system ultimately provided no incentives for efficiency or timely achievement of production goals. Most importantly, the state did not possess the resources to subsidize industrial concerns. Many plants closed for lack of material or fuel. Thus, from August 1921 through 1922, individual enterprises were compelled to operate according to *khozraschet* (cost accounting; self-sufficiency), that is, they were not subsidized by the state. The government converted former glavki into trusts and placed regulation of their financial and production plans under Vesenkha. Factories had to purchase raw materials at cost and produce marketable goods. Workers once again received their wages in cash, and social services were no longer free. Moreover, wages were effectively reduced by inflation. In short, just as it no longer subsidized industry, the government no longer subsidized the industrial worker.

In theory, khozraschet differed little from the profit and loss accounting of private business in the West, except in that the state owned large industrial enterprises. Although in practice, khozraschet was compromised by price-fixing and other aspects of government control, to administrators, workers, and society, Soviet socialist business was beginning to resemble capitalist business. Trusts competed for materials and sold their products to the nepman if he offered a better price. In order to operate commercially, state enterprises needed people with business experience, but these were rare among communist ranks. The government thus depended on *spetsy* (plant directors and technical specialists from prerevolutionary times). Communists had to rely on former businessmen especially for their expertise in procuring supplies, a dependence that some nepmen were able to exploit to great advantage.[32] Soviet businessmen were encouraged to learn from the nepmen how to be capitalists, and to build the socialist society with their profits.

Besides the tension between communists and capitalists, NEP generated other tensions. One that proved critical was competing interests—between industry and agriculture, workers and peasants. Initially, industries forced to finance themselves had difficulty obtaining operating capital. In 1921–1922, few people could afford to buy what goods were available. This led to a fall in the prices of industrial goods compared to foodstuffs. Unable to sell their goods, factories could not make ends meet and closed down, causing in turn a precipitous rise in unemployment. The workers gained the impression that with NEP, the government had abandoned them in favor of the peasantry.

The price disproportions reversed in 1923 with the famous "Scissors Crisis." Reeling from the shock of economic self-sufficiency, from years of neglect and no operating capital, industry took longer than agriculture to recover production levels. Moreover, the system of production trusts became more organized, and so competition for raw materials and markets greatly decreased. In addition, state industries were inefficient and production costs high. These factors contributed to a marked rise in industrial prices. By contrast, the state not only offered the peasant low prices but also was still the principal purchaser of grain. And the harvest of 1922 was a good one. Agricultural prices thus fell sharply in relation to industrial prices; by October 1923, they were as much as three times lower than their prewar parity. The price drop induced the peasants to cut production and withhold grain from sale to the cities. In turn, this shrinkage in agricultural production further reduced the peasants' purchasing power for consumer goods, triggering a new round of decreases in industrial sales. The government had to increase the prices it paid for agricultural goods, particularly for grain, and cut industrial prices.[33] Although the government had overcome the crisis by 1924 and now emphasized a *smychka* (alliance) between workers and peasants, in fact it could not reconcile their contradictory interests, the "petit-bourgeois" concerns of individual peasants against the "socialist" goals of the urban proletariat. The retreat to a consciously pro-peasant policy revealed the government's inability to control food production and distribution, implying the vulnerability of its entire vision for social and economic development. This retreat also brought into sharp relief the tenuous position of the worker, in danger of becoming "the stepchild of NEP."[34]

Throughout NEP, the government—which now controlled neither the means of production nor output and distribution—had to choose between inadequate grain procurements and intolerably high grain prices. Peasants had options: they could cut back cereal production and switch to industrial crops and animal husbandry. Ironically, it was the kulaks who were most productive and held greatest power over the marketplace. Thus, the kulaks produced 13 percent of the grain, of which they sold 20 percent; the remaining peasants produced 85 percent of the grain but marketed only 11 percent. The state and collective farms, on the other hand, accounted for the remaining 1.7 percent of production, but marketed fully half of their produce, thus presenting for the government a tempting alternative for agricultural production in the future.

In the short run, and despite crises and tensions, NEP went far toward a restoration of prewar production levels. Foreign investment remained negligible; given the Bolshevik repudiation of foreign debts and confiscation of foreign property and the apparent political and social instability in Russia, few investors were prepared to accept Bolshevik invitations to invest and obtain concessions. The communists who ruled Russia and the capitalists abroad were mutually suspicious and hostile. Nevertheless, foreign trade did grow, providing the Bolshevik government with the machinery and equipment needed for reconstruction. In 1922, Russia concluded a trade agreement with Britain, followed by other countries. Exports grew to one third their prewar level. Farm machinery, locomotives, and electrical and other parts and equipment were imported. Thus supplied, transport also quickly recovered from a virtual standstill. In 1921, the railroads were paralyzed due to lack of fuel and the poor condition of rolling stock. By the following year, however, the situation improved, and as of the fiscal year 1926–27 rail transport exceeded 1913 levels.

Labor did not share in the benefits of economic recovery.[35] For the workers who were employed, wages recovered slowly from their disastrous levels of 1921–22, almost recovering their prewar parity by the 1925–26 fiscal year. But it was an employer's market: official wage scales were unenforceable and strikes discouraged by the party. The situation was bleaker still for the unemployed. Unemployment rose steadily throughout NEP, presenting a grave problem economically, socially, and politically. The official number of unemployed grew from 1.25 million in January 1924 to over 1.5 million by 1929, a high proportion compared to the employed labor force (8.5 million workers and employees in 1924). Moreover, engineers, specialists, and top administrators and bureaucrats experienced almost universal employment, while manual and clerical workers bore the brunt of unemployment. Women, juveniles, and youth fared the worst; they were the proverbial "last hired, first fired" in the workforce, and often suffered a desperate fate indeed during NEP. In addition to the high number of unemployed were the millions of homeless children who roamed the country, orphaned or abandoned during the years of war and famine. An already saturated labor market offered few hopes to these children for work and rehabilitation.[36]

Moreover, the growth of state industry could not continue indefinitely without state investment. Because of the increase in wages to meet inflation and other production costs, both profits and accumulation for reinvestment were falling. By spring 1926 industrial recovery had begun to slow down. Thus, the government instituted various initiatives to cut the cost of production in order to make industry more efficient and therefore profitable. One initiative was a cost-cutting campaign called the "economic regime," a common source of complaint in appeals to the center. Vesenkha initiated the economic regime in an attempt to promote industrial development without placing undue pressure on the peasantry.[37] The purpose was to lower production costs, increase sales, and raise new capital for reinvestment in industry. Economizing primarily took the form of higher labor productivity, which was to be achieved through increased labor discipline, better management, and higher quality control. But, as early as July 1926, the economic regime provoked sharp criticism from the Left Opposition in the party which denounced the campaign as "a device for putting pressure on the workers"—a criticism that Stalin and the party Right soon conceded. The critics condemned an economic initiative to make production more efficient mainly at the expense of manual workers, while white-collar workers retained high salaries, bonuses, and perquisites, and administrative staffs remained disproportionately large.[38] Although it nominally abandoned the campaign, the government retained the economic regime as a guiding principle.

State Control

NEP reached its apogee in 1925, in both economic and political terms, but plainly suffered from fundamental and irreconcilable contradictions. In addition to those already discussed (the conflicting interests between workers and peasants; the operation of a socialist economy according to capitalist principles), there remained the problem of government control over economic development. That contradiction was embedded in NEP itself, which presupposed that business and industry were to operate independently of government support but under government supervision. Thus, the function of Vesenkha was constantly reassessed and duplicated by other government agencies charged with administration and planning, suggesting not only confusion over the government's economic role, but also a lack of coordination and, ultimately, of control over economic development. Shortly before NEP's introduction, the government had created Gosplan, with the responsibility of creating a general economic plan for the state and a design to implement it. However, it was never Gosplan's role to create an overall economic scheme, only to offer forecasts and guides for setting priorities. Gosplan and Vesenkha even competed in creating plans for economic production and growth, and, from the beginning, Vesenkha sought a much greater degree of economic control. Although Vesenkha gave the government close supervision over certain branches of industry, others operated quite independently, especially in consumer production. As the decade progressed, the issue of planning became central to the debate over the economic and political future of the country.

The possibility of government control over the economy became closer as the decade progressed. Beginning in 1923, when private traders possessed a virtual monopoly of the consumer market, the state and cooperative network steadily gained ground through competition and, increasingly, elimination of the competition. In industry, the state gained steadily as well. It controlled heavy industry from the start but by mid-decade began to make inroads on consumer production. In 1923, the private sector, mostly individual or family enterprises, controlled 90 percent of small-scale production. By 1926, this share fell to 78 percent.

Only in agriculture did the private sector retain control, and thus limit the government's ability to exploit its production. The vast majority of land was occupied by poor or middle peasants, that is, those who merely subsisted or produced only a modest surplus to sell to the state. The kulaks, approximately 5 to 7 percent of the peasantry, provided much of the grain that the state needed for export. Even the kulaks, however, were able to produce much less surplus grain than had prerevolutionary landlords and kulaks combined; the large estates, which had been modernized and were able to exploit economies of scale, had given way to a sea of small, inefficient peasant household producers. Hence, the supply of grain decreased, even as demand rose.

Yet, agricultural development was critical to industrialization, which in turn was essential for military security and the long-term survival of the proletarian state. Many throughout the government, the military, and society as a whole believed that if the Soviet Union was to survive in a sea of hostile capitalist powers, the country had to industrialize rapidly. Beyond that, the kulak was an internal enemy—not just because of his power in the village, but also because of his economic power over the government. To encourage the kulak to produce more grain was, in effect, to encourage the enemy to prosper and become stronger. Thus, under NEP, the state's economic goals conflicted with its political identity. As long as prosperity continued to enrich the private sector, the possibility of building socialism—the cause for which the Bolsheviks had seized power—grew more remote.

The End of NEP

Lenin himself had recognized the tensions between the economic necessity for NEP and its long-term risks. He had hoped to reconcile these tensions by persuading peasants to accept a socialist form of agricultural production and inducing them to join producers' cooperatives. In any case, after 1922, an incapacitated Lenin lost the ability to formulate economic policy, a task that devolved on competing party factions and claimants to power. As Lenin's health continued to worsen, the consistency of government policy increasingly suffered from party debate over a long-term economic strategy and the country's economic future. On the Right, Nikolai Bukharin maintained that NEP would have to last at least a generation to improve Russia's agricultural situation. In 1925, when NEP reached its height, the maladroit politician even encouraged the peasantry to "get rich" in order to improve agricultural production. Bukharin was confident that over time, socialism would win. Trotsky, representing the left wing of the party, demanded NEP's immediate termination, vigorous measures against the kulak, and a much more ambitious program of industrialization. But the Left Opposition conceded that the country could not build socialism in isolation, a problematic position in view of the apparent ebb tide of world revolution. Ultimately, both an increased pace in industrialization and the collectivization of agriculture were accepted by the party in principle, at the Fourteenth and Fifteenth Party Congresses (1925 and 1927, respectively). Stalin did not openly commit to either the right or left until 1929; once he defeated his political rivals, Stalin condemned Bukharin's conciliatory policy toward the peasantry and moved toward the fateful decision to support the collectivization of agriculture in 1930.

The movement toward greater control of agricultural production was also reflected in government policy toward the nepmen. Under conditions of profound economic uncertainty and the apparent revival of capitalism in the midst of a socialist revolution, the nepmen were almost universally reviled by the population and under constant threat of attack by the government, depending on which political faction had the upper hand. Many party leaders and rank-and-file communists were concerned that the government, instead of learning from the capitalists, would be engulfed by them and succumb to capitalist control. The early stages of NEP appeared to confirm the worst fears over the future of communism. If the nepmen gained control of the economy, capitalism would be restored and the revolution would fail.

After Lenin's death in January 1924, the economic moderates led by Bukharin temporarily gained the upper hand in party policy. Bukharin essentially dismissed the dangers posed by the nepmen and leftist warnings that their growing strength signaled the restoration of capitalism. He favored instead peaceful economic competition between the public and private sectors, confident that the socialist state would eventually win the competition and ultimately the consumers. Under pressure from the Left Opposition in the party, however, by 1926 Bukharin was compelled to call for greater regulation of the activity of nepmen. Several measures were undertaken to squeeze them out of business. For example, surcharges for transporting private goods by rail were steadily increased, and taxes on private profits were raised, including one imposed in June 1926 on "super profits." At the same time, taxes on wealthier peasants were also increased. In addition, an amendment to the criminal code

> envisaged imprisonment for up to three years with total or partial confiscation of property for those guilty of evil-intentioned increases in prices of commodities through purchase, hoarding, or non-placing on the market.[39]

By late 1927, Stalin had essentially adopted the militant rhetoric of the defeated Left Opposition and called for a rapid elimination of the nepmen. He warned that an imminent and climactic class struggle would decide whether capitalists or communists determined the revolution's fate. By 1928, mounting grain shortages compelled the regime to seek a final resolution of the economic and social tensions of the countryside by waging war against the kulaks and taking the first steps toward collectivization of agriculture. The government also adopted increasingly harsh measures to eliminate nepmen that mirrored the war against the kulaks. Profit was thenceforth officially deemed antisocial and antisocialist. All of this was closely linked to the preparation in 1927 of the first Five-Year Plan and its vigorous implementation over the next few years. In what appeared to be a revival of War Communism, the party banned private trade as tantamount to speculation, forbade the private use of hired labor, and terminated any remaining concessions and leases for private enterprise.

NEP began as the reintroduction of market relations in the countryside on a limited basis in order to resolve a food supply crisis. But within a few years, the rate of growth of private trade exceeded the communist leadership's wildest expectations. Gone was the radical phase of communism that prevailed during the civil war. The establishment of long-awaited economic and social reconstruction was postponed to a later, unspecified future date.

What follows is a study of the social tensions that attended that postponement. NEP, and the social and economic climate it engendered, soon fostered deep frustrations and resentment throughout society. It was regarded by many both within and outside the party, and by foreign observers as well, as the abandonment of radical communist revolutionary goals and a return to capitalism and the inequities it implied.[40] In the popular mind, capitalism connoted not so much an economic system, as a catalyst of social, cultural, and economic hierarchy. Socioeconomic disparity and social inequality had persisted even under the radically stringent conditions of War Communism. But especially after Lenin introduced NEP, social disparity was allowed to flourish, and the realization of a socialist utopia appeared even more remote. Class war was a reality throughout the 1920s, not just an official policy later declared and inaugurated by Stalin. The issue under examination in the following chapters is how the perception of social inequality caused the mobilization of groups against each other and fed revolutionary tension throughout the 1920s in Russia, culminating in the so-called Stalinist revolution.

CHAPTER TWO

Collective Rights and Interests

FOR the lower classes, the October Revolution promised to bring social justice and material security. Many who supported the Bolsheviks thought that the revolution would ensure a more equitable distribution of wealth and power than had existed previously. Throughout NEP, in letters to party leaders and in political rhetoric, the goals of the revolution were often summed up in a single phrase: building the socialist society. Building socialism meant constructing not only an industrialized nation capable of providing a higher standard of living for all, but also a collective social organism capable of ensuring that that higher standard of living would be enjoyed equally.[1] Building socialism thus could be considered a catchphrase for the creation of an egalitarian society.

The egalitarian impulse was hardly new. The establishment of socialism found its roots in the peasant commune of tsarist times. The commune historically provided material security to the Russian peasant through periodic repartition of land, provision of social security, and a long tradition of law and custom that regulated and stabilized the peasant's existence, marginal as it was. Indeed, nineteenth-century socialists viewed the commune as a proto-socialist institution and hoped to save it from the onslaughts of capitalism and modernity. Neither of these tendencies, however, could be arrested. After the Great Reforms of 1861, the commune began to erode. Under the burdens of taxation and redemption payments they paid to compensate the aristocracy for the land, the peasantry experienced growing economic differentiation. Moreover, the glaring gaps between the existence of most Russians and that of the small elite were hardly touched by the reforms. What communism promised in the Revolution of 1917 was a more equitable division of resources and wealth than had existed under tsarism. Many perceived the revolution as a restoration of justice and equity. Especially following the ravages of war, revolution, and famine, material security became the central goal of communist society.

For many communists and nonparty citizens alike, creating an egalitarian society meant material security not on an individual level, as in the West, but on a collective level. In the West, security has been sought historically through guaranteeing the rights of private wealth and individual freedom and initiative. In contrast, communist society ideally provided security to the individual through membership in a collective that limited individual freedom but ensured provision of life's necessities, which private wealth and individual freedom had failed to provide for the majority in prerevolutionary Russia or, indeed, in the West. Capitalism and the chaos of the free market brought exploitation and social and economic disparity. Supporters of communism hoped to escape these social evils through the establishment of collective security.

The socialist collective would provide material and social security both on a mass level and through constituent organizations such as the Communist Party, the Red Army, and the Komsomol. The collective, it was hoped, would offer the masses the security, sustenance, and protection of a family. As in a family, those who sought membership in the collective expected protection and nurturing in return for an equal share of labor to sustain the family and, when necessary, to defend it from threats to its integrity.

As expressed in letters and appeals to the center, people viewed the roles of the various Bolshevik leaders in different ways. Lenin was the head of the collective family, the founder of the revolution, and the leader of the worldwide struggle against capitalism. Supplicants often addressed him in a tone of deference, acknowledging his genius and his role as mastermind of the revolutionary struggle. Stalin, by contrast, while often addressed with deference, was yet a comrade, an equal of the common man, a fellow fighter among his troops on the revolutionary ramparts. This last image was often evoked both figuratively and literally, as civil war veterans reminisced about their mutual struggle. These reminiscences were not merely sentimental; they often implied a sense that the revolution was far from over, and a conviction that Stalin would lead them in a future battle to salvage the collective and build the socialist society they had been promised.

Historical Roots of the Collective

The desire after 1917 to form a mass collective in Russia that would redistribute wealth and power among workers and peasants drew perhaps on an earlier type of collective that still existed after the revolution, albeit in a much-altered form. This was the peasant commune, the traditional social and economic organization among the majority of Russian peasants.[2] The commune provided social and material security and with a tradition of law and custom around which the whole of peasant society revolved. Traditionally, the commune's functions included the regulation of land use and its periodic repartition among the households of the village; settlement of civil and some criminal disputes according to common law; maintenance of public order within, and of defense from threats outside the commune; mutual aid and assistance; and management of the public, social, and religious life of the village.

The peasant commune was all-encompassing. It regulated all public life in the village and operated according to a legal and moral code that varied with each commune. The purpose was to ensure order and harmony and a modicum of material security. Thus, for instance, land was distributed according to size of household, and taxes were levied according to the ability to pay. In the village assembly (composed of male heads of household), decisions were made only after unanimous assent. Because the purpose of the commune was to ensure collective survival, individual freedom was restricted to minimize conflict with group interests. However, as in the village assembly, members of the commune were not coerced into conformity with the majority, but rather persuaded. Conformity was voluntary. The commune provided all; thus, there was no need to make a distinction between the individual and the group.[3]

After the elimination of serfdom in 1861, the commune acquired another function that would alter its character and effectiveness. Traditionally, the commune had functioned as a social and economic leveler; through periodic repartition of land and distribution of other obligations it had kept disparity within the village to a minimum. After 1861 this changed. The commune became responsible for collecting taxes and redemption payments that the peasants owed to the state to buy their land, obligations that progressively pauperized an ever greater number. The strain on the land became too great to adequately support a growing rural population, and hence over the latter half of the nineteenth century social and economic disparity within the commune grew.[4] The younger generation left the land to find work in the cities or sought desperately to increase their own holdings in the village. Thus, when in 1906 Prime Minister P. A. Stolypin introduced legal reforms to allow individuals to separate their allotments from the commune—in the hope of creating a class of independent, Western-style farmers—it was not generally the wealthier peasants that opted for separation (as might have been anticipated or hoped), but the poorer ones, mainly in order to sell their insufficient holdings.[5]

Throughout the late nineteenth and early twentieth centuries, the peasant commune thus was under assault from the forces of change and modernity. It shared this fate with Russian society as a whole. These forces ultimately toppled an autocracy that could not adapt to change, and created a huge rural and urban population clamoring for a new social construct that would offer the social and material security the commune once had provided.

The Search for Collective Security

The emphasis on the collective, therefore, was a distinctive component of traditional Russian culture that profoundly shaped postrevolutionary attitudes and assumed greater significance in the midst of trauma and dislocation.[6] Russian society in the immediate postrevolutionary years was highly fluid, unstable, and reeling from a decade of war, revolution, and famine. Throughout the 1920s, many in the Communist Party and in society at large sought an escape from overwhelming insecurity. Soviet citizens across the political spectrum expressed in their letters to the party leadership a yearning for security and stability. Describing the nature and composition of the working class in the immediate postrevolutionary period, Soviet historians observed that the

> social structure of the working class of soviet society . . . cannot be presented as a kind of mechanical aggregate of isolated social groups. The main [characteristic] of their social structure is the *cooperation* of socially distinct strata and their unity.[7]

As letters and appeals show, this assertion expressed both the communist ideal and the genuine aspirations of a significant number of Soviet citizens, communist and nonparty alike. A group of printers from Poltava sent their greetings to Lenin in March 1923. They wrote that, because they "did not have the opportunity to see you [Lenin] in their ranks at meetings or conferences of their union, and desiring to present an account to you, as honorary member" of their work, the printers assured Lenin that they were indeed achieving "the material and spiritual well-being on behalf of the great worker-peasant collective of the whole world." The printers swore that this victory would be "secured by the ongoing creative work in the process of our own labor."[8] It was understood that, if they fulfilled their obligation to contribute and commit to the common good, their membership in the collective was ensured.

The Collective as Family

Many communist supporters viewed socialist society in terms of a family. Victor Kravchenko wrote that as a young communist, while being tenderly and carefully treated for injuries he sustained in a mining accident, he "had the sense of having been adopted by all of Russia . . . as the favorite son of a vast and wonderful family."[9] Many workers' clubs formed in the early years of the revolution provided a "second home" for their members because they fed them in canteens.[10]

The urge to form a nurturing family was articulated by revolutionaries long before October 1917. In the aftermath of the 1905 Revolution, shop clerks from Pskov agitated to organize "into a union, into a close-knit, friendly family . . . [in order to] represent a force that will give us the opportunity to attain a better share."[11] The strong bond of a family ensured survival for all its members. This message reverberated throughout postrevolutionary society and was evoked by and understood throughout the ranks of collective organizations. Each soldier inducted into the Red Army swore to defend the revolution "as a son of the laboring people, a citizen of the Soviet Republic," and the Red Army itself was characterized as "one great family of toilers."[12] Red Army veterans (and others) would later employ these images when they appealed to the party leadership for work or pensions, as they would to a "son" or "brother."[13]

In addressing party leaders or in describing the type of party and society that characterized their ideals, supplicants commonly employed family imagery.[14] Messages sent in the early postrevolutionary years displayed confidence in the ultimate victory of the socialist family on the economic front.[15] On the occasion of their union's third anniversary, miners from Shakhty *uezd* (district) in the Donbass sent greetings from their

> mining brothers, and for our part we declare—rest assured that your ideas, proclaimed in October, are firmly guarded and taking root in our workers' family. We miners also declare, be confident esteemed comrades in the victory over worldwide capital.[16]

Similarly, on the occasion of the opening of a new mill, the "workers and employees" of Nizhnii Novgorod railroad wrote to Lenin "[declaring that we are working] as a collective family, not subdividing into classes by profession, and the result is plain—we are united."[17] The difference in images used here is significant: the Donbass miners considered themselves "brothers" and did not appear to include white-collar workers and administrators in their mining family. By contrast, the workers and employees—white-collar workers—of the railroad express a desire to combine into one collective family, "not subdividing into classes," thereby avoiding class conflict.

As the decade progressed, earlier, optimistic images of the collective family successfully uniting to achieve common goals seem to disappear and be replaced with images of longing for a family that might sustain its members. These images were especially pronounced in the appeals of those who had been totally abandoned, or were in danger of rejection by the collective family. Many such appeals came from veterans. Thus, in his appeal to Stalin for work in 1927, a Red Army veteran from Yaroslavl *guberniia* (province) wrote of entering the party: "I joined its ranks . . . like a son in need."[18] Another party member, demobilized after ten years' service, pleaded with Stalin to be sent to fight in the Chinese Revolution, since, apparently, the army had been the only home and family the unemployed peasant had ever known.[19] Similarly, a veteran, who had been expelled from the party because of his father's background in trade, appealed to Stalin for help. Since the veteran had a family of his own, he was in no position to support his sister and brothers. But, he argued, "the three kids could be useful in the future, you know, if they saw that for them, the Soviet power was not a stepmother but a mother."[20]

Similar messages issued from workers and party members. In 1927 a former railroad worker from Minsk guberniia from a poor peasant background wrote after being laid off: "Comrade Stalin, I appeal to you as to my father and mother as well as defender and leader of the working class . . . I have been discarded from the family of workers, as a worthless element."[21] A *komsomolets* (member of the Communist Youth League) studying at a *rabfak* in Leningrad, expelled after refusing to admit his guilt in inciting a strike, appealed to Stalin for help, since "the rabfak was like a home to me, because I have nowhere else to go in light of the fact that I do not have any relatives and had worked as a batrak [agricultural laborer] from 1919 until I entered the rabfak."[22] In yet another appeal to Stalin in 1927 for "any kind of work," a party member from Shadrinskii *okrug* expressed his certainty that Stalin would not "abandon without consideration someone who was like a member of his own family."[23]

Sometimes organizations and institutions of Soviet society were not families but the structures that housed them. In February 1927, a self-described rank-and-file party member from Sverdlovsk wrote a long, rambling, and somewhat incoherent letter protesting the government's cost-cutting measures and class inequality. The party, "according to [his] understanding," was supposed to be "united and unshakable" in following the testament of Lenin. The party was like a house, and all its members stones that were held together by the cement of Lenin's words. That cement held the party together against both the onslaughts of the "worldwide bourgeoisie, with their capital" from without, and of the opposition from within. The main goal was to keep the house sturdy. The supplicant expounded at length on the economy and ended with a request to transfer him and his wife and baby to a healthier climate. For that, he would do "any kind of work you like."[24] Such appeals raised the question of what lengths individuals would go to, in order to gain security and keep the house intact.

The Social Contract between Party and Collective

As the preceding implies, supplicants expected the Bolsheviks to provide refuge for members of the socialist family. In return, family members would contribute their share of work and, if necessary, defend the collective from threats to its integrity. But supplicants predicated that willingness on the party's ability to sustain all family members in equal measure. Security and stability could be attained only through the availability of work for everyone and equal distribution of the fruits of that labor. This was the social contract on which support for the Bolshevik regime was based.

Supplicants recognized their responsibilities to the collective. To remain a member, one had not only to contribute one's fair share of work but also to refrain from taking more than what one needed to satisfy "personal needs and ambitions, and that without foreshortening or stultifying the needs and ambitions of any other." The communist government "set out to awaken the individual intellectually to the fact" that his or her personal happiness depended on the general happiness. General happiness in turn resided in recognition that injuring or taking from another the necessities of life detracted from the quality of one's own life, as a member of the "[social] organism of which he is a part."[25] The message apparently was taking root. An educated peasant, working as a director in the taxation office of a district soviet in Smolensk guberniia, was refused party membership by virtue of his white-collar status. Nevertheless, he wished to be sent to aviation school to become a pilot in the Soviet air force and "give [his] life in defense of the October conquest, when necessary." The supplicant reached this decision upon realizing that "one does not need to live only for oneself."[26]

The revolution's survival was very much in question in the early years, and the socialist collective in jeopardy. Socialism was not so much a system as an ongoing commitment, an organism with a delicate constitution that required constant nourishment and affirmation to survive. A group of working women sent a letter of greeting to Lenin on the occasion of the anniversary of their "freedom . . . from the vestiges of olden times . . . keeping us enslaved and to this day still not eliminated." They "fervently hoped that the liberated women of Kyrgyziia [*sic*] already understood the necessity of active participation in soviet construction, fulfilled by new recruits to the ranks of the communist party."[27] The women's appeal appears to display some apprehension that, lest their sisters not bolster the party with active membership, they might once again become enslaved by "the vestiges of olden times."

Many supplicants appeared eager to show the government they understood that building socialism required active participation. Thus, many appeals are filled with assurances of duties successfully fulfilled. At a meeting of railroad security workers held in September 1922 a resolution was passed to send a greeting to Lenin, wishing for the return of his health and assuring him that,

> regarding the crucial work that has been placed before us, guarding the most valuable property of the Republic—grain . . . we are fulfilling with honor the task set before us, in spite of the fact that we live under the most difficult material conditions—rest assured that not one kernel of grain will be lost from the transport lines guarded by us.[28]

Apparent in many such letters is a significant feeling of incorporation in the task at hand, a sense of pride and a belief that whatever role they played in the survival and growth of the collective was important. In a telegram to wish Lenin a speedy recovery, a group of firefighters assured him that they "[understood] your bidding and promise to fight fires selflessly, firmly appreciating that we are the safe keepers of the property of workers and peasants."[29] Similarly, in a letter to Lenin in August 1923, workers and employees of the local transport union of Kozlov uezd, Tambov *oblast'*, attested that they had fulfilled Lenin's call for worker productivity 100 percent, and quotas for grain export by 100 percent as well.[30]

Clearly, those who expressed their unconditional devotion to the communist government did so because in their own eyes they had a vested interest in the government and the society it represented. Incorporation was key to the revolution's survival, and many were eager to enfranchise themselves in ownership of the new society. Representatives of the "female workers of Archangel" sent Lenin a telegram in November 1923, recalling the time when

> five years ago, at an all-Russian congress of female workers and peasants, you said: "Under Soviet power, even cooks can run the government." Believing your summons, under the leadership of the communist party we, Archangel female workers—wood cutters, metal workers, water haulers, printers, textile workers, seamstresses and cooks—are learning how to govern and consciously taking part in the construction of our workers' country.[31]

These female workers were learning—and were motivated to learn—how to become vested citizens of their country, because of Lenin's faith that they possessed both the ability and the right to do so. They let Lenin know that they took his invitation to them to take an active role in building socialism seriously.

Similarly, a group of "worker-peasant youth awaiting call up" wrote to Lenin in April 1923 to wish him a speedy recovery. The youth, who were following the course of Lenin's illness "with great attention," assured him that they were

> studying the military craft, how to read and write, politically developing, we future conscripts are prepared to enter the ranks of the Red Army, and will prove worthy reserves to strike fear into the enemies of the proletariat—international capitalists.[32]

The young conscripts were eager to become defenders of the Soviet state, that is, to assume their position in the military. They felt they had earned this right to become "worthy" defenders, because they were raising their level of education and political consciousness, which was the responsibility of every active citizen and member of socialist society.

Supplicants took every opportunity to remind their leaders that the socialist contract required the good faith not only of the proletariat but also of their leaders, and to emphasize that their support was based in the Bolsheviks' dedication to them. This understanding comes through repeatedly in letters written in the early postrevolutionary years. In March 1923, a group of factory workers passed a unanimous resolution to send Lenin a greeting on the occasion of the Bolshevik Party's twenty-fifth anniversary. The workers resolved to do this after hearing a speech on the party's longstanding and unrelenting

> activities . . . directed wholly to the betterment of the existence and lives of workers and peasants. We workers . . . mostly nonparty . . . wish the party to thrive and continue, in order to firmly stand in defense of workers and peasants.[33]

Peasants, workers, and government employees bombarded Lenin with the message that their dedication to him and the party's initiatives required a reciprocal commitment. This message appeared to be a product of both a sincere popular belief in Lenin's dedication to the cause of the revolution, and popular manipulation of Lenin's official image as savior of the people as a reminder to Lenin and his government, whose interests they represented.[34] On the occasion of his fiftieth birthday, those present at a meeting of party members and workers on the Kazan railroad sent Lenin a telegram, wishing him "health, energy and strength" for his further work on behalf of the proletariat, "recognizing and appreciating all your fruitful work in the construction of a new, happy life for laborers, and we for our part promise to use all our energy so that the construction . . . takes place successfully."[35] To mark Lenin's fifty-third birthday, a telegram was sent by representatives of a general assembly of party and Komsomol members of the "administration of the worker-peasant militia" of Irkutsk guberniia, to express their deep devotion to their leader. This loyalty stemmed from Lenin's own "dedication to the cause of the struggle to liberate the laboring masses," which resulted in the fact that he was "loved by the millions of oppressed slaves of capital."[36] A group of railroad workers at a regional conference wrote to Lenin to extend greetings from the delegates, "emphasizing their certainty that our Il'ich will give us much more yet in the future construction of the RSFSR," and promising to fulfill their part of the bargain in return.[37] And, a district soviet in Odessa sent Lenin the text of a resolution adopted at a meeting of lumber workers which extended their

> brotherly greetings to the leader of the proletariat, dear Il'ich, with the wish for his soonest recovery, in order that he have the opportunity to guide the ship of communism to the shore of a world where there won't be exploitation of one human being of another.[38]

Lenin was acknowledged as the creative genius and motivating force behind the revolution. During the long period of his progressive physical debilitation that overhung the early NEP years, the leader received countless expressions of grief and anxiety on the part of the laboring masses, who depended on him as on a father to raise their socialist utopia to maturity. His imminent death throughout the early 1920s brought the prospect of their abandonment on a mass level. In May 1923, a telegram to Lenin from a Briansk guberniia conference of the Department of Labor assured him that "the entire proletariat of the world" awaited "with trepidation" his return to steer "the ship of socialism, as an experienced helmsman."[39]

Ubiquitous expressions of anxiety showed supplicants' conviction that the survival of the revolution depended wholly on Lenin's survival. Government and party representatives from Penza guberniia wrote to Lenin on the occasion of the opening of a new Palace of Labor to express their hope for his recovery, since

> at the time when you were treacherously wounded we also followed your pulse and breathing and were confident in your recovery and now we do not wish to hear of your departure from us.
>
> You will be with us, you will lead [us] to the bright days of socialism.[40]

Such expressions of hope for, and confidence in, Lenin's recovery read as much like the authors' attempts to reassure themselves, as words of encouragement for their leader. Young communists especially hoped that Lenin would provide the direction and recognition they needed to bring socialism to fruition, and they expressed deep anxiety at the prospect of losing this direction prematurely. Representatives of a Komsomol conference wrote to Lenin on May Day, 1923, to express concern over his health, reminding him that "you [*ty*] are precious to us. Precious and necessary to the entire international proletariat."[41] And a Komsomol organization in Vladikavkaz sent Lenin a telegram in April 1923, pleading for the sake of those forming the "relief shift" in the struggle to establish communism that Lenin would be "for many years still for us the leader, director and teacher that you were for our older comrades . . . Your health is precious not only to us, but to the proletariat of the entire world."[42]

Many appeals articulated anxiety over the possibility that Lenin might abandon the cause of the revolution. Some read almost like messages of encouragement or inspiration, born out of despair. In May 1920, komsomoltsy from Kazan guberniia wrote to Lenin,

> not with hope that our letter would direct your attention to us, only to make known to you our dream of receiving from you maybe a few words, which would be proof to us that our great teacher was very near to us, and was not forgetting about us.[43]

In November 1922, party conference delegates in Don oblast sent a telegram to Lenin to express their great joy at the news of his recent recovery, since "the Russian and worldwide proletariat received through you reliable and keen theory, strategy and tactics [for the] proletarian revolution." For their part, the delegates assured Lenin that they would "apply all their energy to the practical implementation of all the tasks" that the party had placed before them, "since on this depends the well-being of our Republic of workers and peasants."[44]

Thus, countless supplicants made clear that their support was based in the expectation that Lenin and the party would deliver on their part of the contract. The very nature of that popular mandate, however, created a contradiction that seemingly could not be resolved. In order to fulfill popular expectations of the creation of an egalitarian society, the party would have to be strong. But the party's growing strength inevitably diminished egalitarianism. This inherent contradiction is apparent in an appeal sent in 1921 to the Russian president M. I. Kalinin that listed point by point the various ills that currently plagued the new republic. The supplicant described himself as a railroad worker and old revolutionary, who, although never allied with any particular party, had taken part in the 1905 and 1917 revolutions, and who, "beginning from the time when I was capable of independent thought, was an opponent of the capitalist-landlord system of government." He emphasized that his parents were peasants, and that he was not "an adherent of the bourgeois order." He admonished party leaders to end the class war and to repair the damage done to the country. This would be impossible unless the party could regain its authority and establish genuine power which, however, had to be based "on the voice of the majority"—prescriptions that were clearly contradictory. Indeed, the supplicant bemoaned the party's favoritism of "a small group of official, registered proletariat, to the obvious detriment of the remaining mass of non-registered proletariat." Such favoritism caused "sharp antagonism among the pure proletarian masses."

Nevertheless, it appeared to many both within and outside the government that collective order was required before collective material security could be established. According to the supplicant, two vital tasks stood before the party. The first was to establish better organization in the center to overcome "the lack of system and order and the chaos and chance" that plagued administration with "bureaucratism like never before." But certainly, a weak party could not establish such a level of organization. The second was to create a system that provided equal access to and distribution of goods and work to everyone. The author did not believe that everyone was equal but maintained nevertheless that the party should extend to everyone "equal . . . conditions and rights to work." The people's dissatisfaction came not from a lack of goods, he claimed, but from the government's "inability to distribute what they had." Significantly, he considered the government's "authorization of free trade in grain and . . . goods"—NEP—a "colossal" mistake.[45]

It was clear not only that the party had to establish equal access to goods and work and demonstrate that those who labored were benefiting directly from it, but also that this would require a far greater degree of organization and control. Echoing this message, a citizen from the Donbass systematically outlined to the leadership his recommendations for the organization of production and education in order to achieve satisfaction of the needs of every member of society. He concluded by suggesting that

> the branches of production should absorb all people without exception, so that every person from the day of his birth to the day he dies would be connected with production, counting as one of its reserves, first as a worker and finally as a pensioner.[46]

Thus would the needs of state and citizen be met and a productive utopia be created that satisfied the need for stability, order, control, harmony and, above all, security.

In Defense of the Collective

Like the need for internal order, the need for protection against internal and external enemies also implied a level of central control that threatened to overwhelm the equally strong popular mandate to build an egalitarian society. The desire to establish a secure collective, and willingness to take part in its defense, was a common message in letters to both Lenin and Stalin. A poor peasant from Vladimir guberniia wrote to Stalin in July 1927. Having read an appeal in the newspaper *Bednota*[47] from the Communist Party to party members, workers, and peasants concerning the threat of war with the West, the peasant pledged his support for the government and his willingness to join in the fight "against evil imperialists, against our enemies, who maliciously prepare for war against our honest proletariat and our dear bolshevik communist party." Why was he willing to fight for the government? Because, as he stated:

> I well know that the party works exclusively for us ignorant workers and peasants, it struggles for the betterment of our existence, it endeavors in every possible way to raise the level of our industry and agriculture. . . . For one hundred years the communist party . . . struggled to free us from the yoke of slavery and from the . . . hands of tsarism, in whose grip we remained for 300 years without hope of freedom.[48]

The peasant viewed the party as his refuge, his savior. But more than that, the government was his government, not the government of the nobility or the bourgeoisie. As the peasant saw it, he was not just the first in line, but the only one in line to reap its benefits.

The willingness to defend the workers' state was a common sentiment throughout the 1920s, particularly at times of perceived vulnerability,[49] although this willingness was tested as the decade progressed and it appeared that the government was not fulfilling its end of the bargain. But the message was present from the beginning. In August 1920, a letter to Lenin, Grigory Zinoviev, and Leon Trotsky, "as leaders of the Russian proletariat" from the administration, representatives of miners' committees, and trade unions and "technical personnel as well" of the coal mines of Eastern Siberia pledged their support to the government, specifically because

> during the most difficult days for the Russian proletariat, in the days of mass kulak uprisings, in the days of the unified attack of worldwide capital on the

> Soviet Republic—as well as in the proletariat's moment of victory—the communist party, and for it all Russian workers, closed ranks to form one steel mass, in order to advance forward on the path to total liberation of the proletariat from the yoke of exploitation and enslavement.[50]

The authors supported the party because they perceived that it unified them and stuck with them through the worst. Likewise, representatives of a tanners' union in Turkestan, "in the name of all members of the proletarian mass of Turkestan," wrote to Lenin in 1921, stating their readiness to

> realize the primary goal of the October Revolution. Notwithstanding our isolation from the center in 1918 and 1919, with a handful of proletarians and semiproletarians we had to ward off the attack of international counterrevolution, tsarist generals and elements hostile to us.

The tanners were prepared to defend the revolution and realize its goals, "taking into account the inestimable services of Com[rade] Lenin in the struggle to establish the dictatorship of the proletariat and the emancipation of the Eastern peoples."[51] The tanners once defended the Bolshevik government, because it was their government; presumably, they would fight to defend it once again.

The dedication of Lenin and other party leaders to the collective cause appeared to provoke a deep and unconditional loyalty from their constituents. But there was a clear difference in the nature of the message, depending on the addressee. Earlier appeals to Lenin often expressed a general willingness to defend the revolution against its standard enemies, and sometimes evoked memories of the glorious days of the civil war, when socialism vanquished its enemies. Many later appeals to Stalin, on the other hand, addressed him not only as the leader of socialist society, but as an equal, a comrade who would spearhead the struggle to bring an unfinished revolution to its successful conclusion. A former Red Army commissar wrote to Stalin to request that his weapons be restored to him to fight the approaching battle with worldwide capital. Apparently, in the confusion surrounding demobilization, the former officer had not been able to register his gun and so lost it. But, he said,

> I sincerely appeal to you to give me back the weapons I had with me at the front. I am a front-line fighter and at the first call of the workers' government I will go to the front and kill off aristocrats or anyone you like.[52]

This appeal underscores an important element of popular dedication to the collective on which Stalin could later draw. The officer clearly relished the days of the civil war, when he realized his identity at the front—or, more to the point, when he gained recognition as being valuable to the revolutionary cause. This was another critical aspect of collective pride and inclusion apparent in many appeals. Indeed, to civil war veterans, recognition and acknowledgment of the critical role they played in establishing the socialist government was vitally important. A worker and civil war veteran from Moscow wrote to Stalin in March 1927, fondly reminiscing about the time when Stalin awarded his regiment the Red Banner for their victory over the Whites. The worker requested that Stalin send him a revolver as a memento of this occasion.[53]

Eagerness to enter the fight, however, in many cases was apparently motivated by economic need. For many supplicants, the greatest threat to the country's security lay in its economic situation. A lack of personal economic security enhanced a sense of the country's vulnerability. Conversely, a victory to secure the existence of one member of the proletariat certainly would improve the chances of victory for the Soviet Union as a whole over the forces of international counterrevolution. This critical symbiosis operated in the appeal from a nineteen-year-old nonparty trade union member from Odessa which illustrates how individual and collective security became conflated. The young unemployed worker requested the Politburo's help to admit him into the Red Fleet or Army:

> I feel and believe that I have an . . . inclination [to follow] in the great teachings of Il'ich, and if you give me the opportunity I will gladly lay down my life and soul for the sake of the Soviet Union, which is the only one in the world; and it seems to me that in this country of free soviets work should be given to everyone who wants it. . . . I call out the slogan . . . of the politically conscious unemployed for the strengthening of the economy and construction of the country of soviets, so that every citizen who desires it is given the opportunity to take part in the building of our country.[54]

The supplicant makes no distinction between his desire to defend his country and his desire to feed himself. Indeed, why should he? Such a conflation of interests need not be viewed as a betrayal of revolutionary goals. As the supplicant points out, contribution to socialist construction was predicated on the availability of employment in some capacity within socialist society; employment in the armed forces thus offered both the material security promised by the collective and security for the collective itself. The very purpose of this socialist utopia, unique in all the world, was to provide for its workers, thus armed to protect the collective which sheltered them.

This chapter concerned the ideal socialist society—the collective—that many Soviet citizens hoped would be established under communism, as expressed in letters to the party leadership. The Russian Revolution evoked many expectations. Workers, peasants, and soldiers sought both material betterment from the center and more control over their own affairs, desires that were inherently contradictory. And, when the civil war finally put an end to seven years of fighting and material deprivation, many sought above all else a refuge in the new socialist society. They sought to build a collective organism, in which all the needs of its members would be met, and which would protect them against the onslaughts of an uncertain existence. Indeed, such a society was the promise of communism.

Appeals to the central party leadership illustrate how that collective might function. It was like a family. The government would provide sustenance, shelter, and the equal distribution of work to all. Only through equal distribution of labor, and the fruits of that labor, would the needs of society be met. And the collective required its members to contribute their fair share, and to take only what they needed to sustain themselves. In order to grow and flourish, the collective required from the government and its citizens alike a sense of incorporation and connectedness. This was the social contract by which the Bolsheviks had gained power, and which legitimized the communist government. Indeed, many who appealed to the center during the 1920s made it clear that they were prepared to defend the Soviet government in case of attack from hostile forces. They were prepared to do so, because the government was their government, and because of the perceived dedication of party leaders to the collective. They were prepared to defend the collective, because it bestowed both a livelihood and recognition of their individual and collective worth.

CHAPTER THREE

The Menace of NEP

ALTHOUGH the Bolshevik government intended NEP only as a temporary remedy for peasant revolt and economic breakdown, its adoption signified for many the abandonment of communist ideals. It seemed that the goal of building an egalitarian society was no longer deemed a realizable objective, and the free market brought economic disparity. The new policy evoked great disaffection and led to a dramatic increase in resignations and even suicides among party members, Red Army veterans, and members of the Komsomol. A lack of clear vision among party leaders about NEP's objectives and implications, or even its duration, exacerbated disaffection.

NEP threatened the very purpose of Soviet rule, for it denied its ostensible *raison d'être*—building socialism. By legalizing class differentiation and thus economic disparity, NEP was dramatically opposed to the fundamental goals of collective security and egalitarianism. Appeals to the central leadership emphasized that it was not merely poverty, but poverty in the midst of plenty that caused social and political dissent. The relative extremes of wealth during NEP stood in stark contrast to both War Communism and popular expectations. Class differentiation had not merely survived but intensified—despite the revolution and victory in the civil war. Moreover, social leveling was the core desire among not only party members but also the general population. Conspicuous wealth was deeply resented, especially by the disadvantaged (the unemployed, pensioners, and invalids), and by party members who could not support their families. This resentment was expressed in widespread criticism of unequal pay, especially the relatively high salaries of government officials and of the technical intelligentsia.

Another complaint was that the government sought to raise economic efficiency at the expense not of management, but of workers.[1] Supplicants claimed that workers bore the brunt of layoffs and cutbacks, while management retained their positions and salaries regardless of industry performance. Such criticism was especially intense during austerity campaigns, such as the economic regime launched in 1926 to cut production costs.

The fact that workers were paid less also resulted in their psychological devaluation. Their actual value stood in stark contrast to the regime's official glorification of the proletariat as the preeminent social class in the new society.

The worker seemed a superfluous commodity, disempowered in an era of chronic and growing unemployment.

NEP's Effects on the Party

In its early years, contemporaries observed that NEP appeared to be a capitalist juggernaut that the communists were powerless to stop. They were horrified by the share of trade that quickly concentrated in private hands. There was a definite perception that capitalism was "winning," and a "[growing] conviction . . . that 'free-trading' is here to stay."[2] The implications for the survival of the revolution, and particularly for the party, were clear. Contemporary (pre-Stalinist) accounts portrayed NEP as an abandonment of the hopes and dreams of the revolution, and the end of communism. One communist remarked that the switch to NEP made him and his comrades feel "like officers of a vessel whose compass had ceased to function. 'Has all this bitter struggle been in vain? . . . now when the victory seems won we are ordered to retreat and abandon what we fought for?'"[3] Moreover, NEP's temporary nature, as Lenin had envisaged it, was evident only in retrospect, that is, once it had been dismantled. In the mid-1920s NEP was alive and well, with every indication that it would continue to be so.

Developments within the party, the vanguard of the proletariat, bore out this impression. The party's retreat in the battle with world capitalism had profoundly negative repercussions throughout the organization. Material wealth once again determined social status; those without wealth or the ability to generate it, lost their status, whatever their revolutionary credentials or theoretical worth in the new social order. Indeed, as one communist observed,

> decorated with medals won at the cost of their blood, the heroes of the Civil War discovered in their wanderings about Moscow that everything was beyond their reach, that the profiteers could snap fingers at them with impunity; and they began to wonder whether they had fought in vain.[4]

Radical communists despaired over the new economic direction, which signified the betrayal of communism and the abandonment of their cherished goals, including the nationalization of industry, the destruction of private property, and the elimination of money. One party member noted that "Lenin's arguments in support of NEP bounced off party members like peas off a wall." This opposition did not disappear; on the contrary, "very many" party members simply kept quiet about their "near panic-stricken fear" of NEP.[5] Moreover, opposition to NEP appeared more prevalent among the lower party cadres and rank and file:

> When PUR [the political administration of the army] conducted a survey of its staff in early 1924, 91% of the senior political staff declared themselves to be in favor of NEP. In contrast, a quarter of the lower-ranking political workers and Red commanders considered NEP to be "a harmful turn in the develop-

> ment of the Revolution." Between one fifth and one half felt that their material situation had improved little since the end of the Civil War, and when asked whom they considered to be the winners under NEP, they answered, "The bourgeoisie."[6]

As the survey suggested, opposition to NEP in the lower ranks was based not only on ideological grounds, but also on the realities it generated for them. Red Army soldiers were opposed to NEP not just because of the return to capitalism but because of the pain attendant on demobilization.[7]

This suggestion was borne out by other data as well. Statistics compiled by the Secretariat on party resignations after NEP's introduction suggest both disgruntlement over it and a general loss of purpose, although for obvious reasons government officials did not explicitly state this.[8] To conclude that party resignations were due to NEP would be to criticize Lenin's leadership.

Analyzing statistics compiled in a number of gubernii on party resignations for 1922, the Orgburo (Communist Party Organizational Bureau) noted many interesting trends and reached some predictable conclusions. Such resignations constituted generally a "process of self-cleansing" in the party, since "the main element of those leaving had fallen under the influence of NEP." In other words, statisticians claimed, those resigning were corrupted by the new economic climate, and so the party was left stronger and better off without them. Such interpretations tended to give the impression that anyone disagreeing with NEP was not a good communist, either too ignorant or too capitalist, and so the party was better off without them. According to the report, "a significant number" of those who tendered resignations withdrew them, "after explanation" of what NEP was about. But the actual number of those who withdrew their resignations in such cases was 21 percent, less than one quarter of the total—hardly a significant number. In the end, the central authorities' studies are not helpful in uncovering actual motivations of those resigning from the party.

Moreover, the data indicate a considerable margin for error. In such reports, statisticians tended to consider reasons for resignation based on NEP as "masking" the real causes. Such an interpretation begs the question, how they determined which causes were genuine and which were not. Presumably, if those resigning offered NEP as an excuse to conceal the actual reason, the reverse could also hold true. Indeed, as statisticians themselves admitted, "the materials of the statistical department contain too large a percentage of 'unknowns.'" The statistics on which the Secretariat based its information were by their own admission unreliable, unstandardized, and incomplete. In any case, the results hardly constituted a glowing recommendation of the party's new economic line. Contrary to official claims, the data suggested, in fact, that those who resigned had not so much fallen under the influence of NEP as fallen victim to it. In Tambov and Odessa, dissatisfaction with NEP was connected with "the difficult material circumstances [among] bedniaks [poor peasants] and the backward lower-middle-class strata" of the party organization. In Orenburg, "the transition to a barracks situation prompted appeals for resignation." From Petrograd, the Crimea, and Saratov came reports in the summer of 1922 of a "mass exodus [from the party] of political workers in the army" due to "lack of material support and, indirectly, uncertainty surrounding their fate after demobilization."

Commentary on resignations throughout the country spoke of economic uncertainty, dissatisfaction among the lower depths of the party and, if the conclusions of the statistical department can be believed, a decided degree of moral malaise under NEP's influence. This disaffection pervaded the military as well. In the Red Army, "party commissars heard charges that inequality had become the norm of army life and that 'NEP ethics' was corroding the army's 'comradely cohesion.'"[9]

The malaise among revolutionaries could not be glossed over, even by party officials eager to please the central leadership. In a report to the party Secretariat in February 1923 on "the economic encirclement of communists in connection with NEP," the Cherepovetskii *gubkom* (guberniia-level party committee) secretary noted that

> as a result of the general improvement in the economic situation, an improvement in the material situation of party members undoubtedly may be observed. [However,] individual groups of [communists] continue to find themselves in the most difficult material circumstances; these are the employees of establishments supported by the government, namely: military organizations, the G.P.U., Rabkrin, and so forth.[10]

The *gubsek*'s (guberniia party secretary) list of those who continued to suffer despite a general economic amelioration is an unsettling one, since it included those groups that not only provided external and internal security and control, but also presumably contained the most militant communists—and potentially, the most socially vengeful—among the revolutionary vanguard.

Exacerbating the party's moral malaise was the fact that even party leaders did not clearly understand NEP's implications, a lack of direction that only increased once Lenin was out of the picture. There were great inconsistencies in the expressions of leaders, most notably Lenin himself, on what NEP meant for the future of socialism.[11] Guidelines created for NEP's implementation in trade and industry illustrated this inconsistency. Criteria established in July 1922 by Glavmetall (central administration for the metallurgical industry) were contradictory in nature and light on specifics. The guidelines encouraged various industrial concerns to adhere to the "methods [and] established practices of Private-Lawful Capitalism," but maintained the importance of keeping the periphery "in direct subordination to the Center, which provides the only way to guarantee government-economic regulation of industry."[12]

This confusion left the party at its lower levels in a quandary since, as the Tambov gubkom secretary put it, "NEP in practice raises a mountain of general questions that have not been worked out in party procedure." The secretary recommended that the central government create a commission composed of local officials, who could address the questions raised by the new policy, drawing on "the party wisdom of the Central Committee and the experience of local [party] workers."[13] In practice, NEP presented complications from which the center was removed and insulated, leaving communists at the local level the unenviable task of realizing a vague and seemingly contradictory policy; those who followed the party line did so without a clear notion of what that line was.

Despite this confusion, however, party protocol after 1921 compelled higher officials to show support for the new policy. NEP was the correct line because Lenin said so, and anyone who resigned due to "disagreement with" or "lack of understanding of NEP" turned out to have "hidden motives," or a "hidden inclination to consumer communism," which is to say that they sought to take advantage of the possibilities NEP offered.[14] This explanation seems dubious, since one obviously did not have to leave the party in order to profit from NEP. Instead, the problem was that what was economically or politically necessary for the government or the country as a whole may have been economically disastrous for the individual. Contemporaries saw in NEP the most dramatic illustration of the divergence between the goals of party leaders and those of the rank and file. In introducing NEP, so this line of reasoning goes, the party leadership was the ultimate saboteur of the revolution.

While their leaders may have appeared uncertain about the future of socialism under NEP, many average party members entertained no such doubts. In 1924, Orgraspred (Communist Party Organization and Assignment Department) sent a secret memorandum to Stalin concerning "the increase in incidences of suicide among members of the party and Komsomol."[15] The report began by noting that

> to compile sufficiently complete data for the present memorandum was not possible. This is explained by the fact that on the local level until now not only have cases of suicide not been taken into consideration or clarified, but also in general the necessary attention is not paid to these occurrences.

Nevertheless, information based on data from a number of organizations, including the Political Administration of the Army, the Central Control Commission, the Information Section of the Central Committee, and the Komsomol Central Committee, led to some conclusions as to the increase in suicides. The report noted, first of all, a "considerable number of suicides in the Red Army and Navy," nearly half of which were unexplained; an additional third were the result of "dissatisfaction with life and service." The remainder found their cause in "criminal offense in service," "romantic notions," "serious illness (nervous, coronary)," "difficult material circumstances," and "family disorders."

The report noted that the increase of suicides among party members in the army was so great that "in some party organizations suicide is beginning to assume almost a mass character," and that, with rare exceptions, suicides were caused by nervous exhaustion. Among communists and komsomoltsy who were not serving in the armed forces, according to information compiled by the Odessa guberniia organization, suicides were caused by:

> a) nervous illness and exhaustion; b) illness in general (tuberculosis and other *curable* illnesses); c) failure (in social, political, and personal life); d) difficult family situation (squabbles connected with questions of existence); e) difficult material situation (unemployment, small pay rate for a large family and so on); f) criminal activity on the job (embezzlement, accepting bribes, and other

> types of crime); g) romantic grounds (love, jealousy, etc.); h) moral disintegration (chronic drunkenness, debauchery, sexual perversion, etc.); i) the result of an improper approach by individual party committee workers and other organs; j) various other causes.[16]

The list suggests that many of the suicides not directly attributed to material difficulties can nevertheless be reduced to serious economic problems.[17] This explanation was sometimes offered in the notes left by suicides themselves, whose illnesses, family turmoil, and other problems often were caused by material dilemmas. Appeals from communists and nonparty citizens throughout the decade often reduced their predicament to material need. Many, who appealed directly to the party leadership as a last resort, requested material assistance on the basis of serious illness, nervous breakdown, or family problems due to illness or poverty. Supplicants often warned that if Stalin and the central authorities could not assist them, they would be driven to criminal action or suicide. Judging from Orgraspred's report on suicides in the party, many of these supplicants were not bluffing.

The notes left by suicides to explain their actions bore out the observation that material need, and general lack of support, were the underlying causes of the disturbing epidemic. Indeed, a few of them explained that it was not merely destitution that drove them to self-destruction, but destitution in the midst of plenty, that is, disparity. The report recounted that

> Komsomolets Mamalyga worked in the village. . . . The district secretary dismissed him from work, as being unfit for his position. . . . He fell into dire circumstances and . . . starved. . . . Before his suicide Mamalyga was in Odessa, where he saw the conditions [there], returning to the village, he shared with his fellow komsomoltsy that "we, the young, starve, but there they go mad with plenty."

The report concluded that

> it is undoubtedly necessary to take stock of the emerging tendency toward an increase in the number of suicides among party members and komsomoltsy, especially among the ranks of the Red Army, and to outline a number of measures to eliminate the causes and conditions that . . . cause them. These measures should go toward bettering the material situation, establishing a more sensitive and thoughtful approach toward individual comrades on the part of their respective superiors and directing organs and toward more complete familiarity with the state of health of the lower party aktiv [militants or activists in or outside the party] and outlining more complete measures toward its preservation and recovery.

NEP's Effects on the Collective

Disparity

Ultimately, in confronting NEP and despite their anxiety over the apparent abandonment of revolutionary objectives, both the party rank and file and the general population had no choice but to rely on their faith in Lenin's dedication to the cause of socialism. In December 1921, a telegram to Lenin, Zinoviev, and Smirnov from the "workers of land and forests in Siberia" of Omsk guberniia expressed their gratitude for the leaders' work on their behalf and for their "decisions in the area of the economic life of the republic," presumably referring to the introduction of NEP. But the workers' belief in NEP was not wholly unqualified. They continued:

> We workers of the provinces hope that with the new course of economic policy, with our support you will be able to do everything you can to carry out those principles of the October conquest, which the precious river of our blood achieved.[18]

The workers appeared to harbor a certain anxiety that their leaders would fail to preserve the gains of the October Revolution, that the party might abandon the principles for which they had fought. In August 1921, representatives from trade unions and sovnarkhozy met in Riazan guberniia "to settle questions surrounding the new economic policy in peaceful conditions," and sent a letter of greeting to Lenin to inform him of their decisions. The conference concluded

> with deep certainty that under your leadership, all the gains of the revolution and attainments of the proletariat will be secured for good for the proletariat, and therefore resolve [that] all recent changes in economic policy are wise steps in the achievement of prosperity of the country.

Having thus resolved to trust that the prosperity promised by the party's change of course would accrue to them, the proletariat, the delegates pledged to do their utmost to bring about victory on the economic front, "as our valiant Red Army and Red Fleet emerged victorious on the military front."[19] Approval for NEP seemed thus to be based on faith in Lenin's dedication to their interests, and in the party's ability to steer economic gains in their direction. But this faith was fraught with anxiety. Historian E. H. Carr observed that

> in the autumn of 1922 when the first phase of NEP was complete . . . the Soviet Government . . . decided to introduce a civil code. Lenin described it as [in part] an attempt "to preserve the boundary between what is legitimate satisfaction of the individual citizen under the present economic system of exchange and what represents an abuse of NEP."[20]

But who could say where that boundary really lay?

For many individuals, any threat to collective security was a threat to individual security. Disparity was the gravest threat to the collective, because disparity inherently favored the interests of some individuals over the collective membership as a whole. A Red Army man and party candidate wrote to Stalin in July 1927 to request that "the lower party masses, who implement party decisions in the country and in production" be better informed about the results of their work on the party's behalf. Rank-and-file party members required solid information in order to defend communism in opposition to the petty-bourgeoisie and social democrats, as well as to explain it to nonparty citizens. More precisely, the soldier wanted to know what socialism meant in the real world, or how the classless society could be realized, when in fact "property still existed as the object of private consumption." If private property still existed, so did class differentiation. "To what end," the author wondered, "did highly qualified members of the socialist society receive the greater and better portion of [goods]?" Would this situation not lead naturally to the existence of leaders and led, governors and governed?[21] What the soldier was asking, of course, was how he could justify his support of communism—to himself as much as to anyone else—when the reality did not resemble the ideal.

Indeed, the persistence of privilege and inequality made poor, disadvantaged, and desperate supplicants wonder to what end the October Revolution had been fought. In a letter addressed in the mid-20s to Stalin, a Kiev factory worker summed up the situation in no uncertain terms:

> The worker went to the front to defend the interests of his brothers, but he still sees the bourgeoisie today, those who, at the same time that the worker was defending the interests of the masses, put on balls, feasted and drank workers' blood, and [even though] the revolutionary working class was victorious, the capitalist bourgeoisie lives. . . . As the bourgeoisie grows, so does the oppression of the working class. . . . No one is claiming that unjust laws are issued by the center . . . but why after ten years in power have they not eliminated inequality of rights among people? Why can one [person] eat, drink, promenade, and spend money on foolishness, and another not get enough to eat or drink? Why are the lowly left everywhere to fate? . . . Why are there so many hungry, cold people? . . . These are questions that trouble many millions of the masses. . . .
>
> Ending my appeal I beg you to answer these burning questions, knowing that I appeal to an old comrade, to a former exile and prisoner, to a comrade, at the memory of whose name the whole proletariat brightens up and senses before them a solid future.[22]

For many in NEP Russia, life and its prospects bore an alarming similarity to prerevolutionary times. The socialist utopia was slow in materializing, and only a conspicuously small number of well-placed individuals appeared to benefit under the construction contract. For the rest, poverty and uncertainty persisted. The desperate situation in which many Soviet citizens found themselves, despite their efforts and expectations and the government's assurances, provoked both supplication and indignation.

While many begged for survival, others demanded it. Both their demands and their anger were based not only in the party's failure to deliver, but in the fact that during NEP the party appeared to be delivering only to a small minority. A worker and civil war veteran from Tver guberniia wrote to the central authorities in March 1927 concerning his unemployment. As he pointed out, "I am a human being and I also want to live and I also know very well, that nobody may take that right away from me." Being unemployed was particularly hard, "now, when surrounding him swarm the cherished of NEP."[23] The wealth and prosperity ushered in by NEP was not general prosperity or recovery; wealth reappeared, but only for some—which made the poverty of the rest all the more bitter.

The theme of disparity is ubiquitous. A Leningrad party member, who supported his elderly parents and was laid off after filling a number of party posts, appealed to Stalin for work. He was desperate, facing a choice "either to wait for the end or steal" to survive. Although he had been spurned by his government, the supplicant nevertheless had no wish to defy it. Rather, so the appeal ran, if Stalin would support him, he might be assured that his leader nevertheless "relates to me, as a comrade." The destitute man had been living for six months "on a crust of black bread. And I envy everyone who laughs merrily, and . . . hate all food stores, always causing within me a tempest."[24] In short, the bitterness of having been abandoned seemed particularly unjust, when there was food to be had, and others clearly had access to it. Similarly, a communist from Siberia appealed to Stalin in March 1927 concerning the fact that he lost his job as an accountant. He attributed his layoff to his communist superiors' enmity toward apparatchiki like him. He asked Stalin to suggest where he might find a way out of his predicament, "in order that I won't go hungry, even though there is plenty of bread to be had at the market."[25] Disparity threatened the only tangible benefit that communism supplied, that is, material security. When socioeconomic disparity reached an intolerable degree, the security of the majority was no longer ensured, and social stability was in jeopardy. Indeed, historians and contemporaries alike concluded that the 1917 Revolution itself was inevitable, considering the glaring contrast in wealth between the upper and lower classes of the old regime.

The revolution in Russia was consciously materialist in its objectives, and material well-being was the goal of socialist construction. But general wealth was a long way off. In the meantime, all members of the collective had to adopt an austere existence to ensure collective cohesion. Everyone had to conform to the lowest common denominator in wealth, education, and culture. Appeals to the center suggested a general consensus across the political spectrum that competition and self-enrichment were immoral in an atmosphere of general want. As before the revolution, as long as wealth and comfort were enjoyed by a minority, instead of by the majority, since "individual wealth on the one hand [could] only spell individual poverty and want on the other,"[26] the mere presence of a disparity in wealth and privilege threatened the collective's integrity. Until a socialist society could be built, those who rose above the general standard of living were resented by the majority, who saw no possibility of escaping. This sentiment naturally held true for the worker, and especially the communist worker, on whose behalf the socialist society was being constructed.

The instinct for social leveling, of course, was not limited to communists, but deeply embedded in Russian social tradition. This explains why, as one contemporary observed, the Russian population as a whole appeared to welcome the relative prosperity and relaxation of tensions that NEP brought, but universally despised nepmen and the flaunting of wealth generally.[27] The collective ideal of economic success was general, moderate economic wealth. This ideal left no room for excessive wealth, that is, wealth that exceeded the norm. In 1927 a nonparty representative of poor peasants from the Urals complained to Stalin of the activities of the uezd leadership, former Whites who were promoting their "bourgeois-nationalist line" primarily through "incorrect" land distribution, causing much dissatisfaction, especially among bedniaks.[28] These holdovers from the prerevolutionary system perpetrated acts that discredited the Soviet government. The supplicant requested that the central leadership "liquidate" these "abnormalities."

Unequal Pay

The reemergence of money under NEP was bemoaned by communist radicals, because it meant, as under capitalism, that Soviet citizens would now receive widely disparate amounts of it.[29] This inequity took various forms: unequal pay rates within and among various industries, gaps between workers' earnings and the salaries of management and specialists, and significant differences between the meager pay of local party workers on the one hand and the relatively lavish salaries and perks that higher party officials enjoyed on the other. Indeed, wage disparities caused intense animosity before the revolution, and afterwards a sharp debate at the Eighth Party Congress, which even before NEP affirmed the necessity of higher pay for industry specialists and abandonment of workers' control in the factories.[30] Thus, the material devaluing of labor was accompanied logically by a decrease in workers' power.

This devaluation of labor was so dramatic that in 1923, Narkomtrud (People's Commissariat of Labor) was compelled to establish minimum wages throughout the country by region, indicating that wages in many areas had fallen below subsistence levels.[31] Great disparities existed among different industries and between workers' wages and those of administration.[32] Changes to minimum wage rates allowed for inflation but retained these disparities.[33] Especially the much higher salaries of white-collar specialists and administrators provoked widespread anger and were the source of ubiquitous complaints to the party leadership. The issue was not merely that of higher party apparatchiki versus the lower party aktiv or the impoverished nonparty masses. It also involved the privileges of the skilled versus the destitution of superfluous unskilled workers. While those at the bottom of the heap may have disagreed who benefited most from the policy of unequal pay, their indignation over the basic injustice of the disparity itself was universal and a point of contention throughout the decade.

Thus, in May 1924 a party member and "lowly" office worker appealed to his comrades in the central committee to close the wage gap between party administrators and rank-and-file communists like him. He pointed out that "the question [of wage disparities] stands before not just one individual but, if I may be so bold, before everyone. I will speak of the fate of the rank-and-file party member, offering myself as an example." The clerk's appeal is humble in tone; in fact, the author made a point of acknowledging his "worthlessness" relative to his party leaders. Nevertheless, he argued that such a disparity of pay was unjust, especially considering that those like him did not even earn enough to sustain themselves and their families. The supplicant earned only 12.60 rubles per month and described in detail his family budget and all the necessities they could not afford. The clerk then made his own recommendation for wage adjustments: increasing the lower end by double, and decreasing the higher end (which he defined as 100 rubles per month or more) by a fifth which, he observed,

> should not offend our comrades, especially party members. But the lower classes would have the opportunity to exist. Dear comrades, if you plead [your greater] responsibility [to justify your higher salaries], then I absolutely cannot accept it, because in our cause we are all equally responsible.[34]

Another appeal was sent to Stalin in December 1924 from a former party member from a village in Tver guberniia. The supplicant had been a factory worker in Leningrad and served in the Red Army and a number of party posts, including *volost'* (territorial subdivision of an uezd [district]) party chairman. He had been transferred without his papers, however, and so could not prove party membership. The communist begged Stalin to help him, "as I helped you for six years in the struggle against counter-revolution on various fronts of the republic." He described his means of existence: his family subsisted on one *desiatina* of land (old Russian measure equal to about 2.7 acres) and had no horse, and work was unavailable due to high unemployment. What made his situation especially unbearable, however, was the fact that "a nonparty director at Gubsoiuz [guberniia-level consumer cooperative] . . . lives like a Russian *barin* [gentleman] on 150 rubles per month."[35]

Communists were not the only ones complaining about wage gaps. A peasant complained in March 1927 about several issues, including the huge gap in salaries. He was incensed that a village soviet secretary, "who worked from morning till night," made a mere 20 to 25 rubles per month, while higher officials received from 100 to 500 rubles and did not work nearly as hard.[36] In his eyes, nothing could justify such a disparity in compensation. This was especially true, when many at the bottom of the pay scale or on pensions lived below subsistence. Addressing this issue, a group of "young militiamen of the city of Piatigorsk" appealed in September 1927 for assistance. Their main protest, too, concerned wage disparities; it seemed that they received only 33 rubles a month, on which they considered subsistence impossible.[37]

The cost-cutting mentality in industry that accompanied NEP inevitably led to opposition between white-collar state administrators and blue-collar workers.[38] This was especially true for unemployed workers, who saw that management pleading economic austerity laid off workers, while awarding themselves pay increases and other perquisites. Thus, in 1927, a former Red

Army soldier and nonparty employee at a Leningrad optical factory expressed his dissatisfaction that

> "spetsy" receiving huge salaries, resulting from the excessive labor of lower employees . . . are not held accountable for their mistakes before the authorities. . . . They . . . continue to work, continue to make mistakes, and continue to lay us off . . . under the slogan of "economic regime" . . . never considering . . . cutting their own high salaries if only by five rubles, but . . . cut the pay of the entire lower apparatus.[39]

Labor Devalued

NEP had profound psychological repercussions for the working class. In addition to material difficulties, wage disparities attached widely disparate levels of worth to different workers. With official sanction of the free market, labor once more became a commodity, rather than a social duty or obligation.[40] By extension, the individual laborer became a commodity as well—and in the current state of economic breakdown and competition, a superfluous commodity at that. According to the Left Opposition, NEP lowered the proletariat's political and social dignity.[41] In this new socialist society, management clearly was in control. Moreover, since the worker's devaluation precluded individual material security, collective integrity was compromised as well. Whether party or nonparty, the worker's powerlessness was inconsistent with the values and goals of a communist society and with the official glorification of the proletariat. Mistreatment from management thus formed a common basis of complaint in letters to the party leadership.

Many appeals came from supplicants who claimed to be persecuted by management for their activism in both factory and party. In November 1924, a veteran factory worker from Cherkassy, Ukraine appealed to Stalin when he was fired, allegedly on the basis of a factory administrator's intrigues. This director was ostensibly "a true opponent of communists" and, the worker charged, "did not want to work with lower technical personnel," even though the worker had seventeen years of experience on the bench and "knew production like the back of my hand and [I] am considered one of the best foremen." When the director found out that the worker had applied for party membership, he claimed, the director began a campaign against him, supported by the factory specialists, which ultimately led to the worker being fired. He appealed to Stalin for justice.[42]

Workers' powerlessness, it was claimed, reflected management's disregard for worker input. A party member and miner from the Donbass region with twenty-seven years' experience complained in December 1924 to the Central Committee that the administration of "Donugol" mining operation paid no attention to his many suggestions on raising worker productivity. He claimed he knew how to raise productivity levels to prewar norms and, "bearing responsibility before the party," wished to make these suggestions known "if it would please the party." The miner said that the administration had not even answered his letters.[43]

If communists had little power or authority over administrators, nonparty workers faired no better. In July 1927, a nonparty clerical worker from Novosibirsk appealed to the center to review her case. She claimed that she had been fired from her job after submitting an appeal to be paid for overtime work. Responding to her charge, her employers countered that the woman herself had submitted an appeal to be let go.[44] This claim seems improbable under current economic circumstances. In a similar scenario, a party member from Samara guberniia, a white-collar employee who had held various positions in the local committee, wrote in July 1927 about his dismissal, allegedly due to his complaints about staff cutbacks. The troublesome employee lamented the fact that, although everyone in the party bemoaned careerism and protectionism, no concrete measures were ever taken, and party members generally remained passive in the face of the corruption that plagued government and party alike. Meanwhile, the nonparty masses simply saw one party member being replaced by another, without realizing the significance.[45]

An economic climate in which people were fortunate to be working at all could not help but lower the worker's self-worth. Those who were lucky enough to be employed knew that they could be replaced. Thus, they were compelled to march to the tune sung by management. In June 1927, a komsomolets working for the railroad administration wrote to complain to party leaders about the lengthening of the workday from six to eight hours, with only a twelve percent wage increase. While acknowledging that such a policy might not seem unreasonable, the supplicant expressed his workmates' concern that this was only the first step in a growing trend: an eight-hour workday could be extended to nine or even ten hours. Especially ominous, he felt, was the fact that such a step was taken on the eve of the revolution's tenth anniversary. It did not bode well.[46] Similarly, a nonparty employee with the trade administration clerical union protested against the situation in his industry caused by the economic regime. Office workers, especially accountants and bookkeepers, were systematically laid off. To make up for the loss in labor, he complained, the rest had to work excessive overtime, frequently fourteen-hour workdays. Many were forced to do the job of two workers but compensated only 10 to 15 percent more in wages. They agreed to this state of affairs, however, "seeing before them the mass of unemployed." Such a situation, the clerk lamented, was "fully unjust and completely impermissible" under labor laws.[47]

In the eyes of many supplicants, the situation was especially impermissible, considering the correspondingly high value accorded specialists. Manual workers' resentment of the higher earnings and other perquisites of the technical intelligentsia became readily apparent from the outset, as workers briefly in control of factory management vented their hostility toward both management and specialists in a variety of ways. In the early revolutionary years, former tsarist managers and specialists, both military and civilian, were more likely to be accused under the comrades-disciplinary courts and receive stiffer penalties. The courts were dissolved in 1922 after they lost legitimacy in the eyes of the workers, when the party discouraged prosecution of managers and specialists.[48]

The persistent and growing gulf in wages and benefits in Russia of the 1920s caused extreme resentment among workers. Even party officials who were eager to paint a positive picture of the country's progress under the new economic policy could not mask such problems. In May 1923, the secretary of the Kostroma Gubkom (guberniia-level party committee) sent a private letter to the Central Committee on the economic and political situation in the guberniia. While the workers' material situation and mood had improved over the last two years, observed the secretary, "the only thing that remains bad . . . is the housing crisis." Another development meriting comment was the fact that the technical intelligentsia's mood was "decidedly NEP"; this "element" had grown satisfied and complacent, a trend that would prove worse for "the growth of economic construction."[49] Evidence of this chronic tension came from all sides, for example, in a report to the Party Secretariat by the Chernomorskii *okruzhkom* on the "question of relations with specialists in production." The study found a correlation between the initiative to raise "productive discipline, and the local growth of a hostile relationship to shop-floor managers and specialists . . . in a number of enterprises."[50] A campaign to raise labor productivity and discipline bespoke workers' loss of control and dignity. As their worth plummeted, workers vented their frustration on specialists, whose social and economic superiority had been restored and reaffirmed.

Frustration was compounded when these specialists turned out to be members of the former elites. Thus, a party member from Ufa protested in July 1927 the government's use of specialists and former White officers.[51] At the very least, he argued, specialists should be paid no more than ordinary workers. He asked: "Isn't it time to undertake more decisive support of those in need, and pay [specialists] the minimum necessary for life in comparison with the life of workers and peasants?" Clearly, the government's policy of granting favorable treatment to specialists was at best hypocritical, at worst a betrayal. Indeed, Soviet historians tended to rationalize the regime's early support of "bourgeois specialists," maintaining that the communist government always stood in defense of the interests of the proletariat.[52] The protestation suggests their readers' apprehension that the opposite was true. The party member from Ufa went on in his appeal to criticize the lifestyles of the "trading-industrial bourgeoisie," who used industry's profits "noticeably to create those conditions of life, which laborers of the USSR never see."[53]

The message was relentless: economic disparity was increasing; class differences were reappearing. The comforts of the powerful were out of the reach of common people. Indeed, it seemed that former businessmen and specialists useful to the government were allowed to live in the privileged manner and with all the luxuries they had enjoyed before the revolution.[54] The party appeared to favor specialists and management over the working classes, leading to the inevitable conclusion that the party was abandoning those in whose name it ruled.

In essence, it seemed that with NEP, the party had reconstituted the prerevolutionary status quo and abandoned the cause of building a socialist society. A komsomolets and Red Army veteran, from the city of Bobrov in Voronezh guberniia, appealed for assistance on behalf of his needy family, who owned but few possessions, worth about five rubles, while "others have three or more thousand [rubles] and even thirty thousand." Even under Soviet power he remained a bedniak—nothing had changed. His previous appeals for assistance on the local level had been refused; the *ukom* (district party committee) secretary pleaded "economic regime" and claimed he had no money to give them. The supplicant knew, however, that there was money to be had, if one had the right connections. If "the bosses could go for cures," then money was available. He asked the ubiquitous rhetorical question, to what end had he served in the army? The answer, unfortunately, was clear: "For nothing—they do not even pay attention to me." Finally, the supplicant had decided to leave the party organization, "only because they ignore the poor."[55]

With NEP, it seemed, the party had completely lost sight of the main goal of the revolution. The question then became whether the Soviet government could ultimately fulfill the task entrusted to it. On the occasion of the revolution's first anniversary, Sovnarkom received an optimistic message from representatives of party and worker organizations of the Vanilovskaia factory in Bronnitsa uezd, near Moscow:

> We know that the bourgeoisie lost, due to their extreme egoism, in the face of a new creative force growing before their very eyes, and that now they resort to the most desperate means to halt the flow of the people's life. But there is no such force that can turn the river's tide back to its source. The great deed, esteemed comrades, has already been done; the huge achievement of our freedom is the spiritual resource of the masses.[56]

Many Soviet citizens saw a sharp disconnect between the ideal socialist society—the collective—and the reality of NEP. In 1921, the government was forced to adopt a new economic strategy, meaning that free trade was allowed to flourish and capitalism was restored, in an attempt to bring the country back from economic collapse. The government adopted the new policy because it had neither the power to control the economy nor the resources to provide what the population needed. But for many average citizens, NEP meant that, like industry and trade, they were forced to survive on their own, without the help or protection of the government. Social and economic disparity were allowed to flourish, with the nepman profiting at one end of the social spectrum and the unemployed and the homeless starving at the other. In the wake of this disparity and chronic unemployment, workers, veterans, poor peasants, and even communists were deprived of the benefits that the socialist society was supposed to provide. They were deprived of both material security and dignity, which they perceived as the revolution's goals. The question thus became how these goals might be achieved.

CHAPTER FOUR

Neither Jobs nor Schools

NEP was not merely an economic system.[1] The individualism and private enterprise of the 1920s permeated all aspects of society, as any Marxist would expect: economic relationships were reflected throughout society and culture. Seven years of war and revolution left millions of people indigent and desperate. But with NEP, the communist government apparently abandoned an egalitarian solution to the crisis—in effect, Russia was no longer communist. For many citizens, NEP signified abandonment of themselves and the revolution. Far from constructing an egalitarian socialist society that would ensure material security, NEP unintentionally promoted class differentiation and impeded an equitable distribution of material resources. The revolution thus underwent a mutation; for average people, the collective struggle became an individual struggle, just as in a capitalist state; individuals could not rely on the collective for protection, but were left to sink or swim on their own, competing for work and survival. In short, the collective struggle became an individual struggle to gain admittance into the collective.

The collective per se exhibited stratification. Egalitarianism became passé; social darwinism prevailed; competition replaced cooperation as the predominant economic and social ethic. This change in course dashed the expectations of those who viewed the communist revolution as an antidote to the evils of prewar Russia; supplicants found this new emphasis on individuality and independence inconsistent with socialism. Indeed, it was noted that individual existence in the free market system was more difficult under NEP than it had been before the revolution, or under similar systems in the West.

Growing unemployment during NEP aggravated competition for survival. Among the unemployed, women and youth were disproportionately represented, although even party membership or Red Army service did not ensure employment. Ubiquitous complaints reached the central leadership from communists and veterans, who were worn out from sacrifice and overwork, and now discarded. Their appeals were rife with expressions of incredulity and indignation at their treatment by the government they had brought to power.

Unemployed people shared a sense of hopelessness and uselessness. Supplicants commonly described the pain of being a burden in a system that vilified idleness. The irony of being unemployed in a workers' state was not lost on the unemployed themselves. In the new communist society, idleness was perceived as criminal; thus, even the involuntarily idle often sought to demonstrate in their appeals that they were blameless in their indigence.

Both the party leadership and society at large were aware that high unemployment, especially of communists, presented political and security risks. Political unrest among the unemployed caused weakness and disunity in the party. And a weak party doubtless would encourage opposition both internally and externally. Average communists and nonparty citizens alike, incredulous that a country of such vast resources was unable to support its population, shared the leadership's concern.

Fear of unemployment contributed to demands for education and job training. On the one hand, the jobless hoped to improve their marketability through higher education and specialized courses; on the other, those already employed sought education for job security. Obtaining higher education came to be considered a prerequisite for entering, or remaining within, the newly competitive socialist collective. And in a culture in which education traditionally defined elite status, citizens with ambition to rise above their circumstances and communists newly promoted to positions of greater authority felt inadequate without education. *Vydvizhentsy* (workers promoted from the bench into administration) hoped that education would raise their self-confidence. For their part, cultured citizens and even party leaders held a thinly veiled contempt for the uneducated that discouraged their inclusion in the vanguard of the proletariat.

Because of the limited resources of the early Soviet government, however, education, like other branches of government, operated on a restricted budget. The system could not even remotely satisfy the demand, especially for higher education. This situation further threatened the building of socialist society; unequal access to education meant unequal access to the fruits of education. During NEP, higher education remained especially impervious to the throngs of workers and peasants clamoring for admission. Administrators and professors bemoaned the influx of "zero" students entering universities with little preparation and a working-class background. Since the education system thus could not, or would not, meet the demand, the government made admission to courses and schools more difficult through arbitrary impediments and requirements. Moreover, poverty and, in the case of peasants, simple access to the most basic tools of education impeded advancement.

Both the Bolsheviks and widespread elements throughout society assumed that the Soviet Union would have to raise the general level of education and culture of its population to compete with the West, particularly with the English and Americans, who were used as a yardstick for material success. Thus, many Soviet citizens endeavored to do their duty and educate themselves. Unfortunately, many fulfilled that duty, only to find that they remained unemployed. Their frustration was profound.

Mutation of the Revolutionary Struggle

Lenin's abandonment of radical communism in 1921, intended as a temporary change in economic strategy, meant that both individual businesses and individuals would have to survive on their own.[2] According to one observer, the principal change under the new system was that suddenly "the bulk of the population was obliged to shift for themselves [as in the West] . . . only [it was] vastly more difficult."[3] Security, the real benefit that people hoped to gain in their social contract with the government under communism, no longer formed part of the bargain; the contract was null and void. A young, unemployed woman from Baku, abandoned by her relatives and slowly dying from starvation, pleaded with Stalin for work of any kind, lamenting that "on top of everything else, I am utterly alone."[4]

In effect, with the introduction of NEP and market relations in 1921, the definition of the revolution changed. For the majority, competition for work and survival became the goals of everyday life. In May 1923, the party secretary of Kostroma guberniia noted in a confidential letter to the Central Committee a "great surge of revolutionary spirit" among peasant and working class youth, who were joining the Komsomol in record numbers. The secretary noted, however, that, "in any case, the incentive [to join] is material."[5]

Competition for resources became the route to survival not only on an individual plane, but also on the organizational level throughout the government and party apparatus, discouraging cooperation and consultation among government agencies. Organizations and factories chafing at economic independence became indignant at the suggestion that a socialist government would sooner see the demise of industry and, consequently, of jobs, than subsidize their operations. In a March 1922 letter to an administrator of Glavmetall, the director of the TsUGAZ automobile trust protested the recommendation to turn over auto factories within the trust to khozraschet, arguing that such a measure would sound the factories' death knell. The director appealed to the administrator, "not only as the director of TsUGAZ, but also as member of a party to which we both have the honor of belonging." As it was, the director observed, workers were on the verge of striking at the factories because TsUGAZ did not have the money to pay them and was struggling to fill orders under a shrinking credit supply. The director concluded that

> already in two or three weeks in such a situation, the auto factories will die a natural death from disintegration. Personally, I do not have the least desire to be their gravedigger. . . . For four years I scraped along during the Republic's most difficult time. . . .
>
> In your position you can find obliging people who will not explain themselves to you with long letters, but who will do everything you want them to, but I, happily, cannot. I consider myself responsible to the revolution.

Echoing this message, an auto factory director sent a long discourse to the government on the history of the automobile industry in foreign countries, arguing that nowhere was a national auto industry able to thrive without "consistent government support."[6] But in the Soviet situation, that support was not forthcoming, either for the auto industry or for individual citizens. As the factory director suggested, many found this new emphasis on individualism inconsistent with socialism.

Unemployment and Abandonment

As the preceding discussion implies, building socialism in NEP Russia became not only difficult, but, ideologically, an oxymoron. There was palpable and pervasive concern that many of the revolution's intended beneficiaries were not receiving a chance to participate in the construction of socialism. That perception grew along with the rate of unemployment, described in the mid-1920s by economist John Maynard Keynes as "severe and increasing."[7] The plight of the indigent was exacerbated by the Soviet government's inability to extend financial assistance to all who needed it: the unemployed; pensioners, invalids, workers, and peasants with incomes below subsistence; and the armies of *besprizorniki* (homeless children) that roamed the Soviet countryside.[8]

Rural migration exacerbated urban overcrowding and unemployment. Between 1923 and 1928, unemployment grew steadily, the national rate more than doubling, and in Moscow, almost tripling. The higher rate in the capital was due to a constant rate of immigration of 100,000 per year. Moreover, these estimates were probably low after 1925, when registration with the ineffectual labor exchanges became voluntary. As many appeals to the center indicate, the unemployed held out little hope for finding work through labor exchanges and often did not bother to register with them. After 1925, there was a "free market" in labor, meaning that employers had even more freedom to hire whom they would. In practice, this meant that skilled workers and union members were laid off in favor of migrant labor, peasants who were willing to work under any conditions and for lower wages.[9]

Among the various social groups, women consistently suffered most from unemployment. Employers routinely laid off women to make room for men, as after demobilization in 1921 and 1922, despite the government's decree that women and men should be considered on an equal basis for lay-offs. Nor did women benefit after 1925, when unskilled male peasant laborers were hired in preference to women. Under conditions of severe unemployment, discrimination against women in the workforce held true, even in traditionally female-dominated industries, such as textiles.[10]

By the late 1920s, unemployment had reached nearly 20 percent, about the average rate experienced in the West during the Great Depression. This estimate included only those officially registered by the trade unions and the 281 local labor exchanges. Peasants swelling the urban workforce aggravated Lenin's celebrated smychka, causing resentment that later contributed to worker support for the collectivization campaign under Stalin.[11] Rural overpopulation and competition for land caused friction in the village that would be exploited through divide-and-conquer tactics by party activists and administrators during collectivization.[12]

Competition for work created conflicts not only between workers and peasants, but also among various strata of the working class. The working class was made up of skilled and unskilled workers, who had significantly different goals. The skilled labor force was opposed to wage equality after the revolution and fought to preserve their relatively higher status. Nonetheless, because of a general superfluity of labor, skilled workers scarcely fared better under NEP than the unskilled. Moreover, in the campaign to raise productivity, management aggravated competition among workers, whom they separated into productive "proletarian" workers and "backward" workers, who opposed productivity campaigns. The result was that competition not only failed to heighten "socialist corporate consciousness," but further alienated workers from the means of production.[13]

That lack of a collective consciousness was reflected dramatically in the fate of the besprizorniki. The increasing exclusivity of the socialist collective, operating on both material and emotional levels, becomes clear in the following. In May 1927 the Central Committee received an appeal, "or more precisely a huge request," from a bezprizornik, an eighteen-year-old who had been orphaned at an early age. The supplicant "grew up in train stations," working at casual labor of various kinds to support himself, and saw that "everywhere [there was] injustice, everywhere the influence . . . of NEP." Eventually he found work in construction, and "began a new life, the life of a producer." But this newfound security and sense of purpose proved to be short-lived when he lost his job "because of politics." He apparently spoke out against the factory administration's policies on wage rates and distribution of work among *artels* (peasants' or workers' cooperatives). He was fired, and "the party cell could not do anything about it." Following this, the author found himself once again on the streets, suffering from deep emptiness:

> Now . . . when I see a meeting, hear the "hoorah!," then I am prepared to give everything to the masses, dissolve into them, tears uncontrollably well up in my eyes, but this dream is cruelly choked by the deep root of bureaucratism and narrow-mindedness. Explain to me and help me so that this [dream] in my head will not be in vain, use me, for that, I only need the minimum for life and nothing more.[14]

Notable here is the youth's apparent willingness to fulfill whatever purpose the collective required of him, in return for a chance to survive. The appeal further shows how the loss of work and lack of inclusion caused not only material but also emotional distress.[15]

The number of homeless children in the 1920s ranged from the conservative estimate in the *Bolshaia sovetskaia entsiklopediia* (Great Soviet Encyclopedia) of seven million, to "the precise figure of 9,351,467 children to be found in an émigré source." Soviet officials attempting to find a remedy were stymied in their efforts by the enormity of the problem and their lack of resources. All government agencies saw their budgets drastically reduced, including Narkompros (People's Commissariat of Enlightenment) and others responsible for the besprizorniki. The burden fell on local government agencies that could not afford it. Officials found the causes for homelessness not only in the upheaval caused by war and famine, but also in "the social conditions of the middle part of the decade," specifically, rural youth escaping poverty and abuse or parental exploitation of their labor, or seeking work and excitement in the city; family disintegration; and inadequate schools for both regular and special education. The problem of the besprizorniki was not solved until the 1930s, when Stalin's industrialization drive offered employment opportunities for older children and educational opportunities for younger ones.[16]

Youth comprised one of the biggest groups among the unemployed, since they had neither seniority nor experience.[17] In his letter of greeting to Lenin in October 1922, a Komsomol representative from Kursk guberniia wrote that

> for us this greeting is symbolic. In Il'ich, communist youth sees for itself a model in the struggle against exploiters and, especially, in the current conditions of NEP which sharply aggravate conditions of existence of youth.

The komsomolets wished Lenin a speedy recovery, so that he might continue to be a model for Soviet youth.[18] But to what purpose? Komsomoltsy encouraged to educate themselves in preparation for leadership in the campaign to build socialism had little opportunity for building any future, socialist or otherwise. A komsomolets from a village in Voronezh guberniia wrote to Stalin in 1927, pleading for work. The youth had written previously to Kalinin,[19] but without result. His next appeal, to the head of the Komsomol, "Comrade [Nikolai] Chaplin," was equally fruitless: "his answer was, 'we have in our ranks 1,000 unemployed komsomoltsy, and we cannot get work for everyone.'"[20]

The desperate situation of youth came through to the party leadership in countless appeals for work. A sixteen-year-old from Rostov-on-Don appealed in February 1927 to Stalin for work of some kind. His father, a communist and railroad inspector, had been killed three months earlier under the wheels of a train. Consequently, the supplicant and his sister had to support a family of seven.[21] The boy's appeal appeared to have met with some success. It merited a directive from Stalin to the local party secretary to find him some work,[22] but there is no evidence that the directive actually was implemented.

Another appeal from an orphan came in March 1927, from the eldest brother of a family in Perm. His mother was dead and his father killed by the Whites during the civil war. Since his family had no other means of subsistence, the boy's sisters were entering into a life of prostitution in order to feed them. Their appeals for help were rejected by the local party organization.[23] A seventeen-year-old from Leningrad appealed to Stalin in March of the same year, requesting help to find work, because he possessed neither boots nor a coat to face the Leningrad winter.[24] Another appeal for work or some means of subsistence came from a komsomolets in Moscow who had enlisted in the Red Army at the age of sixteen, and whose family and friends back home in Kaluga guberniia were all dead. The supplicant wanted to avoid "wandering around the city and being considered homeless."[25]

Such a fate was harder still for civil war veterans. Making the transition to the relative insecurity of NEP civilian life was difficult for former soldiers. Once demobilization began in earnest, Red Army soldiers fell into sixth place in priority for food rationing.[26] Distraught, a former Red Army soldier from Nizhnii Novgorod whose monthly pay of 22 rubles was insufficient to sustain his family implored the leaders "to plot to fight nep and strangle it like a dog, so that my mother and sister do not die of hunger."[27] Veterans' level of sacrifice and desperation were at times enormous. In one pathetic case, a former soldier, who had suffered serious wounds and become addicted to morphine, appealed to Stalin to be euthanized.[28]

The government's seeming disregard toward the revolution's most ardent supporters caused bitterness. One civil war veteran, an invalid with ten years of service in the army and a family of four, wrote:

> My family and I live in inhuman conditions. . . . but people are still deaf, the revolution has still not re-educated them. . . . It is not their affair if someone else is dying, as long as their own family enjoys well-being, and to see that causes pain in my heart.[29]

In their frustrated search for employment, those who were not party members often suspected that the latter were favored. Thus ran the appeal from a recently demobilized peasant from Nizhnii Novgorod guberniia. He expressed his indignation in a letter in April 1927, addressed not to Stalin but to Kalinin, "defender and patron of the poor." The peasant explained that he and his fellow peasant-soldiers had been promised a new life upon demobilization. In exchange for fulfilling their duties, they would receive "work without having to stand in line, lumber on favorable terms, privileged access to insurance and living space, and so on." However, the soldiers encountered "just the opposite." The supplicant had already gone four months without a job. In his frustration and disillusionment, the peasant wondered where one could find justice, and asked:

> For what did I serve? The fate of tribulations and contempt of local authorities? And all for what, for what . . . Now, wherever I go to present my services for work they always ask me: "party member, trade union?" What stupid questions. I maintain that all have an equal desire to live. Do party members or trade union members really work more or carry more responsibility in the Red Army? Not in the least.[30]

Yet, while nonparty citizens complained about the advantages enjoyed by party cadres, the fact was that party membership was no guarantee even of survival, let alone privilege. One communist, a former fireman from Saratov guberniia, pointed out his willingness to go wherever the party sent him, and had moved "without complaint . . . when it was necessary for the party." But now he found himself in Saratov, where the *raikom* (district party committee) was unable to find work not only for him, but also for his fellow communists. The fireman ended his appeal by requesting "the opportunity to exist."[31] Another desperate appeal came in September 1927 from a party member in Artemov *raion* (district in the Sverdlovsk region in the Urals). His wife, herself a former party worker, at the time cared for their baby, and both husband and wife suffered from tuberculosis. The husband wrote his appeal to the central government from jail, where he was serving time for assaulting a militiaman in a state of drunken despair. He was concerned that his family had neither winter clothes nor food.[32] Another appeal for financial assistance came from a party member, a family man with a wife and two children, who in 1921, while working for the party, had suffered "psychological damage" at the hands of bandits. The supplicant had been in and out of sanatoria and was unable to work, and his family was starving:

> I should move away, I should go far from home. I should make a clean break in life, because at home I howl, I cry, I tear my hair out, I am a nervous wreck—I see terrible visions. I beg you to save me. I leave home . . . I leave my naked, hungry family. The children cry: "Papa, do not go, we want to eat." . . . It is shameful that a party member should have to write this, but I am telling you this and howling like no one else.[33]

Many found it difficult to comprehend that ten years after the revolution, even party members went untreated and unfed in a socialist state.

This reaction was common in appeals from veterans who were communists. These supplicants commonly expressed astonishment at the party's failure to provide either work or support. One appeal for work came from a komsomolets and red army veteran from Astrakhan. His father and brother had both been communists; the father was killed in the line of duty, and the brother disappeared in Moscow "without a trace." His sister had also been killed by "a band of Antonov's men."[34] The supplicant himself had previously searched for work through the labor exchange without result, and his appeal to the gubkom for work had been refused, with the explanation that he was only a member of the Komsomol. Incredulous over the response, the komsomolets asked: "Would the authorities really allow a revolutionary to die?"[35]

This astonishment is echoed in a letter to Kalinin in May 1927 from a komsomolets from Vladimir guberniia. The author appealed for work or a pension for his family. The father and eldest son had been killed in the war. The family at first received some assistance from the government but subsequently got nothing, and the young communist could not get work at the local factory. He fairly sputtered with indignation:

> And truly, Mikhail Ivanovich, look, we lost two for the cause of the October revolution, and the third worked on behalf of society. But now—they will not give assistance or hire me—no help of any kind from anywhere—and truly we will die—the ones who defended October, who gave up our lives—and now, and now, although I have been a komsomolets since 1921, with pleasure I would go and beat and cut up those communists who are sitting there now at the Kol'chuginsk factory—sitting there sweating and do not know anything else about it. . . . You know there are a lot of rich peasants around here who are working, and they will be able to survive, but our brother-bedniak soon will not be returning.[36]

The young communist's appeal strongly suggests the general suspicion among unemployed supplicants that there were jobs for those with connections. As if in response to this suspicion, the factory cell secretary, who was the object of the desperate youth's wrath, answered his charge by assuring the authorities that he would be happy to hire the komsomolets as soon as there was a vacancy. But, as it was, there were not enough positions open at the factory to hire other party members.[37] Another interesting and common aspect of this appeal is the tendency of exasperated supplicants to turn their frustration on scapegoats or favored groups perceived to benefit, in this case, "rich peasants."

Nevertheless, the soldiers of the revolution had fulfilled their end of the bargain and demanded that the government now do the same. Thus, a party candidate from Zhitomir okrug in Ukraine appealed to Stalin in June 1927 for work. The supplicant had served as a commander and commissar in the civil war and still had bullet fragments in both legs, but could obtain neither work nor a pension. Despite his sacrifice for the sake of the revolution, the veteran became "unnecessary," an outcome that clearly astonished him.[38] Similarly, a former Red Army soldier sent his demands to the central authorities in July 1927. After demobilization, he had been hospitalized for some time but was subsequently unable to secure a place in a sanitarium because he no longer served in the army. The soldier, who had worked as a daily wage laborer in Moscow, had for two months been without work:

> As for relatives, I have not had any since 1914. . . . I gave the best years of my life . . . but now have been thrown out on the street, no good to anybody. I only ask that I be allowed to exist. I need: 1. medical treatment. 2. means for survival. . . . I honestly fulfilled my duty until the last and to the letter [during the civil war]. . . . I am convinced and believe now, as I did then, that we always must defend [the revolution] against the white parasite.[39]

Evident here is the common progression from distress over individual insecurity to the wish or expectation, even demand, to eliminate enemies.

Unemployed party members deeply resented their perceived dependence for work on class enemies. In 1927 a party member from Chernigov guberniia begged the Central Committee

> to answer my question—why . . . is it impossible for a communist to find work anywhere, and only go to meetings from which nothing good comes. I have been out of the army for six months and cannot find work anywhere. . . . I waited as long as I could but now have to go to the nepman for work. Give me an answer.[40]

As the rigors of war service and party work took their toll, veterans and party members often became invalids due to disease, most commonly tuberculosis, or nervous exhaustion. Thus, the party was constantly in need of new blood. On the eve of the Lenin Enrollment (the 1924 recruitment campaign of new party members), the vast majority of old communists were suffering from "physical and moral exhaustion."[41] In early 1924, during internal discussions on party democracy, one party cell in an electro-mechanical plant in Moscow guberniia proposed an addendum to their resolution on unity that was seemingly unrelated. The addendum urged that measures be taken "as soon as possible to provide for party members losing their health on the revolutionary front struggle."[42] The party's appeal for unity, it seemed, prompted a reciprocal appeal from party workers for support.

Besides incredulity and resentment, worn-out revolutionaries expressed a feeling of uselessness. The feeling of emptiness outside the collective was most profound for those who had once belonged to it. A request for work—from a twice-wounded civil war veteran from Cherepovets guberniia—echoed a common refrain:

> Why, comrades, when I was needed by Soviet Russia, then they knew me and found me useful and considered me a son of the proletarian defense, but now that I have been wounded and crippled, I became of no use to anybody?[43]

Along with anger and resentment, unemployed and abandoned communists and veterans often expressed shame. The more desperate supplicants became, the more deeply they felt their disgrace. A party member and civil war veteran, four times wounded during his service, appealed from Moscow in April 1927, as many did, "as a communist," hoping that the center would pay attention to one of their own, "with a request to give me proper advice on how to get myself out of this stupid situation." The veteran and his family had no possessions to sell, and

> to expect help was apparently useless, since I am nothing to the party. If some party member named Tosov kicks the bucket from hunger, you can replace him with anyone you please. . . . In fact, I myself would not be here crying for help, but when you have a family and a hungry baby, you are prepared to do anything. I hope, Comrade Stalin, that all the same you will give me an opportunity to escape from this situation.[44]

Similarly, in March 1927 an old revolutionary and communist from Voronezh guberniia who had worked for many years in the revolutionary underground appealed for assistance, because he and his wife were both ill. Together they received a monthly pension of 11 rubles, 63 kopecks, and found themselves in "the most critical circumstances . . . things could not be worse." A previous appeal addressed to the Central Committee had generated no help. The old communist now pleaded with Stalin personally "not to allow a party member to be subjected to the ridicule of the kulak element."[45]

Another appeal came from a party member from Saratov guberniia, who had been a batrak and served in the civil war and who had contracted tuberculosis. Unable to work or obtain support for medical treatment, he sent an astonished appeal to Stalin:

> How offensive, how disappointing, when I was healthy—I was necessary, but when I became ill everyone turned away from me, did not even give me the means to live, I cannot work. . . . Surely this cannot be! Surely I have earned a cure from the government wherever necessary. Have I really earned this contempt, even though I lost my health for the sake of the workers? Such treatment of a worker is unfair. . . . It cannot be.[46]

Because Soviet society condemned it, idleness, voluntary or not, was perceived as criminal. Those without work often felt that they were being punished for some unnamed crime, their outrage and desperation mixed with guilt over unknown transgressions. As Red Army units were disbanded, soldiers often saw demobilization as a punishment for some error on their part.[47]

Many unemployed thus perceived their situation to be not merely shameful. Idleness in a workers' state implied political unreliability, and so unemployed supplicants often sought to convince their leaders that they should not be blamed, because they were willing to work. In 1927 a komsomolets from Rostov-on-Don appealed to Stalin for work. He had grown up in Penza guberniia, but during the civil war part of "Antonov's band" attacked his village; while defending their home, his father was "cut to pieces with their sabers." The youth became homeless and could not find work: "I want to be a worker, but no one will give me the opportunity."[48] There was great irony in the lack of work in a workers' state, irony not lost on the unemployed themselves. The contradiction between party propaganda and reality was apparent in the appeal of another komsomolets, a former batrak from Ukraine. He complained that in the old days, "when there were landlords," one was at least "free to earn money." But now, ten years after the revolution, there was no work to be had at all, and "to live without work is very difficult." The writer went on to lament that "to beg for help is shameful, only 'cripples' beg, and everyone says that a healthy man needs to work, and not beg. But where do you find work?"[49]

The party's inability to take effective action to ease unemployment was devastating. The unemployed and indigent commonly described their plight as *bezvykhodnyi* (hopeless). This was a far cry from the psychological uplift communism had promised to the proletariat. Supplicants often indicated that their appeals were a last resort, as some of them were even considering suicide to escape the hopelessness of their situation; their very lives depended on action from the center. Indeed, who else was there for them, and thousands like them, to appeal to, when local officials turned a deaf ear? One komsomolets, a bedniak and village correspondent from Smolensk guberniia, appealed for assistance.[50] He was suffering from tuberculosis and expressed no hope of recovery in his current circumstances. For him, a "passionate [desire for] building Soviet power" was closely connected to escaping "cold, hunger, want [and] poverty." He appealed to Stalin:

> For a long time I have been a komsomolets and active within the school cell as head secretary. . . . Comrades! Now, when I look back over this appeal objectively, it is too, too painful. Sometimes I think about killing myself, but . . . I still want to live, I am still only twenty-two years old. . . . Comrade Stalin, I make my request to you.[51]

Supplicants occasionally sought to establish some kind of personal connection with the party leadership in an attempt to escape the killing anonymity. Thus, a komsomolets in Siberia who had formerly served in the Red Army and was now an "invalid of labor" requested only to see "the leader of the Comparty" and meet with him, "to receive advice for further existence."[52]

In order to find work or assistance of any kind, however, one had to warrant inclusion in the family of labor, and so supplicants who apparently were not workers in the strict sense nevertheless were careful to identify themselves as such. Thus, an actress with a worker-peasant theater in Moscow appealed to Stalin for help by emphasizing her working-class status. She had been married to a student in a military academy, but they split up; she continued to live in his dormitory for lack of other quarters. The actress had been rushed to the hospital by ambulance for an operation and, upon returning, she discovered she was evicted. "That is the kind of country we live in," she wrote, "where laborers do not have the right to a place to live!"[53] Notably, the actress identifies herself not as an artist or performer, but as a worker.

Both the superfluity of the unemployed and their attempt to escape it through connections were illustrated matter-of-factly by a party member writing to Stalin in July 1927:

> I am in the Bashkir organization of the VKP(b), which at the present time in one district alone has ninety unemployed party members, the majority of whom are workers, and without hope of receiving work anywhere. I find myself in the most critical circumstances and have no means of existence. I wish to go to Central Asia, or maybe still anywhere you see fit to send me . . . or maybe I need to come to you, in order to get acquainted. . . . I have been a worker and party member since 1919, voluntarily served in the Red Army from 1918 to 1924 inclusive, and finished officers' training with the . . . R.K.K.A. I was demobilized in 1924. I await your answer with impatience.[54]

Political Risk of Unemployment

As the preceding discussion illustrates, the assumption that the communist government would provide for its people was widespread, especially among party members and veterans, who considered both their status and sacrifice beyond that of average citizens. The great numbers of desperate and disaffected communists and Red Army veterans, not to mention nonparty workers, posed a grave political danger of which the party was fully aware. For example, the Leningrad party committee directed the labor exchange to extend special attention to communists and party candidates through quotas, and reminded local party committees of their responsibility in finding work for party members.[55] Those who were unhappy with the party's treatment could be drawn into opposition. Supplicants lost no time in making this point to the center, trying to manipulate the leadership's omnipresent fear of losing their tenuous hold on power.

Disaffection and demands for security appear to have reached a peak in 1927, coinciding with the apparent threat of war with England. Collective insecurity heightened perceptions of individual insecurity and vice versa.[56] A demobilized Red Army soldier residing in Moscow had been placed with his family on a waiting list for an apartment; others like him had been on the list for two or more years. Writing to Stalin in 1927, the soldier wished to speak to the leader personally about the problem since, as he pointed out, "the morale of the Red Army depends on such questions." The soldier wrote that, while serving in the army from 1921 to 1926, the only thing that kept his spirits up was the promise of a good apartment in which to live "and, in case of war, which will come for sure, my wife and baby would have their corner, and no one could throw them out."[57]

The year 1927 was also conspicuous in another regard: it was the tenth anniversary of the October Revolution. The occasion caused many to reflect on how little they, as individuals, had progressed and, by extension, how little had changed for the masses of Soviet citizens. In October a party member and veteran of ten years' service in the Red Army wrote to his comrades in the center to vent his anger. He explained bitterly that he and his family would be celebrating the tenth anniversary of the revolution starving and freezing to death in an unheated attic. Here, they had been waiting in line for housing, having registered with the Krasnaia Presnia district soviet in Moscow, for almost a year. The supplicant appealed to the secretariat "as a communist" and implored the central authorities to rectify his situation "as soon as possible, since it is already getting colder." The veteran warned that if "the highest organs of the party could not take care of their members," then perhaps it was time to take them to court. He found such neglect of those who had served the revolution unacceptable. Lest his readers miss the point, the soldier left no doubt as to the possible consequences of such neglect:

> In my opinion, the Central Committee of the party needs to pay attention not only to me, but to party members in general, and determine their situations and take appropriate measures to get the situation in hand, so that there would be no "aggrieved" people among party members, for, as we say, the "aggrieved" border on opposition.[58]

Just as was the general population, party leaders were especially anxious over domestic problems. In June 1924—just months after Lenin's death—the Moscow party committee discussions showed deep anxiety that the labor exchange was too "remote" from the needs of the unemployed. Committee members suggested that the unemployed be sent to the country to work as field hands, or to sanatoria or rest homes. They also stressed the necessity of paying special attention to unemployed trade union members, and of approaching the question of closing factories with the "utmost care."[59]

Solutions to Unemployment

Concern over unemployment was not limited to the party leadership. As early as August 1923, a citizen from Kiev appealed for the second time to Trotsky to impress upon him the gravity of the problem of overpopulation and unemployment, and the urgent need to colonize Siberia.[60] He reminded Trotsky of Lenin's injunction to "repartition the earth" and criticized party leaders for their eagerness to send people east, "when the talk was of Kolchak," and for their silence now, "when there should be discussion about the economic front in the East."[61] The supplicant continued:

> We have, along with an abundance of vulgar elements that made their appearance especially with NEP and in the presence of an even greater number of scum, . . . a very large number of people (party and nonparty) for whom the revolution is just now beginning.
>
> Many of them are falling into apathy, some driven to disappointment, to despair, nearly to suicide, not being able to reconcile reality with the ideal. This is not just because they are unstable, or for lack of ability. . . . It means that they need to be sent quickly to a different front, not military . . . but where they can apply their energy . . . and where there will not be room for parasitic elements to grow.[62]

Another letter came in 1927 from a Leningrad citizen, with a plan for liquidating unemployment. The plan, based on his assumption that the Soviet Union had almost unlimited land for resettlement, did not take into account the fact that the cities were besieged by peasants looking for work. But to the supplicant, the very thought of unemployment in the Soviet Union was inconceivable. He argued that in Western countries, where every piece of land was privately owned, unemployment was the "inevitable accompaniment" of the capitalist system. But in Russia, "all the land belongs to the laboring people." Each should be able to have his share, and then no one would go hungry.[63]

The party ultimately offered an alternate solution to the question of land and hunger. In 1925, reflecting current party policy toward the peasantry, at a guberniia-level party conference in Smolensk the conferees concluded that

> the unemployment situation is getting worse. To improve it, the peasants must be allowed to become more prosperous, which will enable them to hire more work hands. War Communism must go. One cannot close one's eyes to the fact that the top layer of peasants will become better off. . . . Nevertheless, this policy is necessary for the state.[64]

The party resolution stands in notably stark contrast to the Leningrader's more egalitarian solution.

Another egalitarian solution came from a "former military sailor" from Vladimir, who in 1927 wrote to complain to Stalin that "the great mass of workers and civil servants find themselves in the situation . . . that [NEP] strikes such a heavy blow on the proletariat that one cannot even begin to say."[65] This self-appointed spokesman for the proletariat had several recommendations:

> 1) instead of throwing out such a mass [of people] on the labor exchange, it would be preferable to lower salaries and grant everyone the opportunity to exist; 2) categorically prohibit the concentration of positions, especially in the hands of those civil servants who work in two or more establishments and receive separate salaries from each; 3) in hiring, do not take into consideration seniority or education, but rather capacity to work; 4) prohibit management from hiring workforce from outside of the labor exchange; 5) absolutely give

> preference in hiring to workers and peasants first, since it is not necessary to employ them the way they were . . . [under] the tsarist system, that is, the workers and peasants were needed only for military service, but the rest of the time . . . there was no work [for them].

The author of the appeal was a casualty of staff reductions, apparently in a legal office in which "the son of a priest, the son of a nobleman, an officer, a general, and so on" were employed. Essentially, the sailor was protesting the privileges in pay and employment opportunities of white-collar workers—who were, in his mind, dominated by former elites. Moreover, his frustration in 1927 over hiring from outside the labor exchange is significant, since this practice became legal only in 1925, and doubtlessly contributed to unemployed workers' frustration. Finally, his reference to the presumed advantages of those with education ironically points to both growing anti-intelligentsia sentiment,[66] and growing demand among workers and peasants for education to escape unemployment.

Employment through Education

For those seeking work, the question of acquiring education was more immediate than for party theorists. Lenin and the leadership postulated that raising the general standard of living was impossible without raising the cultural level of the population, and elevating the people's cultural level was impossible without education.[67] Thus, for many individual communists the immediate goal was to obtain an education, which would lead to a better job and a higher standard of living, to more personal freedom and leisure time, ultimately to a culturally richer and more satisfying existence—in short, to the type of existence previously enjoyed only by a small elite. Literacy would grant them independence and control over their lives. It thus became axiomatic that, as the population became educated, a redistribution of wealth would occur—if opportunities for education were distributed equally, then the fruits of education would also be equal.

The education of the masses, however, would not take place overnight. A group of students at a rabfak at the Moscow institute of communications engineers wrote to Lenin in September 1922:

> The October fissure smashed the locks on the doors of this institute, through which had tread only the legs of the bourgeois-noble. At first, workers and peasants timidly began to percolate into the institute in insignificant numbers. These numbers that were insignificant in the beginning now have turned into a wide, working-class torrent.[68]

Thanks to the revolution, the floodgates of education had opened to workers and peasants. The numbers turned out to be overwhelming.[69]

Incentives to Education

In the competitive atmosphere of NEP, education became almost a prerequisite for membership in the socialist collective. Anxiety over the future was omnipresent for communists and nonparty citizens alike. Supplicants hoped that an education, or more education, would assure their future prospects. Building a socialist society was beginning to look a lot like building a capitalist society.

As in a capitalist society, the first consideration was material; most of those appealing to receive an education were motivated primarily by economic considerations. For them, education offered the only escape. Thus, in May 1927, two komsomoltsy from Georgia appealed to Stalin for the opportunity to continue their studies: The translation from Georgian explains that, "from their letter, it is apparent that the boys are very needy; they indicate that their economic situation is so bad that they have considered suicide."[70] Similarly, in September 1927, a komsomolets and unemployed factory and office worker sent an appeal to study to become an "engineer-mechanic," or to obtain work of some kind, "either in the mines or in an office, it does not matter to me."[71] Another unskilled, semiliterate worker requested help from Stalin to take courses in machinery. The worker suffered from a nervous ailment contracted during the civil war, when the Whites attacked his home and family. Now, he had to support his family on an insufficient income and was at the end of his rope. The supplicant's desperation was evident in his concluding words—Stalin could either shoot him or help him; it was all the same to him.[72]

The unskilled and inexperienced were the most desperate in their struggle to obtain work or education. In July 1927, a seventeen-year-old komsomolets appealed to Stalin for help; he was unemployed, unskilled, and without connections. In short, his prospects were bleak. He begged: "Save me from hunger and poverty and thieving and a thousand times I beg you, help me." Pleading "simply from my worker's heart to send me to study," the youth sought to persuade Stalin to assist him by pointing out that "it would not cost you anything to help me, but would bring me great joy."[73]

As in a capitalist society, in NEP Russia individuals sought an edge on their comrade-competitors. A worker from Pskov guberniia appealed for help: he had received permission to attend a rabfak in Leningrad, only to be refused for lack of space. "As a member of the proletariat" the worker possessed a "very strong desire to study," because he felt he was ill-prepared for "white-collar-social-responsible work, and I feared I would become marginalized and unemployed."[74] This was not an idle fear. A Leningrad communist, a vydvizhenets, lost his position in the railroad administration for lack of an engineering degree and appealed, in March 1927, to Stalin for "the opportunity to gain a technical education." Neither the fact that he was a Red Army veteran with a large extended family to support nor his years of work apparently had made much difference in the decision to let the would-be administrator go: "With the coming of [NEP], I entered the ranks of red specialists, confronting and overcoming every difficulty, never dreaming that after five years of work I would be laid off because I did not have an engineering degree."[75]

The incentive to get an education, however, was not only material. Lenin had said that the cultural level of the general population was inadequate to the task of government; thus, several appeals requested financial assistance for projects intended to raise the people's cultural level. In January 1927, a citizen from Ukraine wrote on behalf of a group organizing an "International Academy of the Arts" to provide free education to children of poor workers and peasants in all arts, "from theater to architecture." The supplicant himself, who came from a poor peasant background, had been a railroad worker for thirty years and a political worker in the army, and his brother was in the Komsomol.[76] A similar request came from a red army soldier enrolled at a military academy in Nizhnii Novgorod. The soldier, a Georgian by nationality, asked Stalin for costumes and other necessities to stage theatrical productions for his school club, since, he argued, "Red Army men have great cultural need."[77]

In the early years of Soviet power, the vast majority of party members had little formal education, and elites both in Russia and abroad bemoaned the general lack of intelligence and administrative capability among communists. In describing a local soviet in Simbirsk, one of the famine regions, a Western observer noted that

> the commissars . . . are all young men in their twenties, except the chief, who is perhaps in his early thirties. . . . none of them give the impression of much education, great intelligence, or high character. . . . They are neither serious-minded nor reliable.[78]

This observer described Chekists (Soviet secret police) as "generally unintelligent and . . . likely to misinterpret one's meaning."[79] Another foreigner remarked that the "proletariat, as such, were not fitted to wield supreme power—above all, not the peasant class. . . . Nor was even the artisan class competent as a whole."[80] Komsomol youth were "fully convinced of their ability to rule Russia," despite the fact that, "according to Bukharin . . . 80 to 90 percent of them are political illiterates."[81] These observations were naturally fed by doubts about the lower classes' capability to rule in general, doubts that attached as a matter of course to individual communists, regardless of their inherent or uncultivated abilities or practical experience. Administrative competence was assumed, in short, to be a class rather than an individual quality that depended on a background inaccessible per se to the lower classes.

Many average communists were aware of the assumption that they were inherently unsuited to government or administrative work. A nonparty specialist who worked on the first Five-Year Plan remarked that workers in administrative positions made great efforts to appear educated in the presence of technical specialists and administrative personnel.[82] Such efforts no doubt stemmed partly from the frustration and hostility of specialists forced to take directives from their less-educated directors. At a meeting of the central administration of the Commissariat of Trade held in July 1925, the work of certain vydvizhentsy was discussed. The protocol stated that,

> concerning our vydvizhentsy, it has been indicated that some of them adapt themselves, and some are unsuitable. The main use of the vydvizhentsy was in

> [the area of] inspection. Comrade Shibailo . . . is of the opinion that vydvizhentsy already have practical experience, but lack theoretical preparation to promote them to responsible work.[83]

Thus, semiliterate workers and peasants once placed in positions of authority were perpetually nagged by a sense of their own inadequacy. Party members promoted to administrative positions often felt unprepared. In March 1927, a former factory worker and party member of long standing from Tver guberniia appealed to the center for admittance to an economics institute and for financial aid to support his family. For four years, while holding various administrative posts in the economic sphere, the supplicant had felt his knowledge inadequate to the tasks before him. With study at the university level, however, he felt that he would be able "to cope." The real work of the revolution, of learning how to run the country, had overwhelmed the vydvizhenets: "In the course of my work since the October revolution in various . . . posts, I became convinced that my devotion to the party alone was no longer enough; I needed knowledge, and mine was shaky."[84]

As some appeals suggest, however, party members' feelings of inadequacy stemmed from want not of ability but of a formal education that would legitimize their power and authority; the sense of inadequacy was based not on a lack of education, but on a lack of appearing educated. What vydvizhentsy often requested in their appeals was thus not practical administrative training, but "a good Marxist education." In their position as administrators in a party and a culture that prized theoretical knowledge, they felt a greater need for a theoretical grounding. This was the request of a party member and metalworker by trade who had served in the Red Army and occupied a number of party posts. Although elected to a position in the Tashkent *obkom* (regional party committee), "work with which I am completely satisfied," the supplicant felt deeply inadequate because he had "almost never studied anywhere."[85] There is nothing to suggest that the metal worker's duties actually outstripped his abilities.

Workers and party members aspiring to rise above their social and economic position experienced pressure, from within the party, to acquire theoretical knowledge and culture. In November 1924, Stalin received an appeal from a worker and former party member, who had been expelled during a purge the previous spring due, in part, to "semi-literateness and lack of ambition to replenish his knowledge." Answering this charge, the supplicant argued that his political training was weak, because, while a volunteer on the Polish front in 1920, the party did not allow him to complete any systematic coursework. Nevertheless, noted the worker, he had endeavored to make up for the deficiency on his own by studying "the program of all Russian [political] parties and reading through if not all, then the majority of works published at the time of the revolution." The party had also charged the worker with "carelessness" in his work, a charge that was "sharply contradicted" by recommendations filed on his behalf by the factory cell. In fact, the worker argued, his work record at the factory and as an activist within the party was exemplary; he himself had founded his factory party cell.[86]

In seeking to rise within the new society, education would provide workers and peasants not only theoretical knowledge but also a sense of confidence. In the workers' clubs established after the revolution, spontaneously and independently from the party,

> It was characteristic of the work in these circles [within the clubs] that further education in all fields was envisaged. This did not mean a mere acquiring of basic knowledge, but the opening of new fields which up to then had been shut off from workers because of their economic and social situation. This included a first visit to a theater or museum, learning to read and write, as well as practicing one's own artistic abilities or training in rhetorical skills in order to facilitate one's own confidence in articulating opinions and interests.[87]

What the workers lacked was not only what higher learning might provide for them in practical terms. Education and culture continued to confer status even in postrevolutionary society. Moreover, that value automatically adhered to those who possessed such education and culture. As a batrak and komsomolets from Ukraine stated in his appeal to Stalin for books (especially the collected works of Lenin), he knew that Stalin was a great man, because "you yourself have written many books [and] brochures," in contrast to the supplicant himself, who "cannot write such books and do not even own them."[88]

Thus, self-esteem and respect from others was a powerful incentive to get an education. Both rural and working-class communists harbored a great desire to learn more about their party in order to remain connected to the elite. In 1924 a komsomolets and factory worker from Belorussia appealed to his comrades in the central committee to send him an "outline of Marxism and Leninism, and methods for studying them." The worker wanted

> to understand these things myself; I have already begun to sort out a book of Lenin's on "State and Revolution," . . . and therefore I beg you to send me abstracts of books, some knowledge. . . . I would like to correspond with you; I will write in detail about everything in the country.[89]

Similarly, a peasant from Viatka guberniia, a communist and veteran of both World War I and the civil war, appealed to Stalin for an education. He had no cattle or any other means with which to support his family of three, including his "little daughter Roza." The local party organs would not give him any work. He begged his "dear you [*ty*] our leader, Comrade Stalin Iosif Vissarionovich, [to] help me in this." The supplicant lamented that there were those "in our village who laugh at me."[90] Similarly, a fatherless batrak from Kharkov guberniia appealed to Stalin to help him gain admission to "some kind of school," because he feared he would be unable to do so on his own, due to "weak technical preparation." Before the revolution he had been unable to study, since "those who worked for the kulaks never studied." The batrak, nevertheless, taught himself to read and write, but after the revolution had to work once more "for the kulaks," until he entered the Komsomol. His great desire for a formal education apparently stemmed from a wish to be "on equal footing with intelligent comrades."[91]

The idea that the country's future wealth and prosperity depended on raising the general level of education was widespread. In April 1927, a village teacher from Kursk guberniia appealed to Stalin for financial assistance to build a school. The appeal clearly illustrates the assumption that there was a direct progression from education to culture to wealth to power, for the individual as much as for the country as a whole. As the teacher pointed out, the school would be a testament, on the eve of the revolution's tenth anniversary, to the Soviet government's dedication to enlightenment. He hoped that the school would make available to both children and adult peasants "not only literacy, but also educated management of agriculture." Ultimately, the teacher hoped "to prove that our people could be as educated and rich as, for instance, the Americans or the English."[92]

Obstacles to Education

Educational opportunities were hardly widespread or equal in their distribution. Admission to institutes of higher education was in great demand, as many appealed to the center for assistance to obtain admission, or to overturn a refusal for admission. Supplicants often attributed refusal to the prejudice of professors or administrators, who wanted to keep out historically undereducated and underprepared students. In theory, supplicants argued, higher education was supposed to be available to all those who qualified, not just those "pupils sent there just because parents [could] provide the funds."[93] In fact, it seemed, the competition was such that access once more seemed to be a privilege of the elite.

Yet, even party membership did not automatically entitle one to an education. This fact angered young and old communists alike. A komsomolets and former worker from the Kirghiz republic sent an appeal to the center asking for an opportunity to study in Leningrad. The supplicant had no means to pay for his own education and found it

> extremely offensive that children of former nobility and merchants, as it happens in the city of Osh, formerly had the opportunity to study and still do, sometimes even at government expense, even though they scarcely think to study for the sake of the government.[94]

The author wondered whether he would have to choose between begging or suicide, and could not believe that his government would allow his efforts to come to such an end. Indeed, he maintained that he had "a right to life, but not the kind of life I lead now, when one road remains for me, the road to death." He appealed for help to Stalin "as a party member and as a human being" and, closing his appeal, asked whether "it was really true, that only those who have money and good connections have a right to live?"[95]

Supplicants complained that all types of impediments were placed in the way of party and nonparty citizens clamoring to obtain an education. Competition for places in rabfaky and every other kind of educational establishment compelled the government to create arbitrary barriers to make admission more difficult. Age requirements were one device for limiting access to education. One komsomolets from Baku, whose father worked in oil production, appealed to Stalin for assistance in obtaining a place at a communist university. He had been refused admission because of his youth and lack of party tenure. Yet, the young communist pleaded with his leader to grant him the right to continue his education "while I am still young and I have the energy."[96] A twenty-year-old komsomolets residing in Vladimir, a batrak since the age of ten who had long been unemployed, echoed these sentiments. Despite his lack of means, the batrak was active in party work but was forced to lead a vagrant existence, because of his low pay. The officials had rejected his application to a VUZ, citing his youth. The homeless youth hoped that "Comrade Stalin" could lend him some assistance and answer his plea, in which case he "could say that all the same I have a comradely friend and brother in the TsK VKP(b)" (Central Committee of the Communist Party).[97]

Even though impediments existed for everyone, the young found it more difficult to get an education, just as they did in their search for work. A peasant komsomolets from Tver guberniia requested Stalin's help for admission to study in Leningrad. The gubkom of the Leningrad Komsomol organization had refused to support him in his endeavors, suggesting that he find his own means. The young peasant nevertheless insisted on his right to obtain special training in order to "improve" himself, pointing out that "there is no law in our Soviet, communist, free government prohibiting anyone . . . from studying." He cited Lenin's famous exhortation to Soviet youth to "study, study, and study some more."[98]

Barriers to admission also included various types and lengths of party tenure. For instance, one party member and Red Army veteran from Ukraine appealed to central authorities in September 1927 for the opportunity to obtain training for propaganda work. His appeal with the local authorities had been tossed back and forth, and, "in the end, I came to the conclusion that I would never be admitted, because my one-year party tenure was insufficient."[99] Similarly, a communist from Voronezh guberniia who had been in the party only two years appealed to the center for assistance in May 1927. It seemed that a new rule had been promulgated, providing that acceptance into a Komvuz (communist university) required party tenure of a minimum of five years. The supplicant, son of a batrak, argued that the new rule discriminated against those with lengthy party candidatures. He had been a candidate for four years; for a time, only workers from the bench were being accepted into the party. As a batrak and soldier until 1924, the supplicant felt he had been held back arbitrarily. Although he had received some education in the army, he "naturally considered it insufficient" and thus sought admission for further study.[100]

Yet, for many, neither age, nor veteran status, nor party or class affiliation would suffice for admission to education. A party aktiv, civil war veteran, and former miner from the Donbass appealed for assistance to continue his education. Orphaned as a baby, the supplicant had supported himself from an early age; but after studying at a rabfak for only one year, he left his educational pursuits to do "practical work." He pleaded with Stalin "as a party comrade," since, after all, he wished to study not only for himself, but "in order to be in the avant-garde."[101] Another party member and former Red Army man from Kursk requested help in September 1927 for admission to a rabfak which he had been refused on the basis that he was too old. He argued, however, that it was "better late, than never" for him to get an education and be "of greater benefit to the cause of the working class and peasantry and party in general." He contended that, as a communist, he would need "to lead the masses in the decisive struggle against the worldwide bourgeoisie, and that would be soon."[102] Yet another party member, a student at the Institute of Red Professors in Moscow, wrote to complain that party members younger than he—and not even workers by origin—were being promoted to further study, while he was left behind. This was unfair, the supplicant argued, considering that he had ten years on the bench and fifteen years' active party work.[103]

The fact that the government constantly erected such arbitrary and shifting barriers to education caused great frustration and disappointment for those seeking to better themselves and, in so doing, further the cause of socialist construction. One classic horror story came from a bedniak and komsomolets from Siberia, who wrote in August 1927 that he had been trying to enter a party school for two years. Red tape had held up his application, until he finally was accepted to study for the upcoming fall term. The prospective student was prepared to begin school and anticipated the fulfillment of his dream with great excitement, when at the last minute he was informed that a new central directive would not allow him to study, since he was to enter the army within the year. His disappointment was profound:

> I thought for sure that in 1927 I would be able to go to school, to broaden my knowledge and become a useful member of society . . . thinking that by studying I could raise my low level of education. . . . I cannot describe how happy I was, that a peasant lad would be able to go to study; all the bedniaks awaited the 5th of September, then on the 20th of August they tell me at the district committee that there is a new directive from the Central Committee.
>
> . . . Comrade Stalin, explain to me why they pursue such a policy. . . . For two years I went to the Rubtsovskii okrug with my request, and I cannot understand it.[104]

Ironically, party membership could even be a hindrance to advancement in education. A student at the Kiev Medical Institute wrote to Kalinin in April 1927 to complain about the burden of party work. He pointed out that nonparty students were doing better at school because they did not waste so much time on "social work," endless and nonproductive meetings and lectures, and other distractions. As the exasperated student noted, "even semiliterate workers and peasants would say, if you asked them, that for socialism to be victorious in our country we need professional forces, we need good engineers, technicians, doctors and so on." But the fact, for instance, that, according to the supplicant, party members and komsomoltsy made up only 2 percent of the membership in student science organizations blatantly illustrated the party's confusion of priorities. Armies of skilled personnel—within and under the control and direction of the party—would never materialize under such conditions. The student also discussed the peasant question and added to his criticism of party policy that the opposition was not counterrevolutionary. After remarking on this, significantly, the student reconsidered his boldness and added: "I am afraid to write more. You do not have time to read about things you have known for a long time. But, all the same, I thought it would interest you to know the opinion of the masses."[105] A komsomolets from Komi autonomous oblast was more self-assured in his remarks. He appealed to the central leadership for leave from his party work in order to pursue his education; the oblast authorities had refused him. The author pointed out that, having spent a childhood in poverty as a batrak, he had been unable to receive "even the bare minimum general education," and, as a party worker, "always felt the most extreme lack of theoretical preparation." But, he continued, he had the right to obtain the education necessary to continue his work.[106]

As the batrak and many others suggested, plain and simple poverty remained, for the vast majority of the people, the greatest obstacle to education and self-improvement, despite the government's professed ideals. Most supplicants apparently disagreed with the party leadership's theory that cultural advancement had to precede material improvement. In February 1927, a communist worker from the Urals described to party leaders local living conditions—the general scarcity and high prices of products, such as sugar and meat, the low wages and high cost of living, and the horrible housing (with many workers camped in filthy barracks). The worker concluded:

> The fact is that low wages and the high cost of products do not permit the growth of cultural construction. Workers must concern themselves every minute over a crust of bread, and therefore one almost cannot begin to talk about cultural growth.

Consequently, he lamented, "among party members there are workers whose cultural level and knowledge about society in no way differ from [that of] the rest of nonparty comrades."[107]

Many supplicants reminded the government that its future depended on a timely investment in the working class, which presumably constituted its main political base. Thus, a communist factory worker complained to Stalin of workers' lack of access to education: student stipends were insufficient to support workers with families (the majority of young workers and peasants, according to him). He emphasized that the cultural (not practical) education of young workers and peasants determined the ability to build "our socialist society"; he further maintained that many were frustrated by the gap between the professed ideals of the government and the possibilities that real life offered them. He closed with a warning that if workers were unable to educate themselves simply for lack of means, and if only the privileged, who could afford to study without government assistance, had access to education, then "we will return to the old [system], from which we only recently emerged."[108]

In short, many supplicants believed that the opportunity for education and progress was slipping away from those who deserved it most. Thus, in May 1927 a party member and former Red sailor complained: "In recruitment to institutions of higher education, fewer and fewer workers dedicated to the cause of the revolution receive help from [worker] organizations to enable them to get in somewhere to study." This trend was especially unsettling, "now, when the war front has shifted to the front of the great construction of the Soviet Union," and the country was in need of educated workers. The former sailor, however, would not give up the fight; he maintained that he could not "remain passive and want[ed] to be in the front lines, beating a path to socialism."[109] The language employed here is telling: supplicants frequently expressed the effort to build socialism in militant terms, reflecting not just communist rhetoric but also the years of warfare by which they (and the rhetoric) were shaped.[110]

The special disadvantages of the poor peasantry in gaining an education formed the basis for many complaints to the party leadership. The growth of the Komsomol in villages was spontaneous, driven by a hunger among village youth for education and information about the outside world.[111] A variety of obstacles, however, stood in the way of all peasants seeking education to escape rural backwardness. For many, the basic problem was simple lack of educational materials. One party member working in Voronezh guberniia appealed to Stalin on behalf of a group of village communists. They requested Lenin's collected works; it seemed that they were too poor to buy any books, and the nearest library was eighteen *versts* (about twelve miles) away.[112] Similarly, a komsomolets from "a wild, remote corner of Siberia" sent a desperate appeal to Stalin, in February 1927, wondering how rural youth were to obtain an education. The youth appealed to Stalin "not as secretary of the Central Committee, but as Comrade Stalin, communist." The supplicant had apparently appealed to various government organs without success and lamented that only those who had connections with party cadres got ahead. The rest in the countryside were left to educate themselves under impossible circumstances, perhaps in a village reading room where it was "colder than outside." The komsomolets implored Stalin to turn his attention to the village youth, "who struggled for a future, that is, toward the building of socialism."[113]

Requests for reading materials from rural communists, komsomoltsy, and pioneers were common. One party member and village correspondent from Ukraine sent Stalin a convoluted request for a history of the party, which he could not afford to buy.[114] In another appeal, a schoolboy from Nizhnii Novgorod guberniia wrote on behalf of his friends, requesting books and journals for their Red Corner.[115] He described himself as an orphan, having lost his father in the civil war and with a mother too old to work, but made no material request beyond something to read.[116] Similarly, komsomoltsy from the Minsk region requested literature on political and agricultural subjects, as well as some posters and portraits to decorate their Red Corner. They considered their request part of a bargain, assuring Stalin that if he fulfilled his end, then "we for our part will try to put our knowledge to use and present a good example on how to practice agriculture."[117]

Many supplicants complained that their educational goals were undermined by a system unwilling to make allowances for the traditionally disadvantaged, and that workers and poor peasants never would break into the education system unless it was modified to accommodate them. In 1924 a party candidate, a former batrak and veteran, appealed for help in clearing him of criminal charges leveled against him in his village; he was in the midst of his studies and lacked the time and means to exonerate himself. The supplicant protested this burden, considering the effort he was making to be a communist "not on paper but in deed," and that he had formerly worked unceasingly and had nevertheless "remained illiterate."[118] In another case, a former worker was dismissed from an officers' training school in Orel due to "lack of success," and his military pay was consequently reduced to 3 rubles 50 kopecks per month, on which he had to support himself and his elderly parents. The aspiring officer argued that his dismissal was "unjust," since he was not to blame for his general lack of preparation:

> Like all workers, I created the means for socialist construction, and, therefore, as a laborer I have a right to education, and if my general educational preparation did not provide me the opportunity to become an officer of the RKK, then I am not to blame, and therefore I should not be punished for my failure. . . . Tell me how to support a family on 3.50 rubles.

The worker's tone was respectful but demanding. He knew his rights and was not prepared to see his future ruined due to disadvantages the revolution was meant to correct.[119]

Solutions to Lack of Education

In contrast to the party's prevailing approach to economic and cultural advancement which upheld class differentiation and cultural and economic disparities, supplicants appealing for education commonly argued for a leveling of resources and opportunities. In January 1927, a "union of shepherds and batraks" working in the forestry industry in the Northern Caucasus sent a joint appeal to Stalin. They extended their regards to their "esteemed comrade" in honor of the upcoming anniversary of the revolution, then proceeded to ask him for a grant from his own salary to open a veterinary school:

> We heard that you receive 180 rubles [a month], so we ask you to send us some money . . . so that . . . we could know when and why our cattle become ill. We would start a school ourselves, but some of us workers and peasants receive 5 or 3 rubles a month. If we spent it, our families would have nothing left, and therefore Comrade Stalin we appeal to you.[120]

Similarly, in March 1927, a komsomolets from Tambov uezd wrote of the difficulties of rural party work. The party, he maintained, needed to come to the assistance of bedniaks by cutting party salaries and using the money to buy farm machinery for poor peasants. In addition, standards for admitting bedniak children to institutes of higher education had to be lowered, since only "the wealthy [peasants] passed entrance exams, because they have greater means for preparation." For that reason, bedniaks would never come to power, and their interests would continue to be ignored. The author warned:

> [The bedniak] says that our party and Komsomol have long since diverged from the Leninist path. . . . we need to drive alien elements from power, pay

> lower salaries, beginning with uezd [party] workers and higher, and use this money to improve bedniak agriculture, those who have nothing. . . . But until now they have received nothing, so I decided to write to you, maybe you do not know about it.[121]

Undeniably, the vast majority of the population still lacked the most basic services to raise their level of existence, of which educational opportunity was but one. Supplicants often expressed the belief that, until a general improvement in the standard of living was effected, general access to education and a corresponding rise in the "cultural level" of the population would remain only an ideal. In March 1927, a nonparty citizen wrote to the center on the problems of "provocation, banditism and hooliganism" that generally plagued the country. The author's discussion of the universal shortage of educational materials and books and of hospitals and trained medical personnel suggested a direct connection between shortages and social ills.[122] In a similar vein, in March 1927, a peasant from Saratov guberniia wondered whether socialism could indeed be attained if all or most of the party's attention was not focused on the peasantry who, after all, constituted 75 percent of the population. He stressed the necessity of providing mass education to all of the country's inhabitants, in order to address the peasantry's needs.[123]

Thus, the connection between economic and cultural disparity was central. One factory worker, not a communist, wrote to complain about unemployment of party and nonparty workers and suggested that unemployment was related to bureaucrats' high wages. The worker further lamented that, while there were many schools, relatively few workers were being educated, due to their poor preparation. He, therefore, suggested that highly paid specialists "need to be utilized 100 percent" to teach introductory subjects to workers, without pay. He clearly resented the gaps in opportunities and living standards and advantages in educational opportunities and wages of white-collar workers. The playing field was not evening out, and this, according to the factory worker, was wrong.[124]

Another proposal for leveling the field came in a remarkable appeal from a student at the United Belorussian Military School in Minsk. He advocated the adoption of Esperanto as a common language to facilitate communication among the various nationalities and workers of the world. The student argued that, for lack of time, "our workers" never learned foreign languages: "it is only the bourgeoisie who, out of idleness, sitting on soft couches in sumptuous dwellings, had time to study languages."[125]

Supplicants often argued that it was the government's responsibility to lower entrance requirements. A twenty-two-year-old party candidate appealed to Stalin to waive the requirement for the entrance exam to either a "naval academy or technical institute." The supplicant was orphaned when his father, serving in the navy, was drowned at sea; he wished to study to become "an educated and useful person for the republic." As a factory worker, however, he feared that entrance exams would prove too difficult and effectively put an end to his aspirations.[126] As another unemployed party member argued, the difficulties encountered by unskilled workers in finding work were the fault of the tsarist system. But now, under the new system, the party needed not only to help unskilled party members obtain education and training, but also to encourage "comradely" relations between communists in a position to hire them and rank-and-file party members. Such equality would enhance party unity. The author pointed out that such questions concerned not only him, "but also a number of other comrades, of whom some would be extremely pleased if Comrade Stalin . . . answered." He closed his appeal by asking Stalin to excuse his semi-literateness.[127]

In the short run, however, the creation of hoards of educated citizens often increased frustration and resentment, because there were no jobs for them anyway. Those who were fortunate enough to receive an education discovered, to their profound dismay, that their efforts were in vain. Superfluity of human beings was the problem. In July 1927, a nonparty citizen from Ukraine sent a long, indignant appeal for justice. After having completed an eight-month course for workers in the judicial system, the supplicant related bitterly, he found out that no such work was available. Along with 140 other participants he had been promised a job upon completion of his studies. Instead, all were instructed to register with the labor exchange which, the supplicant observed, amounted to remaining unemployed. As it turned out, his unemployment resulted from a new initiative to hire only those with party or trade union tenure.[128]

Similarly, in March 1927, a VUZ graduate wrote bitterly of his disappointment. Unable to find a job after finishing school, he reckoned that only communists received employment upon graduation, regardless of their merits or abilities, and not even all communists at that:

> Just as before, when those who were not of the nobility or capitalists, etc., but simple muzhiks [peasants] were condemned to eternal suffering, so today those without a party card share the fate of their fathers. . . . You are a nobody, you are garbage. . . . Former priests, clerks, "esteemed citizens" again accommodate themselves.

The collective offered education but little opportunity to put that education to use. The formerly privileged had already infiltrated the party and thus retained their old advantages. Nothing had changed; the situation remained as before the revolution. The supplicant's bitterness and resentment toward elite groups is unmistakable. But beyond that, the graduate concluded, the communists were creating legions of educated citizens they could not use, simply "because here we have a sufficient army of persons immediately available for work."[129]

During the revolution there were great expectations that a new, egalitarian society would emerge and provide work and sustenance for all. NEP disappointed those expectations, altering the revolutionary struggle from a collective effort of oppressed against oppressors to an individual struggle for survival. This competition defined society, promoting a general mood of atomization and alienation.

The change of revolutionary goals did not occur without protest through mass party resignations and numerous appeals to the party leadership.

Official elites—party members, komsomoltsy, veterans, workers, and poor peasants—protested their abandonment by the government, expressing incredulity, anger, and a pervasive sense of hopelessness. They threatened the center with political opposition, playing on the party leadership's fear of losing power. The unemployed and indigent also sometimes experienced a sense of guilt. In a workers' state, those without work felt a particular loss of dignity and self-esteem.

Many without work or those fearing unemployment sought a competitive edge through education. Considering education a prerequisite of material advancement, Lenin himself had exhorted the masses to educate themselves. Moreover, Bolshevik ideology dictated that the proletariat would be led by an educated vanguard, and socialism built by a cultured, educated proletariat. However, the lack of opportunity either for work or education laid bare the contradictions between Bolshevik ideology and Soviet reality. In the short run, the cultural imperative also caused a pronounced sense of inferiority among less-educated party cadres.

Ultimately, educating the population was impossible without sufficient funding or action on the part of the state. Lacking both of these during NEP, the government was inundated with appeals protesting the arbitrary barriers erected to reduce the number of applicants. Many supplicants observed bitterly that poverty was still the greatest barrier to cultural advancement, and, unless the government eliminated the material disadvantages of the majority, the revolution would in fact have changed nothing.

CHAPTER FIVE

The Specter of Bureaucracy

AS the 1920s wore on, bureaucracy and corruption in party and state presented a growing impediment to creating an egalitarian socialist society and a major source of complaint to the central party leadership. The growth of the party and state apparatus made government control ever more difficult, prompting even more government growth. Adding more personnel appeared to be the only solution the government could offer to combat the lack of coordination and communication among its various branches. In addition, besides accelerating the chaos, the center's efforts to control stifled initiative at the lower levels of both party and state.

For their part, Soviet citizens contributed to bureaucracy by employing both state and party as vehicles to satisfy their aspirations and redress their grievances. But the center relied on local administrators to rectify problems, so the power of local officials—and their potential for corruption—was extraordinary. Throughout the period, the party received a multitude of complaints about the ineptitude and corruption of party and nonparty officials. This search for justice, however, presupposed a non-existent consensus on what justice meant in a socialist society, and, indeed, on the revolution's very purpose.

Through its impersonal and unresponsive character, the bureaucracy victimized communists and non-communists alike. Clearly, government and party organs were overwhelmed and crippled by a lack of resources, a poorly coordinated infrastructure, and too much information. Yet, many supplicants suggested that officials used red tape as a means of persecution. Others complained that party and state officials operated as though they were above the law, and used their positions to obtain special benefits. The fact that corrupt officials were not always party members complicated the search for a solution. Nevertheless, since the Bolshevik Party was in power, a search for the source of corruption inevitably led back to the party. Supplicants faulted opportunists, who supposedly flooded the party after Bolshevik power was secure. Critics often connected this opportunism with the general atmosphere of NEP, with its emphasis on, and ubiquitous opportunities for, individual self-enrichment. Moreover, the acute competition for work and survival that characterized NEP society further engendered abuse of power; those employed were reluctant to complain or report on their superiors' abuses. The atmosphere of economic exploitation brought about other forms of exploitation. At the same time, many joined the party simply because they craved the power over others that circumstances lent them.

In the end, intense competition for work not only eroded party purity but also promoted nepotism and favoritism. Even while criticizing the favoritism that plagued the system, the unemployed and indigent themselves petitioned the center for special consideration. Supplicants sought special treatment from the center, based on whatever services or qualities might qualify them for it, including special abilities or training, working-class membership, past service to the revolution, loss of family members to the socialist cause, or simple poverty. In short, widespread need facilitated the growth and corruption of party and state.

Growth of State and Party Bureaucracy

Perhaps the greatest impediment to building socialism was the socialist state itself. Attempts by the Bolsheviks to gain control over a vast and potentially hostile territory helped to create a great and unwieldy bureaucracy. The amorphous state of the new government apparatus complicated the task of gaining control and contributed to the center's impulse to crack down on independent initiatives. This impulse came to the fore very quickly. While in 1919 the Eighth Party Congress supported granting trade unions "quite wide functions," a year later, the Ninth Congress condemned the policy as "syndicalist."[1]

As the party built up its apparatus to gain control over the country, average citizens sought to satisfy aspirations and rectify grievances through government channels, and so contributed to bureaucratic growth. Communists and non-communists viewed the state as protector and benefactor. This perception grew during NEP, as citizens victimized by economic circumstances appealed for government support. Moreover, throughout the 1920s, the state was still the employer of first importance. Under conditions of chronic unemployment, therefore, a drastic downsizing of the state or party apparatus was difficult. Considering these factors, the growth of bureaucracy during NEP is hardly surprising.

Ironically, the more the bureaucracy grew, the more control slipped away from the party. Bureaucratic growth increased the government's lack of coordination. Evidence gathered by the Party Secretariat indicated that from the first, coordination between central and local party organs but also among all party levels was decidedly lacking. Communication and discipline within party ranks were conspicuously absent.[2] This phenomenon contributed to the lack of connection between the party and the people that caused profound concern and criticism within and outside the party.

Party control of the country at large was even more remote. Even coping with such vital problems as unemployment appeared beyond the government's capabilities.[3] The statistical aspect of control alone presented insurmountable obstacles. A 1923 report from the People's Commissariat of Labor on industrial wages throughout the country began with some startling revelations. According to the report, "data on wages were not successfully gathered in all gubernii . . . The cause resided in a shortage of Labor Department personnel and the impossibility of forcing them to compile statistical data."[4] Similar evidence of the government's inability to gather complete, standardized, or reliable data—or even to direct its own apparatus—surfaced in a number of instances, including the party's social composition.[5]

Efforts to strengthen central control also encouraged a lack of responsibility at lower party and state levels, the notorious "fear of the man one step higher in the bureaucracy,"[6] which quickly stifled initiative and innovation within the system. Discussions on the party's tasks in 1923 in Moscow workers' party cells indicate that some rank-and-file members were frustrated over being discouraged from dealing with problems locally. One participant in the discussion emphasized the "necessity [to grant] more initiative, and to stop running to a higher level to solve every stupid thing."[7] Ironically, central intervention could undermine the party's authority. In February 1927, the chairman of the Ivanov volost executive committee sent an angry letter to the Central Executive Committee, protesting its decision to overrule the volost committee and restore voting rights to a citizen disenfranchised by the local organ. This action was an affront not merely on an official but also on a personal level. The volost chairman, clearly offended, reached the conclusion that "the TsIK . . . does not wish to take into consideration lower organizations." Such a position, he pointed out, not only weakened their authority in the countryside, but also caused them "apprehension in their work."[8]

Economic Chaos

The general lack of bureaucratic coordination had disastrous consequences in the economic sphere. With NEP, the party had essentially relinquished its attempts to control distribution, thereby allowing the chaos of the free market to reign supreme. Bureaucratic confusion in the state economic apparatus aggravated this chaos. One official inspecting government economic administration lamented the "disgraceful" level of bureaucratism that characterized the relationship between departments and subdepartments of the glavki, and deemed the accountability and distribution of goods among and within the glavki to be "criminal." The official concluded that "the profundity of this issue resides in the fact that the chaos that rules in accounting and distribution generates economic and every other chaos."[9] This assessment suggests that government officials recognized the destabilizing effect of bureaucracy on society. At times, officials appeared eager to emphasize the "systematic order" that characterized various campaigns within their organizations, suggesting that the opposite was true.[10]

Confusion over the nature and goals of NEP further contributed to bureaucratic disorganization. Government reports pointed to a conspicuous confusion over exactly what the new economic policy was, the relationship between government and industry, and, indeed, the government's very function under NEP. As late as 1926, Vesenkha issued a report concerning the Southern Machine Building Trust and attempts to organize factories within the trust according to the principles of khozraschet. The report found that, in the past year, "the most outstanding defects in the constitution of the trust" came from "the complete lack of administrative organization and of a well-defined relationship with the factories and control over their work." A new administration was installed in the trust to correct these faults.[11] The government appeared confounded over the issue of how it might increase bureaucratic efficiency. A 1927 report by Rabkrin on the textile industry found that "supply . . . proceeds under conditions of red tape due to lack of regulation and the unwieldiness of the system . . . and the numerous stages through which orders pass." The entire system, the report concluded, flowed "roughly and unsystematically."[12] However, the Rabkrin official could only suggest more regulation to simplify and clean up the chaos.

The only alternative was less regulation, which meant simply allowing industry to develop independently. That alternative was unacceptable to the Soviet government for a variety of reasons. Less regulation smacked of laissez-faire capitalism, of aimless industrial development. For a self-proclaimed socialist government to undertake such a course was unthinkable.[13] The chaos of an unregulated economy brought disparities and uncertainties that neither party nor the general population could accept. After all, the purpose of socialism was to eliminate material insecurity. If the government relaxed its hold over economic and industrial development, there was no assurance that industrial performance would improve indefinitely or, more importantly, that social and political requirements would be satisfied.[14] Indeed, NEP appeared to confirm this. Thus, the only apparent option was more regulation and control, and so bureaucracy continued to grow.

Resisting effective control, the bureaucracy soon took on a life of its own. With time, the state came to replace the proletariat as the "bearer of socialism," and the bureaucracy replaced the proletariat as the Bolsheviks' political base.[15] Thus, in a very short time after the party began its task of building the socialist utopia, which would theoretically function without a state, it became apparent that the state itself showed little promise of withering away.

Economic chaos made strong leadership imperative. Underscoring this point was an appeal sent in April 1927 by a citizen from the city of Sergiev-Posad in Moscow guberniia. Two years earlier, the supplicant had asked Stalin to publish a pamphlet he had written concerning "the problems of production and distribution." Now, he wrote to warn that the "maneuvering of socialist construction" according to the plans proposed by Vesenkha would constitute a "great tactical error." The critic lamented, "What a pity that Vladimir Il'ich is no longer here! On you, comrade, lies a profound responsibility—take note of that at this moment."[16]

Bureaucratic inefficiency was caused not only by a lack of strong leadership but also from a simple lack of means. Revolutionary expectations mandated a new state and society, but the Bolsheviks lacked the resources and infrastructure to build them—part of the reason for adopting NEP in the first place. This had disastrous effects on the party at its local, most critical levels. In a confidential report to the center in September 1922, the Kubano-Chernomorskoi oblast party secretary lamented the deplorable state of the regional party organization. Party work was decidedly "weak," because many members were currently out working in the fields and seldom met to discuss party business. The secretary added that, "unfortunately, we are not in a position to pay party cell secretaries, and this affects party work."[17] Similarly, a memorandum on pay for party cell workers from Orgraspred to Stalin in December 1924 noted that industrial concerns were considering taking party workers off their payroll to lower overhead costs.[18] Thus, economic considerations were jeopardizing the building of socialism—and party power—at its most basic levels.

The lack of material support for the builders of socialism was the complaint of a party member and vydvizhenets, who appealed to Stalin when it appeared that his recent "promotion" would cause his family to starve. He was required to take three months of coursework, but was offered no financial aid to support his wife and baby during that time. The disgusted worker asked:

> Why tear people away from production, throw them here and there? If that is promotion from the ranks, then I would rather not be promoted. . . . If they had not taken me from work and sent me to the country, I could have continued to work peacefully . . . doing all the overtime they put before me. I want very little, namely, only to work and net something to live on. In my opinion, this is not a lot to ask.

The supplicant added that, if it wanted to promote workers to its ranks, it should ensure that they were actually employed, so that those "promoted" might avoid ridicule.[19]

Sources of Corruption

The Process of Appeal

Causes for bureaucratic growth did not emanate only from above. Merely through employing state and party organs as vehicles for getting satisfaction, ordinary citizens themselves caused the juggernaut to grow. Soviet citizens had but one route to justice, and so government corruption was practically inevitable. In March 1927, a worker and trade union member from the city of Tiumen' sent a lengthy protest to central authorities about bureaucratic corruption. The supplicant claimed to have been illegally dismissed from his job by a communist official, and that his appeal to be reinstated had been held up by red tape for a year. According to the aggrieved worker,

> Tens of millions of peasants, thousands of white-collar employees, and workers address their complaints to the center, seeking justice and support from you. Millions of these pieces of paper return from the center to localities for verification. You come to have little faith in these masses, and instead put your trust in various individuals sitting at the local level. It may be that the center does not notice this, but it is so. Statistics for the Procurator, statistics for Narkomzem [People's Commissariat of Agriculture].[20] The ones who crank up

> the red tape are naturally those who are seeking justice. And who among those local administrators sitting there would report on their own abnormalities and distortions? Not one would write about it, believe me. And in this way, millions of peasants, white-collar employees, and workers give up on their complaints, because they do not have the endurance, the time, or the means. Whoever seeks justice from the center must have strong nerves, because for that you need time and more time. In this way, that notorious dissatisfaction arises, which must be addressed by the directing organs of the Politburo of the party.[21]

The role of local officials, in fact, was not primarily to satisfy, but to verify; as employees of the party, their primary task was not to serve, but to control. In order to supervise its population, the central government relied on local administrators, whose power was extraordinary. And extraordinary power engendered extraordinary potential for corruption.

Moreover, as the worker observed, the central party leadership relied on local officials to rectify injustices for which they themselves were often responsible. This fact was the subject of innumerable complaints. In one such appeal, submitted in July 1927 from a party candidate from Armavir okrug, near Krasnodar, the supplicant asked Stalin why his previous petitions, concerning his admission to the party and directed to the central control commission, had been returned to the very local powers opposing him. Under such circumstances, "true communist justice" was obviously impossible. As the supplicant remarked, "all of the co-workers in our region vouch for each other on oath, never daring to come forward in meetings against our soviet official, because if you did you would curse the day you were born."[22]

The Problem of Defining Justice

The frustrated supplicant's search for justice was complicated by another important factor in corruption. The appeal presupposed some consensus on the notion of "communist justice," but no such consensus actually existed. As might be expected, references to socialist justice were often vague.[23] In July 1923, the plenum of the Altai guberniia court sent a letter of greeting addressed to Lenin and the country's top judicial figures on the inauguration of new legal training courses. The plenum's members expressed their "belief [in] the triumph of proletarian justice in the near future," but did not specify what that justice meant. The authors indicated only that communism had not yet been achieved, and that the revolution was not complete.[24] Indeed, true communist justice was interpreted in various ways.

These multiple interpretations were due in part to the wide spectrum of revolutionary motivations. For many, justice meant establishing equal opportunity for work and education. But for most, the definition derived from personal experience of inequality that was only later intellectualized and politicized. Thus, even the most idealistic communists might be inspired by self-interest. For others, self-interest occupied a more prominent and cynical place in their notion of justice. Still others considered social vengeance to be the primary goal of revolution. For many such individuals, revolution simply meant being on top; indeed, the revolution promised that the last would be first. A powerful desire for social revenge against unapproachable social elites might be satisfied through exploitation of those more vulnerable, and justified as the revolution in practice. And this desire for social revenge was fueled by resentment over the presence of class enemies in positions of power and privilege throughout party and government long after October 1917.

The Criminal Element

There was a general perception that, within the growing bureaucracy, a growing number of persons with corrupt motives and questionable pasts had insinuated themselves into the party or state apparatus. One citizen complained that the government had become "clogged [with] rowdies and other riffraff composed of petty thieves."[25] Others connected criminality with politically and socially suspect allegiance. In one complaint, a vydvizhenets promoted to work in the railroad administration in Ukraine complained of thoroughgoing corruption. The worker had been wrongly accused of sabotage, suffered a nervous breakdown from stress caused by trying to clear his name, and then was laid off, ostensibly due to his nervous exhaustion. The exasperated supplicant lamented that "the administration of the Southwestern Railroad is criminal from bottom to top, with the support of the local courts . . . discrediting the government and the idea of legality itself." He went on to name a number of top officials who had accepted bribes; a number of these, he claimed, had been White sympathizers during the civil war.[26]

Sometimes, aggrieved employees were not informed of the cause of their dismissal, making the source of their misfortune even more sinister and difficult to explain. In one appeal, a self-described nonparty Soviet worker was laid off from his job in the trade administration and asked central authorities why. He remarked that such arbitrary dismissals and constant changing of the guard bred uncertainty among the nonparty masses, who depended on the goodwill of their uncertain allies throughout the government apparatus.[27]

Under these circumstances, anyone who suffered from a tendency toward directness did not fare well, and often lost their jobs or party membership for their pains. One village correspondent from Tula guberniia appealed to central authorities in August 1927.[28] It seems that he had been refused party membership due to his activities in exposing corruption, but this apparently did not dampen his enthusiasm. His appeal read more like a declaration of war:

> Nevertheless I will remain one of those who will continue the work I began, as a RABSEL'KOR AND WORKER-JOURNALIST. BECAUSE I KNOW that THE PARTY IS BEHIND US, THE PARTY CREATED US.
>
> THE PARTY LEADS THE RABSEL'KOR ARMY, IT DIRECTS ITS WORK, AND SEPARATE ATTACKS AGAINST ME WILL NEVER BREAK MY DESIRE TO GIVE EVERYTHING THAT I HAVE, FOR THAT I WOULD GIVE MY LAST PENNY.[29]

The correspondent's affirmation was both an appeal and a warning to party leaders. He sought reassurance that the party intended to remain dedicated to the goals of the revolution and to the support of revolutionaries. As the 1920s progressed, it became clear that the party leadership's commitment to both had most definitely fallen into question.

The Party Opposition

Of all the questions that troubled the party rank and file, however, none was perhaps greater than how to regard the so-called Left Opposition within the party.[30] If the solution to party and government corruption was greater party unity, then the opposition was a corrupting influence. Conversely, if the remedy was to be found in party democracy, opposition within the party was the last best hope to save the government and the revolution. In short, one could view either the opposition, or its suppression, as the source of the party's corruption.

In a letter to Stalin in November 1927, one communist from Stalingrad wrote on a number of issues "that stand before every member of the party, and that require from the official party leadership clear answers." Among these was the current state of international socialism. The supplicant wondered whether it was true that capitalism was growing stronger, and, if so, what relationship the Soviet Union should have with socialist movements in the West. Following on this query was a challenge: Did Stalin know that his regional party supporters conducted "illegal meetings" closed to opposition members in which they "worked out strategies in the struggle against the opposition"? If Stalin knew about these intrigues, "did [he] consider such a situation normal?"[31] For this communist, normal party procedure meant democratic procedure—even allowing for dissension or opposition that might threaten party unity.

In another appeal in October 1927, a group of factory workers from Poltava reprimanded Stalin for the party's shameful treatment of the opposition. The workers censured so-called party faithfuls for shouting down opposition leaders at meetings and labeling them as hooligans. They suggested that "it would be interesting to know, Comrade Stalin, who the real hooligan was, the one giving the speech or the one shouting him down—probably the one shouting." In the workers' estimation,

> being a member of the government and shouting "hooligan" and "feeble" at meetings [was] shameful! Shameful! . . . Has it come down to that, that we don't have a Central Committee, but "hooligan"? Shameful! Shameful to act that way!

The workers added, interestingly, that they "did not defend" opposition leader Grigory Zinoviev's words, but felt the party was nonetheless obliged to allow him to express himself. The authors requested that Stalin not only make their letter public but also answer them; in conclusion, they asserted that "as workers [we] are for the opposition, and not for hooligans."[32]

But party fractionalism was strongly opposed by Lenin, many other communists, and even nonparty citizens. The opposition's very existence signified party disunity and weakness, which presented for many an intolerable danger. Opposition to the party line threatened not only the authority of the party, but also the survival of the revolution itself. After all, it was Bolshevik unity and determination that had secured the revolution against the threat of civil war and foreign intervention. Advocates of unity feared that a weak party would cause the revolution to fail.[33] Indeed, "the Bolsheviks felt deeply that in a hostile world the survival of the revolution depended on their own unity and the disunity of their opponents."[34] Moreover, according to countless appeals, class enemies were to be found throughout party and society. Facing such insecurity, how could anyone consider democracy a higher priority than the revolution? The fact that the communist from Stalingrad quoted above juxtaposed concerns over the country's external security with questions about party unity was not coincidental. On the contrary, it expressed the obvious connection between the two, a connection drawn over and over again in appeals to the center. If the nascent socialist state became fragmented, its enemies would certainly capitalize on the situation, and its demise would be certain.

In the wake of the party's decision against factionalism during the Tenth Party Congress—when NEP was adopted—there continued to be a great deal of discussion on the crucial question of democracy, and party cell resolutions taken on this issue reflect a surprisingly wide range of opinions and conclusions. Many took the line of the Poltava factory workers, supporting the right of free discussion within the party. In December 1923, the party cell of the Moscow State University Chemistry Department resolved that, although they supported the general line on party unity, they considered "absolutely impermissible" the practice of labeling any criticism of "certain features" of party policy as "fractionalism." Such a practice, they noted, constituted a "struggle against free discussion."[35] Similarly, a meeting of party cell members of the Traffic Division resolved that no appointment made by the cell secretary should be carried through without a general discussion in the party cell.[36]

But the discussion of democracy versus unity often hinged, it seemed, on the level of individual concern over the party's disintegration. Most communists supported free discussion but rejected an outright challenge to the party as a whole. In 1920s Moscow, "party activists in Krasnyi Proletarii and Serp i Molot [factories] had their eyes firmly fixed on the goal of socialism, and any deviation from that path, however caused, appeared to them as a betrayal."[37] Similarly, the Selenskii raikom of Astrakhan resolved that, while "discussion of all questions was necessary," so was a "merciless struggle against grouping and fractionalism," since party unity was of paramount importance.[38]

In the end, the goals of party democracy and party unity appeared to contradict, even cancel out, one another. But the desire to achieve both led to confusion. A general party meeting in December 1923 at the Komintern factory in Moscow guberniia adopted a strong position against disunity and for democracy. The party cell resolved that

> no grouping should take place in our party. This general meeting summons all members of the party to greater unity of activity and, expressing their deepest

> faith in the CC [Central Committee], considers it necessary to move toward practical realization of inner-party democracy under the CC's leadership.[39]

Obviously, democracy was important. The question was how to determine where democracy ended and counterrevolution began.

One possibility was to take a middle course. Many supporters of unity insisted on the right of members to discuss "certain aspects" of the party line. In theory, it was possible to reject the party opposition per se, while supporting certain aspects of its platform. Thus, a Central Committee report on the Kursk guberniia party organization noted that, while it condemned the opposition as a whole, a plenum of the Kursk ukom "vindicated the opposition, in particular regarding the question of the growing danger of the kulak, and expressed their support for a change [in party policy] in the direction of a greater limitation of the kulak."[40]

In any case, outright support for the opposition was clearly dangerous. In April 1927, a party member answered Stalin's response to his previous letter regarding the opposition. The details of the initial exchange are unclear, but the supplicant's backpedaling response is telling:

> Having received from you an answer, I cannot describe the feeling of gratitude that I will have for you my whole life, and your answer not only gave me a clear explanation to my question, but . . . revealed my mistakes, as well as gave me direction at every step of my life and my work.

The contrite communist also inquired whether other oppositionists like Trotsky had admitted their mistakes, and what they were doing presently.[41]

Not surprisingly, many wrote pledging their support for Stalin's fight against the opposition and offered information concerning its alleged leaders and members. Many offers of information appear to be sincere efforts to denounce and expose counterrevolutionaries, while the motives of others, as might be expected, appear less than altruistic. One Leningrad citizen, Lanskii by name, wrote to Stalin in February 1927 that he had information on leaders of the opposition he wished to impart to Stalin personally. The author began his appeal by assuring Stalin that he was "one of your many passionate admirers and one of your most productive communist followers." The appeal merited a directive to OGPU chief Genrikh Yagoda to check on the would-be informant. The resulting report showed that there were two people with that name in Leningrad, one a former count working for the railroad, the other a nonparty worker in a hydro-technical cooperative. Marked on this report in blue pencil are the directions, "make inquiries."[42]

Bureaucracy as Victimizer

The growing bureaucracy was threatening, because it was both corrupt and impersonal. Bureaucrats worked simultaneously for everyone and for no one; the government was often perceived as a monolith, unresponsive to the needs of individuals. One railroad worker from Stalingrad guberniia made a desperate appeal to the central leadership in February 1927, after his application for a pension became hopelessly bogged down by red tape. The worker had lost a leg under a train but received no benefits, and after a year his family was on the verge of starvation. His previous attempts to obtain a pension met with the response, "'we do not know anything about it.'"[43] A similar situation was encountered by a worker on an electrification project in Tula who, as a result of a fall from an electric pole, lost both legs. The invalid had a family of nine but had been unable to secure a settlement through the courts, and meanwhile received a small pension insufficient to support his family.[44]

The impersonal nature of bureaucracy made it more dangerous, because there seemed no way to fight it. A particularly pathetic plea for assistance came in April 1927 from a seventeen-year-old komsomolets from Briansk guberniia. The supplicant had developed an eye condition that was quickly leading to blindness, but he was forced by an impersonal and uncaring bureaucracy to helplessly await his fate. It seemed that he had been tossed back and forth between a doctor, who for some reason refused to give him a referral, and various government health commissions, which refused to admit him to a hospital for treatment without this referral. The young communist had hoped to lead political education circles but was no longer capable of fulfilling his Komsomol duties. Slowly going blind, the youth sat at home without hope of a cure, facing the probability of begging for a living.[45]

Anyone seeking financial support, justice, or even simple information often came up with the same disappointing result. Several appeals came from parents or other family members inquiring after the whereabouts of a son who had served in the Red Army or party and who had simply disappeared. In many cases, the response from Orgraspred or other organs was that no information was available. Indeed, it seemed that the party had a hard time keeping track of its own, much less the country at large.

This became particularly clear in many appeals from those who claimed to have been wrongly expelled from the party in periodic purges.[46] A number of such complaints were received in 1924 from former members claiming victimization through bureaucratic incompetence, either in the course of the purge itself or during the appeal process. One appeal came from a worker's son, expelled in June 1924 for a number of general deficiencies. The expulsion had noted, for instance, that he had not served in the Red Army and lacked political training. Worst of all, lamented the supplicant, all his party work since 1917 had been placed under the rubric of "clerk," thus lending a vaguely white-collar, and therefore suspect, appearance to his position. The supplicant despaired of ever being reinstated.[47] Similarly, a female former party member appealed once again to the center in November 1924, after her first appeal to Vyacheslav Molotov had gone unanswered. She complained of having been unjustly accused of counterrevolution and expelled by a commission in Rostov-on-Don. Her appeal reflected her precarious position and desperation:

> If I am a counter-revolutionary, exile me, if I am a trade union member and citizen, give me the opportunity to exist like all workers, if I am considered a party member, then why have I not received an answer and a resolution?[48]

Yet another supplicant with an otherwise exemplary record as a worker and veteran had been purged due to a female employee's charge of rape. He complained that his appeal had not been properly handled, and that the purge had been botched. Testifying to this was the fact that fully 80 percent of those expelled were subsequently reinstated; the supplicant, however, was not, since all of his documents and testimonies to his innocence had been "lost." More questionable still, he lamented, was that higher party cadres charged with serious offenses had been reinstated, while he was merely rank-and-file.[49]

The victims of bureaucratic incompetence naturally sought a cause for their persecution, but the anonymity of bureaucracy often frustrated that search. As a result, supplicants often instinctively felt compelled to exonerate themselves from guilt over some unnamed crime, simply because no obvious perpetrator was at hand. In November 1927, a party member who moved to Leningrad with his wife and baby wrote a desperate appeal to the central government. He recounted a complicated story of bureaucratic blunder and red tape that resulted in a lost party card. Without it, the supplicant was unable to obtain work through the party and sustenance for his family, and winter was fast approaching. The frantic supplicant lamented:

> As a member of the VKP(b) I consider it wrong that I have been thrown out of its ranks through no crime of my own. If the TsK VKP(b) finds that I really constitute extra ballast in its ranks . . . But I feel I am absolutely not at fault.[50]

Why, indeed, did the supplicant suffer, unless the party suspected him of some wrongdoing?

Ultimately, it seemed, bureaucracy's impersonality made attaining justice hopelessly remote. Two Red Army veterans writing from the city of Armavir in Kuban oblast appealed for help to Stalin as the "defender of the working masses." They were unemployed and homeless, and considered themselves victims of the carelessness and neglect of local authorities. Throughout their appeal, the supplicants lamented the fact that, "for us, everything is closed. . . . Iosif Vissarionovich, where is our victory, when they promised us, 'comrade—everything is yours and in your hands.'"[51]

The Party's Role

Contributing to general frustration over bureaucratic inefficiency was a general consensus that party and state apparatchiks abused their positions. This was a source for complaint even from many communists. In November 1924, a party worker in the Moscow railroad administration appealed to party leaders. After he had complained about corruption and crimes perpetrated by communist administrators, it seems, he had been subjected to ongoing harassment meant to silence him, including a three-week stint of incarceration by OGPU. Eventually, he had to be released for lack of evidence. His case, however, had never been resolved, and at the time of writing the supplicant had no means of subsistence.[52]

Another party member working in a credit union in the city of Kansk in Siberia wrote in March 1927 about the problem of embezzlement. The crime was widespread, and far stricter measures were needed to combat such corruption and fight the demoralization that resulted. The supplicant added that

> every party member is presented with a number of questions, for which he seeks answers that might satisfy him and sustain his spiritual needs and enthusiasm, directing his energies to consciousness of the business of socialist construction of his country.[53]

The conviction and sense of purpose necessary to reform the country were impossible to maintain, if the government leading the reform was itself corrupt. In a similar appeal, a bedniak from Briansk guberniia wrote in July 1927 about a certain party member accused of misusing government funds. Apparently, the communist in question was not being held accountable for his crime, which naturally caused dissatisfaction. The supplicant argued that an honest, hard-working peasant or worker surely presented the party with a more valuable ally in the struggle to build socialism than one rotten party member. Why, then, were party members above the law?[54]

This question troubled many communists and turned many others away from the party. A communist from Donets okrug appealed to Stalin in September 1927 concerning a local party official, who moved into an apartment reserved for homeless families on the waiting list of a living cooperative. The supplicant was indignant that this official simply took the apartment, without asking permission or paying rent. When the cooperative confronted him with the fact that families on the list had been waiting a year for a place to live, the official refused to speak with them, as lower party members, claiming that the district committee had given him the apartment. The district committee in turn denied this, but the co-op was informed by another party official that the apartment had been "reserved." In the end, apparently, the official got to keep the apartment. This was not, according to the supplicant, what communism was supposed to be about:

> Our dear communist party on Il'ich's bidding always and everywhere speaks to and organizes the dark masses, only in order that the poor worker and peasant might have the opportunity of living better and more easily.

This prescription clearly was not borne out in practice, and the supplicant was no longer prepared to condone such activity:

> I don't want to be a member of the party in order to hide behind it . . .
>
> I ask the Central Committee to expel me from the party ranks. . . . It seems to me that from such small fires, large ones flare up, through people like Kheinich and Ivanenko, maybe even through people like me. . . . Soon we will need to find out where the dog buries it.[55]

In an atmosphere rife with suspicion and resentment, any party member suspected of corruption encountered popular hostility. In August 1927, one communist petitioned the government for a transfer. He claimed to have been a worker his whole life and a Red Army veteran, as well as having filled a number of party posts. Recently, however, money had been stolen from the cafeteria he managed, and he was convicted of the crime and imprisoned. The supplicant wished to be transferred from his present organization, since the smear on his reputation would make further work difficult at best.[56] Under conditions of economic desperation and uncertainty, crimes against property were especially resented.

The party's task was to turn a mainly preindustrial, semi-feudal country into a major world power, capable not only of resisting the counter-revolutionary onslaughts of capitalism but also of overtaking it economically. In a country where labor was cheap and a significant portion of the population desperate, those belonging to the party that would effect such a miracle commanded power and respect. Under circumstances that granted an inordinate degree of power and prestige to party workers, as many appeals suggest, power often was sought by those who lacked and craved the prestige that party membership granted.

Thus, the pretensions to power of government and party apparatchiki was the basis for many complaints. In September 1927, a worker in a Donbass miners' hospital sent a lengthy complaint to the central government when the hospital director was replaced by a vydvizhenets and assistant who, the worker claimed, lacked administrative competence. The new director, "from joy at having gone from being a stable boy at 40 rubles a month salary to a director at 116 rubles," promptly entered into a permanent, celebratory state of drunkenness, financed with his entire earnings. To continue the celebration, charged the supplicant, he stole from the till and from his coworkers, and this was only the beginning. The hospital suffered from a lack of leadership. An appeal to the regional party secretary responsible for the change allegedly yielded the reply: "Since I am tsar and god . . . no one may go against [my decisions]."[57] The response was telling. It indicated that questioning the secretary's judgment was intolerable to his fragile ego. On the other hand, the supplicant may also have invented or inflated the response, perhaps betraying his own opposition to party promotees.

A similar situation occurred in a town in Samara guberniia, where a militiaman complained to Stalin about a local party member's offensive behavior. The communist in question was often publicly drunk, diminishing the party in the eyes of the local people. They concluded, remarked the supplicant, that hooliganism was a crime only for nonparty citizens; "but if one was a party member, one could do what one liked." The militiaman related an incident allegedly occurring the previous summer that characterized the offensive communist's attitude. He had been sitting at the bar in the train station's cafeteria, "in military costume." When another militiaman approached the bar, the communist confronted him, insisting that he did not show the communist enough deference. This incident "was well-known to all, since it occurred in public right in front of everyone."[58] Was this an indictment of one party member's arrogance, or of the party's arrogance?

Such communists would be labeled "opportunists" by their more idealistic and devoted comrades. But the label was misleading. Clearly, these party members were not in pursuit of opportunity, but of the prestige and respect that accompanied their position. As these scenarios suggest, such opportunists possessed an almost insatiable desire for respect.

Belonging to the party meant membership in the power elite. That many sought membership in order to raise their status was inevitable, and complaints about them ubiquitous. A komsomolets from the Chechen Republic lamented the arrogance displayed by local communists. The supplicant himself sought to rise above such arrogance:

> Comrade Stalin, I am a komsomolets and always ready to carry out the party's directives, but if they tell me that the party says, "never shake hands with a nonparty citizen in front of a communist," then I am that party's enemy, because it would no longer be a workers' party.[59]

As the appeal implied, an entire apparatus plagued by arrogance and corruption required a deeper explanation than the presence of a few corrupt individuals. Apparently, there existed an inordinately large number of individuals who craved dignity, and who sought respect by joining the party.

For example, another komsomolets, a village correspondent from Ukraine whose father had been arrested on a trumped-up charge, complained of the general corruption of the local party apparatus. He charged them with promoting such crimes as the production of spirits, and encouraging hooliganism and anti-Semitism.[60] Since Ukraine historically witnessed considerable anti-Semitism, such a charge was hardly surprising, but communists were supposed to rise above the local factionalism and chauvinism. When they did not, they strayed from the communist ideal. But they also represented more closely the population within which they lived, and in so doing shed some of the elitism that was also the cause of much complaint about the party. In March 1927, another party member, working in banking in Ukraine, requested a transfer. His request stemmed partly from his difficulties with the language, but mostly from his perception of "refraction" of national policy and chauvinism. The supplicant attributed this chauvinism not to nationalism per se, but to the elitism of the nationalist intelligentsia: the chauvinists, it seems, were not only nonparty, but party members as well, "naturally, those party members [who] entered the party recently, especially intelligentsia." The author requested to be transferred to another location, where he could "work more comfortably."[61]

Among other chauvinistic refractions that, one would expect, characterized the ubiquitous power-hungry official, was discrimination against female comrades. Women were grossly underrepresented in the party membership and leadership. The party officially espoused the doctrine of gender equality, but in practice women were shut out. This was the basis for an appeal in May 1927 from a female communist from Orel guberniia. As a party member and the mother of twin girls, whose father had been killed during the civil war, the supplicant appealed for assistance in finding work. She herself had been a domestic servant from the age of twelve, until the revolution provided new possibilities and "opened [her] eyes." Despite the fact that she had completed her studies at a party school, the supplicant was not given "corresponding work."

Indeed, she had been unemployed for six months, and her family's situation was "hopeless":

> Soviet power freed women and gave them equal rights, and women for their part want to be comrades and help the revolution's cause, but party officials shove them into the abyss without work, [a situation] impermissible under Soviet power.
>
> I beg you dear comrades . . . don't let me die of hunger, your comrade in the VKP, because our goals are the same, the conquest of the revolution and carrying it to the end.[62]

Besides under- and unemployment, female party members encountered other forms of discrimination that militated against their more active participation in party ranks. Information from the party organization in Tver guberniia indicated extraordinary pressures on and complaints from female members, who shouldered the demands both of party work and domestic duty. This state of affairs resulted "either in their alienation from the party or apathy towards party work or rupture of the family," and inevitably caused a mass exodus of women from the party's ranks.[63]

Ultimately, authority meant having power over and discriminating against those who were vulnerable, whether nonparty, Jewish, female, or merely unemployed. The party's attempts to gloss over these abuses only led to a credibility gap. Underscoring this point, in June 1927 a village correspondent from Stalingrad guberniia sent an urgent appeal to Stalin. As the correspondent remarked, "We are not building socialism, if we do not strive to correct irregularities on the local level." The party was corrupted with drunkenness, bureaucratism, and swindling. It was supposed to lead the peasantry, but, in reality, "it was just the opposite," and, as a result, the peasants felt cheated.[64] Another peasant and civil war veteran appealed for assistance in October 1927 when his hut was confiscated by the previous owner's brother, a communist:

> Dear Comrade Stalin! I read "Peasant Gazette" No. 38—Your talk with American workers—where you defended members of the VKP(b). Naturally, you are completely correct to say in front of workers of other countries that no one may say that everything here is bad. Of course you need to say that everything is good and without mistakes. But we among ourselves here in the Soviet Union can say and point to what is bad and what is good. Nevertheless, I personally disagree with the opinion of Comrade Stalin, if you claim that all members of the VKP(b) are so good and defend the interests of the workers and bedniaks so well and are defenders of the RSFSR. There are good party members, but many, many bad ones as well.

He went on to point out that the high salaries party members paid themselves corrupted them, and remarked on the prevalence of alcoholism among party officials. Yet, the Soviet leadership denied these problems, in effect treated its own people as foreigners, lying to them even while the people themselves experienced the reality of corruption on a daily basis. And, despite this corruption, "currently almost all positions in government are filled by communists, and all work goes through their hands."[65] Absolute power had corrupted the party, absolutely.

Supplicants commonly complained that corruption was greater at the local level and sought to inform central authorities of local problems, assuming that the center could not know what was really transpiring. In October 1924, a sympathetic nonparty peasant from a village in Riazan guberniia appealed about the low quality of local communists. He believed that the party made no headway among the peasantry because its leaders failed to clean up the local party apparatus, filled with drunks and petty tyrants who alienated the masses and disgraced the party. The peasant further faulted the party for not paying enough attention to rural activists. Significantly, the supplicant—sufficiently literate to read Lenin's works—complained that "all good, honest, living [communists] are drawn to the cultural center, but here only people who are not fit for serious work remain." He continued: "I know practically all of our volost party comrades, of whom only one reads a newspaper and, it seems to me, even he does so only out of boredom, not knowing what to do with himself." Such local party members, he lamented, were only concerned about their positions and material gain.[66]

The appeal of a komsomolets from Pavlograd in Ukraine also suggested that the center's information rested on unreliable sources. He complained about the corruption of the apparatus, and pointed out that control personnel sent by the center to investigate irregularities dealt only with the party apparatchiki. If they did not pay any attention directly to "the private public," then how could the central authorities possibly know what really went on? Reality was filtered through the reports of corrupt party officials. Consequently, "We are remote from the masses and they likewise are remote from us."[67]

What complicated the situation further was that corruption was not limited to communists. This made the search for the cause of corruption, and its solution, even more difficult. Indeed, party members themselves often were its victims. One communist, a Rabkrin inspector working on the railroad, appealed in March 1927 for a transfer. It seems that he had lost all authority when he criticized the uneconomical procedures employed by a number of local administrators.[68] Similarly, a party member from the Bashkir Republic sent a second appeal to Stalin in August 1927, concerning the loss of his position. His dismissal was due, apparently, to the supplicant's "persistence in the struggle for Soviet authority and the communist party in general" against widespread "criminal behavior" throughout the government. "If you arrest a militiaman," the supplicant lamented, "you hold out against him and his boss and so on and so forth."[69]

Moreover, appeals about corruption often did not involve the party at all. In June 1927, the members of a mechanics' factory cell appealed about their persecution by the shop foreman, a nonparty worker, who was backed by the factory administration.[70]

The Influence of NEP

The party's degeneration did not develop in a vacuum. Apparently, communists' real crime was that they commonly failed to transcend the shortcomings of the society that produced them. This fact notwithstanding, since the party ostensibly controlled the government, the search for government corruption automatically meant a search for corruption within the party. Party veterans and nonparty citizens alike commonly lamented the alleged flood of opportunists into the party. Opportunism was ubiquitous because opportunities were ubiquitous, and survival so uncertain. The population in general viewed the money that began to circulate freely under NEP as a sign of corruption and decadence. Victor Serge commented that he and his fellow communists "felt ourselves sinking into the mire—paralyzed, corrupted. . . . money lubricated and befouled the entire machine just as under capitalism."[71] A foreign observer credited the reintroduction of "quantities of money into circulation" with the reemergence of "all the old criminal elements in Moscow."[72] And, according to many supplicants, these criminal elements surfaced within the government and party as well.

One Soviet historian explained the corruption of the apparatus as a function of NEP, or, more specifically, of nepmen. Indeed, so the argument ran, one reason why nepmen succeeded in circumventing and breaking Soviet laws was that they already had corrupted and demoralized the government.[73] Following Lenin's prescription to learn from the capitalists, the absorption of the prerevolutionary bourgeois professional strata into the government infected the apparatus. And so, presumably, nepmen were able to exploit their advantages and operate outside the parameters of Soviet legality. The Bolsheviks had not invented bureaucracy, but inherited it in both form and personnel from the prerevolutionary tsarist system. Those who had previously exploited their economic positions to the detriment of average citizens were thus able to continue doing so under Soviet power. The historian explained that

> Workers from the worker and peasant [strata] did not know how to manage the economy and needed to "learn how to trade." Greedy rogues and cunning businessmen quickly began to penetrate into government organs, swindling their inexperienced directors and stealing government property.[74]

Significant in this and similar explanations is a clear distinction between the evil nepman on one hand, and his honest but gullible Soviet counterpart on the other. Such an explanation leaves the honest Soviet official blameless in the corruption of the government and its failure to achieve its socialist goals. Of course, the central issue was whether the party had been corrupted from outside or was inherently corrupt.

While NEP contradicted communist theory, individual communists profited from it. The Workers' and Peasants' Inspectorate (Rabkrin) was created because the Cheka (Soviet secret police) had been remiss in dealing with graft and corruption, and "it was found necessary to create the new department for the inspection and correction of abuses."[75] With the coming of NEP, opportunism and speculation flourished on a grand scale. In all ranks of the party, "members [were] intent on exploiting the moment."[76] Economic exploitation translated into other forms of exploitation. In May 1927, a Moscow party member called attention to another communist, a prominent worker in a cooperative, who used his position to extract sexual favors from desperate, unemployed women, in return for work. The supplicant was irate; such an individual

> besmirched the authority of the party he represented. Further similar occurrences at the local level, among the lower classes, deeply anger the masses, who with reason say after this: "What is a worker from the center, but a scoundrel of the highest sort." Such workers should not be [allowed] in local soviet organs.[77]

Similarly, in July 1927 a group of employees of the financial administration of the city of Tula petitioned the central government concerning the communists directing their department. Their directors perpetrated all manner of "irregular activities," including unexplained layoffs and salary cuts, and "nightly orgies." The supplicants lamented the fact that, "just when our best leaders are attempting to effect unity with the masses, [our] directors sow hostility and hatred towards the party and authority."[78]

As countless appeals make clear, such rampant abuse of power occurred under conditions of acute competition for work and survival. While neither bureaucracy nor corruption were the creations of NEP, both naturally were exacerbated by economic competition, chronic unemployment, and the material insecurity endemic in the NEP era. A superfluity of workers in the workers' state meant that for the unemployed, all sorts of obstacles and indignities accompanied a search for work. In an employer's market, those in a position to hire possessed an inordinate amount of power over potential employees. Corrupt administrators could simply fire anyone wishing to expose them. Those lucky enough to find themselves in a job often declined to complain about their bosses' abuses, fearing that they, too, would find themselves on the street. Thus, a Moscow party member appealed for justice in March 1927, after he was fired from an administrative position with the railroad. He claimed that he had been let go due to his complaints against the administration. "Setting about to fulfill my responsibilities," the author remarked, "I observed a series of illegal actions on the part of the administration about which I, as a party member, could not remain silent."[79] The administration responded to the charge of illegal dismissal by claiming that the former employee had simply been too fussy to please, changing jobs often, and finally never showing up for work.[80] In another, perhaps related petition to the center in April 1927, a group of Moscow railroad workers complained about the corrupt practices of their communist directors. The petition, unsurprisingly, was semi-anonymous. One aspect of this particular petty tyranny the petitioners remarked on was that the party member in charge paid top officials exorbitant salaries. As they maintained, "such a thing is allowed only where a bourgeois government is in power, but not a workers' [government]."[81]

Unfortunately, demographic and economic circumstances dictated that it was not a workers' but an employers' government, filled with petty tyrants who enjoyed their power. In September 1927, a nonparty factory worker appealed about corrupt leaders of the factory party cell. He had complained about their "incorrect, perverted work," until they drove him from the factory altogether. Apparently, the factory director was the brother of a Central Committee member; the director and his wife "flaunted" their authority and used it to create a personal fiefdom. The workers' leaders were no help in the situation; the party cell secretary, according to the testimony of older workers, was "a real dog of a boss," while the factory committee chairman was a "scoundrel of the highest mark," who had been expelled from the party in 1921 for turning in the gold rings of famine victims. In short, both the factory administration and workers' representatives were shady characters at best. In workers' meetings, anyone who spoke about the abuses perpetrated by these individuals was shouted down and accused of undermining authority, while party members who toed the line could expect to receive a salary ten times that of the average party member. Inevitably, this state of affairs led to a strike, and the ringleaders were fired. Worst of all, reported the petitioners, "for two years not one of the older workers, not even any workers of the factory in general, have joined the party."[82]

Solutions

Reducing the Bureaucracy

Although complaints about government corruption were legion, few seemed willing or able to offer solutions to the problem. One exception to this came in April 1927 from a communist, who had worked in a *narkomat* (commissariat) for three years and had a plan for reducing government bureaucracy. He proposed eliminating the narkomaty altogether and transferring their functions to the soviet executive committees. Such a move would eliminate "much redundancy in work, [provide] better organization," and ensure that the people's elected officials have more control over implementation of the laws of the land. An added benefit would be that "reduction and simplification of the apparatus would proceed far more quickly and easily than the current process."

The obvious problem with this plan was that reducing the bureaucracy meant cutting jobs. Staff cuts undoubtedly kept such reforms from taking place. This was not lost on the author, who remarked: "I know very well that such a project would meet with the most extreme opposition, especially from cadres." The author even acceded that his proposal itself might become lost or bogged down in one or another government organ. Nevertheless, he felt obliged to make it,

> since the bureaucratism, red tape and nonproductive consumption of the country's resources by a huge army of soviet civil servants that is now taking place itself threatens the socialist revolution, the dictatorship of the working class and the smychka with the peasantry.[83]

In fact, the government continuously made attempts throughout NEP to cut bureaucracy. The task was not easy, however, and various government organs predictably resisted staff cuts. For example, a set of directives in 1922 to the metallurgical industry set the guidelines by which NEP might be implemented. Paramount among the government's concerns was the necessity for industries to become productive and therefore self-financing. This was impossible, however, without cutting staff:

> Together with the question of the use of manpower stands the question of overhead, which is formed mainly by the cost of maintaining nonproductive administrative organizations. That disproportionately huge number of people, which watches over the producers in various ways, forms and steps, and which raises the coefficient of useless work to distorted levels, obstructing the movement of the entire economic apparatus to the point of idleness, must be greatly reduced.[84]

Like so many others, this prescription was easier in theory than in practice. Attempts to cut Glavmetall's staff met with the response that "many departments were unable to keep within the staff norms prescribed to them, and at various times brought petitions before the Board about retaining an entire series of persons in order to continue necessary work."[85] Similarly, when Orgraspred was directed in October 1924 to cut the staff of its Records Section, the responsible official protested that, in order to keep up with the most vital work, much less with proposed projects, the department would require more, not fewer, staff. For instance, the department faced losing one of three staff in charge of party cards. The work of these few people included issuing new cards—a task that greatly increased with the masses of new recruits under the Lenin levy—and keeping track of lists of party members resigning, deceased, or expelled from party ranks.[86]

Faced with the prospect of huge staff cutbacks, administrators in all branches of industry resisted, reluctant to reduce an already overwhelmed workforce and turn employees out on the street. In July 1923, the technical-production department of Glavmetall sent a letter to Vesenkha stating that,

> Concerning the reduction of staff, GPU cannot under any circumstances agree to it, under the existing volume of functions of Glavmetall according to its latest statutes; in the case of the institution of such personnel [cutbacks], naturally, the question would have to be raised concerning a reduction of functions, meaning, probably, a change in statutes.[87]

Despite white-collar resistance, however, it was both economically and politically necessary for the party to respond to calls for government staff cuts. In a letter of September 1926, Stalin made this explicit to his ally Molotov:

> As far as the target figures go, I think that we have to put on the pressure now and definitely reduce the staffs of the commissariats and self-financing bodies from above. Otherwise, talk about economic austerity will remain empty. Industry's share must definitely be increased.

Stalin's recommendation was followed with the appropriate action, as shortly afterwards the Politburo made the decision to "continue work to reduce expenditures on the administrative and economic apparatuses . . . by a minimum of 15 percent."[88]

Connections

If the party or state bureaucracy could not be reduced, one way to circumvent bureaucratic corruption was to join the bureaucracy. It was widely noted that only those with connections received assistance or employment. Thus, a self-described technician and "bedniak-proletarian" from Nizhnii Novgorod guberniia lamented in March 1927 that workers such as he, without "their share" of connections and protection, did not stand a chance of being hired. The supplicant had been unemployed for two years and pleaded with Stalin to intervene personally to get him work with the railroad, since going through bureaucratic channels was useless. The desperate man found such an arbitrary situation "deeply painful"; in a country ruled by the proletariat, one should not have to depend on connections for survival.[89]

Nevertheless, connections were necessary, and many sought the most obvious route for advancement, namely, through party membership. This process, however, was complicated by the fact that prospective members needed recommendations from other members in order to join, and corrupt communists tended to generate their own kind. As corruption increased, it became more difficult for individuals with pure intentions to find supporters. This could be especially true in rural areas, where communists of any type were fewer and farther between. A komsomolets from a village in Kursk guberniia complained in June 1927 that it was impossible for him or any other honest peasant to become a communist, because the only communists in their village were unsavory characters. Local party members worked for the neighboring state farm and were "hooligans" well known to the local militia, routinely visiting the village to threaten and berate the inhabitants. These hooligans obviously sought status and authority through party affiliation; appeals to regional officials to get rid of them had yielded no result. The supplicant remarked that "the peasantry often comes into contact with such party members" and wondered why they were not expelled. Indeed, no "honest guy" could obtain a recommendation under such circumstances.[90] The young communist's lament was corroborated by reports from the Party Secretariat which criticized party organizations for the reluctance of local officials to actively assist candidates in procuring recommendations necessary to advance to full membership.[91]

Even party membership, however, was useless without the right connections. For those without them, it seemed, finding work was impossible. One party member, a civil war veteran from the city of Vinnitsa, appealed in August 1927 for work, since his family was hungry. He was finally forced to decide between starvation and a life of crime and asked "Comrade Stalin, . . . why am I suffering . . . I have been unemployed for 14 months . . . ill with tuberculosis . . . If I were a thief or a drunk it would be different, then I would not be worthy of party membership." He claimed he could not find work because the local party apparatchiks only gave work to their favorites.[92]

Nepotism

Nepotism was another route to employment in the competitive circumstances of NEP society. Like most aspects of Soviet society, nepotism and favoritism had flourished under tsarism,[93] and remained an accepted route to employment and advancement in postrevolutionary society. The revolution had not instituted a meritocracy, although that was precisely the problem, according to aggrieved and unemployed supplicants. Surely, in a workers' state, all those who wanted to work would be given the opportunity, not just those who had an "in." A self-described "distinguished and honest communist" working for the agitprop section of the party in Tiflis complained in May 1927 of "serious defects" within the central party organization of South Ossetia. Specifically, the director of the executive committee in the city of Tskhinvali hired only his relatives to fill important posts, regardless of their qualifications.[94]

Similarly, a decorated civil war veteran, who worked for the party agricultural organ in Tersk okrug in the Caucasus, sent the central leadership and OGPU a series of complaints concerning the widespread corruption in his organization. His charges, from embezzlement to hiring irregularities, applied to party and nonparty administrators alike. He complained that the garage where he worked possessed only "eighteen vehicles, of which fourteen were tractors," but required fifty-two employees to run it. Not surprisingly, these employees included a large number of the director's relatives, "who did not belong to trade unions, not to mention their party or red army status." Moreover, the author continued, there were many vydvizhentsy in the party who practiced careerism and maintained despotic relations with the working masses. The communist related all this to Stalin, "not just out of a desire to write," but in the spirit of the civil war, recalling Stalin's "leadership on the southern front." Stalin had to take measures necessary to ensure that such people would be made to answer "by law before the revolution."[95]

The egalitarian goal for which the veteran had fought had disappeared. Now, it was every man for himself. A group of students from a Jewish trade school in Odessa complained to Stalin in August 1927 that they were unable to find positions after finishing their education. They discussed the causes for this and censured communist officials who "speculated with their power" to secure positions for those seeking them, a practice that only exacerbated the unemployment problem. "We cannot close our eyes to a fact that everyone knows," they wrote; "in many families everyone is working, while in others nobody works." They made a point to exonerate specialists, whom "the government should prize." The problem lay, instead, in the corrupt apparatus, preventing those without "protection or acquaintances" from even hoping to find work.[96]

Special Pleading

Although many citizens complained about the nepotism, favoritism, and protectionism that exacerbated the unemployment problem, no one expressed aversion to receiving special help in the search for work or education. Those appealing for assistance to central authorities were, in effect, arguing either implicitly or explicitly for special treatment, outlining their particular services to the workers' and peasants' state or special qualifications that made them indispensable to the task of socialist construction.

Thus, an apparently distinguished agricultural expert who found himself without work appealed in February 1927 to the center for a position. This member of the technical intelligentsia assured the authorities that he meant no criticism of their attempts to economize through job cutbacks, insofar as he "understood the economic regime, and its necessity for the authorities." He nevertheless contended that attempts to cut expenditures should not apply to those like him, who possessed special knowledge and training:

> For people with initiative and leaders in their profession, the economic regime does not apply, I am not a mere worker or civil servant or bureaucrat . . . I will tell you plainly, that in the old days by my word of honor, I had no equal in my profession. Why I now have not had any capacity within which to exercise my knowledge for more than a year, I really don't understand.[97]

His incredulity was based on the assumption that special knowledge and training made him inherently more valuable than a "mere worker"; on this assumption also rested his argument for special treatment in obtaining employment. The appeal underscores the fact that, despite the revolution and the government's rhetoric on the preeminence of the worker at the bench or the peasant in the fields, the technical intelligentsia themselves still assumed superiority. Their favored treatment by the communist government from the outset in terms of salary and perks appears to bear this out. In the workers' state, special knowledge and education still counted more than manual labor.

This attitude was echoed in February 1927 by an unemployed businessman, who had held a series of government positions and enjoyed the personal patronage of party leader Avel Yenukidze. It seemed that the supplicant had subsequently suffered from an extended illness, during which he was laid off. Now, he was unemployed, and he and his family in Moscow were homeless. He complained of the "criminal bureaucratism on the part of comrades, even party members," who apparently had given his former apartment to their "close friends." He claimed he had been "driven from service only for speaking the truth, for refusing to do the work of a lackey, considering such treatment disgraceful, not only to myself but to the person who hired me." Although he decried such shameful treatment, he nevertheless declared himself ready to engage even in manual work if, "as a nonparty citizen, I for some reason have no right to an administrative position."[98] Considering the political climate, the fact that the businessman had lost his position should have come as no surprise.

However, cultural assumptions about the innate superiority of specialists both fostered the continuing political and social revolution and blinded them to it.

This blindness was pervasive. Thus, a nonparty citizen from Poltava appealed in September 1927 after his pension had been discontinued, on the basis that he had been an officer in the tsarist army. This the supplicant did not deny, but he felt that, as a veteran, he was entitled to a pension anyway.[99]

Not surprisingly, however, most appeals for material assistance came from those at the opposite end of the social scale in terms of their skills, education, and social background. Supplicants lacking special skills were thus compelled to come up with other reasons why the government should assist them. Indeed, poverty itself would seem to have been sufficient grounds for extending assistance in a country where the poor ostensibly came first. Many appeals were based on this assumption. A komsomolets writing from Moscow in April 1927 is a case in point. He made a desperate appeal to the Central Executive Committee for support for his family. His claim rested on the fact that he was a "peasant-bedniak," on whose behalf, of course, the revolution had been fought. The peasant supported his family back home, and he had traveled to Moscow in hopes of finding work there. But the best he could do was a short stint in construction. At the time of writing, he had been "sitting hungry for three days, and received two letters from home, in which they wrote that they've been hungry for three weeks." If his appeal was refused, the supplicant warned, he would have no alternative but to "quit the [Komsomol] organization and turn to crime."[100] Similarly, in April 1927, a peasant from Smolensk guberniia with a family of nine sent a rambling, semiliterate appeal to the government. He was a veteran, first of all. Second, he could not make ends meet. Thus, he requested "seed, bread, or 290 rubles in cash."[101] After all, was the government not established for the sake of workers and poor peasants?

Certainly, those who had actually fought in the revolution and civil war to establish and defend the dictatorship of the proletariat might expect to have some claim on that government's assistance, when they needed it; indeed, many supplicants staked their appeals on this claim. Party members and Red soldiers expected preferential treatment in hiring. In 1927 Stalin received an appeal for work from a civil war veteran with six years of service (a fact he stressed several times), who was indignant that he was laid off due to staff reductions, even though he, among all the employees in his workplace, was the only veteran.[102] Similarly, in April 1927 a peasant and veteran from Iaroslavl guberniia made a request to the central government for wood to rebuild his home. He had seen lengthy military service, from 1914 in the tsar's army and then as a volunteer for the Reds. Indeed, he had been a revolutionary "almost from my schooldays, my father was a fighter for freedom and I got it from him." Jailed in 1917 by the tsarist authorities for refusing to take part in suppressing revolutionary activities in Petrograd, he was freed only in October, when the Bolsheviks came to power.[103] Surely, such a record of service to the revolution merited a small quantity of wood.

Another such appeal came in June 1927 from a nonparty batrak from Kanskii okrug, central Siberia, who complained that wherever he applied for a job he had been refused, because he belonged neither to the party nor to a union. The batrak appealed for assistance to get work nonetheless, since he was certain that the center would not allow "old fighters to be poor and hungry, but do whatever work they were able to."[104] Another veteran, who had served in the army from 1914 to 1923, requested help from Stalin to get work, after he had lost his previous position due to disability. He had been employed in the Moscow militia, but while on night patrol a horse fell on him, and he lost his left foot. After this, the militia would not employ him, nor could he find another job; the pension he received amounted only to 26 rubles a month, on which "no one could survive." The bitter veteran

> did not forget the time, that is 1917 to 1918, . . . when the people in power and the whole communist party valued us volunteers, because we volunteers created the army that was victorious and that will always be victorious. But now, when you appeal to old comrades for assistance with a request that is completely legitimate, and they ignore your request, it really is offensive and difficult.[105]

When appealing for special treatment based on revolutionary service, supplicants commonly sought to strengthen their appeals by emphasizing the deep degree of their sacrifice. For example, in April 1927 a party member and Red Army veteran from Novorossisk sent a request to the center for a prosthesis for his right arm, which he had lost doing machine repair in a factory ten years earlier. He recounted a long history of party work and emphasized that he had twice been arrested by the Whites during the civil war, although he had managed to escape both times.[106]

When supplicants could not appeal for special consideration on the strength of their own revolutionary service, they often did so on the basis of the family record. In July 1924, Stalin received an appeal from the daughter of a Bolshevik who requested financial assistance. She sought to remind Stalin of the party's duty—indeed, its very purpose—to provide members of the collective with sustenance and security. She began her appeal: "My dying father said to me: Things will not go bad for you without me, because the Communist Party will take you under its protection and at every critical moment will lend you practical support." Her father, she continued, was shot "as a communist in 1918 by the White guards" in Voronezh guberniia. His daughter, now much in need of help, sought to collect on her father's trust in the party.[107]

Similarly, in August 1927 a komsomolets from the Donbass pleaded for party work in a village. His health did not permit him to work in the mines, and where he lived no other work was available. His father had died in revolutionary service, and the rest of his family had been sacrificed to socialist construction: his mother worked in the mines, and his two young brothers had died from neglect.[108] Now, he had no one left, and, in effect, was a ward of the party. In another case, the wife of a communist killed in the civil war appealed in July 1927 for an increase in her pension. This was her second appeal.[109]

Party workers disabled through overwork naturally viewed such proof of exemplary service as a passport to social security from the government, since their health was sacrificed for the government's sake. In April 1927, a Red Army administrator from Voronezh guberniia requested a transfer to Yalta or another such resort. He had a wife, baby, and grandmother to support, but was compelled to resign three months earlier on account of his health. It seemed that he was simply worn out after having to work 15 to 16 hours daily, for several years running.[110]

In August 1927, a peasant and party member appealed for a pension to support him in his old age. He had worked in various party positions from 1917 to 1922, when his health finally gave out. During his service as chairman of his village Committee of the Poor, among other functions, he "was subjected to diverse ridicule, threats," and other indignities.[111] Another supplicant appealed in May 1927 for a pension or financial assistance of some kind, as he was an invalid. Although he did not formally belong to the party, the revolutionary nevertheless had worked on the party's behalf. But that was not his only sacrifice: the year before, his wife had poisoned herself in despair over her failing health.[112] The supplicant no doubt wished to escape a similar fate.

One of the greatest sources of complaint to the Soviet government during NEP was the growth of the bureaucracy, accompanied by inefficiency and corruption. The bureaucracy seemed to take on a life of its own, and all efforts to control or regulate it only exacerbated the problem. Within a few years, instead of "withering away," as Lenin had predicted it would, the state replaced the proletariat as the Bolshevik government's main constituency.

Judging from appeals to the center, bureaucratic growth and corruption derived mainly from two immediate causes. The first was the central government's reliance on a huge number of officials at many levels to control a vast territory and economy. This meant that local officials wielded extraordinary powers, because of their distance from the center and their role as filters of information to the center. Local officials were also relied upon to correct abuses for which they themselves were responsible. Government efforts to control the bureaucracy only fostered a lack of responsibility and initiative throughout the hierarchy.

The second cause of bureaucratic growth was millions of citizens' reliance on it as a means of seeking redress for a multitude of grievances. Because it served as virtually the only route to satisfaction, the state's corruption was ensured. Indeed, the bureaucracy itself victimized citizens through its inefficiency, or through officials who used it as a weapon. Moreover, citizens' search for justice was predicated on a common understanding of its definition. In fact, no such understanding existed. The revolution was based on many different conceptions of justice, which demanded different agendas.

Ultimately, there were few practical solutions to the problem of bureaucracy. Simply laying off staff would only contribute to unemployment, already a huge source of discontent and real suffering during NEP. Indeed, many saw the cause of bureaucratic corruption in NEP itself and nepmen, who penetrated government ranks and infected them with capitalistic impulses. NEP encouraged opportunism and criminality, and if NEP and nepmen were the causes of corruption, it followed that the solution lay in their eradication.

Others saw the source of the problem in the corruption of the party. Since the party created and allegedly controlled the government, it had to be the source of government corruption. But this connection was not always clear. Indeed, some of the most fervent critics of party corruption came from within the party.

In the end, both the growth of bureaucracy and its corruption boiled down to a superfluity of human beings. The bureaucracy was large, because there were vast numbers of people to serve and control. Moreover, the government itself was a major employer in a period of economic uncertainty and chronic unemployment. The intense competition for work and for a place in Soviet society also contributed to party corruption, since it gave officials extraordinary power and thus attracted those who craved such power to the party. Finally, while many supplicants complained about corruption throughout party and government, economic desperation compelled them to appeal for special consideration from that same government. Whether on the basis of special qualifications, social background, party or military service, or simple need, supplicants appealed for government assistance, hoping that they might receive satisfaction from the center when none was forthcoming on the local level.

CHAPTER SIX

The Party and Elitism

THE question of party corruption discussed in the previous chapter inevitably leads to a consideration of the widespread criticism of party elitism.[1] In their letters to the central leadership, rank-and-file communists and nonparty citizens alike criticized the higher salaries and perquisites of party officials and their aspirations toward strict central control and hegemony over society. This criticism revealed an apparent paradox in popular expectations regarding the leadership of the party. Throughout the 1920s, supplicants revealed a strong yearning for the formation of an organic, all-inclusive socialist collective. This was an enormous undertaking: engineering a whole new society, even a new kind of human being. Presumably, someone or some group had to create and lead this new society. At the same time, the desire for independence and local control had been a major goal of both factory workers and peasants. How could these two revolutionary demands be resolved?

The answer is that they could not. The desire to form a mass socialist collective that would include all workers (but not necessarily peasants) was predicated on the expectation that everyone within it would benefit equally. But when social and economic disparity persisted and grew throughout NEP, especially when communist officials themselves were seen to benefit disproportionately or to adopt the bearing and attitudes of former social elites, popular expectations were disappointed. Indeed, a great number of appeals throughout NEP spoke to widespread resentment over this development. Moreover, many supplicants connected the formation of this elite with the adoption of NEP.

The rise of the party elite corresponded with the fall of the working class. Within the first years after the October Revolution, it became clear that workers were being shut out of factory administration. Their status continued to diminish drastically after NEP's adoption, as the growth of unemployment dramatically reduced their value. The struggle for workers' control in the factory continued, however, assuming both passive and active forms, revealing the extent to which the interests of government and workers had diverged. Government initiatives to make workers more disciplined and productive faltered, because workers resisted a factory hierarchy that shut them out of administration. A similar battle went on in the party itself, as rank-and-file communists resisted efforts to discipline the party that inevitably reduced democracy and initiative at every level.

For their part, party leaders justified limits on democracy, especially pronounced after 1921, by underscoring the internal and external threats to the Soviet government and communism in Russia. But security concerns were not the only cause. The party's elite nature followed logically from Bolshevik ideology, which held that an educated revolutionary vanguard should lead the benighted masses to a higher level of consciousness and on to socialism. This vanguard was composed not of workers, but of a radical intelligentsia whose superiority was assumed, a widespread elite view in East and West prejudiced against the lower classes and their suitability to govern or even to participate in government. In short, the revolutionaries' philosophy of revolution was not egalitarian. And the line between leading the masses and controlling the masses was exceedingly thin.

Ultimately, raising proletarian consciousness and controlling and directing the proletariat proved to be mutually conflicting goals. Once empowered, the masses inevitably presented a threat to the hegemonic aspirations of Bolshevik leaders. Proletarians conceived of their revolutionary role differently than the party leadership. Appeals to the center throughout NEP show that, whether on the military front fighting the Whites or the economic front building the socialist society, communists, veterans, workers, and peasants considered themselves not passively led, but instrumental in revolution. This difference in perception was crucial.

Popular criticism of communist arrogance was widespread. Complaints arose particularly over the tendency of party members to mimic the behavior of prerevolutionary elites. Criticism of party elitism came not just from nonparty citizens, but from lower-ranking communists as well, especially young, recent recruits to the party who were labeled opportunists by the party elite.

Party leaders were aware of widespread resentment of party elitism but were unwilling or unable to solve the problem. Communists, after all, were the vanguard of the new society and, having attained that position, were loathe to relinquish it. The prerevolutionary gap between elite and masses was very quick to reform and seemed, once again, insurmountable.

In the end, communist elitism was resented, because it defied both tangible and intangible goals of the revolution. Material security and social status were intimately connected. Nevertheless, it soon became apparent that the Communist Party presented the only means of attaining these ends. Thus, while many supplicants condemned the re-formation of an elite in the new society, others viewed the party as a potential route of escape from cultural backwardness and material desperation, and as a vehicle to attain the dignity and social status they had previously been denied. Conversely, those excluded from the new elite experienced resentment and anger at their exclusion.

Sources of Elitism

The Dictatorship of the Proletariat

As many appeals made clear, a pervasive criticism of the Bolshevik regime was its elitism, which manifested itself both in party members' arrogance and privileges as well as in the leadership's aspirations toward strict central control of the party and society. Both were widely viewed as a betrayal of the revolutionary goal to establish an egalitarian society.

After 1917, Lenin and his supporters justified limits on democracy within the party and society by a variety of internal and foreign challenges to the revolutionary government. Indeed, the sheer geographical challenge of managing and controlling such a large territory as the Soviet Union was daunting. A modern observer remarked that

> with that size came great strategic vulnerability and difficulties of rule. How could the USSR secure a border 67,000 kilometers in length? How do you centrally control such a huge nation, over 22 million square kilometers in size for the USSR, 17 million square kilometers for Russia? The answer, in short, is that you do not.[2]

This observation was especially true in the early years, when the fate of the government and the revolution were still much in doubt. Under conditions of domestic chaos and external threat, the communist government quickly reverted to what was familiar: the authoritarian social and institutional relations of prerevolutionary society. The party leadership's objective from the outset was to gain control over the country politically, economically, and socially; its failure to do so resulted in Lenin's introduction of NEP.

Economic chaos and foreign hostility, however, were not the only factors contributing to the party's need for control. As historians have long established, Bolshevik ideology asserted "the right of the 'conscious' to lead those less conscious."[3] Lenin never intended that the party, the vanguard of the proletariat, would be composed "entirely or even necessarily predominantly" of workers, but rather of the revolutionary intelligentsia, who would lead the Russian proletariat to self-determination. The elitist implications of such intentions are clear.[4]

That a government purporting to represent masses of uneducated, politically inexperienced, and potentially violent working-class people had come to rule the vast empire of Russia was considered by educated society—both in the West and in Russia itself—absurd and dangerous. The party leadership's understanding of revolution was a product of this viewpoint. Sergo Mikoyan complained that the revolution's more affluent critics harbored a general prejudice against the poor, proclaiming "all outcasts and 'have-nots' a mob or a rabble with vile instincts to divide everything," and attributing such instincts to the Bolsheviks as well. Yet, Mikoyan apparently shared the sympathies of the Bolsheviks' critics and their contempt for levelers. He acknowledged that eliminating poverty was a difficult problem, but argued that "to take away and to divide has always been a first and primitive temptation of the poor, which should never be encouraged."[5]

Party leaders' elitist posture thus originated in the liberal and radical intelligentsia's ambivalence toward "the masses." Old revolutionaries at once championed and reviled the mob. In describing preparations for the ill-fated Constitutional Assembly in 1918, émigré sociologist Pitirim Sorokin remarked that "it is most democratic, allowing for full proportional representation. Only it seems to me that it is about as suitable for poor Russia as evening dress would be for a horse."[6]

Party Purity

The ambivalence of the revolutionary vanguard toward the masses influenced policy on the party's expansion. Its ranks were at times restricted to maintain the party's elite nature and function, at other times expanded to increase connectedness with the masses in whose name it ruled. But efforts to retain the party's elite composition and role as revolutionary vanguard ultimately prevailed. Statistics reflect this priority. Initially, the party was composed disproportionately of those from white-collar and educated strata, a trend that continued throughout the civil war period,[7] and became more pronounced during the first years of NEP. In 1922, only 12 percent of new party recruits were workers by employment.[8] It was not only necessity that caused Bolshevik leaders to recruit technical and administrative specialists, white-collar workers, and bureaucrats to join the party. As members of the intelligentsia, the vast majority of the central leadership took for granted that the intelligentsia would run the country. To this end, they were prepared to enlist the assistance of prerevolutionary class enemies.[9]

Reports and directives criticizing overly restrictive procedures to admit and promote new party members also contained warnings about the quality of those seeking party membership, reflecting leaders' ambivalence over expanding party ranks. In order to avoid mass dissatisfaction among party candidates, ran one report from Saratov guberniia, local party organs had to promote a significant number to full party membership. But the report concluded that

> recently the party has grown quickly. This has proceeded without the necessary attention from the lower party organization, with the resulting danger that undesirable elements are penetrating the party in significant numbers.[10]

Another report on the condition of the party in the country's northwestern region tallied nearly as many candidates as full party members, 33,307 and 34,334, respectively. At the same time, the report remarked on the "weak discipline and low political level" of the region's rural party organization, characterized by a high incidence of drunkenness and criminality.[11]

The reluctance to promote party candidates to full membership caused widespread frustration. A directive issued to lower organs in February 1925 by the Irkutsk gubkom secretary noted that the promotion of candidates to party membership was "extremely weak." Local party cells required candidates to possess far too much political preparedness, and the cells exhibited too passive a role, waiting for candidates to submit appeals to higher organs before acting on their cases. Such an attitude, noted the *gubsek* (guberniia party secretary), was dangerous, since it caused too much frustration among would-be party adherents. The directive advised local organs to be more active in facilitating prospective members, for instance, by assisting them to find recommendations. On the other hand, the gubsek warned, "under no circumstances" were local cells to admit new members wholesale or mechanically.[12] Reluctance to promote was having a negative effect on party work throughout the country. A central investigator noted in a February 1925 report on the Kaluga guberniia party organization that promotion of rank-and-file party members was very weak. Administrative posts were traded among a small number of cadres, and lower members, frustrated by the closed situation, transferred to Moscow, where the pay was better.[13]

Despite such widespread frustration and dissatisfaction, leaders were reluctant to relinquish control over the party to the large numbers who clamored to enter the ranks of the elite. A report on the Odessa organization lamented the low level of political education of party cell secretaries, who, although they displayed "great proletarian feeling with a desire to work," were nonetheless ill prepared for their administrative responsibilities.[14] A directive from the Ukrainian Politburo basically recommended placing a greater percentage of Old Bolsheviks (those who had joined the party before 1917) in responsible positions.[15]

As the reports above illustrate, the dictatorship's persistently nonproletarian character pressured its leaders to democratize and proletarianize the party. The pressure came from their own members and constituents, who sent many appeals warning leaders about the growing loss of connection between party and people. In December 1924 a former communist from Smolensk guberniia wrote to alert the center that the party was becoming demoralized through lack of connection, causing both the party and Soviet power to lose all credibility vis-à-vis "the laboring people." "Party members," wrote the supplicant, "occupying responsible posts, 90 percent of which are appointed, are completely cut off from the masses, and consider themselves bosses of the situation." Moreover, the beginning of this process could be fixed in time:

> In particular, the Central Committee itself made a huge error that must be corrected. After Soviet power switched [its efforts] to the economic front, the ranks of the party began to see a rift that with time became greater and greater and took on an ever more dangerous appearance. . . .
>
> [From the time of Kronstadt] the Central Committee of the Party and the Central Executive Committee have paid very little attention to the lowest stratum of the population (the peasantry), but this lowest stratum makes up seven tenths of the working force of the state. . . . Into the ranks of the RKP more and more counterrevolutionary elements are worming their way, unnoticed by party administrators, under the cover of the nepman-fog.[16]

The supplicant suggests a link between NEP and the loss of connection between the party and "the lowest stratum" of the population, but it is unclear whether the party lost touch because of the "counterrevolutionary elements" entering the party, or whether those elements entered because the party lost touch with the lower strata, its constituents. Or, perhaps, there were other, unrelated causes as well. Another supplicant, a muzhik from Samara guberniia who addressed his appeal to *Krestianskaia gazeta*, maintained that the party's difficulties in cultivating the nonparty aktiv in rural areas were due "exclusively to antireligious propaganda and prohibitions against the peasant fulfilling [religious] customs."[17]

Under political pressure, the party's social composition began to change during the decade. But these changes were a challenge to the purity and integrity of the revolutionary vanguard, and the party elite did not welcome them. In fact, they mourned the loss of revolutionary idealism, attributing this loss to the lower quality of the post-civil-war recruits, "the wave of latecomers, the comfortable new conformists who, at bottom, cared exceedingly little about the future of the proletarian revolution."[18]

Education and Control

The dictatorship of the proletariat apparently ran counter to Lenin's assurances that every worker could be an administrator. What Lenin intended by this, of course, was that workers could be administrators only after they had achieved a certain level of education and cultural advancement. And this would take time. In November 1923, a central investigator considered that the cultural level of workers at the Krasnoe Sormovo factory in Nizhnii Novgorod guberniia was low; a reading circle had thus far attracted only a small number of the "advanced stratum of workers and principally the young," in a factory employing over 13,000 workers, of which nearly 11,000 were adult males. Despite the small number directly involved, it was noted, the reading circle nevertheless "played a large role in the cultural life of the workers." The workers attending the factory school numbered less than 400.[19] Few workers were considered sufficiently advanced for participation in the socialist polity. It was up to the revolutionary vanguard to raise the cultural level of the rest, and to determine when the masses would be ready to govern themselves. Until then, they would require the guidance of the dictatorship of the proletariat.

While Lenin lived, soldiers in the campaign to eradicate the masses' ignorance wrote to him, their role model and inspiration, to express their dedication to the cause of cultural enlightenment. In January 1924 Lenin received a telegram from the "education workers" of the city and uezd of Vladimir, "meeting . . . for the discussion of pedagogical and other vital questions." The educators expressed their hope for Lenin's recovery, that he might show them "the path leading to complete elimination of ignorance and elevation of proletarian culture to its ultimate triumph."[20] Similar expressions issued from an "army of enlightenment workers" of the city of Kostroma,[21] as well as educators from Novorossisk, looking to Lenin to lead them to "certain victory over the ignorance of the popular masses."[22]

Note that these expressions, reflecting the general posture of the educated strata and party dogma, presumed a clear divide between educators and those they sought to elevate. This was not a separation of equals, but of higher, more advanced beings assisting lower, less developed ones. The division was often explicit. A cultural-enlightenment circle of communists in an army unit from Shlisselburg uezd declared their readiness to Lenin to

> direct all our young energy exclusively to rapprochement with the popular masses, with the aim of training them by the living, concrete example of our entire lives, which would give the masses the opportunity to enter on the broad path leading to the idea of communism and socialist government. And thus all for the masses, that they might be ours.[23]

As these messages suggest, there was a thin line between leading the masses and controlling them. And, social and political control implied disrespect. The leadership wished to invigorate and raise the population to greater heights of consciousness, education, and initiative, but at the same time to maintain control and guidance over it. These goals are inherently contradictory. Political workers in the Red Army were aware from an early date of the possible conflict between the "'creative initiative' that Marxism would awaken" on the other hand, and military discipline on the other.[24] Nevertheless, party leaders were convinced that the Soviet people could build the socialist society only under their direction, and only after attaining the requisite level of discipline and education.

The desire to educate and the need to control were inseparable objects for the Bolsheviks from the outset. Even after they had succeeded in consolidating their power militarily and eliminating political competition, they fought to win the hearts, minds, and allegiance of the population. There were concerns about raising the political consciousness, for instance, of communists in the Northern Caucasus, who were under "considerable influence . . . of priests and national minority intelligentsia."[25]

For party leaders, the true meaning of socialism could be gleaned only from a firm grasp of socialist ideology and theory. According to the director of agitation and enlightenment in the Red Army political administration,

> an illiterate and benighted person is incapable of apprehending with any depth, processing, or consciously mastering the high ideals of Communist morality. . . . [and] cannot understand the complicated tasks of socialist construction, nor can he respond to the undertakings of Soviet power with any understanding of their profoundly vital and moral significance.[26]

The logic here is clear. Individuals who did not respond to the government's agenda were insufficiently enlightened as to the true meaning of socialism. Underlying this was a more basic assumption, namely, that uneducated people were incapable of understanding socialism.

As long as the cultural level of the masses remained low, the Bolsheviks assumed, they could not participate effectively in the government of the collective. And as long as the masses were unfit to govern themselves, the members of the proletarian vanguard—the Communist Party—would retain their elite status. Ironically, if one followed this argument to its logical conclusion, it would be in the party's best interests to keep the masses undereducated and out of the party. As long as it remained relatively small and the preserve of the previously educated, the party would retain its elite status. And, just as any growth in its membership presented a threat to the party's status, any rise in the general cultural and educational level of the population threatened the dictatorship of the proletariat.

In the end, relinquishing control over the party apparatus or over the population as a whole was an impossible proposition to the Bolshevik party leadership, even on the part of the most idealistic revolutionaries. An exasperated village librarian from Siberia suggested to party leaders in July 1927 that the government round up all priests "and give them a good lecture, so that they would not preach religion." The librarian lived in a large village, where, however, no one visited the library, except for a handful of communists and komsomoltsy, whom the villagers rejected as godless. All the villagers attended mass, yet "ignorance, lack of consciousness, drunkenness, houliganism, fighting and abuse" was rampant—so much for religion. The librarian reasoned that, if only they could enlist the help of the priests in the communist cause, they could turn the situation around.[27] This case illustrates well the dilemma inherent in any experiment in social engineering: it could be perceived as an attempt to steer society toward desired social and political goals, or as the curtailment of freedom. Many citizens and even rank-and-file communists leaned toward the latter interpretation, and widespread perception of the party leadership's patronizing attitude toward the party rank and file and the population as a whole was the cause of much complaint to the center.

Popular Notions of Revolution

Opposed to the dictatorship of the proletariat was the instinctual socialism of the masses. The inherent contradiction of a socialist elite was not lost on the larger population, who greatly resented the socialist vanguard's status and privileges. Russian-American socialist Emma Goldman observed that the privileges Bolsheviks accorded themselves soon after the revolution did not go unnoticed by their working class comrades.[28] She noted in her conversations with peasants and workers in Moscow markets that

> the Revolution itself had struck deep into their souls. They knew nothing of theories, but they believed that there was to be no more of the hated barin and now the barin was again upon them. "The barin has everything," they would say, ". . . while we have nothing." "Communism, equality, freedom," they jeered, "lies and deception."[29]

In short, instinctual socialism meant egalitarianism. Whereas theoretical socialism might allow for the temporary existence of an elite vanguard until socialist society could be built and the population's cultural level raised, instinctual socialism made no such allowance. In one appeal, an anonymous, self-described muzhik censured opposition leaders, specifically Zinoviev, for their hypocrisy. Such leaders called for freedom of speech for the party opposition, but would never support such freedom for "the nonparty working masses." The author ended his commentary with ominous and violent threats against the government, from which he predicted the working masses would soon gain their rights.[30]

As the muzhik's appeal suggests, workers and peasants conceived of the process of revolution quite differently than the party leadership. Indeed,

> the spontaneous formation [during 1917] of thousands of lower-level workers', peasants', and soldiers' committees represented a profound structural change in the organization of Russian society, one providing "ordinary people" with the institutional bases for taking control of their own affairs and the presumption that democracy meant both their right and their ability to do so.[31]

After all, the Bolsheviks themselves had encouraged soldiers, peasants, and workers to seize control of their units, land, and factories during the revolution, and had represented the language of social revolution as their own in order to win over adherents to the Bolshevik cause.[32] Whether communist or nonparty, many individuals appealing for justice to the center throughout the 1920s felt themselves to have been instrumental in revolution—when they fought the Whites for the land, when they fought in the Red Army against the forces of reaction, when they took over the factories, and later, when they aspired to education and an active role in building socialism—in short, when they fought for power and control over their own futures. The central government may have conceived of revolution as directing the masses to a brighter future, but the masses themselves viewed revolution as a vehicle for gaining control. In a letter to Lenin in June 1922, members of the executive committee of the Autonomous Chuvash oblast described the revolution there as the successful effort of "Chuvash workers, in union with the workers of all nationalities, [to] determine our own fate, throwing off the age-old national oppression."[33]

The struggle for workers' control in the factories provided an important case in point. Workers' control had been a point of contention within the party, and between the party and trade unions, virtually from the beginning.[34] Despite the communist leadership's efforts, workers sought control throughout the NEP period. An administrator within the textile glavka exerted pressure on factory directors to crack down on workers of a woolen factory in the Simbirsk region, in order to foster greater discipline "in the interests of the Republic and of the Worker Peasant power . . . where the factory's interests are involved," and warned against the influence of "petty-bourgeois peasant tendencies."[35] It was clear that the interests of the workers' government and those of the workers themselves were not necessarily the same. The charge of "petty-bourgeois tendencies" referred to workers who tried to maintain their independence from government direction, or who made a distinction between their own individual needs and the needs of the collective, as the government defined them. Worker control in the factories was dismantled, not just to gain greater economic efficiency, but for the government to gain more control.

As might be expected, however, the continued efforts of the government to raise industrial productivity through control and discipline fostered worker apathy and passive resistance. Some government officials apparently were aware of the cause of this apathy, namely, factory administration disregard for worker input. In a report of November 1924 on the progress of a campaign to raise productivity in a large factory in Tver, an official remarked that, although "the party masses and the overwhelming majority of workers" responded "in general positively and sufficiently consciously" to the campaign, it had not yet met with much success. Among the campaign's goals were attempts to rationalize production, "raise the intensity of labor," decrease absenteeism, and raise worker discipline. In order to accomplish these goals, the investigator made a number of suggestions. In addition to greater clarity and organization of the campaign, he noted that administration and party officials in charge would do well to show greater regard for the suggestions of workers and worker correspondents.[36] Obviously, a hierarchical approach to the task of raising productivity was not successful.

Nor was the problem solved with economic decentralization under NEP, since workers continued to be shut out of factory control. This was especially true under conditions of unemployment, which further diminished workers' power. Loss of democracy in the factory was mirrored in the loss of democracy within the party. During the course of discussions in Moscow late in 1923 on the tasks of the party, one participant lamented that "during war communism a rank-and-file communist had more democracy, but during NEP they have driven him underground."[37] One might argue that the party leadership had to suppress dissension during NEP, because it had relinquished both its ideals and direction. Its need to control increased accordingly.

The relationship between freedom and order was the subject of an appeal from a group of komsomoltsy from Samara guberniia to "Comrade Stalin," requesting that he clarify for them the difference between communism and anarchism. As the author of the appeal pointed out more than once, he and his friends were not referring to the present; neither anarchism nor communism were possible yet because "our cultural level has not grown and the economic level of our country has not been raised to the required level." In a communist system, the authors wrote,

> there is no exploitation by private capital. . . . Here there is no power over the individual, neither is there egotism, because the individual is well-developed mentally and physically; he is fully conscious and does not wish to do himself or his comrades harm. Such is our understanding of communism.

Anarchism, on the other hand, was also characterized by an absence of power ("in that the individual strives his whole life, namely, in order that no one would have power over him, in order that he would be free"). In that, anarchism resembled communism. But the absence of power associated with anarchism also connoted "chaos and disorder," undesirable social characteristics clearly incompatible with the ideal communist society.[38] The young communists plainly were concerned not just about their freedom, their life's goal, but about its possible incompatibility with order and harmony, which they envisioned as the ultimate social result of communism. In the present society, the two definitely seemed to be at odds. It was safer, however, to discuss this problem on a theoretical plane.

Expressions of Party Elitism

Party Privileges

The main criticism of communists in letters from party members and nonparty citizens alike was their tendency to rise above the collective and to grant themselves privileges, material or otherwise. As one party official expressed it, the communist himself could not indulge in luxury, not because "luxury in itself is a sin. It is not. But—at this stage of the Revolution, there are few enough luxuries to be had, and the Communist must not be the one to seek them."[39] This sentiment was echoed in appeals to the center. In March 1927, a komsomolets from Kuban okrug put a question to the party leadership that had been raised in his political class. In answer to his query, "who can be a party member?" someone asked whether one could be a communist if that person lived in a three-room government apartment and owned two homes besides. This challenge referred to the case of a local official, a party member since 1917.[40] Such questions were obviously embarrassing to the lowly komsomolets or party worker, eager to lead the masses to a brighter future through communism. Another appeal, possibly from the same author, inquired why a party member occupying a responsible post could not live just as easily on 100 rubles per month instead of 200. The supplicant wondered how he could justify this state of affairs to the peasantry; such party members obviously were not working for the people, but for themselves.[41]

In another case, a party member from Archangel, suffering from anemia and overwork, appealed in August 1927 for assistance in securing a place in a sanitarium. "It is no secret," he wrote, "that the party organization sends many for cures for obesity or for abuse of alcohol."[42] Certainly, the supplicant argued, those party members who suffered from too much of a good thing must have less claim on the government's resources than workers who ruined their health in the struggle to build socialism.

Many complaints focused on the perceived advantages extended to communists for employment. This is interesting, in light of the demands of communists and veterans for preferential treatment they felt they had earned for extraordinary sacrifice. Apparently, especially considering the intense competition for work, the greater population did not share this sentiment. In August 1927 the nonparty chairman of a workers' committee appealed to "Comrade Stalin" for justice on behalf of a female cooperative worker in particular, and of nonparty workers in general. The communist boss had replaced the worker in question with another female worker, a party member. The supplicant implored Stalin "as an experienced man and old party member" to answer the question, whether "we really have a party so that party members get first pick for jobs or work." As he remarked, "don't nonparty workers want to eat too?"[43] Similarly, an appeal for work came from a sixty-year-old former miner and opponent of "the louts in our industry here in the Urals under [Tsar] Nicholas the Bloody since 1895." The old revolutionary had been unable of late to find work, because he was not a party member; he found this offensive. Younger party members and Soviet workers, he lamented, "did not even know who had fought for a better share for the working class of the people."[44]

In another protest, a "worker of peasant origins" vented his anger on party leaders. He stated that the nonparty masses did not support the party, because its members were the only ones who got employment, and he condemned the party for its hypocrisy in view of the massive unemployment that plagued the country. In addition, the supplicant censured communists who paid themselves high wages and lived in comfort, while most people were unemployed and starving. The worker's anger is apparent, as he ended his protest with threats to burn communists alive and put out their eyes, among other violent fantasies.[45]

Communist Arrogance

For a communist official, newly endowed with authority, potentially unlimited power and prestige could mean the chance to emulate his prerevolutionary social superiors. The elitist pretensions of such communists, although emanating from a self-conception and world view quite different from those of the revolutionary intelligentsia, greatly augmented the party's elitist reputation.

Throughout the 1920s, countless complaints flowed to the center concerning arrogant or abusive behavior of communists. A few appeals even complained about exclusive and elitist behavior on the part of Pioneers, preteen party supporters too young to join the Komsomol.[46] Supplicants often complained that communists adopted the elitist manner of prerevolutionary tsarist officials, officers, or members of the gentry or nobility.[47] For many party members, it seems, the heady consciousness of being in a position of authority and privilege brought with it a desire to adopt the trappings of such a position, a desire untempered by the comradely mood of civil war days. Indeed,

> even the Red [Army] Commanders . . . seemed only too eager to assume the old privileges that went with an officer's rank. . . . the Red Commanders demanded the rights and privileges of officers as understood by "peasants brought up under the old regime."[48]

This posturing pervaded the entire government and party apparatus, down to the lowest level. In 1921 Kalinin received an appeal from a cobbler, a Red Army veteran, who complained about the business manager of a *kolkhoz* (collective farm) near his village in Tula guberniia. The manager treated the poor peasants just as would a member of the former gentry, lording it over other local peasants and fining them. The veteran complained that the manager did "as it suited him." Even though his family had only three members, the manager owned four cows. He was often drunk and, the veteran complained, "the kulaks were all behind him."[49]

Complaints about communists' elitist manner often came down to the question of respect. Respect denied formed a common theme in appeals to the central government. In August 1927, a manager with the sugar trust and former party candidate wrote to complain of the treatment he received from his communist bosses. Previously, he stated, his dealings with communists had "everywhere [been characterized by] the best relations." But certain individuals with whom he now worked treated him as tsarist officials formerly treated the peasantry—that is to say, with disrespect. According to the supplicant, himself of peasant origin, such relations between the government and peasants in tsarist times were understandable. But now that he was theoretically an equal of his bosses, those same attitudes offended him. The author ended his appeal with the recommendation that such people should not be allowed in the ranks of the party.[50]

Another such complaint came from a *rabkor* (worker correspondent) at the Red Sormovo factory who wished to expose the corruption of the factory's erstwhile director and his attempts to silence the rabkor's complaints. Beginning in 1926, the correspondent had written critiques of the Red director's relations with the factory workers.[51] It seemed that the director "addressed the workers not as people, but as dogs." The rabkor's complaints brought no results. Instead, the director moved on to a new position in Moscow, taking with him all the furniture from his apartment, which belonged to the factory. As the worker pointed out, "I'm not against Comrade Kuritsyn using the furniture . . . but he doesn't need to acquire sumptuous belongings at the expense of the working class." When the workers found out about such things, it created "a bad mood and lack of faith in the party."[52]

The population at all levels took hierarchy for granted before 1917. The communists' main crime appeared to be that they had failed to rise above it. Underscoring this theme was a letter in November 1927 to "Kalinin, Stalin, Kirov" from a nonparty worker. The supplicant condemned a current campaign to "communize" the administration of factories that promoted the formation of class distinctions into

> the class of communists, to whom are given the advantages as the nobility, and the class of nonparty [citizens], to whom no advantages for advancement are given, and [who] even . . . are dismissed from those administrative positions they hold.

Such injustice had to be remedied from above. If it was not, then dissatisfaction among the masses would spread.[53]

Elitism within the Party

The party leadership assumed an elitist posture not only outward toward the broad nonparty masses, but also inward toward the party rank and file. This held true especially with regard to those throngs of youth who had joined the party late, either during or especially after the civil war, and who were often considered opportunists, because their dedication to the cause of socialist construction came only after communist power had been established. Not only were the latecomers suspect as to their dedication to revolutionary goals, but also as to their very suitability to join the vanguard of the proletariat. The party leadership conceived of the new recruits as possessing a decidedly low level of culture and consciousness. A central directive to gubernii and lower party organs instructed that these "elements of the Party . . . were motivated to join it more out of class instinct, than conscious orientation in questions of our party program and tactics." The need for such direction was no doubt a product in part of the great burden of responsibility that rested "on the shoulders [of a] very thin layer" of party leaders and directors.[54]

The condescension of party administrators was a common source of resentment. Communists complained about the superior attitude that government and party officials had assumed toward those of lower rank. Thus, in June 1927 a party member from Cherepovets guberniia appealed about the manner in which he had been dismissed from his position as foreman with the paper trust: "The issue was not so much whether I get my job back, since now as an invalid I need very little, but all the same I would like to know whether justice exists only on paper or in reality." He had sought the cause for his dismissal from the administrator responsible; not only did the latter not provide one, but he refused to speak with the supplicant altogether. The worst part about the whole affair, however, was the fact that the offending administrator was a communist, a "party comrade." And, as the supplicant pointed out, "it's bad, when there is no solidarity among comrades."[55]

Building respectful relations within the party brought up the critical question of party democracy. Many party members decried the leadership's censorship of the party opposition, interpreting it as a lack of respect for the rank-and-file communist. As one supplicant put it, constricting access to information about the opposition and their position was like telling the average party member to "go to hell." The debate over the opposition, he argued, raised important questions concerning party unity and direction, questions vital to the country's future. The average communist or worker had a right to learn about the opposition, and "whether or not it was right." Censorship showed the leadership's lack of respect for the average man.[56] A komsomolets argued in March 1927 that such secrecy on the part of the leadership destroyed party unity. He recalled Lenin's prescription that the party could remain strong only if it were united. If an average party member was not permitted to know what went on in his own party, "for which he was always ready to give his last, for which he might sacrifice his life," then the party could hardly remain unified.[57]

Moreover, appeals from rank-and-file party members suggested that the rift between the lower and upper echelons was closely linked to the growing disparity in NEP society as a whole. As early as 1923, communists in the Moscow organization discussing the defects of the party concluded, among other things, that the leadership had "lost touch" with lower party ranks due to their leaders' long party tenure. One member complained that a "communist, if he lives the life of a rich man, conceals his personal life from fellow communists." Another concluded that "all the trouble comes from the different salaries of communists." Party members felt it "necessary for all communists to be united, but many became specialists, made friends with specialists, and no longer want to concern themselves with communists who are workers." The inevitable result was that communists no longer trusted one another: "the higher-ups don't trust the lower ranks, and vice versa."[58]

Letters abounded with complaints that communists and other revolutionaries were not being treated with the respect they felt they deserved. One petitioner wrote of his disappointment when his district organization refused him 5 rubles' train fare to travel to another city to find work. He was offended, and wrote that "when we were surrounded by the white guard bandits [during the civil war], then we were necessary, but now that we live on the peaceful front, we're an unnecessary element." Divisions had arisen within the party, "that is to say, according to dress and who can speak well."[59] The rift between party administrators and the rank and file led the veteran to question his own worth. The line that separated the idealistic communist from the resentful, negative communist was extremely thin in NEP Russia, when the margin of comfort was so small and individual stakes in building the socialist utopia so easily uprooted.

The formation of an elite within the party that split party ranks contributed to the growing mistrust between government and society as a whole. The mistrust that discouraged communication and coordination among communists was repeated on every level and within every branch of the government apparatus, party and nonparty. Central investigators complained of the lack of trust and cooperation throughout the party and government organs, but appeared powerless to correct it.[60]

Thus, it seems, the party succeeded in maintaining its vanguard character at the cost of its connection with those it represented. In March 1927 a komsomolets from Ukraine wrote a long letter to "Comrade Stalin," tracing the history of his disillusionment with the party. He was a self-described bedniak, born in 1905

> to a poor home, and I live in poverty to this day. Living in a proletarian country, I came to read books and magazines in which it was written that bedniaks such as I had been given power, factories, land, in a word, everything in Russia. All workers and peasants. Political as well as economic [power]. At the head of everything is the communist party, it leads all workers and peasants toward communism and equality, leaning on them. But I don't agree with this. True, [the party] leans on workers and peasants . . . but I think this is ruthless. To lean on the poor proletariat, who can hardly breathe . . .

The supplicant decried the hypocrisy surrounding party democracy, in which a core of party aktiv decided who would be elected before elections ever took place. He acknowledged that the party gave the peasants the land but argued that they nullified this by seizing everything the peasants grew on it, with the rationalization that the land belonged to the government. The workers had been given the factories, only to build arms. The supplicant came to realize that the party was only using the workers and peasants: "I took an active part in work, I fought against exploitation, and I didn't see that exploitation breeds exploitation." The desire to control the revolution had mutated into abuse of power. The bedniak criticized the party for its hypocrisy, pointing out that if the workers and peasants really were in power, "they would not be so unhappy," and exhorted the leadership to "look, and see how the powerless live."

Finally, the komsomolets came to the essence of his complaint. He stated that "communism means equality," and wondered whether "Comrade Stalin would really want to be equal with me?" Perhaps, if he was "one of the first idealistic communists," but not a district secretary or party member who was making 50 to 300 rubles per month.[61] Just as before the revolution, the issue clearly was that of the haves versus the have-nots. In failing to realize the one popular goal of communism—establishing equality—communism in power had become a lie.

Echoing these sentiments, in November 1927 a poor Ukrainian peasant wrote, wondering why the communist government had abandoned the interests of the poor, now that they were in power. Apparently, he surmised, the communists had taken the place of the tsar and his ministers, and "live in luxurious homes"—a charge he repeated three times in the course of his appeal. The supplicant assumed that in light of their new circumstances, party leaders "probably considered the simple people 'dogs'" and defended the interests of kulaks. According to the bedniak, only kulaks got work in factories or the army. He concluded from this state of affairs that either all communists were kulaks, or were controlled by kulaks.[62]

Poor or unemployed supplicants deduced that those in power were simply unable to empathize with their predicament. The gulf between the dictators of the proletariat and the proletariat themselves had simply grown too wide. For many, this fact had to explain the cause for their neglect. A citizen from Moscow appealed to Stalin in June 1927 for work. The supplicant had served in the revolutionary Red Guard and Army, with the Cheka in Ukraine, and had since occupied a number of professional posts in the economic sphere. He admitted that it seemed "strange" for him to be appealing to the *gensek* (general secretary of the party); "but," he wrote, "I have no other choice." He doubted that his leaders could imagine his plight:

> Eight months without work, eight months of a famished existence, if you spent even a month like this, then you would know what it means to be out of work. Morally as well as materially my situation is a nightmare; more concrete measures with respect to unemployment need to be taken.
>
> I would gladly go to China, to Harbin, to the "New World" just to find work. . . . Your refusal [to help me] or your silence would mean the end for a man to whom the revolution was everything, and who gave everything for our Republic.[63]

As the former Chekist's appeal shows, the competition for survival could make a short cycle of the move from last to first, and back to last again.

Solutions

The party administration was not blind to the dissatisfaction caused by communists using their status and position to their own advantage. In January 1921, a commission report on the popular mood of the city of Pskov noted dissatisfaction among an otherwise sympathetic population (with the exception of "the wealthy classes"), because of "abnormal" distribution of food and other necessities. It also noted that employees of Gubprodkom (provincial food supply commissariat) arranged evening parties "off limits to workers," where they helped themselves to "various sweets."[64] And in 1925, the Uzbekistan Central Control Commission noted the high incidence of "official and other crimes" committed by party members throughout the organization, including widespread drunkenness and criminal acts committed under the influence of alcohol. Notably, the commission's resolution on the matter concluded that such rampant criminality resulted from weak central leadership and the remoteness of the control commission from the masses, but their only recommendation was "the need to strengthen the struggle against these occurrences."[65] Indeed, it seemed that the leadership had no solutions to offer, perhaps precisely because of their very remoteness from lower party organs, the party rank and file and, indeed, from the general population.

Consistent with the party's view that education would close the rift between party and people, in 1927 a student attending Red Army officers' training courses in Irkutsk outlined a project for using film to educate the public on the history and task of building socialism. He pointed out that while Stalin's theory of building socialism in one country was "sufficiently apparent . . . public opinion was ill-prepared for it."[66] Leaders needed to realize that, if there were many communists who lacked a clear understanding of building socialism, then this was even more so for the nonparty masses. The author lamented the passivity of party members during discussion of party issues and questions, and attributed this to the fact that they simply did not understand what the issues were. As for "the masses of the nonparty population," they did not even know what socialism meant.[67] The student's attitude echoed the Bolshevik ideological assumption that understanding socialism was impossible without education.

For their part, the nonparty population certainly did not believe that the party possessed a monopoly on truth and understanding of the revolution. First and foremost, understanding required communication, which in turn was impossible without freedom of speech. According to a professor from Moscow writing in March 1927, an all-union, independently funded newspaper was necessary to give "the nonparty masses of the population" an opportunity to express their views.[68] Allowing freedom of expression was vital to popular participation in the political process. This was the message of an appeal "respectfully" directed to Stalin in 1924 from a Moscow party member, who lamented the fact that at a recent trade union conference, out of a total of 845 delegates, only 11 were nonparty. He considered this, at a time when the party was attempting to solicit the allegiance of the nonparty aktiv, to be "a political blunder." Instead, the communist opined, 200 nonparty delegates should have been sent, "workers from the bench, our friends."[69]

For many younger communists, however, the source of the rift between party and people lay not in the party per se, but in those older members who viewed the party as an elite. Thus, the fissure would be closed by eliminating those communists who held this outmoded, prerevolutionary outlook. In June 1927, a disgruntled worker and party member wrote to Stalin about the snobbery of "our old communists." The worker described himself as a "Leninist," having entered party ranks in 1924.[70] According to him, old communists in positions of power either did not carry out central directives or fulfilled them poorly. Worst of all, and clearly the basis for this complaint, was their attitude to communists like him. He was an enthusiastic "aktiv," but of late was rapidly losing his enthusiasm. In party meetings, he was dismissed by the old communists as a "rowdy," while his elders carried on "like lords"—treatment he found "offensive." He claimed that such communists, "who have good apartments and received good salaries . . . undermine party work." He assured Stalin that, asked whether he was satisfied with this situation, any young communist would answer in the negative. Stalin needed to "absolutely purge the party" of such elitists, "drive such communists from the party." The young communist said he no longer had the patience to bear the actions of old communists.[71]

The universal cry for an egalitarian society was not just about economic equality. As the preceding discussion makes clear, average individuals aspiring to construct the socialist society also longed for dignity and respect. Although most of those appealing for work or an education did not express it in so many words, their self-esteem clearly was at stake. One appeal that underscored this point was addressed to the Politburo from a factory worker in the Urals. The essence of his appeal was a suggestion to eliminate the Russian word *rabochii* (worker) from the vocabulary of "party and professional organizations," because the root of the word was *rab*, which meant slave.[72] As he pointed out, "in our free country . . . we don't have slaves," and continued use of *rabochii* was inconsistent with this reality. He recommended instead using *truzhenik* (toiler), and made additional suggestions for neutral terminology applicable to peasants.[73] The objective was to disassociate all laborers, both workers and peasants, from the memory and reality of their past identities as social inferiors. Of course, it goes without saying that gaining distance from the past would not have been so important, if the past really were past.

Joining the Elite

The factory worker's appeal was an obvious indictment of hierarchy and its elimination as the solution to the problems that plagued the revolution. Other supplicants adopted a different approach to the existence of a privileged proletariat vanguard. The basic irony of the NEP system was that the universal equality of the ideal communist world on the one hand, and the individualism that flourished under NEP on the other, were essentially incompatible. In a socialist utopia, general equality meant that whatever condition prevailed for the majority had to prevail for all. But the socialist utopia presumed general prosperity. However, in the real world, general poverty prevailed, and no one could foresee when this reality would change. In the absence of general prosperity, those who had the opportunity were left with the option of creating a limited utopia—that is, of escaping poverty on an individual basis.[74]

Thus, it was generally perceived that the party was an elite and, it seemed, the only route to whatever advantages in status or employment might be available. As such, party membership was in great demand, and would-be communists complained about restrictions placed on membership, essentially condemning the party's elitism for refusing to admit them into the party elite. To the Old Bolsheviks, party newcomers were opportunists. But for many prospective communists, idealism was eclipsed by economic desperation. Obviously, "the reason . . . why one might, or might not, wish to join the party [was that it was] almost certain to lead to an assignment to administrative or white-collar work."[75] That such a motivation was deemed "careerist" by older communists and party leaders was ideologically inconsistent. After all, Marxism was consciously materialist; it held that material progress preceded cultural growth. Younger party members recognized that in the hierarchy of needs, eating took precedence over party work, if only for practical reasons. For those wishing to become proprietors and beneficiaries of the brave new world, opportunities for party membership were far too restrictive. In their own eyes, young would-be party members were building the socialist society. Stalin may have been flooding the party with new recruits, but there were more than enough who were desperate to join the deluge.

This mixture of idealism and economic considerations comes through, for instance, in an appeal for work in February 1927 from a Leningrad komsomolets. He had no means to support himself and lived with his father, with whom the aspiring communist did not get along. It seemed his father was a printer and a "man of the old stamp, while I am a person with new views." He wished to continue working with the Komsomol, but needed work "to give me the opportunity to better my material existence, and the opportunity to extend the influence of my work in the Komsomol collective, which is my life." The komsomolets pleaded for help from Stalin, "as an old party member, leader, and member of the old guard," to give him the opportunity "to work in the ranks of the young guard."[76] Indeed, economic and psychological motivations to join the party were closely intertwined and, in some cases, almost indistinguishable. Thus, two Moscow komsomoltsy appealed to Stalin for work in August 1927. They had recently finished a four-year technical course and qualified for skilled positions as mechanics, but no such jobs were available. As a result, despite their education and years of training, they were unemployed and without any means of support. They pleaded with Stalin, "having secondary education and as members of the VLKSM, we will never agree to allow ourselves to sink to the lowest dregs of society."[77]

Such desperation to escape poverty and backwardness was ubiquitous during NEP. The futility of existence and lack of opportunity for most existed alongside visions of unobtainable wealth and comfort flaunted by the few. The collective was being torn apart by two different ethical codes: one for those out to get what they could, and the other for those who embraced poverty by choice or by necessity. And, as implied in the prospective mechanics' appeal, the desire for material sustenance was combined for many communists with a profound dread of the social stigma attached to poverty. A civil war veteran and party member working in Voronezh guberniia appealed for a transfer back to the city. He was frustrated that, in spite of ten years' party and war service, he was essentially left to rot in the countryside without a chance for promotion. He begged Stalin "to take me from the country, in order that I don't fall behind the general level of political development of urban party members." In addition, he lamented, his wife was "completely illiterate," and she needed to get an education.[78]

A similar appeal came from a communist working among the peasants in Tver guberniia. A former factory worker from Kronstadt and Leningrad, he clearly viewed himself as part of the revolutionary avant-garde and pleaded to be transferred back to the city. He wanted his children to be raised "as proletarians," not to be "inculcated with the ideas of petty-possessiveness." He himself had been "active at the time of war communism" and wished to take a more active part in building socialism. In general, it was all the same to him "where or how, only I would like to work and exist like a human being."[79] These communists were not content to serve the cause of the revolution through the slow process of raising the muzhik's cultural level, in part because they feared that rural backwardness would swallow them up instead. As the revolutionary from Leningrad knew all too well, in becoming one with the peasantry he risked being relegated within the party and society to second-class status. One could either beat the elite, or join them. Facing such overwhelming odds, many sought the latter route to salvation.

The Revolution Betrayed

Whatever the causes for the re-formation of an elite in Soviet society, there was no doubt that the revolution's failure in this regard caused no small degree of bitterness and resentment among the vast numbers who were excluded from its ranks. A common reaction to this was self-chastisement. An unemployed veteran of the civil war, several times wounded in the course of service, bemoaned his treatment at the hands of administrative officials. His search for work at various agencies or the labor exchange yielded no result, his service in the revolution no longer of any advantage. When he attempted to appeal to the chairman of the okruzhkom, the veteran was thrown out on the street by the militia. He lamented his gullibility, for having lived so long in "damp, wet barracks" only for the sake of officials, who received high salaries and lived in comfort, while he, a partisan in the revolution, remained in those same damp barracks. When they were fighting for the revolution, he lamented, they believed the promises of their commanders, promises that they "would have everything." Certainly, for believing this lie, he and his soldier-comrades were nothing but "blockheads." He pleaded to Stalin for some type of work.[80]

Individual abasement, and the resulting bitterness and resentment, however, also had political and social implications. The connection between low self-esteem and social instability is evident in the rather pathetic appeal of a worker at a beer factory in the Donbass. He wrote to Stalin in February 1927, apparently out of a profound melancholy:

> I am a half-worn-out thirty-eight-year-old worker, and I have tormented myself to the point that I became convinced that life without struggle is not worth anything, and I have no further desire in what remains of my life besides a good fight. . . . I thought to myself that by satisfying a desire, even a weak-willed, little man could become a little more firm. So I decided to contact gensek Comrade Stalin personally, since I think, to undertake the soonest possible creation of socialism in one country—not from the bottom up, but "from the top down" . . . So I beg you to answer: might not a little, semiliterate, beaten, weak-willed [man like me] personally [join] the staff to see the world struggle and gape at the greatest fighters in the world?[81]

One of the greatest sources of complaint to the center throughout the 1920s was the elitism of the party, and particularly of the party elite. Lower-ranking communists, komsomoltsy, and nonparty citizens resented both the pay and privileges of higher officials, and their aspirations toward hierarchy and control over the lower apparatus and society. The party leadership's desire for control stemmed mainly from two causes, namely, the necessity to organize and administer a huge and chaotic system, and the desire to lead a culturally backward population toward the building of socialist society.

When in 1921 it set upon the New Economic Policy, the party officially relinquished control over the economy that it never actually had possessed. This apparent capitulation to the forces of capitalism required a correspondingly greater degree of control, both socially and politically, and further decreased democracy in the party and throughout society. Democracy was also threatened by the party elite's conception of revolution, informed by their belief that the uncultured, uneducated masses were neither capable of performing the work of government and administration, nor, indeed, of understanding socialism. These assumptions justified the existence of an elite that would direct and control the population for an unspecified period, and diverged greatly from popular conceptions of the meaning of socialism or of the revolution.

The formation of a party elite, and of elitism within the party, were also encouraged by the NEP ethic that fostered opportunism and increased competition for work and position in the new society. Many sought positions in the party merely out of economic desperation. Others sought party affiliation to escape social and cultural marginalization. These new communists were often labeled opportunist by older Bolsheviks, who looked on the new recruits with contempt for their presumed lack of revolutionary idealism and for their lack of culture and education.

Ultimately, party elitism caused the gulf between party and society to grow. Communists were criticized for adopting the posture of the prerevolutionary elite, and for their perceptible contempt for the masses. This contempt in turn promoted self-contempt among those who were shut out of the elite, a phenomenon that portended grave social repercussions.

CHAPTER SEVEN

Foreign Enemies

THROUGHOUT NEP, the possibility of military confrontation with foreign powers was, if not a greater threat, perhaps a more obvious threat to collective security than socioeconomic disparity. This threat was especially apparent at moments of crisis, such as the war scare of 1927, when diplomatic relations with England broke down and war appeared imminent.[1] From the onset of the revolution, however, widespread elements throughout the Soviet Union not only feared but assumed that a hostile confrontation with capitalist powers was inevitable. Memories of foreign intervention in the civil war were fresh. Hence, concern over the country's military vulnerability was pervasive among both communists and nonparty citizens not only in 1927 but throughout the NEP period.

Soviet Foreign Policy during NEP

Besides socioeconomic disparity, a clear threat to the integrity of collective security during the 1920s was that of foreign invasion. Indeed, the threat of invasion was the communist government's primary incentive for instituting rapid industrialization and collectivization at the end of the decade. In this undertaking, according to official Soviet historical analysis, the government was supported wholeheartedly by the proletariat:

> In their speeches [at the Fourth All-Union Congress of Soviets in April 1927], workers unanimously approved the course of socialist industrialization of the country, emphasizing the necessity of its rapid pace under conditions of capitalist encirclement and the threat of military attack on the USSR.[2]

More important, and perhaps more genuine, than the workers' vote of confidence was the support of the military. By the mid-1920s, many throughout the military perceived the collectivization of agriculture as a prerequisite to preparations for a future war. They were opposed to the expansion of the private market under NEP that took control over agriculture and hence of agricultural exports out of the government's hands.[3]

The question of the extent to which the threat of war was legitimate, or a cynical contrivance on the part of the Soviet government to rally support for its agenda and deflect criticism, is not directly at issue here. The central government did propagate the fear of war and capitalist invasion that certainly contributed to support for industrialization.[4] But the fact is that, from the inception of the communist state in Russia, widespread and diverse elements of the population did not merely fear but assumed that confrontation with inherently hostile foreign powers was imminent.[5] In this sense the central government was but one of these elements. Nor could this assumption be said to be groundless. Indeed, the new government had succeeded only in 1921 in ending a civil war in which foreign governments had actively lent their support to the monarchist cause. As the decade progressed and expectations of worldwide revolution diminished, capitalist encirclement of communist Russia became a fact. This caused many Soviet citizens, and doubtless the Bolsheviks themselves, to feel vulnerable and on the defensive. This vulnerability was in turn enhanced by Russia's utter ruination in economic and human terms after seven years of war, revolution, and famine. Defensiveness combined with an implacable and mutual hostility towards the bourgeois governments of the rest of the world to define Soviet foreign policy.

In March 1921, a bid for power by German communists by means of a general strike failed. Thus was the last and best hope for worldwide revolution quashed, and Russia became isolated as the only communist country in the world. At the Third Congress of the Comintern (Communist International) in June and July of that year, it was recognized that worldwide revolution was no longer imminent, and that Russia and the Comintern had to assume a "defensive and preparatory" posture.[6] The year 1921 thus marked a reorientation for Russia not only in terms of domestic but also of foreign policy. The Bolsheviks had to rebuild their economy in order to defend communism in Russia both at home and abroad. The concentration on reconstruction was further hampered by widespread famine beginning in 1921. The Bolshevik government was not equipped to deal with the magnitude of the disaster, and so it accepted vital assistance from the American Relief Administration, formed for the purpose of reconstruction in Europe after World War I. The Americans extended this assistance even though they refused to grant the Bolshevik government diplomatic recognition. Indeed, it was not until 1933 that the American government under Franklin D. Roosevelt recognized the Soviet Union.

The main foreign policy goals of the Soviet government throughout NEP were to establish trade and credit links with the West and gain diplomatic recognition, which would facilitate trade and maintain peace necessary for reconstruction. The Bolsheviks bargained that even though Western powers were opposed to them politically, they would be compelled to trade with them, and in this the communists were proven correct. Western governments were open to trade, because of a crisis of overproduction following the war and an urgent need for markets. Thus, in March 1921 an Anglo-Russian Trade Agreement was concluded, followed quickly by agreements with other Western powers. Trade with Britain preceded diplomatic recognition, which was not granted until Britain's first Labour government came to power in late 1923.

Before that time, both the British and the Americans had condemned the communist government, which had come to power through violent revolution and vowed to facilitate a similar fate for bourgeois governments worldwide. The American position softened when President Woodrow Wilson was replaced by Warren Harding, less judgmental and more open to the economic possibilities that Russia offered. But the British remained intransigent. British foreign secretary Lord Curzon, who was "violently anti-Russian,"[7] prompted the first serious diplomatic crisis between England and Russia in spring 1923 by sending an ultimatum that granted the Soviets ten days to satisfy certain British grievances.[8] This crisis was resolved, however, and when Labour came to power, they quickly granted full diplomatic recognition. The Italian and other Western governments soon followed suit, ending the Soviet Union's diplomatic isolation.

In the meantime, the Soviet Union had sought and achieved economic and diplomatic links with Germany. With the Treaty of Rapallo in April 1922, Germany and Russia established full diplomatic recognition and mutual cancellation of financial claims. Neither had committed to the Treaty of Versailles, and both were diplomatic outcasts in Europe: Germany for its role in the war, Russia for its communist revolution. Western Europe sought to punish the former by exacting an astronomical sum in war reparations; the latter fell out of favor for their nationalization of foreign property and repudiation of national debt, which had greatly increased during the war. Thus, sharing the dubious distinction of international ostracism, the Russians and Germans banded together and formed a mutually beneficial relationship that continued until the Nazis invaded Russia in 1941.

The last vestige of Russia's isolation ended in January 1924 with recognition by England which coincided exactly with the death of Lenin. After his demise, the political and economic liberals around Nikolai Bukharin were briefly in power. Bukharin maintained a much closer relationship with Georgy Chicherin, Russia's foreign minister. Chicherin came from the aristocracy and, although committed to the communist cause, was an equally committed diplomat, accepted and respected in the international diplomatic community. Chicherin, however, was as opposed to the British as Lord Curzon was to the Russians. In any case, the Labour government in England lasted only a year. It fell partly as a result of a forged letter allegedly from Comintern head Grigory Zinoviev to a British communist leader, urging communist intrigue against the British government. This incident snuffed out the policy of rapprochement that had been pursued by the Labour government; the Conservatives returned to power in England, and from that time Soviet-British relations disintegrated. This culminated in May 1927 in a raid by the British government on the offices of the Soviet Trade Delegation in London and the subsequent break of diplomatic ties. Relations were not resumed until 1930, when Labour returned to power.

One last foreign relations incident that profoundly affected both the Soviet government and popular opinion during NEP was the fate of the Chinese communist movement in 1927. The Chinese Communist Party had been formed only in 1920 and lacked as yet a large popular following. They looked to Moscow as the leader of the Comintern for direction. The Soviets, for their part, feared British and Japanese encroachment on China and provided the Chinese communists with advisors and a plan of action in their efforts to topple imperialistic power and establish socialism in China. Specifically, the Soviets advised the Chinese communists to merge with the Guomindang, the Nationalist Party of China, and to fight for control of the country together.

This was a dangerous position after 1925, when Sun Yat-sen, the Guomindang leader, died. It was then that Jiang Jieshi began to fashion himself as the leader of the Guomindang. Jiang displayed a threatening posture toward the communists, who repeatedly requested a new line of direction from the Comintern to allow them to break away from the Guomindang before it was too late. But Stalin, at this point controlling the direction of foreign policy, would not allow the Comintern position to change. This spelled the doom of the Chinese communists. When Jiang and the Guomindang military forces marched in their bid for national control on Shanghai and Wuhan, in April 1927 they also massacred the communists there. The Chinese Communist Party was temporarily obliterated, but now independent from Moscow. It took a decade for Mao Zedong and others to revitalize the Chinese communist movement, and this time, it began to march to its own beat.

The Threat of Foreign Invasion

In 1922, on the occasion of the revolution's fifth anniversary, members of a district soviet in Kostroma guberniia sent their greetings to Lenin and Trotsky and vowed that "not one arm of the powers hostile to the Soviets will dare to make an attempt on the interests of Soviet power."[9] The fear of war and an intense sense of vulnerability compelled the revolution's defenders to adopt what sounded like an aggressive posture. The sympathies of the Soviet populace, however, varied tremendously as to why—and whether—Soviet citizens should fight and defend the communist government.

Most citizens expressing their views on this subject took the probability of war for granted. After all, the West was inherently hostile to the communist cause, and so it seemed logical that a confrontation would develop sooner or later, and probably sooner rather than later. The question, then, was not whether war would come, but whether the Soviet Union would be prepared when it did. Many supplicants expressed deep anxiety that the Soviet Union was not prepared and would suffer grave losses in the coming battle with worldwide capitalism. In this spirit, in March 1927 a director in the State Bread Inspectorate wrote to "Comrade Stalin . . . personally, absolutely secretly." The purpose of his letter was to inquire whether the state was creating an emergency bread supply to feed the populace in case of hostilities. The inspector was concerned, because the government was exporting such huge amounts of grain; in the case of a bad harvest, at this rate, bread would have to be imported to feed the country. What if the imperialists attacked, and formed an economic blockade? People would starve.[10] Memories of starvation and death during the civil war and the famine that followed were still fresh in the popular mind. Inherent this and many other appeals is not only the fear, but the certainty of looming hostilities. Delegates to a conference of Red volunteers declared that they were ready:

> If Anglo-French and American capital drives our country to come forward with weapons in hand for the defense of the interests of the laboring masses, our volunteers will supplement the military forces, and the shot sure and the bullet on target in the struggle with the imperialist predators.[11]

Expressions of enthusiasm in defending the revolution were common in 1927, in response to the government's warning in the press of a pending attack by the British. That year saw a breakdown of foreign relations between the Soviet Union and England, considered by the Soviet government to be the communist power's greatest opponent and threat. England had not only supported the White cause but also directly intervened on the monarchist side during the civil war. England was also the economic and spiritual leader of Western capitalism, and its culture was steeped in the notion of class and socioeconomic hierarchy, antithetical to the cause for which the Russian Revolution had been fought. When diplomatic relations with England were broken off, the war scare that followed prompted many letters to the party leadership from communist and nonparty citizens alike.

Concern over the country's preparedness was pervasive. A Ukrainian komsomolets inquired in June 1927 whether, in case of war that he knew was inevitable, the Soviet Union would be supported by the Western proletariat. He thought that even though Soviet youth were all ready to fight, he considered that the Soviet Union would be outclassed by Western capabilities in such a war. Consequently, the country's existence would be in peril.[12] Such concerns suggested a number of alternatives for the party leadership. If the Soviet Union were indeed militarily inferior, it had two options: either avoid conflict at all costs in order to avoid the country's destruction, or make rearmament a top priority. And, if war really were inevitable, as this komsomolets believed, the second alternative would seem to be the government's only choice.

For many wishing to bring thc rcvolution to a successful end, the best defense was a good offense. Since the struggle to build socialism was an international one, the best way to solidify the revolution at home was to adopt an aggressive stance abroad. On the occasion of the revolution's sixth anniversary in 1923, representatives of the city of Vladimir sent a telegram to Lenin that acknowledged their victory under his leadership, and concluded by saying that "with you [*s toboi*] we arrived at the Russian October, and with you we will soon arrive at the worldwide October."[13] In January 1924, the presidium of a congress of soviets in Nizhnii Novgorod guberniia sent their greetings to Lenin, wishing him a speedy recovery and hailing "the first and most dreaded gravedigger of capitalist society."[14] Representatives of a conference of miners sent Lenin their hopes for his recovery, so that under his leadership "we may soon finish off worldwide capital, and set the first stone in [its] international grave."[15] However, the problem of where the struggle against worldwide capital had to be fought was only complicated by geographical factors. The Soviet Union, comprising the old Russian empire, had a huge periphery to defend, and its internal revolutionary struggle was inherently international in scope. The further removed from the center, the more vulnerable a region was and the more uncertain the fate of the revolution. In October 1922, delegates to a party conference in the Far Eastern region expressed to Lenin their desire to strengthen their ties with Soviet Russia and to weed out the remnants of "maritime reaction and give the decisive rebuff to intervention."[16]

Enthusiasm for battle was not, however, wholly unqualified. Many letters to Stalin regarding the threat of foreign attack express both reluctance and ambivalence to engage the enemy.[17] Memories of seven long years of war still fresh in their minds, both communists and average citizens were concerned about the relative and potentially overwhelming strength of the capitalist powers and the destruction that such a confrontation promised. Clearly, not everyone, not even all communists, were clamoring for a confrontation with the worldwide bourgeoisie. In June 1927, a communist living among the Khakassy in Siberia urged restraint upon the government, entreating his leaders not to declare war on the English. If the Soviets refrained from hostilities, he argued, they would allow the English to reveal to the workers of the world their true colors as the real aggressors.[18] Whether he truly believed this, or whether he simply employed a clever argument in an attempt to persuade party leaders to avoid more bloodshed, is unclear. What is clear is that like many others, the author was certainly apprehensive about the Soviet Union's vulnerability. At the very least, the Soviets needed to be careful. Along a similar vein, in June 1927 a komsomolets from Penza guberniia pledged to Stalin his readiness to defend the Soviet Union in case of war with England, because it was "October that gave us freedom." He wished to let Stalin know, however, that support for a war among the local populace was mixed. According to the komsomolets, "no one desires war, even those who hate the soviet power, for instance, private traders and kulaks." He observed that local opinion was divided mainly into two camps. Middle and poor peasants felt for the most part that the country should fight only if it were attacked, while wealthy peasants thought that only the government elite should fight. The real issue, however, seemed to be the fate of the revolution at home. According to the author, "they still ask, why is there no equality? . . . why does everyone not ride in troikas, in cars, the people say, in place of the old master there is a new one."[19]

Locating the Enemy

Most supplicants agreed that the enemy should be defeated; there was less agreement on who or where the enemy actually was. Often, when discussing the threat of foreign invasion, supplicants pointed to the problem of counterrevolution at home. The logic behind this concern was that a country seething with class enemies was more vulnerable to rapacious foreign powers similarly irreconcilable to the revolution. The two threats thus were inherently connected. In June 1927, a communist from Taganrog in the Cherkass autonomous region urged the government not to allow the country to be drawn into a costly war by bourgeois provocations, such as the assassination that month of Soviet ambassador to Poland Petr Voikov. "War," he argued, "would mean the country's ruin, the sacrifice of people, but we do not want to spill blood and practice fratricide." He expressed his obligatory readiness to defend the country if need be but urged his leaders to avoid confrontation.

That was not, however, the end of the communist's message. In fact, many letters to the leadership expressed contradictory messages, perhaps because the situation itself bred conflicting emotions, or perhaps because the authors did not want to appear lacking in support for their country or government. In any case, the latter interpretation cannot be assumed. In this case, the author could not have been wholly peaceable in his intentions. He summed up his appeal with a provocative message concerning the presence of former officers, landlords, and exploiters throughout the soviet apparatus, admonishing his leaders to "turn their attention" to this problem.[20]

A similar message was extended by two communists writing to Stalin in June and July 1927, respectively. They urged Stalin to protect the country from the English, and pressed the government to sanction OGPU to use stricter methods of surveillance and verification of the population and heavy industry to weed out spies and counterrevolutionary elements. In general, they spurred the government to continue the struggle "against world bourgeoisie . . . for industrialization of the country . . . elimination of opposition within the party . . . for peace . . . [and] correctly to fulfill Lenin's bidding."[21] A difficult order to fill, since certain of these initiatives surely would cancel out others. How could the government simultaneously fight against foreign enemies and internal disunity, and maintain peace as well? Yet, this appeal underscores the inconsistency of the desires of many, an inconsistency no doubt repeated in higher levels of government.

This implicit connection between foreign invasion and internal instability found ubiquitous expression in appeals to the center. In July 1927, a komsomolets from Pskov discussed in a long letter the inevitability of a war with the Western bourgeoisie and the measures the government should take to ensure victory in the struggle. Among these was the "complete neutralization of our interior, [in order that] it would be safe for us to proceed to the final and decisive battle with capital." On this point, the author was adamant, for it was only through neutralization that the communists could be victorious.[22] Apparent in this and other appeals to Stalin is that, in the minds of many communists and nonparty citizens, the hostile capitalists outside and hostile class elements inside the country's borders had become completely conflated. Indeed, why distinguish between them? Since the enemy was a class enemy—the bourgeoisie—then there were enemies in sufficient numbers still lurking among the population and throughout the government and economic apparatus of the Soviet Union. The battlefield was at home.

Complaints to the center abounded on the ubiquitous presence of spies, sometimes equating them with Whites or former class enemies generally. Class enemies betrayed themselves, among other ways, by opulent displays of wealth. In July 1927, an anonymous letter sent to "dear Comrade Stalin" complained about the showy behavior of the Polish envoy in Moscow. It seemed that the envoy's car was frequently observed pulling up in front of a commissioned store on the Arbat. The ambassador and his companion were seen to have "purchased, or better yet bought up, diamonds and silver articles." The author asked Stalin, "what is the Polish ambassador doing here? It is disturbing to watch this."[23] Flaunting wealth in a communist country was no more acceptable for foreigners than for citizens. Moreover, as the informant implied, the wealth of Russia now belonged to the people, and the Polish ambassador therefore had no right to it. Some contemporaries observed that foreigners with foreign money—capitalist money—reentered Russia after NEP was introduced, hoping to reap profits in the newly relaxed atmosphere through concessions, and in so doing, they corrupted the collective organism. Buyers from throughout Europe flocked to Russia to acquire the treasures of the former ruling classes; "moving vans would transport across the frontiers in a few days treasures in furnishings and art objects which it had taken generations to assemble,"[24] pillaging the country of its wealth as the spoils of a war that Russia had presumably won.

The Polish ambassador was a relatively conspicuous enemy; the native variety were harder to spot or control and consequently more dangerous. In July 1927 an elderly Jewish woman from Kiev appealed, presumably to Stalin, not naming him specifically but addressing her letter to the "highly-honored commissar," who was "our defender. The defender of all oppressed and enslaved." The purpose of her appeal was to name and expose a number of "dangerous individuals," former Whites and informers residing in Kiev. These persons presented a security risk to the government, and she recommended that they be rounded up en masse for deportation to Siberia. Dealing with them one at a time would be ill-advised, since they were "terribly cunning, secretive, and dangerous."[25]

Thus, for many, the line separating class enemies from spies working for hostile foreign powers was virtually indistinguishable. In July 1927, a party member from Donets-Shakhty okrug warned the party that bourgeois agents employed mainly in government establishments were sending government secrets to the foreign bourgeoisie, "on the basis of which the bourgeoisie of all countries quickly change the fronts of bourgeois politics to the advantage of the suppression of bolshevism."[26] The author recommended that the government carry out a full-scale verification campaign "of every white-collar worker and administrator" by examining documents from authorities in the employee's birthplace. The objective was to unmask spies and counterrevolutionaries hoping to escape exposure by working where their true identities—their pasts—were unknown. The author was convinced that "these spies have crept into our ranks and work for the sake of counterrevolution."[27]

Such paranoia concerning the widespread presence of spies might be attributed to party propaganda, except that the tendency to equate spies with class enemies appears to be almost instinctive. The hatred for class enemies came from a different place than party propaganda. Class enemies, just as much as foreign spies, presented a security risk to the Soviet government, because their mere presence constituted a threat to the individual and collective aspirations of the proletariat. It is significant that the author of this appeal advised a verification only of white-collar workers—those who occupied favored positions with correspondingly high salaries and perks who were the subject of ubiquitous complaints to the center. In appeals informing the center about espionage, spies frequently were accused of belonging either to prerevolutionary elites or to the favored strata of NEP society, those who continued to benefit from social inequality at the workers' expense. This would explain why the leadership received relatively few recommendations to verify the credentials of the unemployed. How could the unemployed be enemies? They were poor.

Security through Unity

Many expressing their desire to defend the revolution essentially spoke in terms of protecting the collective. This is evident, for example, in an appeal from a Red Army veteran from the Northern Caucasus asking permission to form a partisan band to defend the revolution. The veteran stated that he

> should mention that in the case of a call [to arms], it would be strange for me to go, not absolutely knowing the matter for which we were defending the revolution, but if I were in the midst of partisans and those steeped in the spirit of communism, I could boldly answer the government's call.[28]

The "matter" that required defending obviously was the bond the partisan shared with his comrades, through which he gained courage, resolve, and a sense of purpose. For the veteran, the sense of collective identity itself constituted grounds for answering a call to military action to defend the revolution.

The threat of international hostilities was undoubtedly a great unifier, with both positive and negative consequences. The negative consequences were obvious—including a tendency to reject and fear democracy and discussion, and a heightened paranoia. The positive result, important especially to those who found meaning and worth in revolutionary struggle and civil war, was the unity of the population toward achieving a positive goal.

The desire simply to be included in a unified struggle in itself was a powerful motivator and not to be underestimated. It also formed a common theme in appeals to the party leadership. A group of nonparty Red Army men gathered for a conference in Vladimir guberniia expressed their hopes for Lenin's recovery and their regret at his absence. But they assured their leader that in the wake of his illness, they

> had closed our ranks even more tightly against harm from the enemy, striving to corrupt us. . . . We delegates, discussing problems of the worldwide situation, pledge that the Red Army will vigilantly follow the imperialist policy of the worldwide bourgeoisie, and that every attempt against the peaceful and creative work of workers and peasants of the USSR will be fought with the bayonets of Red fighters.[29]

These soldiers undoubtedly found strength in adversity, a strength harder to tap once the civil war had ended. Indeed, the fulfillment of engaging in a common struggle was not limited to military engagements, but found resonance throughout Soviet life. In September 1923, participants in a party conference of the "distant Bodaibinskii industrial region" sent a telegram to Lenin during his illness to assure him that the "difficult circumstances that the Republic must endure only cause us to close our ranks even tighter."[30] In adversity,

Soviet citizens sought unity because in unity there was strength. It almost appears as though strength and unity were ends in themselves, and foreign threat merely a catalyst. On the occasion of the revolution's fifth anniversary, Komsomol conference delegates expressed their hope that Lenin would "once again appear on the tribunal surrounded by the proletariat, from which could be heard his powerful appeal for the creation of a unified front for the merciless struggle with capital."[31]

As the above appeals suggest, expressions of anxiety over the possibility of foreign attack came not only in response to government warnings in the press but also during periods in which citizens perceived that the collective was particularly vulnerable, including spells of Lenin's illness preceding his death in January 1924. People wrote to Lenin during his incapacitation to express their concern, not so much for their leader as for the country's future. Members of the Orlov city soviet extended greetings to Lenin on the occasion of his fifty-third birthday, expressing their deep concern that the revolution's enemies would capitalize on Lenin's illness. The soviet vowed that any efforts of the "enemies of the proletariat, various double counterrevolutionaries and social-compromisers . . . to sow confusion in the ranks of the avant-garde of the proletariat-RKP(b) [would be] in vain." Indeed, they affirmed, "the illness of our dear and brilliant leader only closes the ranks of the working class more tightly around the RKP(b), which with even greater energy expends all its strength in the construction of the Soviet Republic."[32]

As some pointed out, Lenin's return to health and to the helm of government would present a great disappointment to the forces opposing revolution in Russia.[33] Conversely, Lenin's demise would greatly increase the country's—and the revolution's—vulnerability. The possibility that Lenin would leave his adherents forever was in itself sufficiently threatening to provoke great anxiety and to cause them to seek even greater unity than his presence could evoke. Writing apparently in reaction to the attempt on Lenin's life in August 1918, workers from the Odner factory pledged to their leader and to "the despicable scoundrels of the bourgeois class" that they were prepared "to rise as one man in defense of our leader and [to] destroy to the core the filthy scheme of the bourgeoisie, attempting to regain their old thieves' rights."[34] Similarly, members of the construction workers' union of the city of Petrozavodsk resolved in September 1918 that "with these murders [attempt on Lenin's life and assassination of Petrograd Cheka head Moisei Uritskii] the enemies of the revolution try to disorganize our ranks and inflict a fatal blow to the revolution." The workers pledged their intention to "answer with a mass Red terror, against all enemies of the revolution."[35]

At a point in Lenin's recovery, a group of delegates to a regional party conference wrote that "with the greatest joy we welcome the renewal of your strength, so necessary for us at this time in the struggle against worldwide exploiters." The party delegates almost breathed an audible sigh of relief as they alluded to the danger the country faced without Lenin: "Your return to the post of leader to the avant-garde of the proletariat removes the last hopes of our enemies to undermine proletariat power."[36] Lenin was necessary to the revolution, because his absence lent encouragement to the enemy at a time when the revolution's success was still very much in doubt. Party candidates from Odessa begged Lenin to remain healthy because he was

> not only the ideological leader of our party, but also you unify around yourself the entire party. Dear Vladimir Il'ich you must be healthy, the Communist Party, . . . the proletariat and the poorest peasantry of all countries need you.[37]

In unity, the most vulnerable among the population found strength. In disunity—in Lenin's absence—communists and their supporters, together and individually, faced a hostile world.

Thus, supplicants commonly drew a connection between the danger posed by hostile foreign powers and the lack of unity and security at home. Moreover, this impression seemed not to depend on the supplicant's party affiliation or class sympathies. In July 1927, a group of both blue- and white-collar workers with the railroad stated their readiness "to defend the conquest of October until its victorious conclusion," although in the same breath qualifying their enthusiasm by adding that they "hear the voice of the proletariat, which does not want to fight." If fighting was necessary to defend the revolution, then fight they would; but in order to do so, the supplicants maintained, the whole country had to stand solidly united around the Leninist party. If the country were united, the international bourgeoisie would see that an attack on the Soviet Union would be futile. If the country were united, so the argument ran, fighting ultimately would be unnecessary. And such unity could only be achieved "when the leader of the proletariat of the Soviet Union and Leninist party himself preserves unity within his own ranks, and thereby strengthens his authority among the nonparty proletariat." Only then would the masses be willing to follow the lead of the party. The unity extolled by the authors was, in their estimation, sorely lacking in lower party organs: "Individual party members undermine the party's authority," repelling the allegiance of the nonparty masses. As it turned out, the individual who sparked the group's complaint about party unity, according to them, was none other than a former member of the Okhrana (tsarist secret police).[38]

The message was clear: not only was war inevitable, but the revolution would fail, unless the party leadership cleansed the party of class enemies. Along the same vein, a telegram was sent to Lenin by a meeting of party members, komsomoltsy, and "representatives of the workers, peasants and RA [Red Army] men." The assembly declared that they were

> confident the unified worldwide proletariat will be victorious on the bourgeois front. The disciplined and firm solidarity of workers and peasants calls us conscripts . . . [to achieve] our goal—the bright future of communism.[39]

The soldiers and prospective revolutionaries believed that in order to achieve victory, the party first had to achieve unity and discipline. Without it, the revolution was lost.

Another recommendation to cleanse the party in light of the dangerous international situation came from a rural correspondent who formerly had served as a political commissar with the Red Army during the civil war "on all fronts without exception" and worked in the Special Section in the Caucasus. He had left the party "unwillingly, because of family circumstances." He sent his appeal confidentially to Stalin, informing him that the current "psychology of the kulak element" was counterrevolutionary. At this most serious moment in international relations, "the kulak stratum in the country and city does not sleep, but will conduct brazen policy against the laboring masses with the goal of . . . creating discord among the ignorant and unconscious peasantry." The supplicant appeared to define "kulak" broadly to include both rural and urban elements who opposed Soviet (communist) power, and who rose above the general standard of living through the exploitation of workers and peasants. As he used it, "kulak" was practically synonymous with "bourgeoisie." Thus, the kulak posed both a socioeconomic and a political threat. According to the supplicant, the real danger in the country lay in the lower party organs, filled with those who were neither proletarian nor dedicated to the goals of October or the party program. He specifically mentioned the lower administrative organs of the militia. His appeal closed with a "request to strengthen as much as possible the GPU . . . the buttress of Soviet power."[40] This concern over the infiltration of lower party and government organs by class enemies was echoed in numerous appeals. A regional conference of poor peasants from Khortitskii raion sent Lenin their greetings and hopes for his recovery during the course of an election campaign to the soviets in Zaporozhie guberniia, Ukraine, vowing that "not one parasite will make it into the soviets."[41]

By 1927, Stalin warned that the class struggle was intensifying and would soon culminate in a climactic struggle to decide the fate of the revolution. Indeed, the threat of hostilities from abroad only served to intensify class struggle at home by abetting the search for alien elements throughout the population. The search for spies thus formed part of the class struggle within Russia itself. But there were reasons besides party propaganda why the connection was so easily made for many supplicants. Class struggle was international by definition, because class enemies cut across national lines. It was, therefore, natural for many to see foreign enemies everywhere within the country. As the preceding appeals illustrate, class enemies were suspect as foreign spies by definition, because they were foreign to the collective. As many aggrieved supplicants pointed out, they did not fight the revolution for the sake of those who sat out the civil war behind desks. And because of NEP, those same upper-level bureaucrats and specialists were employed, while party members, workers, veterans, and poor peasants starved. It appeared that it was not the threat of battle with foreign capitalism that intensified the class struggle at home, but the reverse.

Externalizing Internal Insecurity

For many, the greatest threat to the country's external security lay in the country's economic situation. A batrak by origin and former Red sailor, who now served as a chief in the Moscow militia, warned the government that extensive unemployment among the population, especially in larger cities, provided fertile breeding ground for antigovernment sentiment. He pointed out that he was qualified to make such an assessment, since he worked "among the lower masses of the population" and through a variety of sources was privy to their mood and concerns. In the current state of dissatisfaction, "provocateurs" inspired criticism of the government and incited the lower masses against the power of the Soviets. The solution to both foreign and domestic threats to Soviet power thus lay in the liquidation of unemployment.[42] Another supplicant viewed economic weakness as a security risk, indicating that the party would do well to extend more support to village youth in particular and the oppressed in general. Not surprisingly, the author of this appeal was himself a nonparty batrak and Red Army veteran. He wondered whether it was time for the party to go on the offensive for worldwide revolution.[43] Frustration with the failure to effect communism at home seemed closely linked with the impulse to defend communism abroad.

In many appeals, the country's fortunes appeared very much linked to the personal fortunes of the supplicant. Indeed, a lack of personal security enhanced a sense of the country's vulnerability. This connection was clear in the danger posed by dissatisfaction among the unemployed. Conversely, a victory for one member of the proletariat certainly would improve the chances of victory for the Soviet Union over the hostile bourgeoisie. This logic, at times, was explicit in appeals to the central leadership. A number of supplicants requested a chance to be admitted to one of the military academies or branches, which would provide for them an opportunity to fight for the revolution and individual security for the future—the perfect symbiotic relationship between the collective and its members. In this spirit, a batrak from the Crimea requested a place in some kind of military school, since he "found out that our country finds itself under the threat of capitalists and therefore we need to create fighters, to defend the power of the workers and peasants, of the more reliable proletariat."[44] For some reason, the appeal merited a reply, which stated that, regrettably, the Central Committee could not override decisions of local branches of government responsible for placements in various military schools. Each area of the country was allotted a limited number of places that had to be distributed by special regional commissions. Bypassing their decisions would represent an "abnormality" impermissible for effective government.[45]

A similar appeal came from a party member and former Red Army commander who had taken part in the suppression of the Kronstadt uprising. He wished to obtain a place in a communist university in Minsk. It seemed that the school had received such an overflow of applications that they were compelled to turn down anyone with less than a three-year party tenure. When the prospective student showed up for the entrance exam, he was turned away. He argued that for him to return to his village would be shameful. He hoped that the "Central Committee, in connection with the urgency of the new threat of war, would give a son of the revolution the opportunity to study leninism and marxism within the walls of an institution of higher education."[46]

Both the party and the cause of communism had suffered after the Whites had been defeated; after seven years of war and suffering, the population as a whole was exhausted. But now that they had had a chance to rebuild their lives, many who had taken a leave of absence from revolutionary work were prepared to join in the good fight once more. A group of peasants from

Briansk guberniia, "lowly functionaries," appealed in June 1927 to be readmitted to the party at its time of need. It seemed that they had tendered their resignations after the civil war in order to rebuild their shattered homesteads and livelihoods, destroyed by Denikin's forces.[47] At that time, economic circumstances had precluded party work. But now they were "again ready to enter the ranks of the VKP(b), now when the situation is once again difficult and once again the USSR is encircled on all sides by the international bourgeoisie." As members of the revolutionary avant-garde, and "despite their youth," the peasants had once stood in the first ranks and wished to do so once again. They implored the leadership not to consider their "estrangement from the party during NEP criminal," since it was due only to "family circumstances," not to any presumed loss of loyalty.[48]

The allure to join forces and defend the Soviet state can be explained in another way. As one scholar observed, nationalism was "a safe haven in a time of chaos and hardship."[49] As many appeals illustrate, defensiveness and the urge to strike out at internal and external foes alike were often the product of personal and collective failure. Those who had been abandoned by the revolution sought solace in identifying with the myth of a nation that included them to counter the reality of their exclusion. This exclusion made the nation's defense all the more imperative.

Solutions

Many supplicants made it clear to the party leadership that it was their role to galvanize the population and build the armed forces necessary to repel an onslaught of hostile foreign powers. In January 1927, a party member wrote to Stalin, Bukharin, and other party leaders, warning them of impending war and bemoaning the unpreparedness and reticence of the Bolshevik government to develop a "proletarian" military strategy and inform the hostile bourgeois powers of this readiness. The question of war was not whether, but when; as the author pointed out, "No one knows what will happen tomorrow":

> The world situation not only does not rule out the possibility of drawing us into war in one of the nearer periods of the soviet power's existence, but just the opposite. The possibility of this happening is sufficiently near and sufficiently real . . . that the consciousness of the worldwide proletariat and the proletariat of the soviet republic is not limited to a general conception of the danger of intervention, but consciousness of an actual state of war.[50]

A deep insecurity concerning the future is apparent here. War was imminent, of this there was no doubt, and the proletariat of the world could feel it. The fact that no one knew how or when war would break out only intensified this apprehension. In any case, the Soviet government had to be prepared to defend their country and their interests when the attack came.

Several letters to party leaders thus offered recommendations on how best to defend the country. One communist wrote a remarkable letter to the government in September 1927. In it, he presented a detailed outline for strengthening border defenses lying within heavily forested areas, harder to defend in case of attack. He felt it necessary to make these recommendations

> in the matter of the country's defense, as well as the preparedness and military capability along border localities at any moment not only of our Red Army, but also of the local population towards the proper repulsion of opponents.[51]

In the same vein, a suggestion was made in October 1927 to Stalin by the senior engineer, evidently not a party member, at a machine building plant in Voronezh. In response to growing discussion in the press and on the street, he urged Stalin to begin plans immediately for refitting another factory in Voronezh to produce missiles. "Everyone says, and the newspapers discuss increasingly the threat of war. I hope that our chosen leaders will apply all their strength, so that the enemy does not catch us by surprise unarmed."[52] The engineer's admonition warranted a response from Vesenkha, addressed to the party Secretariat, assuring Stalin that "the corresponding work [missile production] in this direction is already being undertaken."[53]

Many supplicants urging the government to greater military preparedness, however, were not responding to any specific threat of war, so much as to the ongoing struggle against their natural opponents. A platoon commander from Chernigov wrote an appeal in January 1927 jointly addressed to the Revolutionary Military Soviet and to Stalin, concerning some type of secret weapon he had created. The inventor must have considered his invention powerful enough, as it "could not be revealed to the bourgeoisie until the final attack of the worldwide revolution." Because of his weapon's decisive potential, the author "decided not to jabber about this project where it would not do any good, but present the question for you to consider and decide on, as the organizer of Leninist ideas among the proletariat."[54] It seemed that if Stalin and his supporters were inclined to promote fear of invasion or attack, they had more than sufficient material to work with.

A large number of komsomoltsy and veterans clamored to wage war against the bourgeoisie in China. They appealed to the leadership to be given the opportunity and means to do so, as it was both a duty to their Chinese comrades and a necessity to preserve the revolution at home. In February 1927, two komsomoltsy from the Chuvash republic expressed their solidarity with the Chinese proletariat. They wondered whether the Soviets should not also help out the foreign proletariat, since they were in the same situation as Russia had been during the civil war. The komsomoltsy admitted that, although such assistance could be costly, Russia could nevertheless afford to extend

> physical assistance . . . that is, procure for them a volunteer army. We guarantee that you could find thousands of komsomoltsy who want to go to China in an army of the Guomindang. . . . We should be of use, we should fight until our enemies are finally defeated.[55]

As discussed above, however, although many appeals urged the government to continue fighting, for many the greatest source of vulnerability for the Soviet Union to foreign threats lay in the foreign enemy at home. The conflation of foreign and domestic enemies was underscored in an appeal for action sent in July 1927 to "Comrade Stalin" from a communist working in the Donbass government fishing trust. He urged Stalin to organize military study groups, as well as security detachments comprised of unemployed communists (an added benefit), to protect the party. GPU forces should be more economically utilized in "direct work and special security." Enemies were active throughout the "political and economic apparatus"; even in Moscow itself, "under our very noses lives whoever wants to and does whatever they want." The country needed to be prepared—for what is not specified. But the author stressed that "we need to be vigilant every minute, in every place, at every step. We need this preparedness to hit our enemies right in the eyes and intimidate them. We need to create a hypnosis of terror." He concluded his appeal by assuring Stalin that his was not

> a proposal bred by panic, but the experience of a worker from the time when we in the Donbass worked for two hours in the Revkoms [revolutionary committees] building life and order, and the rest of the time worked with guns in a barracks situation, both men and women.[56]

Clearly, the memory of the civil war had not faded—nor had it cause to do so. The Whites had not disappeared, but had infiltrated every facet of government and society.

Defending the revolution essentially meant defending the socialist collective. As protector of the collective, the Soviet government elicited deep dedication from communists and communist sympathizers who pledged to defend it at times of crisis and vulnerability. Notable among these were periods of Lenin's illness and death in January 1924. Undoubtedly, the threat of foreign hostilities proved a great unifier. Moreover, the appeal simply of taking part in a great, unified struggle cannot be discounted.

Anxiety over the possibility of war was widespread, but reactions to the impending battle with worldwide capital were mixed. Many supplicants encouraged the party leadership to show restraint and caution. Others, however, opined that the best defense was a good offense, and argued that the Soviet Union should adopt an aggressive posture, promoting and assisting worldwide revolution. Many youth, especially, were eager to fight in China and asserted their responsibility to help their proletarian brothers and sisters. Judging from many of these appeals, aggression often appeared to emanate from perceived individual and collective failure at home. Supplicants often projected a lack of personal, material security onto the country as a whole. Occasionally, they were conscious of this implicit connection and suggested that if the country were strong not just militarily, but also economically and socially, the threat—or need—of foreign aggression would diminish.

Indeed, a greater motivator to continue the revolution lay perhaps in the perceived presence of foreign threats to the socialist collective at home. In the popular mind, former class enemies—many of whom were found throughout the party and state apparatus—were counterrevolutionists and potential spies. Thus, the foreign enemy and the internal enemy were often completely conflated. Ultimately, the pronounced lack of unity and personal and collective security at home made the Soviet Union vulnerable to foreign threat, and prompted many supplicants to call for a cleansing of the party and government apparatus of internal/foreign enemies of the revolution.

CHAPTER EIGHT

Internal Enemies

FOREIGN threats to collective security were easily identifiable, but internal threats were more difficult to pinpoint. The list of internal enemies articulated in appeals to the center included members of prerevolutionary elites, such as the nobility, tsarist officers, bureaucrats, and police; kulaks; nepmen, speculators, and Jews, who were often equated with nepmen; and members of the intelligentsia. Supplicants assumed that these elements were counterrevolutionary, and their anxiety was heightened by a general perception that many of these "former people" had insinuated themselves into the party and state apparatus and thus continued to govern under the guise of communism.[1] The murky nature of internal enemies made them even more dangerous to the state, and more threatening to average citizens, who hoped to raise their social status after the revolution.[2] Moreover, as noted earlier, foreign and internal threats were intimately connected, often conflated in the mind of the party leadership and the population as a whole. Not only were "former people" agitators for the monarchist cause, but their class interests tied them to the international bourgeoisie.

The greatest threat to the new socialist society thus appeared to be the social and economic disparity that comprised in various forms the main complaint of supplicants during NEP. Disparity was not, strictly speaking, a human threat, but in the minds of many supplicants it took human forms. Thus, the common denominator among enemies commonly identified in appeals was that they enjoyed, or were believed to enjoy, a disparate proportion of wealth and privilege.[3] The problem, according to resentful supplicants, was that the revolution was not finished; the classless socialist society had yet to be established. For many supplicants, therefore, the way to establish it was through purging party, state, and society of alien, counterrevolutionary elements that militated against the socialist system.

Internal Invasion of the Collective Organism

Less obvious than the fear of war with England or even foreign spies were internal threats to the integrity of the collective. According to appeals, these threats included members or supporters of former elites (the nobility, military officers, civil servants, police, and tsarist sympathizers, and various social groups or nationalities), Jews, nepmen,[4] the middle class, specialists, and the intelligentsia generally.[5] All groups associated in the popular mind with, or who in reality enjoyed, social and economic privileges were objects of resentment. Because of the purpose of the revolution, its supporters considered the privileged as inherently counterrevolutionary.

Aside from any security risks these groups may have presented, their elite status past or present made them in the eyes of most supplicants an intolerable threat. Throughout the decade it became increasingly clear that the revolution was in trouble. The initial euphoria was replaced by disappointment, when economic policies and realities fell far short of providing what many hoped to gain by revolution. Most supplicants writing to appeal for assistance and vent their anger agreed that there were recognizable social elements responsible for corruption and for the failure of the revolution. Supplicants did not necessarily agree who these elements were, but all those targeted for resentment shared a common characteristic: class enemies were perceived as profiting from socioeconomic disparity; in so doing, they threatened both the collective and the revolution.

The grounds for social leveling are illustrated in the following resolutions of a group of workers at a "general meeting of the main Tashkent and Borodin workshops," probably held in 1918. After hearing a report by a certain Comrade Dubitskii, the participants resolved to instigate a Red Terror against the revolution's enemies and outlined the following measures: All workshops and workers were to unite "as one man" around the party,

> in order once and for all to affirm that all gangs not operating under the proletarian slogan "social liquidation of capital," that is, full freedom for the proletariat from capital and the source of all slavery, we consider to be our bitterest enemies and are prepared to engage with gun in hand . . . in a deadly struggle with them.

The workers proposed to: 1) conduct a census, in order to root out all those who were not engaged in productive labor and put them to compulsory labor; 2) arrest "certain heavy bourgeoisie" to be held as hostages; 3) confiscate wealth and goods of the "heavy and petty-bourgeoisie and speculators" and distribute it among workers' cooperatives; and 4) confiscate the apartments of the bourgeoisie and speculators and distribute them among "those who labor on behalf of the whole proletariat."[6]

It is clear from the measures proposed by the Tashkent workers that the true enemies of the revolution were not determined by their political sympathies but by their functional irreconcilability with the goals of the revolution. Those targeted as class enemies were perceived as possessing wealth and comfort disproportionate to the working population, and thereby defied the dictates of the socialist collective. The proposed measures give other clues as to what constituted a class enemy. The first provision spoke of anyone not engaged in productive labor—the assumption being that anyone who was not a manual worker was living parasitically off the labor of manual workers. Such people did not "labor on behalf of the whole proletariat," and this, combined with their disparate wealth, made them class enemies.

The social and economic disparity that impelled the Tashkent workers was not resolved with the apparent victory over the Whites in the civil war. Throughout the 1920s, it became progressively clear that the socialist utopia was not materializing. Indeed, the apparent growth of social and economic disparity during NEP caused even greater frustration than before. Several supplicants lamented that even by the revolution's tenth anniversary, nothing had in fact changed. A factory worker from Leningrad complained in August 1927 about the administration and the weakness of party leadership in his factory: "we live in the USSR, but in the daily work on the shop floor we do not observe any difference from the old capitalist factory."[7]

Why this was so, led to heated speculation and bitter attacks across the political and social spectrum. Most accusations of counterrevolution in appeals apparently were the product of disappointment and resentment. Many such supplicants protested that the old elites simply obtained—or retained—positions of power and privilege under the dictatorship of the proletariat. There was a widespread sense of anger that "former people" were able to preserve their control over economic enterprises, education, government, and trade. Prerevolutionary elites had infiltrated the government and economic apparatus, and continued to profit relative to, and at the expense of, their fellow citizens in the new republic. The issue for many supplicants thus was not whether the economy had revived with NEP, but to whom the fruits of revival were distributed. There was suspicion that the communist government was held hostage by, or selling out to, the prerevolutionary elite.

The task of identifying social enemies was exacerbated by social and economic upheaval and dislocation endemic during the years of war, revolution, and postrevolutionary reconstruction. For ten years, great segments of Russia's population had experienced a high degree of movement and dislocation, escaping or following conflict, searching for work, prodded by famine. The confusion over social identity was further complicated by a basic lack of effective communication among government agencies spread out over a vast territory. The situation provided ample opportunity for people to evade their past and create new identities, and for the insincere or criminal to further their own interests. Thus, one citizen from a village in Novgorod okrug complained in October 1927 about a communist in his locality, whom he accused of being an opportunist and who in prerevolutionary times had been a *chinovnik* (tsarist civil servant). With the February Revolution the chinovnik transformed into a Socialist Revolutionary and, after the fall of Alexander Kerensky in October, entered the Communist Party through connections.[8] Such a case of changing identity no doubt repeated itself many thousands of times during the years of war and revolutionary upheaval.

The difficulty of determining class origins or revolutionary sympathy was underscored in an appeal of July 1927. The supplicant was a baker by trade living in Odessa, until he was exiled by the GPU for desertion to Siberia, where he now languished with his family, unable to find even unskilled work, because no one was willing to employ a deserter. The supplicant argued, however, that the GPU had acted on misinformation. He recounted his history: He first worked in the communist underground in Poland, where he was arrested by the authorities for his revolutionary activities; then he escaped to Russia, and was transferred by various Soviet authorities first to Minsk and finally to Odessa, where he fell under suspicion with the GPU. A possible source of the Soviet authorities' suspicions lay in the fact that, as he admitted, the baker had served with the Polish border security forces in 1923. But, he argued, this was purely out of necessity, due to severe unemployment at the time in Poland. Indeed, it was then, with the encouragement of party acquaintances, that the baker began to work with the communist underground, since "as a worker I did not forget about my sympathies and solidarity, and feeling the yoke of the bourgeoisie and suffering under their yoke from an early age . . . I began to work . . . for the sake of soviet power."[9] If the self-proclaimed revolutionary truly was what he claimed, then he had been victimized; but what if he was merely an opportunist, or worse yet, a counterrevolutionary?

A similar case was appealed in June 1927. A citizen from a village in the Urals pleaded with Stalin to review the local authorities' refusal to return her home. It seemed her property had been confiscated when she left the village with the retreat of Kolchak's army. A report from the NKVD supported the legality of the confiscation and referred, not without sarcasm, to the fact that the citizen did not deny evacuating the city of Sarapul with Kolchak's forces. The supplicant retorted that she evacuated under threat of her life from a White sympathizer, who lived with her at the time.[10]

The general situation bred confusion and misinformation, as well as suspicion. Class enemies, supplicants claimed, had infiltrated a government and party apparatus only loosely monitored. This is supported by statistics.[11] Attempts to gather demographic information on the party and those resigning from it in 1922, for instance, revealed less than was hoped. Under the all-important heading of "social composition," fully 48 percent of former party members were labeled "unknown."[12] This statistic not only testifies to the problems of directing the growth of party and state in a time of social flux, but also lends credibility to supplicants' claims of the ubiquitous presence of class enemies throughout the apparatus, a persistent theme throughout NEP.

Such an atmosphere made it difficult to determine what constituted a legitimate accusation of past or present abuses or corruption, an allegation based on misinformation, or merely a cynical ruse to eliminate personal enemies or gain power. Indeed, in many appeals it was impossible to ascertain who was the accuser and who the accused. In September 1927, a nonparty citizen complained about his disfranchisement by the local village soviet. He claimed that he had been disfranchised because of his complaints to the volost executive committee charging the soviet with houliganism. For its part, the soviet claimed that the citizen was in the police "for five or six months" in 1904; on that basis he had been disfranchised.[13] One could surmise that the soviet wished to silence the citizen's complaints by digging up (or inventing) some dirt in his past, thereby discrediting him. One could equally decide that the citizen truly was a tsarist sympathizer, hoping in his turn to make trouble for the soviet. Accusations of association with the tsarist police might provide either a convenient vehicle for disposing of those unpopular with local authorities, or powerful evidence of counterrevolutionary sympathies.

There could be other motivations for exposing counterrevolution. Clearly, in a society riddled with enemies of the revolution, those who exposed such threats made a valuable contribution and elevated their own social worth in the process. Another offer of information came in a somewhat garbled message from a peasant and Red Army veteran from Voronezh guberniia. The peasant thought that he possessed some possibly useful information that he wished to impart to Stalin personally. He pointed out, "according to the newspapers it is clear that the bourgeoisie are all grinning at us, and maybe I could be a useful person, advise me in writing, since I have a very important secret."[14] Perhaps the peasant knew of a White sympathizer or class enemy residing in the district, and felt compelled out of loyalty to the revolution to disclose this secret. Perhaps the would-be informant sought, as he said, to be "useful," and this in itself may have been motivation enough.

The task of rooting out counterrevolution was not easy for, as many supplicants indicated, internal enemies were elusive and easily insinuated themselves into government and party. This was the message from a group of militia and allied workers from Eniseiskaia guberniia who wrote to Lenin and Kalinin on the occasion of the Red militia's sixth anniversary. They expressed their commitment to maintaining internal order, and their readiness to join the Red Army when necessary to defend the country against "the murky squall of fascist counterrevolution."[15]

Victims as Accusers

Most supplicants wrote to obtain satisfaction for a personal grievances, such as unemployment, the loss of a job, or refusal of compensation for work or of a pension. As might be expected, a class enemy or counterrevolutionist was most in evidence when a supplicant's interests were jeopardized. Thus, in December 1924 a woman from Simbirsk appealed to Stalin when she was laid off from her job on the Moscow-Kazan railroad after fifteen years' service. The immediate cause for her dismissal was a cutback of railroad staff. But the woman pinpointed the presence of "kulaks, generals, and officers" throughout the railroad's administration as the real source of her problem.[16] Similarly, the son of a "poor, laboring peasant" became a party member in 1925 after several years of service in the Red Army and with the agitprop section of the party. At the time of writing, he was earning a "wretched" salary, while still working for the party. When he was refused compensation for his party work, the supplicant became upset that "the son of a speculator or daughter of a kulak [could] I do not know by what means creep into the party" and come to occupy responsible positions.[17] There was a general perception that undeserving elements were gaining a powerful foothold in state and party, at their expense.

To many supplicants, in the matter of detecting a counterrevolutionary, actions spoke louder than party affiliation. The label of communist was by no means a guarantee of revolutionary or class purity. Thus, a group of factory workers from Briansk guberniia complained about the attitude of their Red director, an Old Bolshevik, whose party affiliation dated from 1912. Party tenure notwithstanding, they claimed, "there was nothing of the party member in him, that is to say, he is coarse beyond description, never views a worker as a human being and does not explain anything to him, a genuine gendarme of the old times."[18] In the eyes of these workers, an arrogant posture was inconsistent with communism at best, and at worst betrayed the elitism of a class enemy. The Red director was a wolf in sheep's clothing; he professed communism, but clearly only parroted the former elite, if he did not in fact belong to it. In another such case, an investigator from the center recommended the removal of a certain high official in the Odessa party organization, who favored and defended the "specialist-bourgeois milieu surrounding him" and consequently had "lost [his] authority with lower party cells."[19]

Counterrevolutionaries were found not only in the party, but throughout the government apparatus. Again, according to many supplicants, proof of this was in the attitudes and behavior of administrators and officials. In June 1927 a party cell secretary from Stavropol okrug appealed to central party authorities to intervene on his behalf. He had fallen ill through overwork in his various capacities as cell secretary, railroad security guard, and rural correspondent. Nevertheless, doctors who allegedly disapproved of his rabkor work refused to recommend the supplicant for a cure. Why would they refuse him help, unless they were reactionaries opposed to his revolutionary work? To add insult to injury, when he traveled to Moscow to present his appeal personally, the various central officials to whom he appealed received him coldly.[20] Such treatment, he concluded, meant that the government apparatus was filled with counterrevolution. It was no wonder that genuine revolutionaries were ignored or even persecuted.

Other supplicants saw proof of counterrevolution in the fact that communist sympathizers were refused support, while class enemies found assistance. A sixty-four-year-old "invalid-pedagogue" from the city of Lebedin, Ukraine, appealed to central authorities to help him secure a pension. Even though he himself was not a party member, he claimed to have once saved the life of a communist pursued by the Whites. This service to the revolution notwithstanding, the supplicant's request for a pension had been refused, and so he was "condemned by the social insurance department to death by starvation." This was an especially bitter pill to swallow, "at a time when former tsarist police and prison wardens receive pensions. . . . Does this conform with your own [notions], and generally with the tenets of communism?"[21]

Identifying the Enemy

The Ambiguous Status of the Peasantry

Its corruption notwithstanding, the party was still the final arbiter on questions of social and revolutionary purity. Thus, the question of how the peasantry fit into the broader communist scheme held great urgency not only for peasants themselves, but also for komsomoltsy and communists of peasant background, and urban workers and party members as well.[22] The leadership received many appeals to resolve this question, such as one in January 1927 from a group of communists from the Kuban who asked Stalin to clarify for them, whether theirs was a "worker-peasant" or a "worker-proletariat" government.[23] For many urban workers and communists, NEP policies favored the peasantry as a whole at the expense of workers. This resentment was exacerbated by competition for jobs between urban workers and poor peasants who flocked to the cities seeking work. Moreover, after mid-decade and the abolishment of compulsory registration on the labor exchange, competition for work favored peasants, who would work cheaply under any conditions. Moreover, young peasants often joined the Komsomol to escape the patriarchal yoke in village agriculture, but both Komsomol leaders and rank-and-file working-class members opposed the party line of peasant rapprochement.[24]

For their part, peasants argued that their status under communism should be equal to that of urban workers. Marxist ideology had introduced a false dichotomy between workers and peasants. The formal exclusion of peasants from the government meant that their status was suspect and their individual futures uncertain. They often sought to emphasize in their letters and appeals that they were not the enemy, but allies of the workers against common enemies. In an undated letter sent to Lenin by the "poor villagers of krasnogradshchina [in Ukraine]," the supplicants referred to the struggle they shared with the working class against the "landlord-bourgeois gang."[25]

Perhaps, thought one komsomolets, poor peasants might obtain recognition from the party by mimicking the workers. He wondered why the government did not organize the peasantry into trade unions. He found all previous answers to his question unsatisfactory, and quoted Lenin, who said that trade unions were schools for teaching communism. Therefore, he argued, the organization of peasants into trade unions would certainly hasten the building of communist society.[26]

For workers, including the peasants as equal partners could cheapen the workers' position as the preeminent social caste and jeopardize their official advantage in benefiting from government policy. Working-class youths viewed the Komsomol as a vehicle to elevate their social status. Membership in the elite brought with it an elevated sense of hope and purpose, which in turn raised self-esteem and contributed to a sense of proprietorship in the new society. Urban youth chafed at the admission of peasants, the very personification of the primitive darkness and ignorance that held Russia back. The peasantry comprised a lower social form, and their presence in the Komsomol and party could only serve to lower the worth of the party—and its members.[27] The "de-peasantizers" within the Komsomol, especially in Leningrad, resented any shift of resources to the countryside, particularly in the wake of increasing unemployment of urban youth during NEP. For their part, peasants criticized urban Komsomol members' attitude of political and cultural superiority.[28]

In their appeals, peasant youth energetically fought against their alienation. In September 1927, one komsomolets, addressing Stalin in the familiar voice, asked Stalin to clarify a passage from his work *Problems of Leninism*. Studying the chapter "On the Tasks of the Komsomol," the supplicant was struck by Stalin's assertion that it was "'necessary as much as possible to attract to the Komsomol all working-class youth and the better elements of the rural poor and seredniaks [middle peasants].'" If the Komsomol was a worker-peasant organization, the komsomolets argued, why then were only the better bedniaks worthy to join? For him, this was a burning question, since he "came from a peasant family," and so he requested that Stalin give him "a more detailed answer."[29]

Another source of anti-peasant sentiment was based on the peasant's perceived independence. Peasants themselves were vexed at suggestions that they were comfortable enough to not require government assistance or were relatively better off than workers. In December 1926, a peasant complained about the high cost of goods compared to the low price of bread. According to him, the workers clearly were much better off than before the revolution, while the same could not be said for peasants. For example, the worker had gained the eight-hour workday, while the peasant, who still worked twenty-four hours a day, "earned precious little, because his labor is not valued." Because of the inequity of the situation, he warned, "in the not-too-distant future the peasant will be forced to rise up against the worker."[30] Such language illustrated the extent to which the peasantry had been alienated by the government, by virtue of a self-fulfilling anti-peasant policy that proclaimed the peasant's inherent hostility to communism.

Similarly, in March 1927 a peasant from Tver guberniia appealed for a higher pension. It seemed that he had been wounded in the "Russian-German" war, but received too little assistance from the government to survive. He argued for greater assistance for all peasant-invalids; the government apparently operated under the erroneous assumption that peasants, as opposed to workers, could make their own way, whether they were handicapped or not. He maintained that, contrary to the government's supposition, he was not self-sufficient and needed help as much as a worker in his position.[31] A similar appeal from a peasant in Viatka guberniia complained about the injustice of the law providing that children of peasants paying more than 6 rubles in taxes were ineligible for educational stipends to attend VUZy (higher education institutions). He argued that peasants such as he were not necessarily wealthy enough to support their children through school.[32] This presented yet another instance in which the government discriminated against the peasantry.

The peasantry was not, of course, monolithic in social composition. All peasants were not created equal, nor were they unified in their attitudes toward communism. Indeed, its heterogeneous nature may have contributed to the government's mistrust of the peasantry as a whole, and to the divisions within the central leadership concerning the degree of danger posed by the kulaks within the peasantry. The difficulty of discerning between a kulak and a seredniak, or a seredniak and a bedniak, was obvious. In November 1925, a "peasant-invalid" sent an appeal written for him by a political commissar, the purpose of which was to voice the grievances of the poor peasant. He lamented the long hours the peasant spent in the fields, his barefoot children working beside him with scythes in hand. He made several recommendations to the party to alleviate the peasant's plight, for instance, by providing "agricultural machinery and tools on favorable terms." Yet, even though he described himself as a poor peasant, the supplicant would not have been so classified by the party: he produced for the market and made use of hired labor.[33]

Some peasants (apparently not bedniaks) even turned the charge of kulakism around on their accusers. If "kulak" in party parlance meant those peasants who profited from others' labor and wielded power over them, then, surely, the true kulaks were to be found in the party. A peasant from Mariupol okrug, Ukraine bemoaned that nothing had changed in the country after the revolution. The peasant had fought for freedom from slavery under the landlords and capitalism, under the banner "All Power to the Soviets," but now was enslaved by the party, which made all the rules and enjoyed all the power and perks. The taxes that peasants paid now were five times higher than under the capitalists. Meanwhile, the communists sat around in "easy chairs," yet

> a muzhik who has a few horses and cows is considered a kulak-exploiter, who eats only bread and onions his whole life, sleeps on bare planks, and on his hands are great calluses from productive work. Where is equality?

The communists accused the relatively prosperous muzhik of counterrevolution, deflecting criticism of their own hypocrisy. Communists did not even work for their comforts. Moreover, complained the muzhik, the party comprised only a tiny percentage of the population, yet controlled the government in order to reap the benefits and live luxuriously.[34] In his eyes, the true kulaks were party bureaucrats.

One study in 1922 by the party on rural communists appears to support the peasant's claim. The study noted that communists in the countryside who had succeeded in establishing their personal holdings economically tended to experience a "psychological shift" in their relationship to the party. Such communists often distanced themselves from the party, or dropped out altogether. But this was not the only possible outcome. Other such peasant-communists sought to remain active within the rural party organization, in order to influence it to the advantage of their own economic interests. The study concluded that the party had to offer support to the poor peasant as an ally to counter the influence of locally powerful peasants, who exerted an inordinate amount of influence within party organizations.[35] The study thus offered an explanation for the presence of kulaks within the party, namely, that a communist's socioeconomic perception might shift once he or she had attained some measure of economic security. Such communists became essentially indistinguishable from socially alien elements within or without the party and, therefore, further obscured the effort to distinguish the pure from the impure.

Complaints to the party leadership from alleged kulaks, however, were rare. Rather, most appeals complained about the presence of kulaks in positions of authority and, as might be expected, came from bedniaks. The party's ideology dictated, and the government theoretically operated on the assumption, that bedniaks would tend to sympathize with the communist cause. In this assumption, party ideology appeared to be correct. But according to numerous appeals from bedniaks, the party was not extending the support they expected and needed. On the contrary, supplicants charged, it was the kulaks who received assistance. One desperate family man, an unemployed veteran from Tula guberniia, lamented his inability to find work six months after his discharge from the army. He had been wounded several times during the war, and yet found himself without support. Echoing a common refrain, he concluded that "probably for the party I have become unnecessary." Intensifying his bitterness and frustration was his perception that kulaks got work with the approval of the local raikom, despite the fact that the raikom knew that party members were unemployed. This was too much for the veteran to bear. He was faced, he claimed, with few alternatives: "finish myself and my family off, or engage in banditism. One of the two." He appealed to "Comrade Stalin" to find him work anywhere, "even in Siberia, wherever you like, but give me work so that I can be of some use and so that my family and I can survive."[36] Similarly, a party candidate from Kursk guberniia requested that the Central Committee intervene to secure for him a place in a rabfak before serving the four years required of komsomoltsy. He had been homeless since the age of six, and had survived by hiring out his labor. He still had no permanent home, and could not live on the 20 rubles per month he received from the party. "In most cases," the supplicant observed, "in my area little sons of former kulaks study and receive stipends, [those who] even now speak against Soviet power."[37]

The party's policy of appeasement of the stronger peasantry had political fallout from the beginning of NEP. Statistics confirmed the notion that the party was losing ground among rural party members. The reason for this appeared to be mainly economic. Most peasant-bolsheviks had to dedicate their time to their own livelihood. Statistics compiled from sixteen gubernii on the period from March 1922 to January 1923 showed that 48 percent of those leaving the party were peasants. The report concluded that the "predominant cause of resignations [resided in] the attraction to peasant farming and material [lack of means]."[38] Reports of peasant recruits to the party yielded a similarly discouraging picture. An instructor from Orgraspred reported in February 1925 that efforts to recruit among the peasant-aktiv of Gomel guberniia were less than successful. In particular, he noted, the number of peasants within the party had increased, but at the level of candidate; elevation of peasant-candidates to full party membership was proportionately low. The report noted, moreover, an extremely low percentage of batraks applying for party membership. As a result of this failure to enlist potential allies among the poor peasantry, antagonistic relations emerged between local party representatives and politically radical peasants. Instead of drawing on such potential support among poor peasants, the party was alienating them.[39]

Other supplicants complained that kulaks exerting inordinate influence over the local party apparatus caused their expulsion from the party. In November 1924, a twenty-eight-year-old batrak from Orlov guberniia wrote to Stalin, "as a serious revolutionary and close friend of Vladimir Il'ich Lenin," "encouraged by my proletarian boldness" and "proletarian impatience." The supplicant had been a communist, volunteered for the Red Army, and was twice wounded. Returning home, he witnessed and exposed "notorious injustice in the freeing of deserters" and was expelled from the party. He claimed, however, that the expulsion committee had been influenced by local kulaks, who had it in for him as a former batrak and because of his previous activities on the Committee of the Poor. A previous appeal to the Central Control Commission had been rejected on the grounds that he lacked "comradely solidarity." The supplicant finally appealed to Stalin for readmission, hoping for a sympathetic ear on the basis of his belief that Stalin himself was a peasant.[40]

A similar appeal came from a batrak from Don oblast who had been expelled on grounds of discrediting the party and for petit-bourgeois tendencies. The charges stemmed from complaints that, while filling various party posts in 1921–22, the batrak had extorted grain from and beaten certain peasants. He countered these charges by arguing that the peasants in question were kulaks, who at the time were hoarding grain while many poor peasants starved. The supplicant argued that he had only done his duty as a communist, and that the charges of assault were brought falsely by kulaks wishing to discredit communists. He defended himself further, asking, "who among members of the party [in those years]" would not have acted as he had; it was, he claimed, "the duty of a communist to carry on a merciless struggle with concealers." The batrak thus admitted having confiscated grain from certain peasants but denied using undue violence. Yet, his hostility toward the alleged kulaks clearly ran deep. Judging from his appeal, the batrak's desperation over being expelled from party ranks was equally profound.[41]

Complaints about kulak infiltration of the party came from nonparty citizens as well. A group of bedniaks from a village in Erevan sent an urgent appeal in April 1927 to the central authorities, requesting protection. They begged the party to expel a certain "Abram Arutynovich Chobanian, son of a well-known and former rich man, himself having secondary education, who in 1921 somehow had the good fortune to enter the party." From that time on, the bedniaks claimed, the communist terrorized the village, committing random acts of violence against the peasants, despite attempts by the local government to remove him from power. The supplicants declined to sign the petition, fearing retribution.[42] According to them, the kulak was real and threatened the party not from without but from within.

There were even complaints from workers about the presence of kulaks in the factory. In February 1925, a Red Army veteran and factory worker from Vladimir guberniia appealed to the center after he had been fired on the initiative of a certain Kasatkin, who, he charged, was "an old black-marketeer and rural kulak," and who "put the workers in chains." Among his other crimes, Kasatkin regularly raped female workers and, if they resisted, put them to hard labor or otherwise threatened them. These facts were well known to the factory party cell and administration, the worker claimed, but nothing had been done. The supplicant called on his comrades to remember the days when together they defeated the White forces under P. N. Wrangel and formed "close ranks."[43] He requested that the center send a commissar to investigate and remove this member of "our internal enemies."[44]

The central leadership received numerous appeals from poor peasants, who claimed to be at the mercy of, or beholden to, their more powerful neighbors. Indeed, most local soviets formed during and in the immediate aftermath of the revolution merely retained their prerevolutionary power structure.[45] When these local powers proved unreliable in providing grain and implementing other orders from the center, Committees of the Poor formed spontaneously to gain local control and authority.[46] As appeals from bedniak-peasants suggested, the struggle between rich and poor in the countryside persisted throughout the decade. Many unemployed batraks felt that they were caught between an unresponsive government on one hand, and the better-off peasant on the other. Poor peasants looked to the central government for assistance and protection; the government's apparent unwillingness to help them prompted bedniaks to complain that they continued to receive short shrift. One komsomolets from Odessa appealed in March 1927 to Stalin for work. He had been an agricultural laborer but joined the Komsomol, for which his "kulak employer" fired him. The batrak then went to Odessa to find work, without success. The Odessa Komsomol recommended that he return to work for his former employer; this he refused to do. The supplicant begged Stalin, "as general secretary of the party," to find him work and save him from a life of crime or hunger.[47] When faced with the choice either of working once again for the kulak or starvation, the komsomolets apparently preferred the latter.

Similarly, in April 1927 a bedniak from Pskov guberniia sent a rambling appeal to Stalin, asking why more attention was not paid to the plight of the horseless bedniak. The supplicant argued, "our greatest poets wrote . . . that all should be satisfied equally." But while workers were much better off than before the revolution, with shorter workdays and better pay, the same could not be said for poor peasants. He assured Stalin that he knew what he was talking about, because he had visited Iartsev and observed how workers lived. Not only were their lives softer, but their drinking knew no bounds. Notably, the supplicant pleaded not for the peasantry as a whole, but only for the poor peasant. He observed that things were worse than before the revolution, because now everything cost so much. "Therefore," he pleaded, "you need as soon as possible to stop organizing the land to the advantage of those who have more, those who are more cultured and clever and always first in line."[48]

"Former People"

As the bedniaks' appeals suggested, and as the vast majority of supplicants implied, the enemies of the revolution simply were those who possessed a disproportionate share of wealth and privilege. Most commonly, those enemies were members of former elites who, apparently, had simply retained their wealth, positions, and privileges. Supplicants often labeled as "bourgeois" anyone whom they perceived to be living off the labor of the working classes. This indictment against parasites is illustrated in the appeal from a group of railroad workers from Tiflis who in March 1927 requested from Stalin the return of their pension fund, which, they complained, had been invested in the construction of an oil pipeline that was "making big profits." They feared that now their hard-earned money would become merged with the "millions [belonging to] bankers, factory owners, princes, landlords, speculators and, in general, robbers." The workers argued that in contrast to the robbers' money, their own savings had been earned through "physical labor of laborers," and thus "could not be considered stolen," and so they requested the state to return it.[49]

This appeal is revealing on many levels. First, it clearly illustrates the working-class morality underpinning socialism. It was inconceivable that anyone could "earn" millions of dollars—that kind of money must belong to other people, to other people's labor, and so was stolen money. According to this logic, and as the workers themselves point out, the only honest money was earned through manual labor. The workers, therefore, list and equate a whole range of groups commonly perceived as parasites—"bankers, factory owners, princes, landlords, speculators."

The Tiflis workers' petition thus also presents a fairly comprehensive summary of those groups commonly pinpointed in appeals as enemies by virtue of their (mis)appropriation of wealth and power, their parasitism. The list not only included the elites of prerevolutionary society who, whatever their sympathies toward communism, were generally despised by workers and peasants; it also referred to speculators, objects of universal contempt during NEP. Finally, the workers implied that the intelligentsia, too, were enemies of the revolution, since, if only money earned through manual labor was honest, then mental laborers, or "brainworkers," were also robbers and parasites.

The most obvious enemies of the revolution were former nobles. In April 1927 a Red Army soldier from a village in Kiev guberniia sent an urgent appeal to Stalin, alerting him to the presence in his locality of none other than the former tsar's aunt.[50] The princess Ekaterina, he claimed, was colluding with "kulaks, bourgeois and priests," and agitating for the burning of communists and killing of Jews. She was "very sly and cunning and elusive, goes around the village and begs from widows and officers' wives and old priests, who are supposedly very poor." Aside from her agitation activities and collusion with class enemies, the soldier was indignant over the manner in which she was treated by her hosts. It seemed that "they treat her like a goddess, kiss her hands and feet, consider her a holy martyr, because she's a princess, the kulaks in the village conceal her." The soldier begged Stalin to rid his village of Aunt Ekaterina, "since soon she will be followed by uncle, and their heirs."[51]

In most cases, however, the enemy was less obvious. Opprobrious terms such as "White guard" were used either literally, to signify those who had fought for the Whites in the civil war, or figuratively, for anyone displaying counterrevolutionary behavior, qualities, or attitudes. The latter meaning was employed by a female communist from Bashkir autonomous republic who appealed to Stalin, after she had been fired from her job as a housekeeper in a hospital. She claimed had become the scapegoat for her bosses, who fired her to cover their own mistakes. She said she was dying of hunger, and appealed for justice and advice on "how to find relief from the White guards Nikolaeva and Shashakhmetova," the managers responsible.[52]

A more literal use of the term occurs in the appeal of a Red Army soldier from the Crimea, a communist, who in June 1927 complained to Stalin about the presence there of "parasites," who collaborated with the Whites during the war and now wanted to wreck the workers' and peasants' government. The Crimea apparently was filled with many such

> scoundrels . . . the types who earlier worked with Denikin, Wrangel, Slashchev, many of them are still here. . . . I am always ready to die for the cause of the workers and villagers. Death to the parasites. . . . We will not allow blood, we do not want war, that is our slogan; but we are always ready to go to the defense of the worker-peasant power.[53]

The language employed begs the question as to what extent the reference to blood-shedding was merely rhetorical. In any case, the message was conveyed.

Another appeal from the Crimea complained of the ubiquitous presence of tsarist holdovers within the apparatus, threatening to spoil the revolution. This appeal came in September 1927 from a former Red Army commander working for the Ukrainian lumber industry who had made numerous unsuccessful appeals to local party organs over having been wrongly dismissed from his position. He now requested that the central authorities reinstate him and investigate the lumber trust administration. According to him, the trust was headed by "a well-known violator of labor laws and suppressor of the working class . . . [who] long ago should have been relieved of his position." The unhappy supplicant had been elected the workers' representative and as such had challenged the administration's policies, making himself unpopular with management in the process. What made the situation harder to bear, he lamented, was the fact that a certain member of the local raikom, who "by chance wormed his way into the ranks of the VKP(b)" and "listened only to the civil servants," sided with management. The result was that he, a former commander of the Red Army, not the traitors within the party, had lost his job and, with his family, was "condemned to die of starvation."[54]

A number of appeals implied or declared outright that remnants of the tsarist past had filled the ranks of party and government. A communist since 1921 from the Leningrad region wrote that, since being demobilized in 1925, he had worked in a number of civilian establishments and organizations. In the past few years, he claimed, he had come into contact with a number of workers in elementary schools, "50 to 40 percent" of whom were "still not so close to the Soviet power and party."[55] Among these suspect individuals were a number of former officers and civil servants who "deliberately distorted" the lessons of current events.[56] Implicit in this appeal are two important elements: a distrust of the intelligentsia (schoolteachers), and a pronounced haziness with regard to identifying enemies. Were the educators in question assumed to be White sympathizers because of their counterrevolutionary interpretations, or did they spread counterrevolution because they were, in fact, White sympathizers? In any case, to the former soldier the question was possibly irrelevant. After all, if one was spreading counterrevolution, one was a counterrevolutionary.

Other charges against enemies of the revolution were not so vague, but stemmed from firsthand experience. Ubiquitous complaints about the presence throughout party and government organizations of known enemies from the past lent credibility to less concrete charges and fears. Thus, a party member and former Red partisan from Ufa guberniia informed party leaders about an unsavory character residing at the time in Moscow. During the civil war, he claimed, this person had worked for the Whites and Czechs against the communists. The supplicant knew this, since he himself had been captured by the person in question and handed over to the Whites.[57]

A similar warning came in July 1927 from a worker in the Partisan wood pulp factory in the city of Kingisepp who reported that the Red director there was none other than a former White officer, who during the civil war had perpetrated crimes against the worker's own family. Moreover, the supplicant charged, the director's behavior at the factory further testified to his past identity and political sympathies. The director would fire any worker who "[kept] an eye on him," and even dared to strike an old watchman not once, but repeatedly. Such an action unmistakably revealed the director's true identity, as a carryover from the mentality and social system of prerevolutionary times.[58] Another such complaint came in September 1927 from a nonparty journalist, who appealed to Stalin for protection. He was working in the city of Kremenchug in Ukraine, but had been harassed and finally driven from the city by the party secretary and the editor of the Red press. The cause of the reporter's persecution was that he had leaked a story about the editor, who had headed a tsarist paper shut down during the revolution for anti-Bolshevist and counterrevolutionary tendencies.[59]

Sometimes, as many appeals demonstrated, a government functionary's actions alone could foster suspicion about his past. Thus, a Georgian wrote to the GPU in November 1927 to inquire about a certain financial inspector named Chernukhin,

> who severely suppresses petty artisans but lends assistance to kulaks and bourgeoisie, and therefore I am very interested to find out in detail who he is [and] . . . where he served in the revolution, as it is obvious that Chernukhin is a suspicious character, and therefore I request that you investigate, since such an individual should not be permitted to serve under soviet power, since Chernukhin suppresses the poor class.[60]

Eventually, class enemies would show their true colors, and so expose themselves; it was a revolutionary's responsibility to point them out.

Most often, it was the poor, those for whom the revolution had ostensibly been fought, who were most threatened by and resentful of former class enemies still in positions of authority or privilege after the revolution. Thus, a former Red Army soldier and batrak appealed in June 1927. After waiting for three years following his demobilization, the batrak finally received an allotment of land for himself and his family of seven. Awaiting his first harvest, he was informed that he had to remit all the proceeds to pay rent. Indignant, the batrak mourned the fact that as a nonparty citizen, "no one protects my interests." The situation was even more offensive, however, when "you see alongside you some White guard or some merchant's wife from Moscow using the land, and not just three, but six or seven desiatinas of land."[61] The disparity was harder for the soldier to bear, because former elites were profiting from it.

This was the message conveyed by a worker from Stalingrad writing to Stalin in April 1927. Among other things, the correspondent discussed how workers in the city thought it should have been renamed simply "Stalin," because

> in the period of the civil war we saw Stalin on the streets of the city, how he ran without a cap and without a belt from armored car to armored car and yelled the victory of October is ours comrades do not give it up to the generals . . . every worker and peasant in the USSR can verify this.

In addition to praising Stalin, the worker vented his disgust over embezzlement, especially considering the masses of unemployed and homeless in the country. According to him, it was the bourgeoisie who wasted the government's resources; but, he warned, "the proletariat will not put up with this waste."[62] The battle lines had been drawn. Now, it was only a matter of dealing the final blow to all the White sympathizers and bourgeoisie who remained, and bringing the revolution to a successful conclusion.

Solutions

In April 1927, a communist named Gorianov wrote to Stalin on the importance of educating the youth about their country's past. Revolutionary iconoclasm had destroyed the old society, obliterating not only its structure but also its history. There was a danger, the communist feared, that the new generation and those to come would suffer from ignorance concerning their "shameful tsarist past," why, in fact, the revolution had been fought in the first place. This ignorance posed a threat to the revolution's existence; Soviet youth needed to know what the party was defending. In particular, he maintained, the government should publish the newest work by White Russian émigré Vasily Shulgin, *Three Capitals*.[63] The communist argued that the government had nothing to fear by publishing this counterrevolutionary work, since it would educate Soviet youth about reactionary goals and sentiments. He closed by reminding Stalin of Lenin's admonition: "We need to remember more often, in order more intensely to hate!"[64]

For most supplicants, however, the problem was not that the past might be forgotten, but that the past was not past, the revolution incomplete. As Sergo Mikoyan observed,

> actually the [Civil] War did not stop in the minds of its main belligerents: the reds, whites, pinks or even greens. The harsh feelings of being exposed to death, the habit of solving problems with a Mauser in the hand, the continuous sense of a decisive struggle against some kind of enemy, practically without any limit as the means of struggle is concerned

persisted in the minds of many throughout the 1920s.[65] Judging from most appeals, the continuing struggle to which Mikoyan referred was due not just to residual trauma from the civil war experience, but also to a widespread perception of the enemy's continuing presence throughout state, party, and society.

There could be many causes for the failure of the revolution. One could blame the Bolsheviks per se, or one could blame the Bolsheviks for allowing party and government ranks to be infiltrated by alien elements. If, as many supplicants claimed, the problem lay in corruption of the party, state, and military by individuals hostile to the goals of the revolution—in a word, counterrevolutionaries—then the solution lay in a widespread purge of the party and government apparatus to eliminate these enemies and opportunists. One communist wrote to Stalin sometime in 1923 or 1924 about the corruption of the party apparatus and Cheka of Alash-Orda (Kazakhstan). Among those exposed were a number of White officers, mere careerists who had "dirtied" the party apparatus.[66]

Many supplicants thus suggested limited or widespread purges. In November 1924, a komsomolets from Briansk guberniia advised the center to undertake yet another purge of its ranks, since "in the period of time [from the last purge] a lot of garbage has collected that undermines further economic and industrial construction, and creates ruptures in the village that are undesirable to us." He could not give more detail in his letter, he explained, since he "would have to write a lot"; but he sent his "fervent greetings," adding that he would travel to Moscow to fill in "Comrade Stalin" on the whole story, but lacked the means to do so. He could only repeat his admonition that the party purge its ranks of the rubbish that filled it.[67] A similar complaint about the riff-raff ruining the party came in July 1927 from a militant communist from Odessa. The cadre had been working in a number of capacities since the civil war, including relocating workers into vacant homes of the bourgeoisie. He was also involved with exposing "criminal elements" within the apparatus itself, with the result that those same elements began to conduct a smear campaign against him. The supplicant pleaded with Stalin to take the necessary steps to remove those elements in order for the party's authority to remain intact.[68]

Another party member wrote from the city of Minusinsk in Siberia, to which, he claimed, "all the counterrevolutionaries ran off." Many of those same counterrevolutionaries, he warned, had entered the ranks of the party. The supplicant himself was currently unemployed, but had worked since he was small as a batrak for the kulaks. He observed that "most of the peasants are well-off, in the city as well as in the country. In relation to their convictions and connection to Soviet power—I consider them enemies."[69] In his mind, the party was not opposed by kulaks, but comprised of them. A similar warning came in July 1927 from a party candidate, who urged Stalin to direct his attention toward those applying for party membership in general, and specifically toward certain "kulak appeasers and wealthy peasants" in his own village.[70]

The question was how these corrupting elements might be exposed. An answer was furnished by a former Red Army officer appealing to his comrades within the party Secretariat in July 1927. He urged the party to implement his suggestion to form cells called "Tight ranks around the VKP(b)" throughout all government agencies and industrial concerns. Their purpose would be to distinguish "among the intelligentsia and, in my opinion, even among the peasantry . . . the pure and the impure." Significant in this appeal not only are the groups he singled out for cleansing, but also his motive. As it turned out, the author himself was the son of a priest, and as such was refused party membership despite his voluntary service in the Red Army. The supplicant's apparent motive for thus encouraging the party leadership to monitor and purge certain groups was so that those (like him) who were sympathetic and "who want to give themselves honestly to the party" would be allowed to serve its interests without fear of suspicion.[71]

In effect, the supplicant was arguing that revolutionary purity could not and should not be determined purely on the basis of social background. Yet, he appeared to contradict himself in the same breath by suggesting that extra vigilance was required for select social groups. The former officer's recommendation begs the question: if party membership ideally should have been based only on loyalty and not on social origin, then why was it necessary to purge only the intelligentsia and, perhaps, the peasantry? Could one really presume the revolutionary purity of workers or soldiers? Why were the intelligentsia suspect?

Identifying internal enemies during NEP was complicated by the extreme social upheaval and fluidity that characterized society following seven years of war and revolution. Determining social identity was confounded by a chronic lack of information, and by misinformation, itself the product of social upheaval. The situation bred paranoia; it presented the opportunity for class enemies to evade their past identities and thus insinuate themselves into the power structures of postrevolutionary society.

The center was flooded with complaints that class enemies had invaded the party and government apparatus. These enemies often were officials who denied the supplicant a pension or benefits, or factory administrators who fired communists and outspoken workers. Moreover, complaints were made that communists and communist sympathizers were denied work or financial assistance from the government, while former class enemies were not.

In response to these "abnormalities," many supplicants called for greater vigilance within and outside the party and government, in order to weed out undeserving and dangerous elements. As the party and government grew, the task of quality control became ever more difficult. Supplicants who had been somehow victimized economically often found a class enemy at the root of their troubles, but other accusations of counterrevolution undoubtedly came from more sinister motives. A charge of counterrevolution could be a powerful weapon. As such charges abounded, separating the suspect from the genuine also became more complicated. Sometimes, however, class enemies betrayed themselves through their elitist manner, or through their prerevolutionary attitudes and sympathies.

Ultimately, the unified party was the final arbiter concerning who might be considered an enemy and who not. In this light, the position of the peasantry was especially problematic. First, the peasantry as a whole suffered from their characterization as the "dark people" by social elites, who over the course of centuries had adopted a patronizing stance toward the peasantry. The peasant, it was felt, was stubborn and ignorant of the forces and processes that brought economic and social development. After the revolution, the Bolsheviks' charges of counterrevolution against peasants seemed to be connected in turn to their traditional and frustratingly persistent efforts at independence from government control.

Second, from the outside the peasantry was viewed socially as a monolith. Even though party rhetoric embraced the poor peasant, the party formed its economic policy in terms of "the peasant" at least until 1926, when the new economic policy began to be reversed. What that meant in practice was that until 1926 or 1927, the party officially supported the interests of the stronger peasants (the so-called kulaks), neglecting the needs of poorer peasants. This neglect brought a great number of complaints from poor peasants, who harbored deep anxiety over whether they were to be included in the proletariat. Poor peasants often complained not only of being deserted by the party, but of suffering continued abuse at the hand of kulaks. According to many poor peasants, kulaks had found their way into the party. Perhaps, some thought, this explained why the poor peasant had been abandoned. Finally, a few peasants who wrote to the government turned the charge of kulakism around on their accusers among the party leadership who, the peasants claimed, were the real kulaks, since higher party officials themselves did no work, but earned many times the salary of a poor village party worker. Among appeals to the party leadership, however, such charges were rare.

In general, the majority of appeals to the center identified class enemies as those possessing an inordinate share of material comfort or social privilege. This list of enemies included members of prerevolutionary elites; kulaks; nepmen, speculators, and Jews, who were often equated with nepmen; and members of the intelligentsia. This last category commonly, but not exclusively, referred to the technical intelligentsia, the industrial specialists in the factories and in government. The case of the intelligentsia is special and forms the subject of the next chapter.

CHAPTER NINE

The Intelligentsia as Scapegoat

BESIDES kulaks, the bourgeoisie, and tsarist sympathizers, a popular scapegoat of the failed revolution in the 1920s were the intelligentsia.[1] After the revolution and the fall of autocracy, the term "intelligentsia" referred broadly to professionals of all kinds who possessed higher or specialized education and training. This meaning comprised both the cultural and technical intelligentsia. However, in many appeals to the center during NEP, the intelligentsia were even more broadly defined. Included under this heading were specialists, white-collar workers and administrators of all kinds, and even those who were merely educated or literate.

The intelligentsia were accused, among other crimes, of sitting out the civil war (if not actively fighting the Bolsheviks) and living generally soft lives. Supplicants criticized the technical intelligentsia and the higher party apparatus, in particular, for earning far greater salaries than the working-class elite of the country, and this was the source of much bitterness on the part of unemployed or underpaid communists, workers, poor peasants, and veterans.[2] Especially for veterans, the irony of having fought the civil war for the sake of spetsy, who received high salaries and privileges caused deep resentment.

Popular resentment of the intelligentsia was intensified by the contrast between official glorification of manual workers and the reality of workers' position during NEP. Widespread unemployment of workers and peasants and their powerlessness under the NEP system stood in stark contrast to their revolutionary expectations. At the same time, white-collar workers and "brainworkers"—the manual worker's antithesis—were in great demand by the Soviet regime and were compensated accordingly. Moreover, throughout the 1920s, workers and peasants alike experienced relatively low opportunity for upward social mobility, while former elites to a great extent retained their positions in the white-collar segments of the economy.[3] The Bolsheviks' "psychological uplift of the proletariat," much commented on by contemporaries, caused workers' disappointment to be that much more profound, when they perceived that the working class in fact was not master in the new society.

The Intelligentsia and Revolution

Over time, usage of the term "intelligentsia" changed with events and depending on who employed it.[4] Before the revolution, it signified not intellectuals in general, but particularly those individuals engaged passively or actively in the improvement of Russian society and the human condition generally. This usually meant opposition to Russian autocracy under the Romanovs, and especially a commitment to more radical solutions for the improvement and direction of society, including populism, terrorism, and socialism. The majority of the Bolshevik leadership thus were members of the radical revolutionary intelligentsia before the October Revolution; when they gained power, in the minds of many, they quickly became allied with the forces of reaction.

Not all members of the prerevolutionary intelligentsia were on the left. Especially after the 1905 Revolution, many Russian intellectuals criticized left-wing revolutionaries for their contempt for law and religion and for encouraging extremism and destructiveness as the means of reforming society. These criticisms were expressed in a collection of essays published in 1909 entitled *Vekhi* (Signposts). Politically, some of the intelligentsia thus turned away from radical solutions to Russia's problems and sought change through moderately conservative or liberal channels. However, political liberalism—indeed, political moderation—had little chance of surviving in Russia before 1917, given the irreconcilability between democracy and autocracy. Moreover, on the eve of 1917 the intelligentsia itself, though expanding and diversifying with the growth of the professional classes and the new bourgeoisie, still included in its ranks almost no workers or peasants—the vast majority of society.[5]

According to petitions during the 1920s, much of the resentment towards the intelligentsia among these workers and peasants derived from an apparently widespread assumption that the intelligentsia did not support the October Revolution—or by extension, the proletariat's pretension to power. Early communist Victor Kravchenko observed that

> party men of the new generation accepted uncritically the assumption that many of the engineers and technicians educated before the revolution would as a matter of course be partisans of the old order—potential if not actual enemies of the industrialization effort.[6]

The historiography on the subject suggests that popular perceptions were mostly correct.[7] In the case of the technical intelligentsia, those who supported the Bolsheviks (even belonged to the party) did so because of the party's authoritarian stance toward industry, and for protection from workers and radical communists. The technical intelligentsia were almost universally opposed to workers' control of industry.[8] Soviet historian S. A. Fediukin remarked on the heterogeneity of the intelligentsia with respect to their acceptance of the Soviet regime, and attributed to the Stalinist mentality the erroneous notion that all intelligentsia were hostile to the communist government. Yet, even Fediukin noted that while many of the intelligentsia expressed "passionate acceptance" of and devotion to the new government, others emigrated and abandoned it, and some of those who remained, specifically engineers, were even guilty of sabotage. He also commented that engineers opposed worker control in factories and instead advocated unity with factory owners and administration to oppose both workers and nationalization.[9]

Moreover, as Fediukin conceded, other members of the prerevolutionary intelligentsia were less willing to cooperate with the Bolsheviks than the engineers. After being imprisoned and then offered a post as commissar of universities and institutes of Petrograd, sociologist and former Socialist Revolutionary Pitirim Sorokin wrote:

> [The communists] thought that Lenin's scheme for converting me and others into [their] allies . . . that is, making us tools in their hands, a feasible matter. But if my colleagues and I were powerless to stop their physical and moral suffocation of our country, we had conscience enough not to encourage or to participate in their murderous activities.[10]

In 1922, Sorokin was exiled from Soviet Russia, along with many other prominent intellectuals who opposed the communists. As for those who remained, according to one communist official, many who had refused Lenin's invitations to join the government during the years of War Communism changed their stance only when the party adopted a more moderate stance with NEP.[11]

The Psychological Uplifting of the Proletariat

Contemporaries observed that one of the immediate and most remarkable results of the Russian Revolution was the psychological uplifting of the proletariat. The consequences for them of becoming the preeminent social caste—at least officially—were both profound and potentially explosive. In their letters to the center, supplicants confidently and outspokenly demanded their due, for, with the revolution, came heightened expectations of social benefits and social worth. It was assumed that common people had gained the right to speak their minds and make demands of their government. The right of self-expression alone reflected their newly won dignity. The Soviet citizen, therefore, should not supplicate. It was inappropriate, an archaic and painful reminder of a time when only those in power had a right to speak out.

This was the substance of a letter to Stalin in November 1924 from a komsomolets from Ul'ianov guberniia about a speech published in *Izvestia TsIK* (Central Executive Committee News) Stalin made at a gathering of rural party cell secretaries.[12] As to the content of Stalin's speech, on the party's tasks in the countryside, the komsomolets was "completely satisfied . . . since [the article] accurately, directly pointed out the mistakes of party work in the countryside, indicated the path needed to correct them and the path of work in the future." There was only one point with which the young communist took issue:

> Everything was how it should be as Lenin would have said, except one place in your speech sowed in me a seed of doubt . . . in my opinion, expressed not as

> Lenin would have said. Here it is: "Once again, I excuse myself for the truth that I tell you." . . . In my opinion, Lenin would never have spoken like that. I've read a few of his speeches and everywhere you see that he delivers his speeches directly, accurately, deeply thought out and harshly, without any apologies for speaking the truth.
>
> I do not doubt for one moment that you have a superlative grasp of Leninism, only that one place . . . created the impression . . . that nobody besides dear Il'ich should speak [the truth] without apologizing.

The komsomolets clearly was disturbed that Stalin, the secretary of the party, should adopt a self-deprecating tone. He criticized him not just because Stalin was the leader of the party, but because he identified with Stalin. That Stalin should adopt such a tone of humility implied that "nobody [else]"—meaning those like the komsomolets—possessed the right to make demands.

One of those demands was the right to be treated with dignity. Indeed, the popular demand to be treated with dignity predated October 1917. When the first Duma in Russia convened in the wake of the 1905 Revolution, numerous groups of citizens petitioned their representatives with lists of demands and grievances they hoped to have addressed in the new democratic atmosphere. These petitions were filled with complaints of degrading treatment. Among the most politicized petitions were from transport and communication workers. The Moscow Post-Telegraph employees demanded wages above subsistence level, leisure time, and escape from the "arbitrariness of various superiors":

> We are not given a single free day during all our service, and to get time off, we must either humiliate ourselves or deceive.
>
> All these conditions deny us the chance to live like human beings: we cannot devote even a little time to our families, give our children upbringing, or supplement and sustain our own development.[13]

Of special significance in this appeal is the notion of what constituted a dignified human existence. This was defined not solely in material terms, but in the possession of leisure time necessary to enhance one's existence culturally, and to improve and elevate the status of one's children.

Cultural improvement was necessary to ensure not only the proletariat's quality of life but also the legitimacy of their political power. The proletariat that brought the Bolsheviks to power was described by one contemporary as "'human scum.'"[14] Another called Bolshevik supporters an "army [of] thousands of workmen and criminals . . . equipped for battle."[15] If these rough creatures were not only to retain but also to legitimize their hold on power in the new society, they would have to raise both their material and cultural standard of living.

The communists expected to facilitate this elevation of the material and cultural existence of the Russian masses. They were to transform Russian institutions and the Russian people into a dignified, productive, and fully modern social organism. In order to realize this transformation, the lower classes were inculcated with a sense of their own human worth; indeed, the 1922 Red Army manual defined military honor as "the consciousness of one's own dignity."[16]

Even rank-and-file soldiers went from being "pariahs" under tsarism to being the champions and defenders of the revolution.[17] After 1917, striking any person became a serious offense, because in prerevolutionary times, members of the elites could strike a social inferior with impunity.[18]

Most importantly, after 1917 the communists promoted a connection in the popular psyche between manual work and social esteem, by officially elevating the proletariat to the highest social caste. Bolshevik propaganda sought to convince the world in general, and the Russian people in particular, that the meek finally had inherited the earth as communism's Chosen People. And indeed, the Bolsheviks appeared to have succeeded in making workers feel important and instrumental in domestic and world events. A British observer remarked with some amazement that compared to workers in his own country, Russian workers in general possessed a surprising consciousness of, and interest in, the outside world.[19] Russian workers had a greater sense that their personal well-being was intimately connected with the greater scheme of things.

As Marxism proclaimed, however, and as the Bolsheviks well knew, social advancement would not occur without tangible evidence that the working classes—manual laborers—were truly preeminent. By declaring the workers and peasants as masters of the new society, the Bolsheviks raised popular expectations that this would actually be realized in material terms. The implication was that workers and peasants would cease to be invested in society, if it became apparent that their efforts accrued to the interests of an elite, as before the revolution. In the short run, as long as benefits were shared, temporary hardships would be tolerated. In the long run, elevated social status depended on tangible rewards. Without them, members of society collectively and individually would lose not only their sense of revolutionary purpose but also their dignity. During NEP, the Bolshevik government failed to deliver on millions of individuals' material expectations, causing those millions to lose faith in the party, in the collective effort to build socialism, and in themselves.

Disappointment

As the decade progressed, it became apparent that for a significant number of Soviet citizens, party and nonparty alike, the revolution had failed to deliver on its promises of a brighter existence, materially and otherwise. In the late 1920s, one observer wrote that

> the revolution still appears to hypnotise and fascinate the Russian mind. The horrors and sufferings of the civil wars are still fresh in their memories. And perhaps they find some compensation for to-day's less acute but more dreary misery in the contemplation of the tragedies and heroisms of the immediate past.[20]

Many Russians looked back with nostalgia on the civil wars years, when communism fought and triumphed over its foes.

Disappointment over the revolution's failure to deliver brought uncertainty over how the socialist revolution might proceed. Especially after Lenin's death, there was much debate in high party circles on this question. The Left Opposition, headed by Leon Trotsky, argued that socialism could be realized only through rapid industrialization based on forced grain sales from the peasantry. Moreover, the Left insisted that socialism in Russia could not flourish in isolation, but necessitated fomenting revolution abroad to aid in the formation of socialist allies. The so-called Right Deviation, led by Nikolai Bukharin, envisioned gradual growth of the economy based on a strong and prosperous peasantry, and the eventual development of industrialization and an industrial working class to support socialism. The proposals of both the Right and Left had weaknesses. The plan of the Left depended on the success of worldwide revolution, while the Right encouraged strengthening the kulak—a politically unpalatable solution. Yet, the issue would have to be resolved, and quickly.

While party leaders debated the fate of socialism, the population at large doubted when—or if—the Bolshevik government would or could build the socialist society they had promised. In January 1927, a komsomolets from Moscow wrote to Stalin, criticizing an article in which Stalin had claimed that according to Lenin, the worldwide victory of socialism could be achieved within ten to twenty years. The critic considered this scenario to be "highly unlikely," due to the fact that "we have certain economic difficulties [to overcome] in order to attain great strength, and the worldwide bourgeoisie is very strong." He believed Lenin had meant that only within Russia could socialism be built within such a time, and then only on the basis of a strong union between the workers and peasants that could withstand a White uprising. Significantly, the komsomolets opined that Stalin had made such a claim only in response to Trotsky, who doubted that socialism could be built within twenty years even in Russia itself.[21] Expressing the same concerns, another komsomolets from a workers' club in Poltava guberniia discussed the possibility of building socialism in Russia and bemoaned the party's lack of factual statistics and data. The debate, he felt, was too theoretical.[22]

Another tenet of Bolshevik propaganda that remained too much in the realm of theory was the exalted position of workers. As a number of appeals illustrated, the realization that the workers did not in fact dictate the terms of Soviet society brought great disappointment. In one appeal, a former party member explained to Stalin why he had left the party. The ex-communist's main complaint was that the party had lost faith in the cause of victory over the bourgeoisie.[23] Faced with their economic powerlessness on the microcosmic level, most supplicants concluded that the task of building socialism on the macrocosmic level was jeopardized by privilege and corruption.

Targeting the Intelligentsia

One contemporary observed that the cementing force in the Red Army was not any particular political belief or partisanship, but a common hatred of the barin.[24] But who exactly was master in the new society? NEP made clear that it certainly was not the manual laborer. To many supplicants, it followed logically that those who profited from NEP were the actual masters of Soviet society and, by extension, the cause for the revolution's failure. For many, the actual masters were the worker's antithesis. Thus, in the postrevolutionary years, "hatred of the bourgeoisie [was] transferred to the intellectuals."[25] The sentiment behind the October Revolution was "anti-authoritarian, anti-elitist, and often anti-intellectual."[26] In the late 1920s, it was observed, fear of the GPU was not general but limited to class enemies,[27] to members of "the Russian intelligent classes."[28]

Appeals expressing anger against the intelligentsia, broadly defined, were common.[29] The causes for resentment against specialists and white-collar workers were both tangible and intangible. A group of komsomoltsy from Viatka guberniia wrote to "Comrade Stalin" in April 1927 concerning a number of questions "that interest not only us alone, but all the Komsomol masses and even the peasantry." Their main complaint was over the government's austerity measures under NEP. The komsomoltsy protested the fact that workers were being laid off from their jobs in the name of economic expediency, while the government bureaucracy "wasted resources to impossible lengths."[30] Moreover, they complained, there were few genuine workers in the bureaucracy.[31] Most egregious of all, however, was the issue of compensation. How was it possible that white-collar specialists received up to 500 rubles a month, especially those who

> sat on their chairs with their cup of tea and their French roll . . . and ran around with their briefcases (akh! actually, they do not run but ride in cars), why pay [them] money of workers and peasants—it doesn't follow. We believe that factory workers should be paid 100 to 200 rubles (since they do the work) and reduce the pay of "responsible and most responsible," paying them 40 to 50 rubles and that's it. . . . The Central Committee of the Communist Party should not just talk about these questions, but do something about them.

The komsomoltsy continued their lament, decrying, among other things, the state of education for peasant youth, and ended their appeal by condemning the bureaucrats, who filled Soviet organs and treated the peasantry in the same manner as did "the old Tsarist officials." Significantly, the supplicants recommended that, in order to clear up the situation, the party should undertake "the most severe measures, even shooting [these bureaucrats], because the peasantry is very discontented with such occurrences."[32]

Popular resentment of specialists hinged on the perception that they were the new bariny, the unofficial elite of the new society. As the komsomoltsy implied, their resentment derived partly from the fact that intellectual work was still valued over manual labor in a very tangible sense. Specialists and white-collar bureaucrats were paid far more than workers, who did the actual work, that is, manual labor; all intelligentsia thus were classed among the parasitic elements of society, because they did not engage in manual labor. Moreover, the gulf between the intelligentsia and the rest of society, between intellectual and manual labor, was all the greater in Russia, because of the relatively primitive conditions in Russian industry.

In the eyes of many communists, the crime of being white-collar was magnified by the large number of bureaucrats and administrators who were not party members. Nonparty administrators earning high salaries under Soviet power, it was implied, robbed the government even while undermining it. In August 1924, a worker and party member since 1905 appealed when he was fired by a nonparty administrator. The communist had a stellar record, having headed his factory soviet and served in the Red Army, where he rejected the post of commissar, "considering it my duty to remain among the soldiers' ranks." The supplicant later became a party functionary but voluntarily returned to the factory bench in 1921 "to improve industry." Finally, he was transferred to work as the director of a *sel'khoz* (village farm), when a nonparty administrator fired him for unknown reasons, and now, out of work for a year, his family of eleven was in dire straits. He lamented that "the majority of those sitting in soviet establishments are nonparty, enemies of soviet power, receiving decent salaries and stealing on top of that."[33]

This resentment of white-collar workers in particular, and the intelligentsia in general, also stemmed from intangible causes. After all, intellectual workers' higher pay merely reflected the value accorded them by the Bolshevik leadership in the struggle to build socialism—a value that, according to manual workers and peasants, they did not deserve. In December 1924, a member of a district party committee in Smolensk guberniia asked Stalin to clarify certain issues "of interest to local comrades" raised in his work *On Lenin and Leninism*. The supplicant was angered in part over Trotsky's "incorrect" evaluation of the roles played by the peasantry and the intelligentsia in the 1905 Revolution. "It is apparent in his 1910 article 'Intelligentsia and Socialism,'" wrote the supplicant, "that Trotsky overrates the intelligentsia and underrates the revolutionary role of the peasantry."[34]

The workers at the bottom resented the privileges of those who were valued and well compensated. They resented specialists' higher wages and their higher status as well. Despite the rhetoric of the new regime, the intelligentsia continued to demand and receive the respect that rightfully belonged to the worker. The average intelligent was an "aristocrat . . . with [a] tradition of personal superiority"[35] unassailable by and inaccessible to the uneducated, uncultured, and unsophisticated worker. Factory wall newspapers criticized those who were getting too "high hat,"[36] and criticisms were "usually directed against members of the old intelligentsia."[37]

As many appeals suggest, however, resentment of the intelligentsia also resided in simple envy of the softer lives the educated were thought to lead. Manual laborers resented brainworkers, because they did not engage in real work—physical labor. But to what did many average communists and workers aspire? An education; in fact, a cultural education. In short, in the new socialist society, many manual laborers aspired ultimately to rise above the hardships and degradation of manual labor. In prerevolutionary Russian society and, indeed, throughout history, manual work was reserved for the lower classes. The upper classes were free to pursue intellectual interests, because others labored on their behalf. Brainworkers, the intelligentsia, carried both the privilege, and the stigma of privilege, into postrevolutionary society, and they were envied and reviled accordingly.

Thus, many supplicants complained about the ubiquitous privileges of managers, specialists, and higher party and state officials. Industrial workers and rank-and-file party members felt they were denied the most basic health care and benefits because upper level officials and bureaucrats abused the privileges that were supposed to accrue to the worker. This was the message from a party member, a village librarian, who complained that he could not obtain the recommended treatment for his advanced tuberculosis. He was told there was no room for him at a sanitarium, but he retorted that "[those] working for the ukom or uispolkom [district executive committee] and various managers and specialists in the uezd are almost never refused a cure." Indeed, he fumed, these people sometimes were admitted to sanitaria merely for a vacation. The supplicant feared he would share the fate of the previous librarian, who had been diagnosed with tuberculosis in 1925 and died the following year. Even though "the doctors considered him a social inferior," the librarian "still wanted to live," especially considering the fact that he had a wife and a three-year-old daughter. He also wanted to enjoy the fruits of the struggle to build a new society:

> In 1918 I returned from the old army and volunteered for the Red Army, was at the front near Leningrad, and fought for the happiness not just of the managers and specialists, most of whom at the time were against us, but just as much for myself and those like me . . . and I will serve as long as I live for the sake of society and the party. This is my last request to the TsK VKP(b), that they perhaps will find it possible to get me admitted to a sanitarium.[38]

Many veterans similarly expressed resentment that their needs went unsatisfied, while bureaucrats who presumably sat out the war received special treatment. In February and March 1927, a party member and former Red Army platoon commander sent two appeals to Stalin pleading for work. The second letter was sent because the first got no response, and the supplicant's position was becoming increasingly desperate. He had been discharged from military service in 1926 due to illness and now, at the age of twenty-five, was classified as an invalid. Despite his sacrifices, the veteran's government stipend was insufficient to support his family. In his second and more urgent appeal, he wrote that he had considered turning to criminal acts,

> But I decided I could not [steal], as a member of the VKP and as a former commander in the Workers' and Peasants' Red Army. Comrade Stalin! I beg you . . . to give me work. Comrade Stalin! Say openly, there are those who spent the whole civil war warming themselves in establishments, and many still who warm themselves without want, while we who bore the whole civil war on our shoulders and suffered in the most dire straits are cold and hungry. Once again I beg you Comrade Stalin! As general secretary of the Politburo of the VKP, only your words will have an effect.[39]

The message was clear: the real heroes of the revolution, defenders of the country, were dying on the street, while the soft, white-collar elite ate and stayed warm, just as they always had done.

As many such appeals make plain, animosity toward white-collar workers was also based on the conviction that members of the intelligentsia generally did not support the workers' and peasants' government that had seized power in 1917.[40] Indeed, being white-collar automatically made one politically suspect. In October 1924, Stalin received an appeal from a worker and party member from Minsk guberniia who claimed to have worked with Stalin before the revolution.[41] The supplicant complained that he had been expelled from the party "for speaking the truth" by a corrupt party secretary, who thereby "cleared a path for himself." What was hardest for the supplicant to bear was that he "was a worker . . . from childhood, twenty-two years in production . . . and I am not in the party? But Khrustal' is white-collar. And nobody at work knows what he was before."

As a final insult, therefore, brainworkers were granted the right in the new socialist society to adjudicate the fate of the workers and soldiers who had fought to establish it. The profound indignation caused by this state of affairs was illustrated in an appeal from a party member, who had a long record of service as a Red Army commander, from the civil war to 1925, when he was demobilized due to advanced tuberculosis. He managed to work in a civilian capacity for another two years, until his health finally gave out, and his military pension of 36 rubles a month was insufficient to support his family of five. When he appealed for a raise in his pension, however, a medical commission refused his request, on the basis that his disease was not directly connected to his military service. The former army commander was indignant:

> That, Comrade Stalin, is what led me to appeal to you [*tebe*]. It really made me ill, when those doctor-specialists sitting there at the Central Medical Commission claimed that my illness was not connected with my past military service. You know, you would have to be a real blockhead to call it that, you would have to have lived underground during the civil war and not known what it was like. What do they think happened, I was just playing around in the Red Army as a rank-and-file soldier and a line commander until 1920, and that I got this disease as a gift from the White guards? Only people who never saw anything and do not know anything about how it was for a soldier in the civil war could make such a judgment.
>
> I have a legal right to government assistance as an invalid of the second group . . .
>
> I think that I have earned it.[42]

The supplicant's contempt for and resentment of doctor-administrators is echoed in numerous appeals from civil war veterans. Apparently, the veteran found a receptive audience for his argument, since his appeal prompted a reconsideration of his case that ruled in his favor.[43]

A similar message came in March 1927 from a peasant and party member who appealed to Stalin for work. He had returned from his long tenure as a commander in the Red Army to his farm, only to find it destroyed by the Whites; since his demobilization, he had been unemployed for three months, with a family to support. The local ukom could only tell him to wait, "which was fine for [them], since they received money." His attempts to persuade local officials that they owed him some kind of work fell on deaf ears. The supplicant was especially bitter that

> wherever you go in these establishments, you see sitting there and working this worthless type, but you cannot say it, because he is well-spoken. But we in the Red Army educated ourselves, and yet no one pays attention to us. I request that the TsK VKP(b) settle this matter as soon as possible, because I have been unemployed for three months already, and I need something to eat, but I am not getting any help from anywhere.[44]

According to Lenin's plan, the conflict between blue-collar and white-collar workers would be resolved through *vydvizhentsvo* (promotion of workers into managerial ranks).[45] Indeed, many workers aspired to rise above their class and enter those ranks, but often found that their path was blocked by a lack of education and training. Moreover, many supplicants claimed that prerevolutionary professors, administrators, and specialists were unwilling to educate, train, or admit them into administrative ranks.

Specialists who were perceived to bar communists from administrative posts were wreckers of socialism and labeled as counterrevolutionaries and spies. For instance, in August 1927 an unemployed party member and former factory director claimed to have been refused a number of positions on the basis that he was a communist. He had gained his training in factory management at textile factories in England before the war, but was not blinded by his former association with that country: "In connection with the open attacks against us," the supplicant warned, "England does not sleep, and our enemies in the form of old specialists in the factories . . . obviously are all firmly united with one another and lead a campaign against the party."[46]

Similarly, specialists reluctant to promote and train the communist relief shift were often automatically considered counterrevolutionaries. One vydvizhenets from Kiev recounted how he had been promoted to learn banking and finance, but had been laid off, allegedly due to the opposition of old specialists. He had worked during the day and studied bookkeeping at night at his own expense, "knowing that the party's task was to create new cadres of proletarian administrators and organizers of the economy." But the bank administration and all the specialists save one, a Comrade Rozorenov, continuously exhibited "veiled opposition" to admitting him to their ranks, refusing him help and advice necessary to learn the business. Ultimately, the supplicant was laid off, despite the fact that no one had ever complained about his work. Indeed, he claimed, they never even checked up on him. The would-be banker lamented sarcastically his "promotion" to the labor exchange to find another position, "only because I was always outspoken and did not brown-nose or suck up to the administration."[47] This last admission hints at one probable cause for the worker's fall. As a working-class communist, the vydvizhenets had no experience in how to succeed in the white-collar world.

Another vydvizhenets, working within the Commissariat of Trade, made a similar appeal concerning the reluctance of old specialists to train the new shift of bureaucrats. The aspiring white-collar worker complained at a meeting in November 1924 that

> when we took part in investigations under the direction of old inspectors, the processing of materials was conducted by them without our participation, and we only had the opportunity to become acquainted with materials that had already been fully processed.

One of his fellow promotees felt that because of the inspectors' reluctance to include them, vydvizhentsy could learn relatively little working with specialists, and could gain far more by working independently.[48]

Undoubtedly, as these appeals illustrate, much of the resentment against the technical intelligentsia in particular was based not only in disparity of value and compensation, but also in the frustration of personal ambitions. Individuals generalized their frustration to signify obstruction of communism or of the working class as a whole, or a conspiracy against the government. From the point of view of vydvizhentsy aspiring to take part in constructing socialist society, specialists who obstructed their advancement indeed struck a blow against the effort to build socialism.

The tendency of frustrated supplicants to generalize their situation is illustrated in another complaint, submitted in March 1927 by a young researcher working for the paper trust in Moscow. This appeal was far more strident in tone than many, almost fanatical in its condemnation of specialists. The young inventor warned the government about a conspiracy among the old specialists in his area, the object of which was to squelch the efforts of young researchers like him and so, indirectly, serve the cause of counterrevolution. He listed the reasons for their conspiracy, including a fear of losing their authority and having their own ways and contributions superseded by new ones. This alleged obstruction stirred the author to such an intensity of indignation and paranoia that he filled fully half his appeal in slogans and battle cries in an attempt to rally the leadership behind his cause, including "Down with the old! Build on the new!" The "new" included a project of the author's own creation, a carton that allegedly would save the government huge sums but, the supplicant charged, was given short shrift by the specialists in question.[49]

The party leadership also received several complaints about the obstructionist tactics of professors and educational administrators. Professors of the prerevolutionary system emigrated to universities in Germany and elsewhere, rather than teach under the new system of mass education. Those who stayed lamented the type of students that became the norm after 1925 who hailed from "quite a different class, and were distinctly poorly grounded."[50] Working-class students, admitted to universities without having to pass entrance exams for which they were unprepared, were labeled "zero students" by their prerevolutionary professors.[51] In the eyes of many supplicants, educators' lack of enthusiasm in assisting workers and peasants to obtain higher education identified them as enemies of the revolution.

In July 1927, a communist and "provincial peasant . . . from the most godforsaken and poverty-ridden corner of Transbaikal" wrote to appeal the fact that he had been failed in his final year at a rabfak in Krasnodar due to weak performance. The supplicant explained, however, that he had contracted malaria, causing his grades to suffer. He pointed out that his record was good—he had spent his first three years at another rabfak in Vladivostok, had gained the opportunity to study there through a promotion by his local party organization. But due to his bad health, inherited from civil war days, the student was obliged to transfer to Krasnodar and finish his education. And when the rabfak administration in Krasnodar refused to cut him any slack when he became ill, his hopes to further his education and study at a university were ended, his dreams for the future dashed. He was "amazed" that the administration could have done this to him, a party member since 1920, and concluded that the directors clearly lacked "faith in the capabilities of the worker-peasant masses." Indeed, his own record testified to workers' ability to improve themselves. He had earned "better than average" grades, despite a complete lack of preparation upon entering the rabfak. The administration's refusal to support him individually, concluded the peasant-communist, could only mean that they opposed the advancement of the workers and peasants generally.[52]

In a similar vein, a peasant from Ivanovo-Voznesensk guberniia appealed to Stalin to help him gain admittance to a rabfak either at home or in Moscow. It seemed that he had already taken the entrance exam but failed. The peasant's failure was based, however, "only on trifles, the cause due to the presence of professor-bureaucrats, only because I was weak on a few of the requirements, because I did prepare." Perhaps, as the aspiring student admitted, he was not first rate; nevertheless, he felt he surely would have advanced but for the professors' unwillingness to allow him to do so. The supplicant, who had literary aspirations, wished to speak with Stalin personally and "intimately" about the plight of the peasantry. Having been disappointed in his efforts to further his ambitions through the rabfak, he apparently sought another route. He wished to know if he could work in some capacity in the Kremlin, as Stalin would not find "a better or purer proletarian, bedniak youth" to serve him. The supplicant thought that perhaps he could prove useful to Stalin in the future.[53]

Less common than specific criticisms of specialists or educational administrators were indictments of the intelligentsia as a class. In one such appeal, once again prompted by a refusal for admittance to a sanitarium, a party candidate, Red Army veteran, and son of a bedniak from Voronezh guberniia vented his resentment. He suffered from tuberculosis, contracted as it commonly was during army service. In addition to his illness, he had been wounded as well. He found his situation "offensive," and remarked with some bitterness that fewer and fewer places in sanitaria were reserved for those "of the lower classes." The truly deserving were supplanted increasingly by the intelligentsia, he claimed, while those who had served and suffered at the front became "forgotten comrades":

> Party comrades say that Comrade Tkachev does not belong to a union, and therefore they do not send him to a sanitarium. Comrade Stalin, I belong to

> the union of the communist party, but not to a trade union. Mainly the old intelligentsia belong to trade unions, and so only they get to go to sanitaria.[54]

According to other appeals, the intelligentsia's infiltration of the party accounted both for its corruption and for the consequent neglect of workers and peasants. This infiltration was diverting the party from the path Lenin meant it to follow. A party candidate and worker from the city of Tul'chin, Ukraine wrote in July 1927 to complain that a miner, a genuine worker, had been driven from the directorship of his cooperative. The supplicant himself had served in the army, which, "when I left [it], had produced an absolutely honest and pure individual, with all the correct views of the party and soviet power, which to me is my whole life." The cooperative where he worked had suffered under corrupt management until recently, when they received a new director. This man was a vydvizhenets, a former miner who "himself knew what it means to be a worker," and he soon set things straight. He established an eight-hour workday and "normal pay, without overtime." Moreover, he made it a point to hire not only communists but also demobilized soldiers. In short, the miner made the best director, because, as a worker himself, he ran the cooperative honestly, competently, and in the workers' interests.

All went well for several months, according to the supplicant, until "some kind of party fraction" agitated among the cooperative's nonparty workers and held secret meetings to plan the new director's expulsion through a purge of the management. The supplicant attributed this anti-working-class development to the lamentable fact that "the entire party organization in the city consists mainly of white-collar workers and intelligentsia." No wonder, then, that actual workers and soldiers were not advancing to those positions that they were meant to occupy under the new social order. The supplicant pleaded with Stalin to conduct an investigation of the local party organization.[55]

As some appeals suggest, anti-intelligentsia sentiment was reinforced by widespread anti-Semitism.[56] In the popular mind, intellectual laborers often were identified as Jews, heightening their alienness and remoteness from average people. According to a peasant from Gomel guberniia appealing to Stalin in July 1924, the local peasantry were opposed to the party mainly because of the type of workers the party sent into the countryside. The peasant claimed that local party workers "did not do a damn thing, thanks to their unsuitability for work in the countryside and because their work is of a purely administrative character, the peasants do not understand them." The party could not solve the problem, he thought, because "[as] we see, . . . who studies at party schools for work in the country excuse me for saying this [but they are] cobbler-Jews, who do not have any idea what the countryside is." The supplicant remarked that Jewish communists met with extreme anti-Semitism from local peasants, who complained that "the Zhids seized power" through the party, which in turn explained the poor position of the peasantry after the revolution.[57] In the face of such rampant anti-Semitic sentiment, of course, many communists from Jewish backgrounds worked to disassociate themselves from their heritage, at pains to prove that their loyalties fell squarely and exclusively with the communists and those they represented.[58]

Ironically, anti-intelligentsia sentiment and policies could also backfire on those workers and peasants, who were educating themselves through the channels opened to them by the revolution. Many supplicants bemoaned the fact that, having risen above humble beginnings, they now had become targets of resentment. A party candidate from Kazan appealed to central authorities to intervene in his case after his local party committee refused him membership, based on the fact that he was a white-collar worker. He pointed out, however, that it was only because of the revolution that he had gained administrative competence. He was, in fact, the son of a bedniak, and the only education he received previously was through a "village missionary school that I attended as a child, and where I [learned] nothing besides the law of god." Only thanks to the revolution did the aspiring communist become "an intellectual laborer." As he maintained, however, "at the moment of the reorganization of economic life (NEP), things became as they were before . . . which explains [my] poor progress politically."[59] A similar appeal came from a komsomolets and party candidate, a factory worker from Ivanovo-Voznesensk guberniia, who pleaded for assistance to enter a party school to which his factory collective recommended him. Apparently, the guberniia admissions commission had refused him a place, owing to his youth (twenty-two years old) and the fact that they classified him as a white-collar worker on account of his party work.[60]

In addition to discrimination, vydvizhentsy often experienced an identity crisis in the course of their metamorphosis from blue- to white-collar worker. Aspiring intellectual workers sometimes condemned the lifestyles of their nonparty class enemies, hoping to distinguish themselves from the prerevolutionary intellectual elite. In July 1924 a party member studying at the Moscow Institute of Civil Engineers appealed to Stalin concerning his persecution at the hands of a fellow student and roommate, who was "clearly, if not counterrevolutionary then hostile towards the party, one of those elements who tries with all his power to undermine the authority of party members in the eyes of the nonparty masses." The supplicant pointed out that he worked diligently at his studies and other duties, while his bourgeois persecutor led the classic wild student existence, drinking to excess and wasting money on road trips to Kharkov, "all the time receiving a government stipend" to study. Finally, the supplicant brought this waste of resources before the student stipend commission. In response to the attack, his roommate framed him before a purge commission, and the supplicant was expelled from the party. This experience apparently caused him apprehension that his social standing had been "degraded" to that of an intelligent, since he had been sent by the party to attend the VUZ.[61]

As many such appeals indicate, those who aspired to further their educational and cultural ambitions were aware that such aspirations in themselves might count against them.[62] A peasant komsomolets from Sverdlovsk requested in March 1927 an opportunity to travel to China to take part in the revolution there. It seemed that he was studying the revolutionary movement in China, and hoped to produce a "great literary work" on the subject. Therefore, it was necessary for him to immerse himself in the revolution, to experience and understand it through active participation and life among the Chinese proletariat. In his appeal, however, the aspiring author was quick to point out that, despite his literary aspirations, he should "in no way" be considered "an intelligent, with a starched collar." His only objective was to serve the cause of the revolution, he claimed, and he assured his leaders that "if necessary, at your first summons I will go anywhere you like."[63]

Many other appeals hinted that the supplicants' woes were caused by anti-intelligentsia discrimination. There is the case of a "rank-and-file party worker since 1919" whose troubles began after his speech at a meeting of his collective, in which he argued against the Stalinist initiative for building socialism in one country. The supplicant had been unemployed for some time, since no party organ was willing to hire him. Perhaps not insignificant was the fact that among his professional qualifications, he listed "teacher, lawyer, and journalist."[64] Another appeal came from a teacher and his family, who were repeatedly refused heated living quarters by a Moscow housing authority. The teacher described himself as "one of those intelligents, those cultural workers who always have worked with the Soviet power." Yet, he lamented, his family was literally dying of cold in an unheated attic. He appealed to Stalin to help him, adding that "if you want to help, help soon, because I am afraid that soon it will be too late."[65]

Solutions

In their disappointment over the revolution's failure, supplicants offered diverse solutions to the problem of how to build socialism. Some suggested that the solution was purely material; the mandate to build socialism was taken quite literally to mean building a socialist economy. And, indeed, building the economy would give the tangible results so necessary to the revolution's survival. One party member from Moscow wrote to "Comrade Stalin" in November 1927, wondering why the party did not speed up production by employing two to three shifts in factories, instead of one to two.[66] This would not only accelerate the economy, but also increase employment opportunities—and the party needed more factory workers for political as much as for economic reasons.

As another supplicant suggested, however, building socialism did not involve merely the construction of factories. This party member from Kiev argued that the workday should be shortened to seven hours. He pointed out that on the occasion of the October Revolution's tenth anniversary, when the Soviet Union would be under particular scrutiny worldwide, such a measure would "underscore the socialist nature of our government."[67] The revolution had brought a shorter workday to the Russian worker, but this gain was obscured by the general powerlessness of workers during NEP. Although the 1922 Labor Code had mandated an eight-hour workday and limited the amount of overtime and the number of consecutive workdays, these mandates were often violated or ignored by factory managers and directors. High unemployment meant that employers could demand any terms, including overtime. Along with wages, the length of the workday formed an important issue for workers. It determined how much free time a worker had for leisure and self-improvement. The appeal of the communist from Kiev underscored the fact that no solution was purely economic, because every alteration in economic circumstances had social and cultural implications.

As a result, most solutions were likewise framed in social terms. This did not necessarily mean social violence. One supplicant from Tambov guberniia, who described himself as "the simplest, most natural peasant-Christian," wrote that the answer lay in peace. The peasant's appeal, addressed to Soviet president Mikhail Kalinin, quoted Tolstoy and Herzen, and expressed confidence that "the U.S.S.R. is a country whose subjects can freely express their opinions to their leaders."[68] The majority of appeals to the center, however, did not adopt a pacifist tone. In the face of seemingly insurmountable obstacles, as evident throughout this study, many appeals voiced "solutions" that were both implicitly and explicitly violent. Most who sought the intervention of the party leadership were jobless, homeless, starving, or simply frustrated in their quest for a future. In their desperation, they sought causes for their misfortune. Removing the immediate obstruction for one individual, it was argued, would also advance the collective future. As one discouraged worker had suggested, perhaps the solution was "a good fight."[69]

There was a pervasive sense in appeals to the party leadership throughout NEP that the revolution simply was not complete, and that in this fact lay the root cause of the country's economic woes. Letters written to Lenin in the early 1920s are replete with vague but nonetheless powerful references to unfinished business in the social revolution that he spearheaded. Thus, a union of tanners from Viatka guberniia wrote to Lenin, assuring him that "the banner of the communist party and Soviet power" would not fall from their hands until "the hearts of honest proletarians beat within our breasts, which we are always prepared to present in defense of the victory of October."[70] A plenum of the Altai *gubsud* (provincial court) wrote to the party leader in July 1923, declaring their "firm belief in the triumph of proletarian justice [that will take place] not far away," and their dedication to the cause of "deepening and strengthening the victory of Great October."[71] The presidium of a district committee in Astrakhan raion wrote to Lenin shortly before his death, assuring their leader that his revolutionary ideas were the beacon "by which we look to the revival of the leader of the proletariat, in the steadfast hope that the hour is not far away when the Russian proletariat may boldly and loudly hail our seizure of power."[72] And in December 1923, participants at the third Kabardino-Balkarskii Conference of Soviets sent a telegram to Lenin to assure him that the "working masses of Kabardy and Balkarii . . . will steadfastly until the end usher in all of your undertakings, displaying the maximum enterprise and initiative." The workers and peasants of the soviets further expressed their hopes for Lenin's "complete and full recovery," that he might accompany them in the "struggle with the enemy, until their complete extermination." Exactly who the enemy was went unspecified.[73] But as most anti-intelligentsia appeals implied, for the worker to gain preeminence in the new society as the revolution promised, the worker would have to supplant those who usurped the worker.

The urge to bring the revolution to a successful conclusion seemed to reach a point of urgency by 1927. The mood was summed up in an appeal in January of that year from a communist from Sverdlovsk regarding the current party debate about the possibility of building socialism within one country. "It seems to me," he wrote, "that the time has come for radical socialist reforms."[74] The supplicant did not specify what those reforms might be. But this was the same year that saw the komsomoltsy's plea for the party to undertake "the most severe measures, even shooting" bureaucrats.[75]

Some members of the intelligentsia apparently grasped the danger posed by widespread animosity toward them and sought a more secure position in the alliance to build a socialist society.[76] In an appeal to Stalin addressing the precarious status of brainworkers in the new proletarian society, one engineer went so far as to suggest that a new government emblem be created to include a hammer, a sickle, and a pencil. This, he claimed, would signify the revolutionary commitment of the "laboring intelligentsia." It would also signify what Lenin had known "better than anyone": that "the proletarian revolution depended on victory on the economic front, only [possible] through the tripartite union of workers, peasants, and laboring intelligentsia." The supplicant sought to assure Stalin that, in the matter of destroying the capitalist system and "[spreading] the principles of Soviet power, brainworkers were no less interested than physical laborers."[77] In the eyes of many manual laborers, however, brainworkers themselves were the main obstacle that stood in the way of Soviet power.

With the revolution, the Bolsheviks had sought not only to include the lower classes in the government, but also to elevate them to the highest caste in the new socialist society. The working classes' new social status stood in stark contrast to that which they had enjoyed in tsarist times, when the majority of the Russian population constituted a distinct, and distinctly lower, class. Appeals to the Russian Duma after the first revolution in 1905 from a variety of workers essentially demanded equal rights; this demand was honored by the Bolsheviks in theory.

Many observers noted in the 1920s that by far the greatest gain made by the working classes in the revolution was not material, but rather psychological. One important component of the workers' and peasants' newly won social dignity was that they gained the right to self-expression. This right, of course, could be exercised in both a constructive and a destructive manner. That is to say, the right of expression could elicit positive suggestions for building socialism as well as give vent to pent-up resentments, expressed in the form of violent social revolution that the Bolsheviks allowed and encouraged.

The Bolsheviks also sought to instill in the working classes a sense of proprietorship in the new society, a sense of incorporation in building socialism. This mission would have been successful, however, only insofar as the fruits of labor accrued to the majority. During the course of NEP, however, it became apparent that this general amelioration was not taking place.

In the appeals to the center, supplicants commonly expressed the view that something had to be done to correct the situation. In the matter of rooting out the cause of the failure to realize socialism, the majority of appeals directed to Stalin during NEP did not adopt a pacifist tone. Rather, when average citizens failed in their individual and collective efforts to realize the social identities to which they aspired, their self-esteem was undermined, and they sought individuals or groups to blame for this failure. Many advocated a return to radical socialist reforms, in effect, a continuation of the unfinished revolution. Uneducated and unemployed workers often found a scapegoat in their antithesis, the intelligentsia.

There were several reasons why the intelligentsia were singled out for blame. First, "brainwork," as it was called, was still valued over manual work, in both tangible and intangible ways, despite party rhetoric to the contrary. Second, as many appeals reveal, manual workers simply envied the softer lives that brainworkers were thought to lead. Manual workers resented brainworkers because they did not do real work, yet an escape from the hardships and degradation of manual labor was precisely what many workers sought.

Manual workers' resentment also was grounded in their perception that the intelligentsia had not supported the October Revolution and the aspirations of workers and peasants to political power and social equality. Workers and veterans denounced bureaucrats, who denied them pensions or medical benefits and for whose sake the revolution most decidedly had not been fought.[78] Many supplicants expressed a mistrust of the revolutionary commitment of the intelligentsia in general, and white-collar workers or specialists in particular. They resented the specialists and bureaucrats for having sat out the civil war and, in any case, suspected that all brainworkers were counterrevolutionary beneath the surface.

Finally, many supplicants found proof of the intelligentsia's counterrevolutionary intent in their apparent reluctance to actively support workers' and peasants' material and cultural advancement. They believed that prerevolutionary bureaucrats, administrators, specialists, and educators, inside and outside the party, were actively holding the proletariat down, discriminating against them in job promotions and admittance to universities. This essentially amounted to what would be termed "obstruction" and "wrecking."

Later, in order to gain true sovereignty in the new socialist society, the proletariat would fashion their own intelligentsia. This movement was the so-called Cultural Revolution at the end of the decade, during the Stalinist war to collectivize the peasantry and accelerate industrialization. But during NEP, due to acute competition for work and education, the proletarian intelligentsia would be an exclusive one. In the short term, this exclusivity would have the ironic result, as a few supplicants lamented, that popular resentment against the intelligentsia was used even against those workers and peasants who managed to obtain an education.

CHAPTER TEN

Above and Below

THE main source of discussion in this study are letters and appeals sent to the Communist Party leadership during the crucial stage of development of the Soviet state under NEP. The central question is, how did these letters and appeals influence the Soviet leadership and the course of events? How can we determine the connection between the aspirations and frustrations of common citizens and the development of the state and politics? The connection, in other words, between the popular will and Stalin's program?

The purpose of this study was to see why the early Soviet state developed as it did, why Stalinism emerged and not something else. The best way to determine this was to view society as a whole—to understand Stalinism by looking not at Stalin, but at the wider society and the wider world that made him, to contextualize Stalinism within the Soviet Union of the 1920s as Stalin was rising to power.[1] This approach rejects Soviet history as *sui generis*,[2] and discards, to a certain degree, earlier working models in scholarship on the Soviet period which viewed the Soviet state either from above (in the Cold War model) or from below (in the revisionist model), but never together, as one.[3] In short, this study attempts to eliminate the dichotomy between above and below, based on the premise that both state and society emanated from the same conditions.

The analysis of how these letters influenced Stalin is based on both direct and indirect, or, perhaps, more tangible and less tangible connections. There is evidence that, like Lenin, perhaps to an unusual degree among the party leadership, Stalin actually read appeals to the center. This, in turn, raises the question of which appeals were read—and used. Were the appeals in this study collected precisely because of the messages they conveyed? It is impossible to know. It is also difficult to determine precisely whether, or to what degree, the messages from below anticipated policy above, passed to the general public through the press and to the party through directives. We must consider, however, the position of the Bolshevik leadership in theory and practice. After all, it is not as though politicians generally, but especially the Bolsheviks (or Stalin particularly), who endeavored to show they were in control of Soviet society, would say, "You know, the other day I read a letter . . ." More likely, they would say, "Such and such is the will of the proletariat . . ."

On a more intangible level is a wealth of evidence of connections between leader and led. These include thematic links—evidence of shared goals, concerns, and agendas; implied links through shared backgrounds and experiences; and, finally, what might be considered psychological links, a sort of mutual identification. In this regard, much work has been done in the case of Nazi Germany and Hitler's connections with the German *Volk* that could profitably be applied to the Soviet case.[4]

Many historians and biographers have commented on how Stalin's early life shaped his character and his leadership. But there is little analysis on how Stalin's experiences and attitudes might have connected him to average people, political supporters or segments of Soviet society later on, or how these attributes might have helped others to sense or form a bond with him. Judging from appeals, a bond did exist between Stalin and his constituency, as it were, that might be summarized as a similarity of grievances and goals, combined with a fanatical hatred of elites (including the party elite) and a mutual connection felt and expressed on both sides: Stalin's personal bond with the masses.

These links and commonalities are considered below as five related aspects: direct connections, thematic connections, experiential connections, social connections, and Stalin's role as leader. Taken together, when we see the remarkable convergence between Stalin/ism on the one hand and certain segments of popular opinion in early Soviet society on the other, a final question suggests itself: who, in fact, was leading whom? We have it on Stalin's authority that the abandonment of NEP and the Great Turn was a revolution from above, but why take Stalin's word for it?

Direct Connections

Modern biographies of Stalin note that, contrary to traditional notions about his intellectual inferiority to his rivals for party leadership, he was extremely bright and widely read. One study noted that he was a "voracious reader" of history and politics, especially on matters that concerned Russian historical political and economic development.[5] Another study describes Stalin as "a super-intelligent and gifted politician for whom his own historic role was paramount, a nervy intellectual who maniacally read history and literature."[6]

But that is not all he read, apparently, since, as noted above, there is evidence that Stalin actually read correspondence and appeals from average citizens. This evidence comes both from occasional data in the archives noted in this study, as well as from observations made in his biographies.[7] It is also useful here to compare Stalin's attitude toward popular appeals with that of other Soviet leaders.[8] Relevant to this is Stalin's own conception of his special, even unique role in the revolution, discussed below.

Thematic Connections

On a more indirect or intangible level, it is evident that popular and Stalinist agendas converge and intersect in many ways. There is a startling, even ominous, connection between messages to the center in the mid 1920s—long before the so-called Great Turn—and later developments under Stalin. We can even see a convergence in language and ideals, a correspondence of interests and identity, between appeals to Stalin in the mid 1920s, on the one hand, and Stalin's own prerevolutionary agitation and personal appeals to the tsarist government on the other.

For instance, there is the theme of anti-elitism, imagining elites as vampires feeding off the blood of laborers. Agitating among factory workers in 1902, Stalin was instrumental in staging a strike against factory management. The slogans used in leaflets calling for the successful strike that followed included: "'Others live off our labour; they drink our blood; our oppressors quench their thirst with the tears of our wives, children and relatives.'"[9] Compare this language with the letter quoted earlier from a communist factory worker writing in the mid-20s to Stalin:

> The worker went to the front to defend the interests of his brothers, but he still sees the bourgeoisie today, those who, at the same time that the worker was defending the interests of the masses, put on balls, feasted and drank workers' blood, and [even though] the revolutionary working class was victorious, the capitalist bourgeoisie lives. . . . As the bourgeoisie grows, so does the oppression of the working class. . . . No one is claiming that unjust laws are issued by the center . . . but why after ten years in power have they not eliminated inequality of rights among people? Why can one [person] eat, drink, promenade, and spend money on foolishness, and another not get enough to eat or drink? Why are the lowly left everywhere to fate? . . . Why are there so many hungry, cold people? . . . These are questions that trouble many millions of the masses. . . .
>
> Ending my appeal I beg you to answer these burning questions, knowing that I appeal to an old comrade, to a former exile and prisoner, to a comrade, at the memory of whose name the whole proletariat brightens up and senses before them a solid future.[10]

Another theme is hardship, ubiquitous in appeals used throughout this study. Note the similarities between many appeals used herein and this appeal to the governor of the Caucasus made by Stalin after his arrest in April 1902 and sentence to three years' exile in eastern Siberia:

> A humble petition. My choking cough is worsening. My old mother, abandoned by her husband twelve years ago and in a hopeless situation, sees me as the sole support of her life. . . . I beg the chancellery of the chief authorities not to ignore me and answer my petition.[11]

There is another way in which Stalin is uniquely connected to the masses. Like many of them, he viewed both the party and the greater socialist utopia as family. One historian noted: "A loner always, Stalin was never really alone. The party was his society, his group of meaningful others."[12] This was also demonstrated at a celebration of his fiftieth birthday in December 1929, when Stalin responded with gratitude to

> the great party of the working class that bore me and reared me in its own image and likeness. . . . You need have no doubt, comrades, that I am prepared in the future, too, to devote to the cause of the working class, the proletarian revolution and world communism, all my strength, all my ability and, if need be, all my blood, drop by drop.[13]

References to the party or other organizations as providing a parent or family are common in appeals examined in this study, for instance, when a Red Army veteran from Yaroslavl guberniia wrote to Stalin for work in 1927 about entering the party: "I joined its ranks . . . like a son in need."[14]

The idea of party as family may also explain the importance of party unity for Stalin and others throughout the party. Perhaps unity meant something more than maintaining control and saving the revolution, as it certainly did for Lenin, or about saving one's position, as it surely did for many others.[15]

Another critical theme to consider was identifying enemies and using terror and violence to remove them. Historians have long noted that use of terror became ingrained in the early Soviet state.[16]

> When an armed uprising took place in Penza in August 1918, Lenin ordered the local authorities to use "merciless mass terror against kulaks, priests, and White Guards." Then came the "Red Terror" decree of 5 September 1918, which specified that "the Soviet republic should be made secure against class enemies by isolating them in concentration camps." Terrorist acts by Socialist-Revolutionaries in 1918 . . . [including] the attempted assassination of Lenin, were met with terrorist response on a large scale. Lenin and most other Bolshevik leaders saw state terror—summary justice, shooting on the spot, taking of hostages, arbitrary imprisonment, and the like—not simply as a necessary response to terrorist provocation, but also as a legitimate instrument of revolutionary action from above.[17]

However—and this is often left out in studies of the postrevolutionary communist state—terror certainly was long a part of both Russian revolutionary culture and tsarist government practice. In other words, the Bolsheviks generally, and Stalin particularly, were not exceptional in their use of terror and violence, both as a means of social control and for removal of dangerous elements.

As to the question of identifying enemies, one biographer noted that "the category of persons subject to terror and other forms of repression as class enemies was ominously elastic in Lenin-inspired thought and practice of the revolutionary period."[18] Note the reference to "Lenin-inspired thought and practice." This statement can be made without challenge only on the assumption—still prevalent in scholarship on the Soviet period—that the totalitarian model of the state controlling society is legitimate. If we hypothesize, however, a different model of Soviet government, namely, that both state and society emanate from the same conditions and grew out of the same influences, then the problem of the genesis of violence, and the language used to describe and engender it, is resolved. Thus, if we do not assume that the Bolsheviks invented either the language or the practice, where does it come from?

Experiential Connections: Stalin as a Product of Past and Future War

According to one recent work, Russians have long agonized over the meaning of violence in their culture.[19] More immediately, the influence of the civil war experience on language, method, and, indeed, virtually every aspect of the early Soviet state, has also long been recognized by historians:

> The Civil War . . . was a formative time in Stalin's political life. The militarized culture of the Civil War later showed in his authoritarian propensity to issue commands, his ex-political-commissar's ruthlessness, his habitual style of dress (party tunic and high Russian leather boots), his ready coarseness of expression, and even in later reminiscences, as when he recalled with relish how a unit of Red Army soldiers scoured Odessa in 1920 in search of the insidious "Entente" that they had heard was responsible for the war they were fighting.[20]

As countless appeals show, this was true not only for the party rank and file and veterans,[21] but also for the population as a whole.[22]

The war influenced both rhetoric and social and political experience in many ways: the omnipresence of violence in social discourse, the tendency to view every challenge as a military campaign, the search for enemies, the need to root them out. All of these themes are played out both in the party leadership in their struggle to construct and govern a new and powerful society, and among the general population, in individual struggles to be included in that new society.[23]

But, of course, the battle against enemies foreign and domestic did not end with the conclusion of the civil war in 1921 and the reversion to a capitalist social and economic order under NEP. Judging from appeals, for many people there clearly was another, more eternal source for the violence, namely, class resentment and anger.

Social Connections: Stalin as the Champion of Joe Six-pack

In seeking to explain the origins of violence in the ongoing revolution and Stalin's special role in this regard, we must consider how Stalin more closely represented the common man through a common background. Biographies provide ample evidence—albeit not intentionally—that Stalin was connected with the masses in ways that other Soviet leaders could not have been.

Common Social Background

First, Stalin came from a common background: his father and mother were born serfs and belonged to the peasant estate after emancipation.[24] This matters, because it meant that Stalin was one of the few Bolshevik leaders who knew from personal experience what poverty and struggle meant, what it meant to come from what we would today call a disadvantaged background.

His background, however, was beyond common. That Stalin's childhood was filled with physical abuse from both father and mother has been used by many historians to show the psychological basis for his ruthless and sadistic tendencies as leader. But these beatings also fostered in him a vengeful nature that squared with certain revolutionary tendencies expressed throughout the appeals in this study. A friend noted that "from childhood on, Soso was driven by a desire for revenge."[25] It also naturally fostered in Stalin lifelong feelings of anxiety and insecurity. As one historian put it,

> His wretched childhood, particularly the beatings inflicted on him and on his mother in his presence by the heavy-drinking Vissarion, evidently generated in young Stalin the basic anxiety that can lead a child to develop a neurotic personality. What does this mean? A person whose adverse emotional experiences in childhood cause basic anxiety, meaning a sense of being isolated and helpless in a potentially hostile world, tends to seek and find a rock of inner security by forming an idealized image of himself, for example, as a great warrior. Gradually and unconsciously . . . the young person moves from self-idealizing to adopting the idealized self as his true identity, the person he believes himself to be. From then on his energies are invested in the unceasing effort to prove the ideal self in action and gain others' affirmation of it. Karen Horney calls this the search for glory.[26]

What did this mean for his position in the Bolshevik leadership? It meant that Stalin was uniquely equipped to comprehend the deep insecurities among the general population during NEP and the anger and frustration, evident in countless appeals, and use it to his political advantage.

And, like many survivors of childhood abuse, Stalin learned to fight back. One reason why young Stalin abandoned his religious education was a crisis of faith: as a student at a church school in Gori (where Russian was compulsory and he received further beatings for speaking Georgian), Stalin was apparently intellectually bright but defiant; he was devout but turned against Christianity, because he could not understand why Jesus did not fight back against his tormentors.[27]

Instinctive Socialism

Stalin's understanding of socialism and its purpose seemed to be based on a basic, instinctive sensitivity to, and resentment of, the gap that separated the haves and have-nots. For him, the purpose of socialism was not so much to level society, as to eliminate and replace his and society's oppressors (the last shall be first), starting with his rivals among the party leaders who dismissed him. This is a critical point of connection between Stalin and the common man, and one, again, that sets him apart from the party elite. In other words, unlike other leaders, for whom building socialism, eradicating social injustice, was an intellectual exercise, for Stalin, social injustice and exclusion was part of his personal experience.[28] Most Bolshevik leaders (and most historians) clearly understood social injustice only on an intellectual level, having no experience of it themselves and thus no personal stake in its elimination, as it were.[29] This lack of understanding registers at times as snobbery, or even mockery:

> Unfortunately, little is known about what attracted Soso to social democracy. Nationalism could have provided a solution to the problems he saw in Georgia: salvation through a particular group called a "nation." Indeed, Soso so admired the hero and avenger, Koba, of the Georgian nationalist writer A. Kazbegi's *The Patricide* that he later took his name. Marxism offered a different solution, however: the universal salvation of human society through a particular group called a "class." . . . Clearly, Soso, of humble origin, was keenly aware of social injustice, not just national injustice: at the seminary he had been caught with works by the French writer and republican Victor Hugo and was punished accordingly. . . . Marxism, with its universal salvation for all mankind, proved more attractive than nationalism, cutting across national lines and presenting a radical, international solution: a new rule by the oppressed and exploited class of workers.[30]

Here is a tragic irony: historians from elite backgrounds cannot grasp the driving force behind revolution, because it is for them an intellectual problem. But this dichotomy between above and below, from the point of view of the common man, was precisely what the revolution was meant to destroy.

This instinctive class resentment and hatred is often expressed violently throughout letters and appeals. Like those supplicants, Stalin's understanding of socialism was personal. Stalin thus had a basis for connection with common people that other leaders could not.

Moreover, a particular understanding of socialism would determine revolutionary method. Within the prerevolutionary Russian Social Democratic Workers' Party, Stalin favored political action and agitation among workers over their education. Indeed, political agitation among workers led to his first arrest in 1900.[31] This preference for action above theory seems to account partially for his well-known anti-intellectualism and contempt for (party) intellectuals—a sentiment echoed loudly in numerous appeals.

Mutual Mistrust

It was noted that, when Stalin met Lenin for the first time at a party conference in Finland 1905,

> Koba was deeply disappointed to find that Lenin, whom he had admired as the "mountain eagle of our party," was, unlike himself, "of privileged birth."

> Koba entertained a class prejudice towards the privileged and intellectuals, whose very social position, in his view, determined their political wavering.[32]

Stalin clashed with Lenin many times leading up to the October Revolution on Lenin's ambivalence, his apparent mistrust—indeed, his elitism—toward popular activism:

> On several issues of critical importance, Koba clashed with Lenin. The first concerned the state Duma, . . . set up by the decree of the Tsar in October 1905. It was to be a parliament based on indirect, unequal and incomplete manhood suffrage, a curia or council system discriminating heavily in favour of the propertied classes (one gentry vote equalled 15 peasant votes and 45 worker votes). . . . All this afforded the revolutionaries an opportunity to bring their underground work into the light and engage in open politics. While attacking parliamentary politics, Lenin was also tempted to use the Duma elections for the party cause. Koba took the opposite position, supporting the boycott of the Duma. Before the party conference, Koba attacked the Duma as "a negation of the people's revolution." After the conference, he called the Duma a "parliament of enemies of the people," contrasting it with the "street" and the "dictatorship of the street," which the autocracy could not disband.[33]

Here, once again, Stalin is the revolutionary on the ground, so to speak. And this was not an isolated case.[34] In several instances, and as opposed to Lenin, Stalin supported activism and the elemental, spontaneous forces of revolution.

Connected with this preference for agitation was the fact that Stalin felt more comfortable among the riff-raff. In prerevolutionary exile, Stalin consorted with common criminals:

> Unlike other "politicals," Stalin is known to have associated with common criminals while in exile. "There were some nice fellows among the criminal convicts," Stalin once remarked, they "were nice, salt-of-the-earth fellows. But there were lots of rats among the political convicts. They once organized a comrades' court and put me on trial for drinking with the criminal convicts, which they charged was an offence."[35]

And, as chaos took over during 1917, while Lenin distrusted spontaneous mass action, Stalin supported it:

> Neither the Bolsheviks nor the Soviets could contain the popular anger. Lenin was cautious about spontaneous mass street actions (which the party could not readily control), whereas Stalin was more supportive (as he was in 1905).

And, unlike Lenin, during 1917 Stalin trusted and maintained ties to the soviets. Lenin's mistrust was based in his inability to control and direct them.[36]

Stalin's Role as Leader

What of Stalin's own perception of his role as leader? To what extent did that self-perception converge, or facilitate connection, with the popular will? Here, it is helpful to compare Stalin's role in the Soviet leadership and the formation of Stalinism with the voluminous research on the nature of Adolf Hitler's leadership of German society and the Nazi rise to power.

One area of research that has produced an enormous amount of helpful scholarship on Germany but has been little explored in the Soviet case, undoubtedly due in part to its marginal acceptance among mainstream historians, is a psychohistorical approach toward understanding Stalin/ism. Although fine psychohistorical biographies have been done of both Hitler and Stalin,[37] more could be gained from studying the psychohistorical underpinnings of the development of Stalinism in Russia.

Consider, for instance, the influence of wartime trauma on the rhetoric and methods of building socialism in Soviet Russia. A seminal study in the German case examined the psychological trauma of World War I as a formative experience, rewoken during the Great Depression, for the children who would grow up to form the bulwark of Nazism. *Mutatis mutandis*, this analysis could be taken for a description of the "Stalinist Youth Cohort":[38]

> The historical relationship between the events of World War I and its catastrophic aftermath in Central Europe and the rise of National Socialism has often been postulated. The causal relationship is usually drawn from the savagery of trench warfare on the western front, the bitterness of defeat and revolution, to the spectacular series of National Socialist electoral victories beginning in 1930, as if such a relationship were historically self-evident. It is the thesis of this paper that the relationship between the period from 1914 to 1920 and the rise and triumph of National Socialism from 1929 to 1935 is specifically generational. The war and postwar experiences of the small children and youth of World War I explicitly conditioned the nature and success of National Socialism. . . .
>
> This essay . . . will focus not on the leader but on the followers, not on the charismatic figure but rather on the masses who endow him with special superhuman qualities.[39]

And it concludes:

> A return to the past is always unreal. To attempt it is the path of certain disaster. There was no glorified father who went to war and who could be recaptured in Hitler. He existed only in fantasy, and he could never be brought back in reality. There are no ideal mothers and fathers; there are only flawed human parents. Therefore for a World War I generation seeking restitution of a lost childhood there was to be only bitter reality in the form of a psychotic charlatan who skillfully manipulated human needs and left destruction to Germany and Europe. What the youth cohort wanted was a fantasy of warmth, closeness, security, power, and love. What they re-created was a

> repetition of their own childhoods. They gave to their children and to Europe in greater measure precisely the traumas they had suffered as children and adolescents a quarter of a century earlier.[40]

In the task of understanding the relationship of leader and led, we can gain further understanding of Stalin's role by examining Hitler's. Voluminous scholarship in the German case could profitably be applied to the Russian. Hitler's psychobiographer wrote:

> The hold that Hitler gained over Germany was like a spell that began lifting piecemeal once the tide of conquest turned, then massively in the final debacle. That spell had been prophesized in 1932 as "a reign of the collective beast" and decried as "a mass madness" in 1937 . . . Just such a spell was alleged afterward on all sides amid the rubble and ashes—and the exposed horrors—of Hitler's rule. Ribbentrop only went the limit when in captivity he "pleaded with everyone who came within earshot . . . to explain what had happened during the 'mass psychosis' of Hitlerism." The intent of such post-Nazi talk was always at least a little apologetic. Yet the question did repeatedly arise whether that mass phenomenon was Hitler's creation or he its creature, whether it was a mass bewitchment or a mass seizure. . . . Thomas Aich's *Massenmensch und Massenwahn* ("Mass Man and Mass Madness") of 1947 argued at once mass hypnosis by Hitler, a "mutual" "frenzy" between Hitler and his public, and a mediumistic pitch of Hitler's voice: "Out of it speaks the collective, the irrational, of the mass soul. . . . It was . . . a diffuse sense of empowerment through Hitler and of powerlessness against him."[41]

Hitler's magic was not inherent but a product of his investiture as savior of the German *Volk*. This analysis concludes that "Hitler's uncanny personal power over Germans came from his having coordinated his private traumatic fury with the national traumatic need."[42]

Several biographers inadvertently lend support to the idea of a special connection between Stalin and the masses by showing how it was done: like Hitler, Stalin subsumed his individual personality to virtually become the vehicle through which a certain version of socialist revolution could be realized. For instance, one classic biography examines how the traumas of Stalin's childhood led him to formulate a heroic self-image as avenger, how his personal struggle became a national struggle:

> His inner world, it appears, was one of dramatic fantasies in which he played a heroic part as a fighter for the just revolutionary cause in a protracted struggle culminating in triumph over powerful, scheming, hatefully villainous hostile forces. These counterrevolutionary forces also had to be anti-Stalin because in him, as in Lenin before him, the revolutionary cause was personified . . . by 1929, . . . his power position and capacity to manipulate policy were sufficiently potent that he could make all sorts of things happen in Russia by enacting his self-designed roles. His hero-scripts, we may call them.[43]

Another biographer noted that "Stalin lived by politics alone. . . . He lived for the purpose of shaping the body politic through the pursuit and exercise of power," and that

> Once in power, Stalin maintained that he was the personification of the epic struggle for socialism. He even said that he, the person, was not Stalin. . . . His identification with the Soviet regime was such that he did not distinguish between the personal and the public.[44]

In yet another biography, the connection is more explicit:

> Like Hitler, Stalin was able to stamp his character on the style and substance of state politics—personality and power cannot be separated. Indeed, in Moshe Lewin's view, "Stalin actually *became the system* and his personality acquired therefore a 'systemic' dimension."[45]

Moreover, Stalin possessed certain personality traits that facilitated his connection with the common man:

> Soso did, however, learn something valuable at the seminary [at Gori], as he later noted: "One thing priests teach you is to understand what people think." . . .
>
> From the very beginning of his revolutionary career, it is often said that Soso did not tolerate those who disagreed with him, often reacting with fists even to innocent remarks. Yet he was also known to be an extraordinarily patient listener, an "ideal listener". "Patience is a rare trait in men of action," as one observer noted. "That rare combination is the principal key to his character."[46]

In none of these biographies, however, is there a sense of mutual connection or identification between Stalin and the masses of Russian people.

In pondering the question, then, of the connection between the agendas of average people and that of the Bolsheviks and Stalin particularly—the question of who leads whom—one interpretation might be that leaders and led pursued similar ends, even supported similar means to those ends, but for different reasons. This presents a basis of popular support for Stalinism even while resolving the greater issue of connection between leader and led in this government system, or, indeed, in any system.

Or, are their reasons so different after all? A leitmotif throughout the appeals used in this study is a lack of personal, individual security. On a government level, this lack of security is simply experienced and expressed in different ways—the idea is to erect not personal but national security.

What was the revolution about, anyway? For those party leaders who came from privilege, building socialism was about constructing a utopia, according to a master plan guided by (the correct interpretation of) ideology. But judging from countless letters and appeals, for average people, building socialism was about getting social justice for themselves, that is, being included, and attaining some modicum of security by virtue of their inclusion, in a new state created precisely and finally for them, for common people, instead of for elites, as throughout history. It was about security. And for Stalin, on a national level, the need for security would be expressed accordingly. On a national level, Stalin's idea of building socialism in one country was

> an October of his own. It was the historically most consequential of his hero-scripts. He would engineer a breakthrough in the world's history comparable in significance to Lenin's October.

In his famous speech to Soviet industrial managers in 1931, Stalin explained the need for the Soviet Union to industrialize as quickly as possible with the oft-quoted line, "We have lagged behind the advanced countries by fifty to a hundred years. We must cover that distance in ten years. Either we'll do it or they will crush us." According to his biographer:

> This famous passage was not only an astute appeal to Soviet Russian patriotism but also a revelation of the speaker's inner world. Here was the Stalin whose Bolshevism blended with Russian nationalism. Here, too, was the self-dramatizing Stalin seeking to realize his hero-script by leading the party and country in a revolution of socialism's construction and thereby saving Mother Russia from the fate of once again being beaten by foreigners.[47]

But was Stalin incorrect in his assessment, both of hostile encirclement and the need for Russia to modernize or be crushed? Certainly, he did not invent the hostility of Western, capitalist powers against communist Russia—it was there from the start. Of course, it turned out to be Germany, not England, that invaded. Even so, in the long run, Russia's technological backwardness, combined with its inherently threatening ideology, made it increasingly vulnerable to Western aggression and expansion. How that would play out, no one could tell, but Stalin (like Hitler) certainly understood the trajectory of history. In the end, we might conclude that Stalin was the "right" leader for the times. Moreover, and related to that, is that his personal and public/collective sense of vulnerability—and his conflation of the two—clearly was not unique to him but generally felt.[48]

For Stalin, then, national security would be achieved through embracing socialism, not abandoning it, as apparently happened with NEP. It would be achieved by beating the aggressors at their own game, by trading places with them. Judging from numerous appeals, he was not alone in this goal.

Indeed, it would appear that gradualist party leaders like Nikolai Bukharin were out of touch—not just with Russia's international vulnerability, but also with the popular desire to achieve personal security. Ultimately, therefore, Stalin was consonant both with the international position of Russia and with the popular will, both in his motives, and in the way he conflated his personal agenda with the needs of Mother Russia.

It seems, however, that a study of Stalin/ism cannot free itself from the Cold War, judging from the persistence of a modified cold-war outlook apparent in recent historiography,[49] and the continued assault on the revisionist perspective, that is, on the effort to view the development of the Soviet system more broadly.[50] In spite of evidence to the contrary, mainstream historians stubbornly insist that the Bolshevik revolution generally, and Stalinism particularly, was a top-down phenomenon whose source is to be found in a narrow, uniquely vicious stratum of Soviet society, unconnected from the general population. Why is this so?

An earlier biographer argued,

> State terror is triadic. One element of the triad is a political leadership determined to use terror for its purposes. The second is a minority chosen for victimization in so frightful a form that the third element, a far larger body of people, seeing what can happen to the victims, will be motivated to fulfill the leadership's purpose, which may be to render it quiescent or, alternatively, to induce it to take actions that it otherwise would not be disposed to take.[51]

Note that in this interpretation, both the victims and the perpetrators are almost entirely passive tools in the government's hands.[52]

This top-down causation is retained in more recent biographies of Stalin, even those that seek to humanize and contextualize the leader. In assessing historical explanations of Stalin and his rise to power, one historian asserted that "Stalin should not be seen as some super-natural demon or God. He was a product of his times and to a large extent shared the concerns, preoccupations and dilemmas of any politician of his era," but also that,

> Although the input of lower-ranking regional bureaucrats, even ordinary Soviet citizens, in the Great Terror should never be ignored, the signal organising role of the 'centre'—Stalin and his top party and secret police collaborators—is surely beyond doubt.[53]

Later, he notes that, "Perhaps, ultimately, [Chris] Ward's overall verdict on Stalin's triumph is the most persuasive." Quoting Ward:

> Given Lenin's death (which threw the leadership into disarray), a modicum of popular support (evident amongst the metropolitan proletariat in 1928) and his mastery of the apparatus (staffed by the new cohort of sub-élites thrown up after 1917), circumstances ensured that inside the mutating body of the party-state [Stalin] would succeed and his rivals fail.[54]

Note the reference to "a modicum of popular support"—an exceedingly vague statement that would not hold up to scrutiny, unless one assumed the top-down model of causation.

Ultimately, the question about the relevance of popular letters and appeals used in this study is undoubtedly hampered by the same insistence on the totalitarian model as the discussion of revolutionary causation generally—and for the same reason, that is, a profound reluctance to place motivation, agency, and, therefore, blame, beyond the party leadership.[55] It is problematic to place agency beyond the leaders, because that means that, perhaps, the Soviet system was not as totalitarian as we thought, or even that the model itself is flawed. It is also problematic to place motivation beyond the top, because that would mean that socialism and social revolution in Russia may actually have had a genuine popular basis. And finally because, of course, the suffering connected with the revolution and Stalinism was immense, and someone needed to be blamed for it.[56]

One could argue that these problems also characterized the German case, and, yet, historians of Nazi Germany—and the Germans themselves—long since have acknowledged the devils of their past and their collective guilt over Nazism. But of these three problems hampering explanation of the Stalinist past, one of them is still problematic in the present, namely, the possibility that there was genuine popular support for social revolution and class warfare. The problem remains problematic for two reasons. First, the Cold War is not over: If anything, political and ideological opposition to what socialism represents is more virulent and emboldened than ever, partly because the fall of the Soviet Union was interpreted to confirm capitalism's virtues. Connected to this is a second reason: The idea of popular support for establishing social justice, for leveling, will always be extremely threatening to those who seek to maintain their privileged positions in a dramatically unequal world. This, more than anything else, hampers our understanding of Stalin/ism.

The explanation that seems to hold this entire discussion together is this: Stalin, unique among party leaders, seems to have formed a connection with a significant portion of the population, which endorsed, even requested, the destruction of NEP and the renewal of radical, violent revolution, and a renewed effort to build socialism in Russia. Social resentment and violence, the anger of those below, had always existed. But whereas before, tsarism—which existed by virtue and for the purpose of maintaining elite privilege—suppressed and punished such resentment and violence, the Bolsheviks, and Stalin particularly, simply legitimated it, used it, even encouraged it, precisely in order to destroy the old order and build a new one. This task—building socialism—was necessarily expressed in different ways at the center and by individual citizens who wished to take part. But it was done at both levels to achieve essentially the same goal: security. And that was a goal that virtually everyone, above and below, even those who opposed the Bolsheviks, shared.

CONCLUSIONS

SOME historians have argued that the Bolsheviks prevailed in the October Revolution for two reasons: because they acceded to popular demands for control over the factory and the land, and because they sought to incorporate workers and peasants into the power structure. Though later repudiated, these strategies pointed to perhaps the key aspect of Bolshevik propaganda: its elevation of working people to the preeminent social caste, making workers feel that their contribution to society was important, even vital to society's well-being. In a country where manual labor had always been cheap and plentiful and where individuals thus counted for little, this message had the potential of making a great transformation in the psychological makeup of the Russian people as a whole. A new system that gave average people a sense of their own importance might also, it was hoped, awaken a sense of responsibility to society as a whole—to the nation—that had previously applied to the peasant commune. In a word, the new Soviet citizen would be invested, would become proprietor of the new socialist society.

Thus invested, however, the average Soviet citizen held enormous expectations of material and cultural progress after the revolution and civil war were over. The reality of NEP Russia fell shockingly short of satisfying those expectations. The basic structural problem of Russian society that fueled the ongoing revolution was the huge gap that separated the elites from the masses of people, in political, social, economic, and cultural terms. Once they came to power in October, however, the Bolsheviks were no more successful in closing that gap than the tsarist government had been, particularly after the introduction of NEP, that is to say, of a quasi-capitalism and the increased disparity and insecurity it brought. Those particularly disaffected by the change in course were the party's most prominent supporters, such as rank-and-file communists, civil war veterans, and youth. Competition for work and resources during NEP heightened radicalism and revived revolutionary sentiment. Russian social reality throughout NEP was characterized by persistent and growing economic disparity, a crippling and ineffective bureaucracy, and an intense competition for jobs and opportunities that fueled chronic, severe unemployment and the corruption of party and government. In addition to these were a host of social problems, which the government had neither the resources nor the personnel to solve.

In an atmosphere of general poverty and disparity, competition for the opportunities that existed was acute. Under such conditions, establishing an egalitarian society was not possible. Thus, as apparent from the letters quoted throughout this study, social leveling of wealth and opportunity became a prominent theme, especially among young communists, who hoped to make something of themselves. Hence the paradox: the have-nots wanted to level the playing field, so that they might become haves. Only a small percentage of the population was going to have a chance for a place in the new elite. Supplicants' appeals to the central party leadership spoke of too many competing for too few posts, opportunities, and positions. Crushed by competition and disparity, many supplicants sought a solution in drastic, even violent measures.

The outspokenness of appeals to the central government notwithstanding, determining supplicants' perceptions of social inequality is a delicate task. Their fears, desires, and aspirations, however real and powerful, often are not explicit. The stated purpose of a particular appeal may have been obtaining work or an increased pension, or admission to a particular school. The implicit messages were the authors' ultimate aspirations, how the disappointment of those aspirations affected them, and what—or who—they blamed for that disappointment. Peasants in general, and bedniaks in particular, felt at a grave disadvantage in receiving help or attention of any kind from the central government, insofar as they were not considered on an equal footing with workers. This complaint, along with the practical obstacles of rural existence in the quest for education and inclusion, formed the basis of many peasants' appeals. Workers, on the other hand, had been promised work and expected to contribute to socialist construction, but throughout the 1920s, work often was not to be found. Unemployed workers thus were denied not just sustenance, but their very identities as workers and members of the proletariat. This irony was not lost on the unemployed themselves, an irony that became more bitter if they also were communists, or veterans, or both. Communists and Red Army veterans who became incapacitated through strenuous service considered the government to be their government; they had fought for it and built it. In their indignant appeals demanding work or medical attention, they often addressed Stalin and the party leadership as comrades and equals.

Widespread unemployment and disparity of wealth and privilege and the desperation that accompanied them grew throughout NEP, intensifying class antagonism. Moreover, unemployment afflicted communists and other theoretically favored groups within Soviet society, such as Red Army veterans. For them, unemployment and economic desperation were especially bitter, because they believed that they had earned special consideration, and in too many cases were shown none. In January 1925 one communist in 100 was unemployed, and by January 1927 the proportion had risen to one in 25. By 1927, one industrial worker in four in Moscow was unemployed. NEP-generated unemployment in the cities in 1927 had reached 1.5 million, or double the figure for 1924. Average workers, communists, and civil war veterans perceived as the decade wore on that the socialist society for which they had fought bore little resemblance to the society of reality, a realization that caused intense disillusionment, bitterness, and resentment. Such attitudes moved them to petition, calling for purges or worse—suggesting, in other words, a revolution from above demanded from below.

As the decade progressed, the promise of building the socialist society became more remote and more exclusive. What the appeals in this study show is a profound sense of abandonment, anger, and sometimes violent sentiments—especially among key constituents but also among the society at large—over their disappointment at the failure of the government to provide even basic sustenance, much less deliver an egalitarian communist utopia. Letters to the center were filled with uncertainty, despair, and frustration that seemed to reach a high point in 1927. But the search for enemies and wreckers of the revolution had begun much earlier, a persistent message that resonated throughout the 1920s. Communism was not delivering on its promise, and most supplicants were concerned with finding those responsible for personal and collective failure. Peasants and nonparty citizens often blamed communist administrators for their predicament. Party members sometimes accused nonparty specialists and administrators of obstruction and counterrevolution. Both party and nonparty citizens alike faulted personnel held over from the tsarist system or White sympathizers for the corruption of the party and state bureaucracy. Ultimately, the frustrations that people experienced frequently led them to propose "solutions" of various kinds. These solutions often amounted, first, to identifying enemies and obstacles to individual and collective success and, then, to proposing that the government remove or purge those obstacles or enemies. The common denominator is the identification not merely of an enemy, but of an enemy that must be eliminated. This is the leitmotif that runs throughout the letters and this study.

To be sure, not everyone—perhaps not even the majority of the population—saw the solution to the country's persistent and growing socioeconomic problems in the purging of enemies. Supplicants' recommendations and critiques varied widely. Society, however, need not have been wholly dissatisfied with the conditions of NEP for a revolutionary mood to linger or reemerge. Indeed, revolution was more certain when a disparity of wealth and security existed, just as before October.

Popular resentment naturally concentrated in the lower strata of society. Both before and after the revolution, Mensheviks found greater support among skilled workers, who traditionally enjoyed higher status materially and socially as members of the worker aristocracy. The Bolsheviks, by contrast, were historically most popular among unskilled workers in the heavy and textile industries, that is, those at the bottom of the heap. Below them were the unemployed. Perhaps there was some connection between the Bolsheviks' appeal to the unskilled and unemployed on the one hand and, on the other, contemporary perceptions that the lower social strata were more susceptible to the "propaganda of hate." The point is not that all unskilled workers were social radicals, but rather that the lower the social status, the greater the propensity for resentment and bitterness toward the elites.

There remained only the problem of identifying these elites. While communists and non-communists alike blamed the party for the revolution's failure, others looked to the most apparent cause—those inside and outside the party who benefited from persistent inequality. And for many poor and unemployed blue-collar workers, those who benefited were the white-collar workers—specialists, bureaucrats, and professionals of every kind. To the lower classes and their communist allies, the fact that the party needed to rely on specialists and educated members of prerevolutionary elites for economic and industrial expertise and educational advancement after the revolution was a bitter pill to swallow. Hence, the endless efforts of Lenin and the party leadership to justify this policy of reliance to the party rank and file and working class, and the ubiquitous rationalizations of Soviet historians of the party's decision to abandon working-class control. Industry specialists in particular were clearly valued over regular workers and were compensated accordingly. In a country supposedly ruled by the proletariat, such an anomaly did not go unnoticed.

The propaganda of hate was cathartic in its appeal to those who occupied the lowest socioeconomic strata and were frustrated in their attempts to escape. One contemporary remarked that for those who remained at the bottom after the revolution, placing the bourgeois-intelligentsia below them relieved their suffering, indeed, even amused them. The creation of a social class still lower than the proletariat, it was observed, made their own existence brighter. The purpose of discrimination against the intelligentsia was to make the worker feel superior by lowering those who were the worker's antithesis. Because intellectual labor continued to be valued over manual work—and the intelligentsia over manual workers—the proletariat had to develop its own intelligentsia, in order to gain true sovereignty in the new society. Many communists and nonparty citizens hoping to raise their social and economic status concluded that the proletariat would "firmly retain in proletarian hands the victory of the Great October Revolution"[1] only by supplanting the prerevolutionary intelligentsia.

Thus, the darker aspirations of the revolution seemed to originate in frustration of more positive goals. In the revolution there operated two distinct impulses, each occupying opposite ends of a continuum. One was an idealistic striving for the establishment of an egalitarian society, a socialist collective. The idealistic communist envisioned a society based in universal brotherhood and equality and a pseudo-Christian philosophy that championed the poor.

The other impulse that impelled the revolution was vengeance, an impulse dominated by resentment toward past and present elites, one that saw the revolution as an opportunity to pound those heads rising above the norm not just back into the collective, but out of existence entirely. This was the impulse often expressed by supplicants whose material existence was threatened, whose dignity had been assaulted by abandonment and disappointment, and whose revolutionary aspirations had thus been squelched.

The vengeful revolutionary aspired to all the good things of life that the socialist society promised, but not through the creation of an egalitarian society. The egalitarian society was a utopia. The object, rather, was to reverse roles with those who had once been superior, who once had all the advantages in material comfort, education, and freedom, indeed, in all those things to which the average Soviet citizen aspired. The vengeful revolutionary sought to supplant the preexisting elites, who had retained power and privilege despite the ostensible victory of the working class in October 1917. These elites were not distinct, but had permeated the party and state apparatus by virtue of their positions prior to the revolution and their education and expertise. The vengeful sought to rise above these elites and destroy them, exchanging places with them in a social system that in any case had retained its stratification. The vengeful sought to destroy those who were considered superior, and in so doing, gain superiority themselves. Once they had dethroned their social superiors, vengeful revolutionaries could adopt the position of the social and cultural elites. For the idealistic communist, material and emotional security could be enhanced through construction of a nurturing socialist society, in which every member would contribute and reap the harvest equally. For the vengeful communist, dignity and security would be sought in the destruction of the sources of insecurity. Thus would the egalitarian collective, the classless socialist society, be built.

The propaganda of hate was dynamic: it gained in appeal as each individual's disappointment and resentment grew. Few communists or nonparty Soviet citizens conformed exactly to either revolutionary prototype. But during the course of NEP, many egalitarian-minded communists and citizens became increasingly vengeful as their dreams and expectations were disappointed. Indeed, many appeals illustrate the individual's metamorphosis from the idealistic to the vengeful revolutionary. Dreams of working to build the new society or of gaining an education and joining the socialist vanguard were dashed in millions of cases, and those millions seethed with resentment.

At a certain point along the continuum of revolutionary impulses, it becomes difficult to speak in terms of "aspirations," since the word usually carries positive social and ethical connotations. But aspirations come in all varieties, and some are neither expected nor welcomed. The right of self-expression inherent in revolution had unleashed resentments and a desire for revenge that was smoldering long before October 1917.[2] These negative aspirations were part of the revolution as well, not merely an aberration or a betrayal of it, as has often been argued by those sympathetic to communism. Such aspirations could hardly be surprising, considering that the gross disparity and violence of prerevolutionary Russia and the ravages of war and famine were compounded by the disparity and disappointments of NEP.

We usually consider violence as physical, but the language of many supplicants implies that they experienced social hierarchy and disparity as a form of violence, by which they had been assaulted and victimized. The physical violence that escalated throughout successive waves of revolution, therefore, might simply be a response to social violence that its victims seemingly could neither fight nor escape.

The Bukharinists in the Communist Party considered NEP a viable program for peaceful economic development to the end, denying the inherent contradictions between NEP and communism and the social conflict that NEP generated. Judging from appeals, throughout the 1920s civil war lay just beneath the surface, and any solution predicated on peace was not based on reality. Numerous appeals suggested that the work of the revolution was far from over. This large and growing political constituency sought a leader who would bring the revolution to a successful conclusion. Many supplicants explicitly entrusted that task to Stalin.

Unlike Lenin, a member of the intelligentsia and the recognized genius behind the revolution, Stalin was popularly viewed as an equal, albeit one in a position of authority. He was a champion of the common working man, and especially of the working man without work. Many appeals, especially those from veterans and rank-and-file communists, suggest that the writers sensed—

or sought to show—a bond of commonality with Stalin, an average man like themselves. Stalin was unique among party leaders, and his non-intelligentsia status set him apart. But it also set him with the mass of the population.[3] As appeals illustrate, hostility toward social enemies was widespread. Stalin's resentment, paranoia, and desire for revenge were impulses found throughout the population, increasing in intensity with each indignity, as disparity between the favored and unfavored of NEP widened.

This discussion begs the critical question: what, then, is the precise connection between the letters used in this study and the policies later pursued by the central party leadership known as Stalinism? As noted in the introduction, determining how popular opinion influences political leadership—whether in a "democracy" or a "dictatorship"—is exceedingly difficult. The evidence here shows at least a clear though indirect relationship between messages sent to, and the agenda under, Stalin, beginning in the late 1920s. But was the central party leadership actually responding to popular desires?

First, to prove such a response would seem nigh on impossible—even if a politician were to claim explicitly and publicly that popular wishes were the basis for policy, that of course might not be true.[4] But here we might turn to what would seem one obvious resolution to the problem of the relationship between government and people, an option that seems rarely to be considered explicitly, namely, the possibility that party leaders and Stalin on the one hand and significant segments of the population on the other both sought NEP's demise, but for different reasons. Thus, the "masses" would have supported Stalin/ism for reasons other than those of Stalin himself (e.g., maintaining the party in power; the survival of Russia internationally vis-à-vis the West, apropos Stalin's perceived need for rapid industrialization; Stalin's desire to maintain his own power).[5] So that while motives may have differed, the goals and means may not.

Alternatively, one might argue that if one takes into account the context, namely, the scarcity and resulting disparity that prevailed throughout NEP, the trauma and paranoia bred by years of war and revolution, it would seem logical to observe that both the party/state and the people of Russia were products of the same context. Of course, such an interpretation means blurring the distinction between the party and the people.

The apparent reluctance to find the origins of Stalinism in the wider society suggests a further, deeper reluctance preventing clarification of the origins of Stalinism, that is, the problem of blame.[6] To "bring the people back in," as one historian recently put it, would be not only to risk blaming the victims, average Russians, for crimes committed under Stalin, but also to admit that the darker motivations and manifestations of social violence were, and are, much more widespread than one would like.[7] And here, perhaps, we find the true origin of the persistence of center-based explanations of Stalinism.

This study shows that messages directed to the center during the 1920s anticipated, even demanded, much of what soon transpired under the so-called Stalinist Revolution. It argues that the turn in revolutionary direction was fueled in part by forces outside the party elite. Appeals to the center show that radicalism grew after 1921, when the goals of the October Revolution were repudiated, and Lenin essentially reinstituted a capitalist system with the New Economic Policy.[8] The dismantling of the NEP economy and society and the institution of the Stalinist system were undertaken in part at popular request, a conclusion supported by other studies on political evolution during NEP.[9] It raises the paradoxical question, to what extent the party's relative liberalism during NEP contributed to the victory of Stalinism. The evidence here supports the conclusion that the party's apparent abandonment of socialism and the communist utopia during NEP, and the insecurity this generated among significant groups of the population, led to the victory of the "control freaks" over revolutionary direction, away from liberal solutions. In short, it suggests not that Stalinism destroyed the liberalism of NEP Russia, but rather that NEP's liberalism brought Stalinism about.

Thus, the following scenario: There were widespread expectations with the revolution that as a socialist society was being formed, social inequities would disappear. This anticipated redistribution of wealth, opportunity, and social status did not take place, causing increasing anger and resentment among those who failed to attain security within the new society. Their resentment was directed toward the privileged classes of the new society who bore a striking resemblance to prerevolutionary elites in both manner and personnel. A particular target of resentment was the intelligentsia, and especially the technical intelligentsia, both because of their favored status in the new society and because they were perceived as passively and actively impeding the progress of those attempting to improve their social position. Stalin represented, validated, and vented the resentment of those left out against the intelligentsia and other class enemies. He was the prototype, the champion, the vehicle of vengeful revolution.

As a collective organism in crisis and under siege, NEP society required resolution of the conflicts and contradictions that were tearing it apart. Diverse elements of Russian society, particularly the more vulnerable elements, had long clamored for a society that was organically whole and secure. In 1906, artisans sought to create a party seeking "a strong, authoritative power with the assistance of the people; it alone can lead the country out of social chaos, after attaining Russia's unity, internal peace, and external security."[10] Supplicants appealing to the center during NEP demanded that this unity finally be achieved, but their frustration and resentment indicated that it would not be achieved peacefully.[11] Thus, it was observed, the essential social dynamic that came to operate under Stalinism was the "violent suppression of all contradictions in society, ruling out any expression of ideological or political disagreement or difference."[12] Thus, "liquidation of the nepman bourgeoisie and kulaks as a class, collectivization of agriculture, [and] formation of a new, popular intelligentsia led to the creation of social unity of Soviet society."[13]

NOTES

Preface

1. Alex Pravda's comment, paraphrased by Elizabeth Teague, *Solidarity and the Soviet Worker: The Impact of the Polish Events of 1980 on Soviet Internal Politics* (New York: Croom Helm/Methuen Publishers, 1988), 74-75.

2. For documentary evidence of this evolution, see Gregory L. Freeze, *From Supplication to Revolution: A Documentary Social History of Imperial Russia* (New York: Oxford University Press, 1988). In his study of peasant petitions to the tsar and the Duma during the 1905 Revolution, Andrew Verner noted that, except under Catherine the Great, the right of petition extended to individuals. Collective petitions were restricted to the private grievances of the petitioners and could not discuss political matters. This constraint on political appeal ended in 1905 ("Discursive Strategies in the 1905 Revolution: Peasant Petitions from Vladimir Province," *Russian Review* 54, no. 1 [January 1995]: 66-68).

3. For the tradition of supplication in Russia and its use by the Bolsheviks, see Margareta Mommsen-Reindl, *Hilf mir, mein Recht zu finden: Russische Bittschriften von Iwan dem Schrechlichen bis Gorbatschow* (Frankfurt a. M.: Propylaen, 1987), 111-18.

In a study of the press during NEP, Jeffrey Brooks noted that the government considered letters to the editor "an accurate reflection of public opinion [which] were frequently used to evaluate policies" ("Public and Private Values in the Soviet Press, 1921–1928," *Slavic Review* 48, no. 1 [spring 1989]: 16-35). Alter Litvin noted that various types of correspondence "which Soviet citizens sent between 1917 and 1927 to representatives of authority . . . up to a point may be seen as an expression of public discourse, a sort of dialogue with the state power," while "[p]etitions submitted in the 1930s and later are quite different from those of the NEP era" ("Sources," *Stalinism: Russian and Western Views at the Turn of the Millennium*, 24).

The critical question of the connection between state and society in the Soviet Union is explored in chapter 10.

4. Studies on the 1930s include Sheila Fitzpatrick, "Supplicants and Citizens: Public Letter-Writing in Soviet Russia in the 1930s," *Slavic Review* 55, no. 1 (spring 1996): 78-105; Sarah Davies, *Popular Opinion in Stalin's Russia: Terror, Propaganda and Dissent, 1934–1941* (Cambridge: Cambridge University Press, 1997); and the articles in *Russian History* 24, nos. 1-2 (spring/summer 1997) edited by Fitzpatrick from a conference held at the University

of Chicago in 1996 on "Petitions and Denunciations in Russia from Muscovy to the Stalin Era." John Keep noted that a "veritable explosion of knowledge stems from the opening up of the former Soviet archives since 1991" which "tended to confirm what independent researchers had long suspected; for example, that the hyper-centralized administration creaked badly, or that there was a good deal of grumbling among the mass of Soviet citizens, which co-existed with genuine enthusiasm among zealots and those eager to rise up in the social hierarchy. Efforts made to establish the degree of support for Party policies among different segments of the population, on the basis of correspondence, petitions and official opinion surveys (*svodki*) are still in their infancy, but seem to show that the scale of disaffection was greater than had previously been thought" (Alter Litvin and John Keep, eds., *Stalinism: Russian and Western Views at the Turn of the Millennium* [London: Routledge, 2005], introduction, viii).

5. The letters used in this study are located primarily in the Rossiiskii gosudarstvennyi arkhiv sotsial'no-politicheskoi istorii (Russian State Archive of Socio-Political History, hereinafter RGASPI; the former Central Communist Party Archive in Moscow), fond 17, the collection of the Secretariat of the Central Committee of the KPSS. Letters addressed to Stalin and other Central Committee members in the possession of the Secretariat and for the period under question number in the tens of thousands. The total number of letters in all fondy combined and for a broader period runs into the millions. The letters in this study will be referred to by fond, opis, dela, and list. Unless otherwise stated, all translations from the Russian are by the author.

6. Freeze, *From Supplication to Revolution*, introduction; see, also, the informative discussion on using petitions as a source for determining social consciousness and relations in K. B. Shustov, "Zhaloby i prosheniia kak istochnik po istorii politicheskogo soznaniia krest'ian zapadnoi Sibiri vtoroi poloviny xix v.," in *Sibirskoi istochnikovedenie i arkheografiia*, ed. N. N. Pokrovskii and E. K. Pomodanovskaia (Novosibirsk: Izd-vo Nauka, 1980).

7. Freeze, *From Supplication to Revolution*, 8.

8. Jeffrey Brooks discussed the centrality of the press in the 1920s before the Great Turn, arguing that although it "was not coterminous with all public expression, . . . it contextualized the Soviet experience and imposed a structure on thinking even among non-believers" (*Thank You, Comrade Stalin!*, prologue, xiii-xiv). In another study of the development of the press ("NEP Newspapers and the Origins of Soviet Information Rationing," *The Russian Review* 62 [October 2003]: 614-36), Matthew Lenoe argued that the difficulties of newspaper distribution during NEP led to a central rationing system of information and, indirectly, contributed to the formation of new elites in Soviet society.

9. A number of scholars have remarked on this rise in tension. See, for instance, Fitzpatrick's comment that "[t]he frenetic collectivization drive and mass expropriation of kulaks that burst forth in the winter of 1929–30 were the climax of two and a half years of rising political and social tension" (*Stalin's Peasants: Resistance and Survival in the Russian Village after Collectivization* [New York: Oxford University Press, 1994], 37), and trade union reports of "the sharp rise in disaffection among Russia's cotton workers" beginning in the same

period (Jeffrey J. Rossman, "Weaver of Rebellion and Poet of Resistance: Kapitan Klepikov [1880–1933] and Shop-Floor Opposition to Bolshevik Rule," *Jahrbücher für Geschichte Osteuropas* 44, no. 3 [1996]: 374-408).

10. Sheila Fitzpatrick has written extensively on this. See Fitzpatrick, *Russia in the Era of NEP*, 12-33, "The Problem of Class Identity in NEP Society"; eadem, "Ascribing Class: The Construction of Social Identity in Soviet Russia," *Journal of Modern History* 65 (1993): 745-70; and an updated and reworked version of various articles in her collection, *Tear Off the Masks!: Identity and Imposture in Twentieth-Century Russia* (Princeton, N.J.: Princeton University Press, 2005).

11. See the introduction.

12. Leopold Haimson, "The Problem of Social Identities in Early Twentieth Century Russia," 1. In an earlier study, Gregory Freeze pointed out that the continuity between the traditional Russian system of *sosloviia* and the tendency of the postrevolutionary system to classify persons on the basis of "social origin" was behind the disfranchisement of the *lishentsy* ("The Soslovie [Estate] Paradigm and Russian Social History," *American Historical Review* 91 [February 1986]: 11-36).

13. This is the method used in A. K. Sokolov, gen. ed., *Golos naroda: Pis'ma i otkliki riadovykh sovetskihk grazhdan o sobytiiakh 1918–1932 gg.* (Moscow: ROSSPEN, 1998). In one study, Sheila Fitzpatrick organized the letters she used according to type rather than subject, reflecting the tropes employed and intentions of the authors ("Supplicants and Citizens").

Introduction

1. The epitaph quotes an appeal sent in February 1925 to the party leadership from a party member and miner in the Shakhty region of the Donbass who wrote to protest workers' low wages (RGASPI, f. 17, op. 84, d. 646, ll. 287-88). Unless otherwise specified, all translations of primary and secondary sources used herein are by the author.

2. NEP was a term used to describe an ad hoc policy

3. See Richard Stites, *Revolutionary Dreams: Utopian Vision and Experimental Life in the Russian Revolution* (New York: Oxford University Press, 1989). For a recent study comparing the attempts of twentieth-century communist regimes in Russia, China, and Cuba to create new, superior human beings on which the construction of new societies would depend, see Yinghong Cheng, *Creating the New Man: From Enlightenment Ideals to Socialist Realities* (Honolulu: University of Hawai'i Press, 2009). Another recent work argues that the effort to construct new human beings was based not in Bolshevik ideology but in modern Western state practices that both the Russian and Soviet governments imitated: David Hoffman, *Cultivating the Masses: Modern State Practices and Soviet Socialism, 1914–1939* (Ithaca, N.Y.: Cornell University Press, 2011). See, also, Sarah Badcock, "Talking to the People and Shaping Revolution: The Drive for Enlightenment in Revolutionary Russia," *The Russian Review* 65 (October 2006): 617-36.

4. A major collection of articles on the problems of NEP is Andrei K. Sokolov, ed., *NEP v kontekste istoricheskogo razvitie Rossii XX veka* (Moscow: Russian Academy of Sciences, Institute of Russian History, 2001). In his introduction ("Istoricheskoe znachenie NEPa," 6-12), Sokolov bemoans the tendency to view NEP outside its historical context, namely, the inherently unstable Soviet government and society immediately following the revolution. He is not specific about what caused NEP's demise but suggests, among other causes, unemployment.

5. See, for instance, Leopold Haimson, "The Problem of Social Stability in Urban Russia, 1905–1917 (Part One)," *Slavic Review* 23, no. 4 (December 1964): 619-42; and idem, "The Problem of Social Stability in Urban Russia, 1905–1917 (Part Two)," *Slavic Review* 24, no. 1 (March 1965): 1-22.

6. Soviets were councils of elected representatives that arose spontaneously during the first Russian Revolution of 1905 and formed the basis for the government of the Soviet Union. A comprehensive and interesting, if partisan, early history of the soviets was by Spanish communist Andrés Nin Pérez, "The soviets: Their origin, development and functions" (first published in *Cuadernos de Cultura*, Valencia, 1932; English translation at https://libcom.org/library/soviets-their-origin-development-functions-andreu-nin).

7. Leopold Haimson, "The Problem of Social Identities in Early Twentieth Century Russia," *Slavic Review* 47, no. 1 (spring 1988): 6.

8. On bridging gap between the intelligentsia and the masses and official Stalinist rhetoric on this, see Vadim Volkov, "The Concept of *Kulturnost'*: Notes on the Stalinist Civilizing Process," in *Stalinism: New Directions*, ed. Sheila Fitzpatrick (London: Rutledge, 2000), 210-30. The problem of the cultural gap in Soviet society and the intelligentsia's position in the revolution is the subject of chapter 9 below.

9. George Fischer, "The Intelligentsia and Russia," in *The Transformation of Russian Society: Aspects of Social Change since 1861*, ed. Cyril Black (Cambridge, Mass.: Harvard University Press, 1960), 262-63. On the composition of the intelligentsia, see also Richard Pipes, ed., *The Russian Intelligentsia* (New York: Columbia University Press, 1961); Elise Kimerling Wirtschafter, *Social Identity in Imperial Russia* (DeKalb: Northern Illinois University Press, 1997), "Middle Groups"; and R. W. Davies, ed., *From Tsarism to the New Economic Policy: Continuity and Change in the Economy of the USSR* (Ithaca, N.Y.: Cornell University Press, 1991).

10. See, for instance, V. M. Selunskaia, ed., *Izmeneniia sotsial'noi struktury sovetskogo obshchestva: Oktiabr' 1917–1920* (Moscow: Mysl', 1976), 268-70. The author asserts that most members of the prerevolutionary intelligentsia were provided by the "bourgeois-landlord order," since "only those deeply interested in the preservation of the interests of the ruling classes could defend them." See also S. A. Fediukin, *Sovetskaia vlast' i burzhuaznye spetsialisty* (Moscow: Mysl', 1965), where the author describes specialists as "people who, in the recent past, were either exploiters of the workers in the person of specialists closely connected with the commanding heights of capital, or accomplices of the bourgeoisie in the exploitation of the working class in the person of the main body of specialists, or defenders of the exploiting classes in the person of officers" (250).

11. See B. I. Kolonitskii, "Antiburzhuaznaia propaganda i 'antiburzhuiskoe' soznanie," *Otechestvennaia istoriia*, no. 1 (1994): 17-27; Eng. trans. in *Russian Review* 53, no. 2 (April 1994): 183-96. Kolonitskii traces the development of anti-bourgeois consciousness through the propaganda of all revolutionary groups in Russia as well as general usage. However, the author does not address the issue of why the appeal of such propaganda was so strong, or why it formed the basis of a sort of social contract between the Bolsheviks and other revolutionary parties on one hand, and the masses on the other, nor why the political usage of anti-bourgeois language developed into more general pejorative usage among the masses. See, also, Orlando Figes' study on peasants' efforts to understand and employ the language of the revolutionary parties, where the author observed that the revolutionary intelligentsia ultimately, ironically, were forced to employ peasant language in their propaganda ("The Russian Revolution of 1917 and Its Language in the Village," *Russian Review* 56 [July 1997]: 323-45).

12. Michael Voslensky, *Nomenklatura: The Soviet Ruling Class*, trans. Eric Mosbacher (Garden City, N.Y.: Doubleday, 1984), 22. Recent studies on the Soviet government's attempts to culturally reform Soviet citizens include Jeffrey Brooks, *Thank You, Comrade Stalin!: Soviet Public Culture from Revolution to Cold War* (Princeton, N.J.: Princeton University Press, 2000); Charles Clark, *Uprooting Otherness: The Literacy Campaign in NEP-Era Russia* (Selinsgrove, Pa.: Susquehanna University Press, 2000); and Igal Halfin, *From Darkness to Light: Class, Consciousness, and Salvation in Revolutionary Russia* (Pittsburgh, Pa.: University of Pittsburgh Press, 2000). These studies assume the "revolution from above" stance, which continues to dominate Western historiography on the Soviet period (see note 25 below). On the Bolsheviks' early attemps to make workers and peasants into Soviet citizens, see David Brandenburger, *National Bolshevism: Stalinist Mass Culture and the Formation of Modern Russian National Identity, 1931–1956* (Cambridge, Mass.: Harvard University Press, 2002). A thoughtful discussion on the use of ideology in the Bolshevik state can be found in Christina Kiaer and Eric Naiman, eds., *Everyday Life in Early Soviet Russia: Taking the Revolution Inside* (Bloomington: Indiana University Press, 2006), where the editors argue that, as opposed to Western societies, the Bolsheviks made ideology into an explicit and conscious tool with which to reshape the Soviet people: "Neither governments nor ordinary people in Western democracies talked about 'capitalist ideology' because the ideology was so embedded that it did its work without being named, while the Soviets explicitly placed ideology at the center of all their programs." This meant that "Ideology, in its traditional, naturalizing, unconscious function, may have been the handmaiden of exploitation, but it also allowed subjects to cope with the conditions of their exploitation. . . . The result was, especially by the 1930s, a widely shared anxiety over the extent to which the individual was alienated from an ideal community of Soviet subjects" (6-7). In the end, ideology becomes reality: in their effort to become included in the new Soviet community, the two become (imperfectly) merged; it is therefore difficult for historians to determine "what Soviet subjects really felt beneath the ideological mask [because] . . . the mask became the face itself" (11).

13. For a general summary and critique of the main historiographical trends concerning Stalinism, see Chris Ward, *Stalin's Russia*, 2[d] ed. (1993; reprint, New York: Oxford University Publishing, 1999).

14. Soviet scholars also maintained that NEP lasted much longer. Whereas Western historians date NEP roughly from 1921 to the late twenties, ending with the collectivization of agriculture and the first Five-Year Plan, for the Soviets NEP extended at least until 1936, when Stalin declared the achievement of the classless society, suggesting that the social aspects of the Stalinist Revolution were more important than the economic ones. See, for instance, M. B. Blanka, "Sovetskii istoricheskii opyt osushchestvleniia NEPa i ego znachenie dlia kubinskoi revoliutsii" (kand. diss., Moscow State University, 1981).

15. See, for instance, Merle Fainsod, *How Russia is Ruled* (Cambridge: Harvard University Press, 1953); idem, *Smolensk under Soviet Rule* (Cambridge: Harvard University Press, 1958); Leonard B. Schapiro, *The Communist Party of the Soviet Union* (London: Eyre and Spottiswoode, 1960); idem, *The Government and Politics of the Soviet Union* (New York: Random House, 1965); and idem, *The Origin of the Communist Autocracy: Political Opposition in the Soviet State, First Phase, 1917–1922* (New York: Praeger, 1965). In his study of Moscow metal workers, Kevin Murphy noted that the "Cold War shaped the framing of the history of the Russian Revolution in the latter half of the twentieth century. . . . Both schools promoted the notion that Stalinism was a natural and inevitable outcome of 1917, both schools identified socialism with Stalinism, and both schools viewed the working class as a social force easily manupulated by the state. . . . fifteen years after the archives of the former Soviet Union opened their doors, not a single archival-driven study has been produced to support either of the Cold War interpretations" (*Revolution and Counterrevolution: Class Struggle in a Moscow Metal Factory* [2005; Chicago: Haymarket Books, 2007], 224).

16. See the biography of Bukharin by Stephen F. Cohen, *Bukharin and the Bolshevik Revolution: A Political Biography 1888–1938* (New York: Alfred Knopf, 1973); for a reinterpretation of Bukharin's position on NEP, see Lars Lih, "Bukharin's 'Illusion': War Communism and the Meaning of NEP," *Russian History/Histoire Russe* 27, no. 4 (winter 2000): 417-59. On collectivization, see the classic studies of Moshe Lewin: *Russian Peasants and Soviet Power: A Study of Collectivization*, trans. from French by Irene Nove and John Biggart, preface by Alec Nove (London: Allen and Unwin, 1968); *The Making of the Soviet System* (New York: Pantheon Books, 1985); and *Political Undercurrents in Soviet Economic Debates: From Bukharin to the Modern Reformers* (Princeton, N.J.: Princeton University Press, 1974).

17. Reflecting the growing Western influence, O. P. Korol'kov ("Sovremennaia sovetskaia istoriografiia ekonomicheskikh problem NEPa" [diss., Moscow Academy of Social Sciences, 1990]) sought to reassess NEP and provide a framework, or "methodological orientation," for perestroika, dating NEP in various stages throughout Soviet history, with the 1920s constituting only the initial phase. Here, Bukharin emerged as the "true" Leninist.

18. V. P. Mishakov, "Razoblachenie fal'sifikatsii 'ostforshungom' leninskikh printsipov ekonomicheskoi politiki perekhodnogo perioda" (kand. diss.,

Moscow State University, 1971). The author criticized Western "so-called" Sovietologists, obsessed with NEP because it was a time of competition between capitalism and socialism which the latter presumably won. The West was eager, therefore, to falsify this history in order to discourage the worldwide spread of socialism.

19. See, for instance, I. V. Bystrova, "Gosudarstvo i ekonomika v 1920-e gody: Bor'ba idei i real'nost'," *Otechestvennaia istoriia*, no. 3 (1993): 19-34, where the author maintained that during NEP, the realism of economists and the intelligentsia was pitted against the political and social agendas of party leaders, specifically Stalin. The author also maintained that the debate over NEP reflected only the power play within the party leadership.

20. See Robert Tucker's summation of a conference of Russian and American scholars held in Moscow in 1989 which focused on "[t]he question of alternativnost', the possible 1920s alternatives to the course history actually took in the 1930s" ("Soviet History in the 1920s," *Slavic Review* 50, no. 2 [summer 1991]: 239-40). For the use of NEP to legitimize reform under *perestroika*, see Lars T. Lih, "Perestroika's Revival of NEP: A Contemporary Chronicle 1985–1990," *The NEP Era: Soviet Russia 1921–1928* 3 (2009): 1-35.

21. See, for instance, John Hazard's interpretation in *The Soviet System of Government*, 5th ed. (Chicago: University of Chicago Press, 1980).

22. Stephen F. Cohen, *Rethinking the Soviet Experience: Politics and History since 1917* (New York: Oxford University Press, 1985), 22. J. Arch Getty criticized the "Westernizing approach" which "discourages locating historical problems or evils lower down in the apparatus and [thus] will have little interest in emphasizing unseemly social problems like class conflict, specialist baiting, populist hostility toward the intelligentsia, or wage and status conflicts" ("The Politics of Stalinism," in *The Stalin Phenomenon*, ed. Alec Nove [New York: St. Martin's Press, 1993], 114-15). The work of Sheila Fitzpatrick, a central figure among revisionists, provoked much controversy. On the causes of this controversy, see the discussion led by Fitzpatrick in *Slavic Review* 67, no. 3 (fall 2008): 682-723, and the response in the "Letters" section, *Slavic Review* 68, no. 1 (spring 2009): 219-24; see, also, chapter 10 below.

23. See Sheila Fitzpatrick, ed., *Cultural Revolution in Russia, 1928–1931* (Bloomington: Indiana University Press, 1978). For the historical debate on the new social history, see note 22 above and the "Discussion," *Russian Review* 45, no. 4 (October 1986): 357-414.

24. Notable studies focusing on social discontent and radicalism during NEP include Sheila Fitzpatrick, *Education and Social Mobility in the Soviet Union 1921–1934* (New York: Cambridge University Press, 1979), where she examined the Soviet education system during NEP and showed that higher education first retained its prerevolutionary character in instructors, students, and philosophy but in the Cultural Revolution opened its doors to a new generation of Red specialists and administrators, who would form the future Soviet ruling class; see, also, Peter Konecny, "Chaos on Campus: The 1924 Student Proverka in Leningrad," *Europe-Asia Studies* 46, no. 4 (1994): 617-35. On worker-peasant tensions, see Douglas Weiner, "Razmychka? Urban Unemployment and Peasant In-Migration as Sources of Social Conflict," in *Russia in the Era of NEP: Explorations in Soviet Society and Culture*, ed. Sheila

Fitzpatrick, Alexander Rabinowitch, and Richard Stites (Bloomington: Indiana University Press, 1991), 144-55. Other contributions to the same volume include John B. Hatch, "Labor Conflict in Moscow, 1921–1925"; Diane P. Koenker, "Class and Consciousness in a Socialist Society: Workers in the Printing Trades during NEP"; and Wendy Z. Goldman, "Working-Class Women and the 'Withering Away' of the Family: Popular Responses to Family Policy." See, also, Lewis H. Siegelbaum and Ronald G. Suny, eds., *Making Workers Soviet: Power, Class, and Identity* (Ithaca, N.Y.: Cornell University Press, 1994); William J. Chase, *Workers, Society, and the Soviet State: Labor and Life in Moscow, 1918–1929* (Urbana: University of Illinois Press, 1987); David L. Hoffmann, "Land, Freedom, and Discontent: Russian Peasants of the Central Industrial Region prior to Collectivisation," *Europe-Asia Studies* 46, no. 4 (1994): 637-48; Lynn Viola, *The Best Sons of the Fatherland: Workers in the Vanguard of Soviet Collectivization* (New York: Oxford University Press, 1987); and Mark von Hagen, *Soldiers in the Proletarian Dictatorship: The Red Army and the Soviet Socialist State, 1917–1930* (Ithaca, N.Y.: Cornell University Press, 1990). For a study of the NEP period generally, see Lewis H. Siegelbaum, *Soviet State and Society between Revolutions, 1918–1929* (New York: Cambridge University Press, 1992).

More recent is a journal devoted to the study of NEP: *The NEP Era, 1921–1928*, edited by Alexis Pogorelskin. On NEP discontent, see my essay in that volume based on this study, "Petitioners and Their Discontents: The Lost Generation of the 1920s," *The NEP Era: Soviet Russia 1921–1928* 2 (2008): 61-80. In a special issue of *Russian History/Histoire Russe* devoted to the journal's inauguration in 2007, Pogorelskin noted that during the 1990s, NEP historiography was sharply divided between East and West, the Russians concentrating on politics and Western scholars, particularly Americans, focusing on social history ("Guest Editor's Introduction: The Politics of NEP and the Politics of Its Historiography," *Russian History/Histoire Russe* 27, no. 4 [winter 2000]: 377-79). However, by the end of the decade the social history of NEP was addressed in documentary collections edited by Russian scholars, including Andrei Sokolov (see note 4 above).

25. See note 12 above. For instance, Halfin (*From Darkness to Light*, xi) attributes violence under the Communists "directly" to marxism as a "dangerous political doctrine." For a "revolution from above" interpretation of the evolution of Soviet society sympathetic to socialism, see Murphy, *Revolution and Counterrevolution*, where the author makes a distinction between socialism and Stalinism: "[The NEP period] was also the period in which Stalinism clashed head-on with the ideals of 1917" (6). See, also, the edited collection, Niels Erik Rosenfeldt, Bent Jensen, and Erik Kulavig, eds., *Mechanisms of Power in the Soviet Union* (New York: St. Martin's Press, 2000), where the debate over which forces controlled the formation of the early Soviet state (the party or Stalin) continues to focus on the center: "A basic contention of all the contributions to [this book] is that the Communist Party of the Soviet Union (CPSU) became the lynchpin of the system, its tentacles firmly tying all parts of the diverse country and its burgeoning politico-administrative structure into the one integrated and disciplined apparatus. In other words, the CPSU became the core of statehood itself in the Party-state system" (Robert Tucker,

"Foreword," vii). Irina Pavlova's essay in the collection offers a more nuanced interpretation ("The Strength and Weakness of Stalin's Power," 23-39), suggesting that through Stalin's manipulation, ordinary people became his accomplices. In her introduction to *Mekhanizm vlasti i stroitel'stvo stalinskogo sotsializma* (Novosibirsk: Izd-vo CO RAN, 2001), Pavlova offers an insightful critique on historiography concerning the relationship of the party to power. For general histories with a center-based interpretation, see: Woodford McClellan, *Russia: A History of the Soviet Period* (Englewood Cliffs, N.J.: Prentice-Hall, 1986); Geoffrey Hosking, *The First Socialist Society: A History of the Soviet Union from Within*, enlarged ed. (Cambridge, Mass.: Harvard University Press, 1990); Richard Pipes, *The Russian Revolution* (New York: Alfred A. Knopf, 1990); idem, *Russia under the Bolshevik Regime* (New York: Alfred A. Knopf, 1993); Martin McCauley, *The Soviet Union 1917–1991*, 2[d] ed. (London: Longman, 1993); and Martin Malia, *The Soviet Tragedy: A History of Socialism in Russia, 1917–1991* (New York: Macmillan, The Free Press, 1994). Even studies seeking to embed the formation of the Soviet state in the context of NEP's problems (thus implicitly emphasizing the limitations of state control) mainly focus on the center, specifically the relationship between Bolshevik ideology and economic developments: see, for instance, E. G. Gimpel'son, "NEP: Byla li vozmozhnost' 'vyzhit'"?" in *NEP v kontekste istoricheskogo razvitie*, ed. Sokolov, 39-56; Robert Service, "Stalinism and the Soviet State Order," in *Redefining Stalinism*, ed. Harold Shukman (London: Frank Cass, 2003), 7-22; and Iu. Goland, *Krizisy, razrushivshie NEP/Valiutnoe regulirovanie v period NEPa* (Moscow: Fond ekonomicheskoe knigi "Nachala," 1998). One study that diverges from this general trend is William B. Husband, "The New Economic Policy (NEP) and the Revolutionary Experiment, 1921–1929," in *Russia: A History*, ed. Gregory Freeze (Oxford University Press, 1997), 263-90, which emphasizes the problems of NEP and rank-and-file radicalism. The question of the continuing appeal of the totalitarian model is discussed in chapter 10.

26. In *Stalin's Peasants: Resistance and Survival in the Russian Village after Collectivization* (New York: Oxford University Press, 1994), Sheila Fitzpatrick observed that while the Bolsheviks did not "singlehandedly invent the idea of conflict along class lines in the villages," the situation was confusing, because class differentiation "had as much to do with political allegiance and historical memory as . . . with current economic status" (31), suggesting that class conflict was based in something more than economics.

27. See the translation of a 1994 roundtable discussion at the Russian Academy of Sciences, "Current Problems of Historical Theory," *Russian Studies in History* 35, no. 3 (winter 1996); and a summary of the conference proceedings, "Revolutsiia i chelovek: sotsiial'no-psichologicheskii aspekt" (*Otechestvennaia istoriia*, no. 4 [1995]: 211-18).

28. See, for instance, L. N. Pushkarev, "Chto takoe mentalitet?" *Otechestvennaia istoriia*, no. 3 (1995): 158-66; E. Iu. Zubkova and A. I. Kupriianov, "Mental'noe izmerenie istorii: Poiski metoda," *Voprosy istorii*, no. 7 (1995): 153-60; and "'Mentalitet i agrarnoe razvitie Rossii v xix-xx vekakh': Mezhdunarodnaia konferentsiia v Moskve," *Otechestvennaia istoriia*, no. 1 (1996): 195-204.

29. A. I. Kuriianov, "Istoricheskaia antropologiia v Rossii: Problemy stanovleniia," *Otechestvennaia istoriia*, no. 4 (1996): 86-99.
30. Gareth Steadman Jones, *Languages of Class: Studies in English Working-Class History 1832–1982* (Cambridge: Cambridge University Press, 1983), chap. 4, "Working-Class Culture and Working-Class Politics in London, 1870–1900: Notes on the Remaking of a Working Class," 196.
31. Ibid., chap. 3, "Rethinking Chartism," 94-95.
32. Lynn Hunt, *Politics, Culture, and Class in the French Revolution* (Berkeley: University of California Press, 1984), 10-11; for an exhaustive study of French revolutionary language, see François Furet and Mona Ozouf, eds., *A Critical Dictionary of the French Revolution*, trans. Arthur Goldhammer (Cambridge, Mass.: Belknap Press/Harvard University Press, 1989 [1988]).
33. Advocates of the totalitarian model assumed that communication operated virtually in one direction—policies came from above, were transmitted downward, and implemented through terror. See, for instance, T. H. Rigby, *Communist Party Membership in the U.S.S.R. 1917–1967* (Princeton, N.J.: Princeton University Press, 1968), 39. But even Rigby concedes that "it would be a serious oversimplification to conclude that Soviet policy making is totally uninfluenced by pressures from below" (40). Similarly, John Hazard wrote that "public opinion can be effectively expressed only through a licensed agency. This is not to say that the Communist Party wants to hear no public opinion. The contrary is true. The party has always been attentive to restlessness among the masses" (*The Soviet System of Government*, 66-67).
34. In her study of messages and values imbedded in workers' essays submitted to a *Pravda* contest during 1922 ("Factory Tales: Narratives of Industrial Relations in the Transition to NEP," *Russian Review* 55, no. 3 [July 1996]: 384-411), Diane Koenker observed that "[t]hese narratives . . . helped to construct an operative language of industrial relations in this liminal period of the definition of socialism" (386), and that, in the process of negotiation and communication, "[t]here came to be no clear demarcation between 'official' values and 'authentic' values, for each influenced the other" (407). On the blurring of "above" and "below," see, also, Michael S. Fox, "Political Culture, Purges, and Proletarianization at the Institute of Red Professors, 1921–1929," *Russian Review* 52, no. 1 (January 1993): 20-42. In a recent study on the Rabsel'kor movement in the 1920s ("From Conduits to Commanders: Shifting Views of Worker Correspondents," *Revolutionary Russia* 19, no. 2 [December 2006]: 131-49), Jeremy Hicks noted a gradual shift in the rabsel'kors' role and relationship to the party toward Stalin's desire for greater control: "the power of the worker correspondents to scrutinize abuses by Party members was gradually eroded and then put an end to altogether when they were placed under the control of local Party bureaux in August 1926" (135), but also that the call for greater control came in part from "the floor" at the Second Rabsel'kor Conference, in order to protect the correspondents (140). In another study in the same volume ("Class Ascription and Class Identity: *Komsomol'tsy* and the Policy of Class during Nep," 175-96), Matthias Neumann noted that during NEP, the "process of becoming aware of class fragmentation and class conflict in society was mutually driven by the political discourse from above, though not al-

ways intentionally, and through experience, traditions, expectations and autonomous discourses from below" (190).

35. In "Supplicants and Citizens: Public Letter-Writing in Soviet Russia in the 1930s," *Slavic Review* 55, no. 1 (spring 1996): 78-105, Sheila Fitzpatrick noted that many of the letter-writing conventions of the 1930s clearly predated the Soviet period, including "[c]onstruing an authority figure as a 'beloved father,' appealing for justice (without reference to law), complaining to higher authority about local abuses, writing pathetically of 'the crust of bread' that was so often lacking" (92). Her observation that much of the language used in letters came from *Pravda* (94) begs the questions, why *Pravda* used that language, and where it originated.

36. David Hoffmann, "History and Literary Criticism," *Russian Review* 55, no. 3 (July 1996): vii-viii.

37. Mark D. Steinberg, "Stories and Voices: History and Theory," *Russian Review* 55, no. 3 (July 1996): 347-54.

38. In addressing the origins of Stalinism, J. Arch Getty remarked on the gap of experience and thus of understanding between "educated, comfortable people" and "those at the bottom of society" that affects both history and historical analysis ("The Politics of Stalinism," 116). On this problem, see chapter 10 below.

39. Major documentary publications include collections of letters to the center: A. Ia. Livshin and I. B. Orlov, comps., *Pis'ma vo vlast', 1917–1927: Zaiavleniia, zhaloby, donosy, pis'ma v gosudarstvennye struktury i bolshevistskim vozhdiam* (Moscow: ROSSPEN, 1998); and two collections, covering the 1920s and '30s, respectively: A. K. Sokolov, gen. ed., *Golos naroda: Pis'ma i otkliki riadovykh sovetskihk grazhdan o sobytiiakh 1918–1932 gg.* (Moscow: ROSSPEN, 1998), especially chapter 6, "Liudi i vlast'" ("People and Power"), chapter 7, "Narodnyi sotsializm" ("Popular Socialism"), and chapter 8, "Velikii perelom" ("The Great Turn"); and Lewis Siegelbaum and Andrei Sokolov, eds., *Stalinism as a Way of Life: A Narrative in Documents*, abridged ed. (New Haven, Conn.: Yale University Press, 2004). In his preface to *Golos naroda*, Sokolov justifies using the voice of "common people" to understand events of the period and how various aspects and structures of society were built, and to address the problem of the connection between/influence of letter writers and government. An important work containing the stenographic records of party Central Committee plenums when the decisive discussions concerning the abandonment of NEP took place is V. P. Danilov et al., *Kak lomali NEP: Stenogrammy Plenumov TsK VKP(b) 1928–1929 gg.*, Rossiia XX Vek: Dokumenty, A. N. Iakovlev, gen. ed., 5 vols. (Moscow: Mezhdunarodnyi fond "Demokratiia," 2000).

40. This appraisal of post-Soviet historiography in both the former Soviet Union and the West can be found in Alter Litvin and John Keep, eds., *Stalinism: Russian and Western Views at the Turn of the Millennium* (London: Routledge, 2005).

Chapter One

1. Traditional historians, focusing analysis on the Bolshevik leadership, support the former interpretation. See, for instance, Richard Pipes, *The Russian Revolution* (New York: Alfred A. Knopf, 1990), chap. 11. A post-Soviet history by Russian scholars also supports the coup d'état theory: Alexander A. Danilov et al., *The History of Russia: The Twentieth Century*, trans. Galina Ustinova, trans. and ed. Vincent E. Hammond (n.p.: The Heron Press, 1996).

2. The term "war communism" was first used by Lenin only in 1921.

3. NEP was also a belated term to describe an ad hoc "policy."

4. Marc Ferro, *October 1917: A Social History of the Russian Revolution*, trans. Norman Stone (London: Routledge and Kegan Paul, 1980), 3; on popular revolutionary aspirations, see, also, idem, *The Russian Revolution of February 1917*, trans. J. L. Richards (Englewood Cliffs, N. J.: Prentice-Hall, 1972). For a post-Soviet assessment of 1917 that is more balanced and less ideologically driven, see F. A. Gaida, "Fevral' 1917 goda: Revoliutsiia, vlast', burzhuaziia," *Voprosy istorii*, no. 3 (1996): 31-45.

5. Orlando Figes, *Peasant Russia, Civil War: The Volga Countryside in Revolution (1917–1921)* (Oxford: Clarendon Press, 1989), 5. The growing body of work on the Bolsheviks' early attempts to integrate Soviet citizens into a new socialist society includes David Brandenburger, *National Bolshevism: Stalinist Mass Culture and the Formation of Modern Russian National Identity, 1931–1956* (Cambridge, Mass.: Harvard University Press, 2002), where the author argues that the Bolsheviks were unsuccessful before the 1930s and Stalinism in forming a sense of national consciousness, both because citizens' loyaties were regional at best, and because of the internationalist emphasis of radical communism. For party influence through the press, see Jeffrey Brooks, *Thank You, Comrade Stalin!: Soviet Public Culture from Revolution to Cold War* (Princeton, N.J.: Princeton University Press, 2000); for efforts at social reform through literacy, see Charles Clark, *Uprooting Otherness: The Literacy Campaign in NEP-Era Russia* (Selinsgrove, Pa.: Susquehanna University Press, 2000). Other studies on the use of ideology include Igal Halfin, *From Darkness to Light: Class, Consciousness, and Salvation in Revolutionary Russia* (Pittsburgh, Pa.: University of Pittsburgh Press, 2000); and Christina Kiaer and Eric Naiman, eds., *Everyday Life in Early Soviet Russia: Taking the Revolution Inside* (Bloomington: Indiana University Press, 2006). For more on this, see the introduction n. 12.

6. Stephen A. Smith, *Red Petrograd: Revolution in the Factories 1917–1918* (Cambridge University Press, 1983), 256.

7. Ferro, *October 1917*, 4.

8. Stephen Smith observed that while factory committees tried to gain the support of technical and clerical staff, even clerical workers opposed workers' control, eliciting the animosity of blue-collar workers (*Red Petrograd*, 234).

9. Ibid., 261.

10. See Figes, *Peasant Russia, Civil War*; and Dorothy Atkinson, *The End of the Russian Land Commune, 1905–1930* (Stanford, Calif.: Stanford University Press, 1983).

11. On the persistence of power structures in the village after the revolution, see Orlando Figes, "The Village and Volost Soviet Elections of 1919," *Soviet Studies* 40, no. 1 (January 1988): 21-45; and David L. Hoffman, "Land, Freedom, and Discontent: Russian Peasants of the Central Industrial Region prior to Collectivization," *Europe-Asia Studies* 46 (1994): 637-48.

12. Alec Nove, *An Economic History of the U.S.S.R.*, 2[d] ed. (Harmondsworth, England: Penguin Books, 1989), 24. Information and figures on war communism and the NEP era that follow are derived from Nove, *An Economic History of the U.S.S.R.*; E. H. Carr, *A History of Soviet Russia: The Bolshevik Revolution 1917–1923*, vols. 1-3, *The Interregnum 1923–1924*, *Socialism in One Country 1924–1926*, vols. 1-3; and, with R. W. Davies, *Foundations of a Planned Economy 1926–1929*, vols. 1-3 (New York and London: Macmillan, 1950–1976); R. W. Davies, ed., *From Tsarism to the New Economic Policy: Continuity and Change in the Economy of the USSR* (Ithaca, N.Y.: Cornell University Press, 1991); Figes, *Peasant Russia, Civil War*; Smith, *Red Petrograd*; and Maurice Dobb, *Russian Economic Development since the Revolution* (London, 1929).

13. See, for instance, Alexander Rabinowitch, "The Evolution of Local Soviets in Petrograd, November 1917-June 1918: The Case of the First City District Soviet," *Slavic Review* 46, no. 1 (spring 1987): 20-37.

14. Smith, *Red Petrograd*, 259-60.

15. Nove, *An Economic History of the U.S.S.R.*, 37.

16. Smith, *Red Petrograd*, 225, 236. The nationalization of industry in June 1918 occurred mainly under pressure from workers' factory committees, which had called for national control of industry from the beginning, in order to coordinate numerous, spontaneous factory seizures. Ironically, the seizure of factories by worker committees was more common in provincial areas than in radical Petrograd.

17. Nove, *An Economic History of the U.S.S.R.*, 38.

18. The word was an acronym from the Russian: Vserossiiskii Sovet Narodnogo Khoziaistva.

19. See Figes, *Peasant Russia, Civil War*; Atkinson noted that peasants struggled against those wishing to separate from the commune and tried to eliminate individual holdings (*The End of the Russian Land Commune*, 129, 155-59).

20. See Figes, *Peasant Russia, Civil War*, chap. 6, "The Rural Economy under War Communism," 246-73, especially the section on food procurement and prodrazverstka from 1919 to 1921. On the intentions of the Bolshevik government during war communism as expressed in Bukharin's work *The ABC of Communism*, Lars Lih pointed out that the Bolsheviks neither invented prodrazverstka—it was first used in tsarist times—nor considered it a "centerpiece" of their peasant policy ("The Mystery of the ABC," *Slavic Review* 56, no. 1 [spring 1997]: 50-72).

21. Although the Bolsheviks defined a "kulak" as a relatively wealthy peasant who employed hired labor, they were generally poor by Western standards. Such peasants might, however, act as usurers to poorer peasants—hence the pejorative term "kulak"—by lending them grain when they ran out over the course of the year. Kulaks were also able to sell when the market offered

higher prices, and they owned whatever machinery or livestock was available, and benefited from hiring it out (Nove, *An Economic History of the U.S.S.R.*, 98). As Nove implies, the kulak was essentially a rural businessman, whose relative commercial success put him in a position of power in the village and of control over the grain. This last aspect more than any other evoked the animosity of the Bolshevik government, which deemed wealthier peasants as "petty-bourgeois," a term essentially used to connote anyone who asserted independence from the Soviet government and society. But the term also carried a moral implication: businessmen placed the good of the individual ahead of the collective. Unsurprisingly, Western accounts tend to take an opposite view, assigning positive moral value to the "strong" or "solid" peasant, whose moral opposite is the shiftless bedniak, or poor peasant, who often supported communism in the countryside. See, for instance, Sheila Fitzpatrick, *Stalin's Peasants: Resistance and Survival in the Russian Village after Collectivization* (New York: Oxford University Press, 1994), 11, 30-31.

22. Ibid., 45-46.

23. See Diane P. Koenker, "Urbanization and Deurbanization in the Russian Revolution and Civil War," in Diane P. Koenker, William G. Rosenberg, and Ronald G. Suny, eds., *Party, State, and Society in the Russian Civil War: Explorations in Social History* (Bloomington: Indiana University Press, 1989), 81-104.

24. On the militarization of labor, see Jonathan Aves, *Workers Against Lenin: Labour Protest and the Bolshevik Dictatorship* (London: Tauris Academic Studies, 1996).

25. For peasant revolts against the Bolsheviks, see Figes, *Peasant Russia, Civil War*, chap. 7; see also *Krest'ianskoe Vosstanie v Tambovskoi Gubernii v 1919–1921 gg. "Antonovshchina": Dokumenty* (Tambov, 1994).

26. See Paul Avrich, *Kronstadt 1921* (Princeton, N. J.: Princeton University Press, 1970); and Israel Getzler, *Kronstadt 1917–1921: The Fate of a Soviet Democracy* (New York: Cambridge University Press, 1983). Several documents on Kronstadt from Russian archives were published in *Voprosy istorii*, nos. 4-7 (1994).

27. Nove, *An Economic History of the U.S.S.R.*, 74.

28. See Alan Ball, *Russia's Last Capitalists: The Nepmen, 1921–1929* (Berkeley: University of California Press, 1987).

29. Ibid., 104; Nove gives a more conservative estimate of 78 percent for the fiscal year 1922–23 (*An Economic History of the U.S.S.R.*, 93).

30. Nove, *An Economic History of the U.S.S.R.*, 75.

31. See F. A. Golder and Lincoln Hutchinson, *On the Trail of the Russian Famine* (Stanford, Calif.: Stanford University Press, 1927); Harold H. Fisher, *The Famine in Soviet Russia* (New York: Macmillan Company, 1927); and Benjamin Weissman, *Herbert Hoover and Famine Relief to Soviet Russia, 1921–1923* (Stanford, Calif.: Hoover Institution Press, 1974).

32. See Ball, *Russia's Last Capitalists*, "Building Communism with Bourgeois Hands," 15-37.

33. See Carr, *The Interregnum*, "The Scissors Crisis."

34. Ibid., 39.

35. See William J. Chase, *Workers, Society, and the Soviet State: Labor and Life in Moscow, 1918–1929* (Urbana: University of Illinois Press, 1987); and Carr, *The Interregnum*, chap. 2, "The Plight of Labour," and *Socialism in One Country*, vol. 1, chap. 7, "Labour." On the impact of unemployment on women, see Wendy Z. Goldman, *Women, the State, and Revolution: Soviet Family Policy and Social Life, 1917–1936* (Cambridge: Cambridge University Press, 1993). On the crisis of the working class and its contribution to the end of NEP, see Hiroaki Kuromiya, *Stalin's Industrial Revolution: Politics and Workers, 1928–1932* (Cambridge: Cambridge University Press, 1988). See also Lewis H. Siegelbaum, *Soviet State and Society between Revolutions, 1918–1929* (Cambridge: Cambridge University Press, 1992). The six-volume Soviet history of the working class (S. S. Khromov, et al., *Istoriia sovetskogo rabochego klassa v shesti tomakh* [Moscow: Nauka, 1984–88]) devotes all of six pages to the problem of unemployment during NEP, emphasizing the factor of rural migration in the growth of unemployment and the subsequent solutions to this problem in collectivization and industrialization. The problem of unemployment and is discussed in chapter 4 below.

36. See Alan M. Ball, *And Now My Soul Is Hardened: Abandoned Children in Soviet Russia, 1918–1930* (Berkeley: University of California Press, 1994); and Margaret K. Stolee, "Homeless Children in the USSR, 1917–1957," *Soviet Studies* 40, no. 1 (January 1988): 64-83.

37. E. H. Carr, *Foundations of a Planned Economy, 1926–1929*, vol. 1, pt. 1 (New York: Macmillan, 1969), 333-38.

38. Ibid., 335-36.

39. Nove, *An Economic History of the U.S.S.R.*, 128. The author notes that this amendment, Article 107 of the Criminal Code, would "be used by Stalin two years later" in the war against the kulaks.

40. Chapter 3 is devoted to this problem. Alexandre Barmine and his communist contemporaries viewed a return to market relations and the use of money as precursors to the reappearance of "rich people"—social disparity—and an inevitable slide down "the slippery slope that led back to capitalism" (*One Who Survived: The Life Story of a Russian under the Soviets* [New York: G. P. Putnam, 1945], 124-26). Commentaries on Soviet Russia written or published before the Stalinist period and NEP's demise, especially in the early 1920s, proclaimed that with NEP, communism—if not the communist government—was all but dead. See, for example, Edwin Ware Hullinger, *The Reforging of Russia* (New York: E. P. Dutton, 1925), 20-27; Walter Duranty, *I Write as I Please* (New York: Simon and Schuster, 1935), 105-6; and Markoosha Fischer, *My Lives in Russia* (New York: Harper, 1944), 10-15. Russian historian I. Ia. Trifonov asserted that many contemporaries hostile to Bolshevism, including Russian liberals, Mensheviks, and European social democrats, concluded from the introduction of NEP that the communist "experiment" had failed (*Klassy i klassovaia bor'ba v SSSR v nachale nepa*, vol. 2, *Podgotovka ekonomicheskogo nastupleniia na novuiu burzhuaziiu* [Leningrad: Izd-vo Leningradskogo universiteta, 1969], 4). Soviet historians often attempted to rationalize the party's decision to adopt NEP, providing a further indication of its unpopularity among those sympathetic to the communist cause

(see, for instance, V. P. Dmitrenko, *Torgovaia politika Sovetskogo gosudarstva posle perekhoda k nepu: 1921–1924 gg.* [Moscow: Nauka, 1971], 265).

Chapter Two

1. These comments can be compared with Lynn Hunt's observations on what "the Nation" meant in the minds and rhetoric of French revolutionaries (*Politics, Culture, and Class in the French Revolution* [Berkeley, Calif.: University of California Press, 1984], introduction and chap. 1).

2. This was not true in Ukraine or Belorussia, where private property and individual inheritance were the rule (Boris Mironov, "The Russian Peasant Commune after the Reforms of the 1860s," trans. Gregory Freeze and Carol S. Leonard, *Slavic Review* 44, no. 3 [fall 1985]: 455). The literature on the peasant commune is vast. On the question of the peasant commune after the reforms of 1861 and 1906, see Dorothy Atkinson, *The End of the Russian Land Commune, 1905–1930* (Stanford, Calif.: Stanford University Press, 1983); eadem, "The Statistics on the Russian Land Commune, 1905–1917," *Slavic Review* 32, no. 4 (December 1973); John Keep, "The Agrarian Revolution of 1917–1918 in Soviet Historiography," *Russian Review* 36, no. 4 (October 1977); Basile Kerblay, "The Peasant," *Survey* 64 (July 1967); V. Maklakov, "The Agrarian Problem in Russia before the Revolution," *Russian Review* 9, no. 1 (January 1950); John Maynard, *Russia in Flux: Before October* (London: V. Gollancz Ltd., 1946); Oliver Radkey, *The Agrarian Foes of Bolshevism: Promise and Default of the Russian Socialist Revolutionaries February to October 1917* (New York: Columbia University Press, 1958); Geroid T. Robinson, *Rural Russia under the Old Regime: A History of the Landlord-Peasant World and a Prologue to the Peasant Revolution of 1917* (New York: Macmillan, 1949); Teodor Shanin, *The Awkward Class: Political Sociology of Peasantry in a Developing Society, Russia 1910–1925* (Oxford: Clarendon Press, 1972); George Tokmakoff, "Stolypin's Agrarian Reform: An Appraisal," *Russian Review* 30, no. 2 (April 1971); Nicholas Vakar, *The Taproot of Soviet Society* (New York: Harper, 1962); Eugene D. Vinogradoff, "The Russian Peasantry and the Elections to the Fourth Duma: Estate Political Consciousness and Class Political Consciousness" (Ph.D. diss., Columbia University, 1974); Sir Donald Mackenzie Wallace, *Russia on the Eve of War and Revolution*, ed. C. E. Black (New York: Vintage Books, 1961); George L. Yaney, *The Urge to Mobilize: Agrarian Reform in Russia, 1861–1930* (Urbana: University of Illinois Press, 1982); and idem, "Some Suggestions regarding the Study of Russian Peasant Society prior to Collectivization," *Russian Review* 44, no. 1 (January 1985).

3. Mironov, "The Russian Peasant Commune," 441-50.

4. On the pauperizing and differentiating effects of the 1861 Reforms, see Atkinson, *The End of the Russian Land Commune*, esp. chap. 2; and R. W. Davies, ed., *From Tsarism to the New Economic Policy: Continuity and Change in the Economy of the USSR* (Ithaca, N.Y.: Cornell University Press, 1991). Orlando Figes also noted this long-term trend but emphasized that general impoverishment characterized mainly the central black-earth regions, in contrast with the periphery—the Baltic, western Ukraine, southern Russia,

the Volga steppe, and western Siberia (*Peasant Russia, Civil War: The Volga Countryside in Revolution [1917–1921]* [Oxford: Clarendon Press, 1989], 16-18). For an alternative interpretation, which views the reforms as raising rural living standards, see Boris N. Mironov, "The Myth of a Systemic Crisis in Russia after the Great Reforms of the 1860s-1870s," *Russian Studies in History* 47, no. 4 (spring 2009): 40-52.

5. Robinson, *Rural Russia under the Old Regime*, 233; and Atkinson, *The End of the Russian Land Commune*, 91-92. On agricultural effects of the Stolypin reforms, see, also, A. V. Efremenko, "Agronomicheskii aspekt stolypinskoi zemel'noi reformy," *Voprosy istorii*, no. 11-12 (1996): 3-15.

6. Particularly among Russian historians but also in the West, post-Soviet historiography has emphasized the profound influence of postwar trauma and dislocation in the formation of the early Soviet state. See, especially, various works by A. K. Sokolov, including "Istoricheskoe znachenie NEPa," in *NEP v kontekste istoricheskogo razvitie Rossii XX veka*, ed. Sokolov (Moscow: Russian Academy of Sciences, Institute of Russian History, 2001), 6-12, and other essays in the collection; and Irina Pavlova, *Mekhanizm vlasti i stroitel'stvo stalinskogo sotsializma* (Novosibirsk: Izd-vo CO RAN, 2001), 3.

7. V. Z. Drobizhev et al., *Rabochii klass Sovetskoi Rossii v pervyi god proletarskoi diktatury: Opyt strukturnogo analiza po materialam professional'noi perepisi 1918 g.* (Moscow: Izd-vo Moskovskogo universiteta, 1975), 210. Emphasis in the original.

8. RGASPI, f. 5, op. 1, d. 1716, l. 4.

9. Victor Kravchenko, *I Chose Freedom: The Personal and Political Life of a Soviet Official* (New York: C. Scribner's and Sons, 1946), 40.

10. Gabriele Gorzka, "Proletarian Culture in Practice: Worker's Clubs, 1917–1921," in *Essays on Revolutionary Culture and Stalinism: Selected Papers from the Third World Congress for Soviet and East European Studies*, ed. John W. Strong (Columbus, Ohio: Slavica Publishers, 1990), 38, 41.

11. Gregory L. Freeze, *From Supplication to Revolution: A Documentary Social History of Imperial Russia* (New York: Oxford University Press, 1988), 262.

12. Mark von Hagen, *Soldiers in the Proletarian Dictatorship: The Red Army and the Soviet Socialist State, 1917–1930*, Studies of the Harriman Institute (Ithaca, N.Y.: Cornell University Press, 1990), 35; 281-82.

13. On unemployment and abandonment, see chapter 4 below.

14. In her study of workers' essays on factory directors submitted to a *Pravda* contest during 1922 ("Factory Tales: Narratives of Industrial Relations in the Transition to NEP," *Russian Review* 55, no. 3 [July 1996]: 384-411), Diane Koenker noted the many traits that workers attributed to "good" directors. Descriptions of the fatherly director who cared for his workers bear a striking similarity to the traits attributed to Lenin in the letters used here.

15. This is not to imply that Lenin received no critical correspondence; on the contrary, from the very first, there was widespread criticism about Lenin's government and complaints about the course of the Revolution. See, for instance, letters from Lenin's personal archive published in *Neizvestnaia Rossiia: XX Vek*, vol. 1 (Moscow: Istoricheskoe Nasledie, 1992), "Leninu o Lenine: Pis'ma 1918–1921."

16. RGASPI, f. 5, op. 1, d. 1709, l. 7.
17. RGASPI, f. 5, op. 1, d. 1680, l. 5.
18. RGASPI, f. 17, op. 85, d. 517, l. 91.
19. RGASPI, f. 17, op. 85, d. 517, l. 25.
20. RGASPI, f. 17, op. 85, d. 516, ll. 224-26.
21. RGASPI, f. 17, op. 85, d. 520, l. 143.
22. RGASPI, f. 17, op. 85, d. 518, l. 98. A *rabfak* (workers' faculty) was a department in a higher educational institution preparing under-educated workers and peasants for coursework.
23. RGASPI, f. 17, op. 85, d. 517, l. 177. An okrug was an administrative subdivision of a republic, krai, or oblast; here, in Kurgan oblast, Russian S.F.S.R.
24. RGASPI, f. 17, op. 85, d. 516, ll. 121-22.
25. Theodore Dreiser, *Dreiser Looks at Russia* (New York: H. Liveright, 1928), 12-13.
26. RGASPI, f. 17, op. 85, d. 516, l. 86.
27. RGASPI, f. 5, op. 1, d. 1726, l. 9.
28. RGASPI, f. 5, op. 1, d. 1748, l. 6.
29. RGASPI, f. 5, op. 1, d. 1718, l. 4.
30. RGASPI, f. 5, op. 1, d. 1697, l. 7. An oblast' (region) is an administrative subdivision of a union republic; here, in Tambov oblast, Russian S.F.S.R.
31. RGASPI, f. 5, op. 1, d. 1660, l. 4.
32. RGASPI, f. 5, op. 1, d. 1715, l. 4.
33. RGASPI, f. 5, op. 1, d. 1660, l. 1.
34. For a study of the development of Lenin's cult image, see Nina Tumarkin, *Lenin Lives! The Lenin Cult in Soviet Russia* (Cambridge, Mass.: Harvard University Press, 1983); and eadem, "The Myth of Lenin during the Civil War Years," in *Bolshevik Culture: Experiment and Order in the Russian Revolution*, ed. Abbott Gleason, Peter Kenez, and Richard Stites (Bloomington: Indiana University Press, 1985). Tumarkin observed that while the Bolshevik leadership consciously built the Lenin cult around key events and crucial times in the early Soviet years to bolster support and devotion to the party, there was no reason to assume that popular expressions of love for Lenin, or those of the leaders themselves, were not genuine; rather, Lenin's Christlike image seemed the result of "some historical process" ("The Myth of Lenin During the Civil War Years," 81). In a conflicting interpretation, Benno Ennker argued that the Lenin cult was carefully orchestrated and infused with religious meaning and thus artificially imposed by the party leadership on the population ("Leninkult und mytisches Denken in der sowjetischen Offentlichkeit 1924," *Jahrbücher für Geschichte Osteuropas* 44, no. 3 [1996]: 431-55; and idem, "Die Anfänge des Leninkultes," *Jahrbücher für Geschichte Osteuropas* 35, no. 4 [1987]: 534-55). See, also, O. V. Velikanova, "Obraz Lenina v massovom soznanii," *Otechestvennaia istoriia*, no. 2 (1994): 177-85.
35. RGASPI, f. 5, op. 1, d. 1663, l. 3.
36. RGASPI, f. 5, op. 1, d. 1673, l. 4.
37. RGASPI, f. 5, op. 1, d. 1694, l. 1.
38. RGASPI, f. 5, op. 1, d. 1714, l. 6.
39. RGASPI, f. 5, op. 1, d. 1662, l. 6.

40. RGASPI, f. 5, op. 1, d. 1685, l. 3.
41. RGASPI, f. 5, op. 1, d. 1668, l. 3. Supplicants' use of the familiar form (*ty*) in addressing party leaders is noted in the translations of appeals.
42. RGASPI, f. 5, op. 1, d. 1721, l. 3.
43. RGASPI, f. 5, op. 1, d. 1738, l. 1.
44. RGASPI, f. 5, op. 1, d. 1669, l. 5.
45. RGASPI, f. 78, op. 1, d. 47, ll. 50-51.
46. RGASPI, f. 17, op. 85, d. 521, ll. 150-53.
47. *Bednota* was a daily newspaper for peasants, issued by the Communist Party Central Committee in Moscow from March 1918 until January 1931.
48. RGASPI, f. 17, op. 85, d. 514, l. 34.
49. This issue is discussed at length in chapter 7 below.
50. RGASPI, f. 5, op. 1, d. 1673, l. 1.
51. RGASPI, f. 5, op. 1, d. 1731, l. 7.
52. RGASPI, f. 17, op. 85, d. 514, l. 271.
53. RGASPI, f. 17, op. 85, d. 516, ll. 283-86.
54. RGASPI, f. 17, op. 85, d. 515, l. 123.

Chapter Three

1. In his study of Moscow metal workers, Kevin Murphy noted "the fundamental tension between the pursuit of economic efficiency and the defense of workers' rights and interests" during NEP (*Revolution and Counterrevolution: Class Struggle in a Moscow Metal Factory* [2005; Chicago: Haymarket Books, 2007], 83).
2. Paul Scheffer, *Seven Years in Soviet Russia* (London: G. P. Putnam, 1931), 4. This assessment was made in November 1921. For an interesting discussion on the ambiguous position of advertising during NEP that sheds light on party members' discomfort at the reversion to a capitalist economy, see Randi Cox, "'NEP without Nepmen!': Soviet Advertising and the Transition to Socialism," in *Everyday Life in Early Soviet Russia: Taking the Revolution Inside*, ed. Christina Kiaer and Eric Naiman (Bloomington: Indiana University Press, 2006), 119-52. The inherent incongruity between NEP and socialism is highlighted in Cox's comment on the "tension between the need to raise revenues and efforts to use advertising for agitational purposes, which limited advertisers' ability to integrate their work into officially recognized propaganda" (121). The discussion brings into focus an even more basic problem, namely, the ambiguity during NEP of consumption itself. A recent study on advertising focusing on the continuity between the prerevolutionary and Soviet periods is Majorie L. Hilton, *Selling to the Masses: Retailing in Russia, 1880–1930*, Pitt Series in Russian and East European Studies (Pittsburgh, Pa.: University of Pittsburgh Press, 2012).
3. Quoted in Walter Duranty, *I Write as I Please* (New York: Simon and Schuster, 1935), 130. Duranty served as the Moscow bureau chief of *The New York Times* (1922–36) and won a Pulitzer Prize in 1932 for a series of stories on the Soviet Union, but he was criticized for his uncritical reporting on the Soviet regime. Sheila Fitzpatrick noted that "we should be wary of jumping to the

conclusion either that all Western visitors of this period fell into the 'progressive intellectual' category, or that all were 'political pilgrims' whose primary purpose in coming to the Soviet Union (as [Paul] Hollander and others have suggested) was to have their political prejudices confirmed and who thus connived at their own 'duping' by the Kremlin" ("Foreigners Observed: Moscow Visitors in the 1930s under the Gaze of Their Soviet Guides," *Russian History/Histoire Russe* 35, nos. 1-2 [spring-summer 2008]: 216). In the same vein, see Michael David-Fox, *Showcasing the Great Experiment: Cultural Diplomacy and Western Visitors to the Soviet Union, 1921–1941* (Oxford: Oxford University Press, 2012); the view that Western visitors were manipulated by the Soviet government is supported in Ludmila Stern, *Western Intellectuals and the Soviet Union, 1920–1940: From Red Square to the Left Bank*, BASEES/Routledge Series on Russian and East European Studies, no. 31 (New York: Routledge, 2007).

4. Alexander Barmine, *One Who Survived: The Life Story of a Russian under the Soviets* (New York: G. P. Putnam, 1945), 124-26.

5. N. Valentinov (Vol'skii), *Novaia ekonomicheskaia politika i krizis partii posle smerti Lenina: Gody raboty v VSNKh vo vremia NEP; Vospominaniia* (Stanford, Calif.: Hoover Institution Press, 1971), 28-32. The author quoted the speech of a "seredniak" communist named P. N. Murav'ev. According to E. H. Carr, because the crisis of the Kronstadt uprising dominated discussion at the Tenth Party Congress in March 1921, the significance of NEP was "scarcely realized at the time by most of the delegates" (*The Bolshevik Revolution 1917–1923* [New York: Macmillan, 1951], 2:282).

6. Mark von Hagen, *Soldiers in the Proletarian Dictatorship: The Red Army and the Soviet Socialist State, 1917–1930* (Ithaca, N. Y.: Cornell University Press, 1990), 195.

7. Mark von Hagen, "Civil-Military Relations and the Evolution of the Soviet Socialist State," *Slavic Review* 50, no. 2 (summer 1991): 273.

8. RGASPI, f. 17, op. 11, d. 301, l. 4.

9. von Hagen, *Soldiers in the Proletarian Dictatorship*, 190.

10. RGASPI, f. 17, op. 11, d. 341, l. 1. Rabkrin was the Workers' and Peasants' Inspectorate, a grassroot-level government monitoring agency.

11. Carr, *The Bolshevik Revolution*, 2:275-77.

12. Rossiiskii gosudarstvennyi arkhiv ekonomiki (Russian State Archive of the Economy; hereinafter RGAE), f. 4086, op. 1, d. 95, l. 15.

13. RGASPI, f. 17, op. 11, d. 125, l. 70.

14. RGASPI, f. 17, op. 11, d. 122, l. 22.

15. RGASPI, f. 17, op. 84, d. 668, ll. 135-45. In a study on suicide during the NEP era (Kenneth M. Pinnow, *Lost to the Collective: Suicide and the Promise of Soviet Socialism, 1921–1929* [Ithaca, N.Y.: Cornell University Press, 2010], the author discusses the problem of suicide not as a product of NEP, but as a challenge for the Soviet authorities in their quest to remake society.

16. Emphasis added. Tuberculosis was a common affliction among party members, especially among army veterans appealing to the central leadership for intervention in obtaining a cure in a sanitarium who often were bitter over their perception that such cures were restricted to top party administrators and

even members of the intelligentsia (presumably the hated spetsy), and that workers and veterans by contrast were left to suffer an avoidable death.

17. Discussing press and information censorship in the early Soviet state, Jeffrey Brooks noted a 1925 directive from Glavlit (the Chief Administration of Literary and Publishing Affairs) which "banned reports on . . . suicides or cases of insanity resulting from unemployment or hunger" (*Thank You, Comrade Stalin!*, 5).

18. RGASPI, f. 5, op. 1, d. 1683, l. 2.

19. RGASPI, f. 5, op. 1, d. 1690, l. 3.

20. Carr, *The Bolshevik Revolution*, 2:341-42. Popular and party rank-and-file anxiety over NEP was reflected in the leadership's debate over NEP throughout the period. See, for instance, Moshe Lewin, *Political Undercurrents in Soviet Economic Debates* (Princeton, N.J.: Princeton University Press, 1974); and Stephen F. Cohen, *Bukharin and the Bolshevik Revolution: A Political Biography 1888–1938* (New York: Alfred Knopf, 1973).

21. RGASPI, f. 17, op. 85, d. 514, ll. 25-27.

22. RGASPI, f. 17, op. 85, d. 514, ll. 198-203.

23. RGASPI, f. 17, op. 85, d. 522, ll. 194-97.

24. RGASPI, f. 17, op. 85, d. 517, l. 156.

25. RGASPI, f. 17, op. 85, d. 516, l. 185.

26. Theodore Dreiser, *Dreiser Looks at Russia* (New York: H. Liveright, 1928), 12-13.

27. See the exhaustive study by Alan Ball, *Russia's Last Capitalists: The Nepmen, 1921–1929* (Berkeley: University of California Press, 1987). For contemporary accounts, see, for instance, Alexander Berkman, *The Bolshevik Myth: Diary 1920–1922* (New York: Boni and Liveright, 1925), 304-5; and Archibald Forman, *From Baltic to Black Sea: Impressions of Soviet Russia Today* (London: S. Low, Marston, 1932), 19, where the author states that the nepman was "an object of hatred and derision by all," yet the Soviet government had to employ "indirect . . . measures" to eliminate private trade, in order to avoid a public outcry. Markoosha Fischer contended that especially after the introduction of NEP, the old middle class anticipated with relief a return to the "good old days," even though they "abhorred the Nepmen, the nouveaux riches who fattened on the misery of others." She maintained further that "many Soviet citizens had disliked the NEP period with its concessions to capitalism," and that even though the communists numbered only a tiny minority throughout the Union, "large numbers of Soviet men and women who did not join the adult party or the [Komsomol] League sympathized with communism. They disliked the NEP and the unemployment and luxury-living of the few which accompanied it" (*My Lives in Russia*, 14-15, 32-33). Another observer described NEP speculators as "an exceedingly unscrupulous, crooked species"; this author, generally unsympathetic to communists, stated that "even if, at the beginning of [NEP], private trading had been proclaimed a lawful means of livelihood, yet, after all, traditions from the time when individual freedom of trade was looked upon as a repulsive feature of capitalism were still in the air. To tolerate the return to the capitalist economic system implied in nep was, alas! compulsory, yet it was not necessary to go so far as to look upon the nepmen as anything else but capitalistic blood-suckers and exploiters" (Karlgren,

Bolshevist Russia, 141). Writing on conditions in Russia during the famine, Frank Golder described the "new rich class" of profiteers as "more unscrupulous and more grasping" than the old (Frank Alfred Golder and Lincoln Hutchinson, *On the Trail of the Russian Famine* [Stanford, Calif.: Stanford University Press, 1927], 150). The fact that the early years of NEP were also famine years would, if anything, tend to accentuate bitterness toward the economically privileged, as Golder and Hutchinson indicate.

28. RGASPI, f. 17, op. 85, d. 518, l. 234.

29. The issue of wages was a major cause of worker unrest and strikes in the prerevolutionary period. Although there were large disparities between workers' wages and the salaries of specialists and management, workers' complaints tended to focus more on low pay or nonpayment of wages by factory management than on disparity. Strikers, however, often demanded some equity among workers' wages, suggesting that workers before the revolution were concerned with survival more in absolute than in relative terms. See, for instance, Theodore H. Friedgut, *Iuzovka and Revolution: Life and Work in Russia's Donbass, 1869–1924* (Princeton, N.J.: Princeton University Press, 1989–1994), 1:299-314, 2:104; and Michael Melancon, "The Ninth Circle: The Lena Goldfield Workers and the Massacre of 4 April 1912," *Slavic Review* 53, no. 3 (fall 1994): 766-95.

30. Olga Narkiewicz, *The Making of the Soviet State Apparatus* (Manchester: Manchester University Press, 1970), 5.

31. RGAE, f. 4086, op. 1, d. 160, l. 38.

32. RGAE, f. 4086, op. 1, d. 160, ll. 1, 41-42.

33. RGAE, f. 4086, op. 1, d. 160, l. 43.

34. RGASPI, f. 17, op. 84, d. 645, ll. 410-11.

35. RGASPI, f. 17, op. 84, d. 646, ll. 115-17.

36. RGASPI, f. 17, op. 85, d. 522, ll. 122-24.

37. RGASPI, f. 17, op. 85, d. 524, l. 293.

38. Carr, *The Bolshevik Revolution*, 2:327.

39. RGASPI, f. 17, op. 85, d. 518, l. 156.

40. Carr, *The Bolshevik Revolution*, 2:318.

41. Robert V. Daniels, "The Left Opposition as an Alternative to Stalinism," *Slavic Review* 50, no. 2 (summer 1991): 277-85.

42. RGASPI, f. 17, op. 84, d. 647, ll. 25-27.

43. RGASPI, f. 17, op. 84, d. 645, l. 244.

44. RGASPI, f. 17, op. 85, d. 518, ll. 203-6.

45. RGASPI, f. 17, op. 85, d. 518, l. 181.

46. RGASPI, f. 17, op. 85, d. 514, l. 132.

47. RGASPI, f. 17, op. 85, d. 520, l. 195.

48. Lewis H. Siegelbaum, "Defining and Ignoring Labor Discipline in the Early Soviet Period: The Comrades-Disciplinary Courts, 1918–1922," *Slavic Review* 51, no. 4 (winter 1992): 705-30. The courts were instituted spontaneously by factory committees from 1918 to 1919 and thereafter under statute by Sovnarkom, ostensibly to adjudicate alleged infractions of labor discipline.

49. RGASPI, f. 17, op. 67, d. 109, ll. 163-71.

50. RGASPI, f. 17, op. 67, d. 472, ll. 2-5. Chernomorskii okrug was an administrative subdivision of Krasnodar *krai* (territory) in the Russian S.F.S.R. in the North Caucasus. An *okruzhkom* is a district party committee.

51. The use of former tsarist officers in the Red Army was widely resented (von Hagen, *Soldiers in the Proletarian Dictatorship*, 30, 110-11, 160-61, 176-77).

52. See, for instance, S. A. Fediukin, *Sovetskaia vlast' i burzhuaznye spetsialisty* (Moscow: Mysl', 1965), 252-53.

53. RGASPI, f. 17, op. 85, d. 514, ll. 287-91.

54. Emma Goldman, *My Disillusionment in Russia* (New York, 1923), 178-79.

55. RGASPI, f. 17, op. 85, d. 523, l. 201.

56. RGASPI, f. 5, op. 1, d. 1678, l. 4.

Chapter Four

1. This chapter was published as "From Scylla to Charybdis: Discontent with Employment and Education in the Early Soviet State," in *Thresholds into the Orthodox Commonwealth: Essays in Honor of Theofanis G. Stavrou*, ed. Lucien J. Frary (Bloomington, Ind.: Slavica, 2017), 489-526.

2. In his study of Moscow metal workers, Kevin Murphy concluded that as NEP matured, the threat of unemployment eroded worker solidarity and collective action and paved the way for Stalinism (*Revolution and Counterrevolution: Class Struggle in a Moscow Metal Factory* [2005; Chicago: Haymarket Books, 2007], 226).

3. Edwin Ware Hullinger, *The Reforging of Russia* (New York: E. P. Dutton, 1925), 7.

4. RGASPI, f. 17, op. 85, d. 517, l. 65. There is evidence that Stalin actually helped the woman; at least, he gave instructions to that effect: l. 64 is a directive to Narkomtrud (People's Commissariat of Labor) to find her work. But this type of attention, especially to a nonparty citizen, appears to have been unusual. Moreover, in the large sample of letters used for this study, appeals from women to the central party leadership on any subject were rare.

5. RGASPI, f. 17, op. 67, d. 109, ll. 163-71.

6. RGAE, f. 4086, op. 1, d. 33, ll. 20-22, 24.

7. John Maynard Keynes, *A Short View of Russia* (London: L. and Virginia Woolf, 1925), 21.

8. Unemployment assistance from the Moscow government was well below the minimum wage and did not extend to migrant laborers (who had to demonstrate three months' residency to obtain assistance). William J. Chase, *Workers, Society, and the Soviet State: Labor and Life in Moscow, 1918–1929* (Urbana: University of Illinois Press, 1987), 140, 159.

9. Ibid., 136-38, 144. Chase noted that economic necessity was the biggest cause for rural migration to the cities. He also noted that, until 1925, employers hired workers illegally—evading the labor exchange—in order to hire whom they wished. The trade unions exerted pressure against this trend until November 1924, when peasant migrants were granted equal rights on the

exchange. From January 1925 to March 1927, the free market in labor gave employers total control over hiring. The worsening of employment conditions for urban workers after 1925, combined with the general rise in unemployment, may account for the fact that appeals to the center concerning unemployment appear more numerous during the later NEP years.

10. Ibid., 149-50. For a comprehensive discussion of women's unemployment and poverty during NEP—which in many cases drove them to prostitution—see Wendy Z. Goldman, *Women, the State, and Revolution: Soviet Family Policy and Social Life, 1917–1936* (Cambridge: Cambridge University Press, 1993), especially chap. 3.

11. Douglas Weiner, "Razmychka? Urban Unemployment and Peasant In-Migration as Sources of Social Conflict," in *Russia in the Era of NEP: Explorations in Soviet Society and Culture*, ed. Sheila Fitzpatrick, Alexander Rabinowitch, and Richard Stites (Bloomington: Indiana University Press, 1991), 144-55.

12. David L. Hoffmann, "Land, Freedom, and Discontent: Russian Peasants of the Central Industrial Region prior to Collectivisation," *Europe-Asia Studies* 46, no. 4 (1994): 637-48. Discontented landless peasants made inroads throughout the decade into rural soviets, which remained dominated by "peasant farmers" for some time after the revolution (Orlando Figes, "The Village and Volost Soviet Elections of 1919," *Soviet Studies* 40, no. 1 [January 1988]: 21-45).

13. John B. Hatch, "Labor Conflict in Moscow, 1921–1925," in *Russia in the Era of NEP*, 58-71.

14. RGASPI, f. 17, op. 85, d. 518, l. 23.

15. Robert Conquest, *The Harvest of Sorrow: Soviet Collectivization and the Terror-Famine* (New York: Oxford University Press, 1986), 293, claims that orphanages became fertile recruiting grounds for the NKVD, the Soviet secret police. Alan Ball notes that while Narkompros administered 90 percent of the *detdoma* (orphanages) during the 1920s, other government agencies, including OGPU, also operated detdoma, colonies, and clinics. The primary difference between the detdoma run by Narkompros and those by OGPU was that the latter stressed discipline in reforming street children. Ball also notes that Felix Dzerzhinsky, head of OGPU, was notorious for his concern for homeless children. Dzerzhinsky approached Narkompros head Lunacharsky as early as 1921 and insisted that the GPU assist in the task of saving them (Ball, *And Now My Soul Is Hardened: Abandoned Children in Soviet Russia, 1918–1930* [Berkeley: University of California Press, 1994], 137, 157). A less sympathetic assessment of Dzerzhinsky and his motives for helping abandoned children is made by Lennard D. Gerson, *The Secret Police in Lenin's Russia* (Philadelphia, Pa.: Temple University Press, 1976), 128-29. The source for the claim that the NKVD recruited from the detdoma apparently came from the U.S. Air Force interviews of defectors from the Soviet secret police (Gerson, 296 n. 129).

16. Margaret K. Stolee, "Homeless Children in the USSR, 1917–1957," *Soviet Studies* 40, no. 1 (1988): 64-83. As Stolee observed, Stalinist initiatives, such as collectivization and the resulting famine, caused new waves of besprizorniki.

17. Juvenile unemployment became increasingly severe during NEP. The number of juveniles employed in industry dropped from 120,000 in 1921 to only 5,000 by 1923. High unemployment exacerbated the plight of the besprizornye. Youth also faired poorly; by 1928, 75 percent of registered unemployed nationwide were aged eighteen to twenty-nine. Like women, juveniles often were not hired for lack of experience, while older workers and union representatives often viewed youth who received some job training as threats, since they were trained and willing to work more intensively (Chase, *Workers, Society, and the Soviet State*, 150-52).

18. RGASPI, f. 5, op. 1, d. 1677, l. 2.

19. Mikhail Ivanovich Kalinin was the nominal head of state of Russia and the Soviet Union from 1919 to 1946 and one of the few Bolshevik leaders of peasant background.

20. RGASPI, f. 17, op. 85, d. 516, l. 291.

21. RGASPI, f. 17, op. 85, d. 516, l. 135.

22. RGASPI, f. 17, op. 85, d. 516, l. 134.

23. RGASPI, f. 17, op. 85, d. 516, l. 274.

24. RGASPI, f. 17, op. 85, d. 516, ll. 35-37.

25. RGASPI, f. 17, op. 85, d. 517, l. 206.

26. Mark von Hagen, *Soldiers in the Proletarian Dictatorship: The Red Army and the Soviet Socialist State, 1917–1930* (Ithaca, N.Y.: Cornell University Press, 1990), 8, 130.

27. RGASPI, f. 17, op. 85, d. 517, l. 152.

28. RGASPI, f. 17, op. 85, d. 518, ll. 207-10.

29. RGASPI, f. 17, op. 85, d. 517, l. 38.

30. RGASPI, f. 17, op. 85, d. 517, l. 34.

31. RGASPI, f. 17, op. 85, d. 516, l. 192.

32. RGASPI, f. 17, op. 85, d. 524, l. 201.

33. RGASPI, f. 17, op. 85, d. 523, l. 118.

34. A. A. Antonov was a Socialist Revolutionary and the leader of a major anti-Bolshevik peasant revolt in the Tambov region at the end of the civil war. The revolt was crushed in 1921, but Antonov survived another year with a small band of followers. See Erik C. Landis, *Bandits and Partisans: The Antonov Movement in the Russian Civil War*, Pitt Series in Russian and East European Studies (Pittsburgh, Pa.: University of Pittsburgh Press, 2008). On the Socialist Revolutionaries generally, see Scott B. Smith, *Captives of Revolution: The Socialist Revolutionaries and the Bolshevik Dictatorship, 1918–1923*, Pitt Series in Russian and East European Studies (Pittsburgh, Pa.: University of Pittsburgh Press, 2011); and Elizabeth White, *The Socialist Alternative to Bolshevik Russia: The Socialist Revolutionary Party, 1921–1939*, BASEES/ Routledge Series on Russian and East European Studies, no. 68 (London: Routledge, 2011).

35. RGASPI, f. 17, op. 85, d. 524, l. 116.

36. RGASPI, f. 17, op. 85, d. 523, l. 42.

37. RGASPI, f. 17, op. 85, d. 523, l. 38.

38. RGASPI, f. 17, op. 85, d. 523, l. 142.

39. RGASPI, f. 17, op. 85, d. 523, l. 199.

40. RGASPI, f. 17, op. 85, d. 517, l. 83.

41. T. H. Rigby, *Communist Party Membership in the U.S.S.R. 1917–1967* (Princeton: Princeton University Press, 1968), 117.
42. RGASPI, f. 17, op. 11, d. 205, l. 9.
43. RGASPI, f. 17, op. 85, d. 516, l. 303.
44. RGASPI, f. 17, op. 85, d. 517, l. 57.
45. RGASPI, f. 17, op. 85, d. 516, l. 249. Apparently, the government was not unwilling to extend assistance but cautious in its response. The appeal merited a directive to the Voronezh gubkom to verify the author's history (ibid., l. 247).
46. RGASPI, f. 17, op. 85, d. 523, l. 203.
47. von Hagen, *Soldiers in the Proletarian Dictatorship*, 176.
48. RGASPI, f. 17, op. 85, d. 524, l. 145.
49. RGASPI, f. 17, op. 85, d. 517, l. 186.
50. The so-called Rabsel'kor (worker and peasant correspondent) movement was instituted in the early Soviet state to enlist workers and peasants in contributing articles to Soviet journals and thus become actively involved in the production of Soviet literature and propaganda.
51. RGASPI, f. 17, op. 85, d. 524, l. 157. On the high party debate in the 1920s over the role and function of the Rabsel'kor movement, see Jeremy Hicks, "From Conduits to Commanders: Shifting Views of Worker Correspondents," *Revolutionary Russia* 19, no. 2 (2006): 131-49. On Rabsel'kor correspondence as a literary genre and the issue of proletarian culture, see idem, "Worker Correspondents: Between Journalism and Literature," *The Russian Review* 66 (October 2007): 568-85.
52. RGASPI, f. 17, op. 85, d. 517, l. 203.
53. RGASPI, f. 17, op. 85, d. 523, l. 52.
54. RGASPI, f. 17, op. 85, d. 523, l. 57.
55. RGASPI, f. 17, op. 67, d. 352, ll. 36-37.
56. See chapter 7.
57. RGASPI, f. 17, op. 85, d. 521, ll. 139-40.
58. RGASPI, f. 17, op. 85, d. 515, l. 75.
59. RGASPI, f. 17, op. 67, d. 122, ll. 1-2.
60. Russian colonization of Siberia began in the Imperial period. Major works on peasant resettlement include Donald Treadgold, *The Great Siberian Migration: Government and Peasant in Resettlement from Emancipation to the First World War* (Princeton, N.J.: Princeton University Press, 1957); Richard Pierce, *Russian Central Asia, 1867–1917: A Century of Colonial Rule* (Berkeley: University of California Press, 1960); L. F. Skliarov, *Pereselenie i zemleustroistvo v Sibiri v gody Stolypinskoi agrarnoi reformy* (Leningrad: Izd-vo Leningradskogo universiteta, 1962); M. S. Simonova, "Pereselencheskii vopros v agrarnoi politike samoderzhaviia v kontse xix-nachale xx v.," in *Ezhegodnik po agrarnoi istorii vostochnoi Evropy 1965 g.* (Moscow, 1970); B. V. Tikhonov, *Pereseleniia v Rossii vo vtoroi polovine xix v.: Po materialam perepisi 1897 g. i pasportnoi statistike* (Moscow: Nauka, 1978); Barbara Anderson, *Internal Migration during Modernization in Late Nineteenth-Century Russia* (Princeton, N.J.: Princeton University Press, 1980); B. V. Ananich et al., *Krizis samoderzhaviia v Rossii, 1895–1917* (Leningrad: Nauka, 1984); and E. E. Leizerovich, "Kolonizatsiia i razvitie Kazakhstana i Srednei Azii v xix-xx vekakh: Dinamika

natsional'nostei, transformatsiia khoziaistva, perspektivy regionov," in *Rossiia i Vostok: Problemy vzaimodeistviia* (Moscow: Institut vostokovedeniia RAN, 1993).

61. Alexander V. Kolchak was a commander of the Imperial Russian Navy who established an anti-communist government in Siberia and led White Russian opposition to the Bolsheviks during the civil war from 1918 to 1920.

62. RGASPI, f. 17, op. 84, d. 646, l. 464.

63. RGASPI, f. 17, op. 85, d. 519, l. 170.

64. Olga A. Narkiewicz, *The Making of the Soviet State Apparatus* (Manchester: Manchester University Press, 1970), 88-89.

65. RGASPI, f. 17, op. 85, d. 516, ll. 123-26.

66. See chapter 9.

67. On the Bolsheviks' attempts to integrate and reform Soviet citizens through a government literacy campaign during the 1920s, see Charles E. Clark, *Uprooting Otherness: The Literacy Campaign in NEP-Era Russia* (Selinsgrove, Pa.: Susquehanna University Press, 2000). The author begins by citing (anti-Soviet/émigré?) scholarship suggesting that, contrary to Soviet government claims, literacy was on the rise in the late tsarist period. Clark asserts that peasants resisted attempts to politicize education under the Socialist campaigns and concludes that the people generally resisted reformation attempts by the government during the 1920s. His thesis is at odds with appeals used in this study; Clark also appears to treat the various groups within Soviet society as monolithic (e.g., "the peasant"), with a common, unified agenda (i.e., to use Soviet power to their own individual ends). On similar efforts to enlighten and remake Russian citizens by the Provisional Government and the soviets during 1917, see Sarah Badcock, "Talking to the People and Shaping Revolution: The Drive for Enlightenment in Revolutionary Russia," *The Russian Review* 65 (October 2006): 617-36.

68. RGASPI, f. 5, op. 1, d. 1678, l. 45.

69. Sheila Fitzpatrick (*Education and Social Mobility in the Soviet Union 1921–1934*), examined the lower classes' struggle for access to and control especially over higher education. Many of the appeals that follow shed light on the political trends and developments that Fitzpatrick discussed. William Chase (*Workers, Society, and the Soviet State*, 151-52) noted that the numbers of unemployed who required job training far exceeded the capacity of technical schools to accommodate them. For an important discussion on the rabfaky as social, political, and cultural battlegrounds during NEP, see Christopher Read, *Culture and Power in Revolutionary Russia: The Intelligentsia and the Transition from Tsarism to Communism* (London: Macmillan, 1990), chap. 5, "Compromise or Confrontation? The Contours of Cultural Policy, 1923–5," esp. 220 29, "Cultural Policy in Practice: The Workers' Faculties (*Rabfaky*)."

70. RGASPI, f. 17, op. 85, d. 523, l. 5.

71. RGASPI, f. 17, op. 85, d. 524, l. 245.

72. RGASPI, f. 17, op. 85, d. 514, l. 303.

73. RGASPI, f. 17, op. 85, d. 523, l. 122.

74. RGASPI, f. 17, op. 85, d. 523, l. 224.

75. RGASPI, f. 17, op. 85, d. 516, l. 267.

76. RGASPI, f. 17, op. 85, d. 521, ll. 9-10.

77. RGASPI, f. 17, op. 85, d. 521, ll. 188-89.
78. Frank Alfred Golder and Lincoln Hutchinson, *On the Trail of the Russian Famine*, 43-44.
79. Ibid., 100-101.
80. Anton Karlgren, *Bolshevist Russia*, 12-13.
81. Ibid., 57-61.
82. Vladimir V. Tchernavin, *I Speak for the Silent* (Boston: Hale, Cushman and Flint, 1935), 34-35.
83. RGAE, f. 5240, op. 1, d. 4, l. 25.
84. RGASPI, f. 17, op. 85, d. 516, ll. 182-83.
85. RGASPI, f. 17, op. 85, d. 517, l. 210.
86. RGASPI, f. 17, op. 84, d. 647, l. 103.
87. Gabriele Gorzka, "Proletarian Culture in Practice: Workers' Clubs, 1917–1921," in *Essays on Revolutionary Culture and Stalinism: Selected Papers from the Third World Congress for Soviet and East European Studies*, ed. John W. Strong (Columbus, Ohio: Slavica, 1990), 39.
88. RGASPI, f. 17, op. 85, d. 517, l. 72.
89. RGASPI, f. 17, op. 84, d. 647, ll. 117-18.
90. RGASPI, f. 17, op. 85, d. 517, l. 188.
91. RGASPI, f. 17, op. 85, d. 517, l. 66.
92. RGASPI, f. 17, op. 85, d. 517, l. 196.
93. George A. Burrell, *An American Engineer Looks at Russia* (Boston: The Stratford Company, 1932), 184.
94. Although the government set quotas for admitting workers, peasants, and communists into higher education in 1921–22, apparently the individual VUZy (higher educational institutions, still dominated in the 1920s by non-Marxists) set their own ratios among party, soviet, Komsomol, military, trade union, and individual candidates. This meant that universities were able to enroll large numbers of class-alien students. Moreover, under pressure from Vesenkha, beginning in 1926, "academic criteria had equal or greater weight" than social origin in admission to higher education (Fitzpatrick, *Education and Social Mobility in the Soviet Union*, 89-90, 106).
95. RGASPI, f. 17, op. 85, d. 517, l. 197.
96. RGASPI, f. 17, op. 85, d. 523, l. 238.
97. RGASPI, f. 17, op. 85, d. 523, l. 10.
98. RGASPI, f. 17, op. 85, d. 516, l. 145.
99. RGASPI, f. 17, op. 85, d. 524, l. 113.
100. RGASPI, f. 17, op. 85, d. 523, l. 30.
101. RGASPI, f. 17, op. 85, d. 523, l. 15.
102. RGASPI, f. 17, op. 85, d. 524, ll. 120-21.
103. RGASPI, f. 17, op. 85, d. 524, l. 263.
104. RGASPI, f. 17, op. 85, d. 524, l. 43.
105. RGASPI, f. 17, op. 85, d. 522, l. 228.
106. RGASPI, f. 17, op. 85, d. 523, l. 99.
107. RGASPI, f. 17, op. 85, d. 522, l. 90.
108. RGASPI, f. 17, op. 85, d. 513, l. 257.
109. RGASPI, f. 17, op. 85, d. 517, l. 194.

110. Recent studies on this include Ol'ga Mikhailovna Morozova, *Dva akta dramy: Boevoe proshloe i poslevoennaia povsednevnost' veteranov grazhdanskoe voiny* (Rostov on Don: Isdatel'stvo Iuzhnyi tsentr RAN, 2010); and Sean Guillory, "The Shattered Self of Komsomol Civil War Memoirs," *Slavic Review* 71, no. 3 (2012): 546-65. Kevin McDermott noted the influence of civil war experience on the party leadership, but not on the population at large: "War and revolution were inextricably interrelated in Marxist-Leninist theory . . . but for Stalin war became also a central tenet of his *domestic* policies—the idea of an internal 'class war' against ubiquitous 'enemies' seemed to take possession of him by the early 1930s." And further: "Wars, civil wars and the threat of war and social unrest formed a constant leitmotif in the political careers and personal experiences of all top Bolsheviks" (8). For more on this, see chapter 10.
111. Isabel A. Tirado, "The Komsomol and Young Peasants: The Dilemma of Rural Expansion, 1921–1925," *Slavic Review* 52, no. 3 (1993): 460-76.
112. RGASPI, f. 17, op. 85, d. 524, ll. 193, 196.
113. RGASPI, f. 17, op. 85, d. 516, l. 46.
114. RGASPI, f. 17, op. 85, d. 522, l. 297.
115. In prerevolutionary Russia, a red corner was a space for Orthodox worship containing icons; under the Soviet government, it was co-opted for veneration of Lenin and the study of communism.
116. RGASPI, f. 17, op. 85, d. 516, l. 96.
117. RGASPI, f. 17, op. 85, d. 523, l. 96.
118. RGASPI, f. 17, op. 84, d. 646, l. 204.
119. RGASPI, f. 17, op. 85, d. 515, l. 122.
120. RGASPI, f. 17, op. 85, d. 521, l. 5.
121. RGASPI, f. 17, op. 85, d. 522, l. 76.
122. RGASPI, f. 17, op. 85, d. 522, l. 48.
123. RGASPI, f. 17, op. 85, d. 522, ll. 102-4.
124. RGASPI, f. 17, op. 85, d. 513, l. 128.
125. RGASPI, f. 17, op. 85, d. 516, l. 272.
126. RGASPI, f. 17, op. 85, d. 517, l. 253.
127. RCASPI, f. 17, op. 85, d. 515, l. 185.
128. RGASPI, f. 17, op. 85, d. 518, ll. 62-88.
129. RGASPI, f. 17, op. 85, d. 522, l. 126.

Chapter Five

1. Olga A. Narkiewicz, *The Making of the Soviet State Apparatus*, 7.
2. See, for instance, RGASPI, f. 17, op. 11, d. 18.
3. RGASPI, f. 17, op. 67, d. 122, ll. 1-2.
4. RGASPI, f. 17, op. 11, d. 264, ll. 2-3.
5. RGASPI, f. 17, op. 11, d. 301, ll. 3-4.
6. Dorothy Thompson, *The New Russia* (New York: H. Holt and Co., 1928), 36.
7. RGASPI, f. 17, op. 11, d. 306, ll. 1-6.
8. RGASPI, f. 17, op. 85, d. 521, l. 212.
9. RGASPI, f. 17, op. 11, d. 18, ll. 53-55. The report may date from 1921.

10. See, for instance, a report made by the Nizhnii Novgorod gubkom secretary on his organization's results in the effort from August to December 1924 to promote workers from the bench, nonparty workers, and peasants to responsible positions (RGASPI, f. 17, op. 67, d. 129, ll. 70-72).
11. RGAE, f. 4086, op. 1, d. 226, ll. 3-9.
12. RGAE, f. 3338, op. 1, d. 309, l. 12.
13. The literature on economic planning is vast. See Maurice Dobb, *Soviet Economic Development Since 1917* (London: Routledge and Kegan Paul, 1948); idem, *On Economic Theory and Socialism: Collected Papers* (London: Routledge and Kegan Paul, 1955); idem, *Political Economy and Capitalism: Some Essays in Economic Tradition* (1945; reprint, Westport, Conn.: Greenwood Press, 1972); E. H. Carr and R. W. Davies, *Foundations of a Planned Economy 1926–1929*, vol. 1, pt. 1 (New York: Macmillan, 1969); C. H. Feinstein, ed., *Socialism, Capitalism and Economic Growth: Essays Presented to Maurice Dobb* (London: Cambridge University Press, 1967); Isaac Guelfat, *Economic Thought in the Soviet Union: Concepts and Aspects* (Liège: C.I.R.I.E.C., 1969); and Aron Katsenelinboigen, *Studies in Soviet Economic Planning* (White Plains, N.Y.: M. E. Sharpe, 1978).
14. In 1928, Rabkrin wrote up a working plan to determine whether greater freedom for textile manufacturers would "increase initiative and improve production" (RGAE, f. 3338, op. 1, d. 499a, l. 47).
15. Moshe Lewin, *The Making of the Soviet System: Essays in the Social History of Interwar Russia* (New York: Pantheon Books, 1985), 261.
16. RGASPI, f. 17, op. 85, d. 522, ll. 220-22.
17. RGASPI, f. 17, op. 11, d. 343, l. 38.
18. RGASPI, f. 17, op. 84, d. 668, ll. 14-18.
19. RGASPI, f. 17, op. 85, d. 517, l. 209.
20. The Office of the Procurator (public prosecutor) was established in May 1922 to ensure the application of a uniform system of law throughout the Soviet Union, established in December. The Procurator was under the jurisdiction of the Commissariat of Justice of each constituent republic until 1933, when an all-union Procurator's Office was established to centralize legal administration. Narkomzem was the Commissariat of Agriculture.
21. RGASPI, f. 17, op. 85, d. 516, ll. 217-18.
22. RGASPI, f. 17, op. 85, d. 518, l. 202.
23. For Lenin's conflicting views on legality and natural law, see Jane Burbank, "Lenin and the Law in Revolutionary Russia," *Slavic Review* 54, no. 1 (spring 1995): 23-44; I. A. Isaev ("Kollektivnoe bessoznatel'noe i predstavlenie o zakonnosti v revolutsii," paper presented at a conference in 1994, "Revolutsiia i chelovek: sotsial'no-psikhologicheskii aspekt," *Otechestvennaia istoriia*, no. 4 [1995]: 211-18) maintains that conceptions of legality mutated during the revolution as a reflection of growing social pathology, wherein "rational bases" of legality were replaced by "an understanding of law as 'revolutionary intuition,' supplanted by principles of 'revolutionary justice' [and] 'revolutionary expediency'."
24. RGASPI, f. 5, op. 1, d. 1659, l. 1.
25. RGASPI, f. 17, op. 85, d. 514, l. 381.
26. RGASPI, f. 17, op. 85, d. 518, l. 226.

27. RGASPI, f. 17, op. 85, d. 518, ll. 17-18.

28. On the tenuous position of rabkors, see Diane P. Koenker, "Factory Tales: Narratives of Industrial Relations in the Transition to NEP," *Russian Review* 55, no. 3 (July 1996): 384-411; and Michael S. Gorham, "Tongue-tied Writers: The Rabsel'kor Movement and the Voice of the 'New Intelligentsia' in Early Soviet Russia," *Russian Review* 55, no. 3 (July 1996): 412-29. See also Jennifer Clibbon, "The Soviet Press and Grassroots Organization" (Ph.D. dissertation, University of Toronto, 1993).

29. RGASPI, f. 17, op. 85, d. 518, ll. 215-24. Emphasis in the original.

30. On the continuing underground activities of the Left Opposition after the Fifteenth Party Congress (December 1927) and its influence on politics, see A. V. Gusev, "Levokommunisticheskaia oppozitsiia v SSSR v kontse 20-x godov," *Otechestvennaia istoriia*, no. 1 (1996): 85-103.

31. RGASPI, f. 17, op. 85, d. 515, l. 127.

32. RGASPI, f. 17, op. 85, d. 520, l. 154.

33. Eric van Ree observed that Stalin possessed almost a "mystical interpretation of party unity" shared by many of his political opponents, who recognized that "'collectivist thinking'" among the party rank and file accounted for their lack of support for the Left Opposition (comment attributed to Alexandra Kollontai in October 1927; "Stalin's Organic Theory of the Party," *Russian Review* 52, no. 1 [January 1993]: 43-57). The editors of a five-volume Russian documentary collection on the demise of NEP observed that party functionaries desired party unity among the top party leadership above all to protect their own positions, since a shake-up among leaders would cause chaos among the lower ranks (V. P. Danilov et al., *Kak lomali NEP: Stenogrammy Plenumov TsK VKP(b) 1928–1929 gg.*, vol. 1, *Ob'edinennyi Plenum TsK i TsKK VKP(b) 6-11 Aprelia 1928 g.*, Rossiia XX Vek: Dokumenty, A. N. Iakovlev, gen. ed. [Moscow: Mezhdunarodnyi fond "Demokratiia," 2000], "Aprel'skii Plenum 1928 g.," 19). For more on the question of party unity, see chapter 10 below.

34. Lars T. Lih, "Political Testament of Lenin and Bukharin and the Meaning of NEP," *Slavic Review* 50, no. 2 (summer 1991): 243.

35. RGASPI, f. 17, op. 11, d. 205, l. 2.

36. RGASPI, f. 17, op. 11, d. 205, l. 8.

37. Catherine Merridale, *Moscow Politics and the Rise of Stalin: The Communist Party in the Capital, 1925–32* (New York: St. Martin's Press, 1990), 224-25.

38. RGASPI, f. 17, op. 11, d. 218, l. 10.

39. RGASPI, f. 17, op. 11, d. 206, l. 8a.

40. RGASPI, f. 17, op. 67, d. 117, l. 265.

41. RGASPI, f. 17, op. 85, d. 522, l. 198.

42. RGASPI, f. 17, op. 85, d. 522, ll. 42-44.

43. RGASPI, f. 17, op. 85, d. 516, l. 103.

44. RGASPI, f. 17, op. 85, d. 523, l. 167.

45. RGASPI, f. 17, op. 85, d. 517, l. 5.

46. For a systematic study of the early history of and issues surrounding party purges, see J. Arch Getty, *Origins of the Great Purges: The Soviet Communist Party Reconsidered, 1933–1938* (Cambridge: Cambridge University Press, 1985).

47. RGASPI, f. 17, op. 84, d. 647, ll. 143-49.
48. RGASPI, f. 17, op. 84, d. 645, l. 133.
49. RGASPI, f. 17, op. 84, d. 645, ll. 267-69.
50. RGASPI, f. 17, op. 85, d. 515, l. 109.
51. RGASPI, f. 17, op. 85, d. 524, l. 2.
52. RGASPI, f. 17, op. 84, d. 647, ll. 132-34.
53. RGASPI, f. 17, op. 85, d. 522, ll. 147-49.
54. RGASPI, f. 17, op. 85, d. 518, l. 108.
55. RGASPI, f. 17, op. 85, d. 520, l. 16.
56. RGASPI, f. 17, op. 85, d. 523, l. 288.
57. RGASPI, f. 17, op. 85, d. 520, ll. 23-24.
58. RGASPI, f. 17, op. 85, d. 520, l. 141.
59. RGASPI, f. 17, op. 85, d. 518, l. 96.
60. RGASPI, f. 17, op. 85, d. 518, l. 8.
61. RGASPI, f. 17, op. 85, d. 517, l. 6.
62. RGASPI, f. 17, op. 85, d. 517, l. 214.
63. RGASPI, f. 17, op. 67, d. 235, l. 19.
64. RGASPI, f. 17, op. 85, d. 513, l. 254.
65. RGASPI, f. 17, op. 85, d. 520, l. 114.
66. RGASPI, f. 17, op. 84, d. 645, ll. 371-73.
67. RGASPI, f. 17, op. 85, d. 514, l. 5.
68. RGASPI, f. 17, op. 85, d. 517, l. 43.
69. RGASPI, f. 17, op. 85, d. 518, l. 247.
70. RGASPI, f. 17, op. 85, d. 518, l. 145.
71. Victor Serge, *From Lenin to Stalin* (New York: Pioneer Publishers, 1937), 38-39.
72. Edwin Ware Hullinger, *The Reforging of Russia*, 268.
73. V. A. Arkhipov and L. F. Morozov, *Bor'ba protiv kapitalisticheskikh elementov v promyshlennosti i torgovle, 20-e–nachalo 30-kh godov* (Moscow: Mysl', 1978), 77-78.
74. Ibid., 229.
75. Emma Goldman, *My Disillusionment in Russia* (Garden City, N.Y.: Doubleday, Page and Company, 1923), 183.
76. Hullinger, *The Reforging of Russia*, 63.
77. RGASPI, f. 17, op. 85, d. 518, l. 14.
78. RGASPI, f. 17, op. 85, d. 518, l. 110.
79. RGASPI, f. 17, op. 85, d. 516, ll. 263-64.
80. RGASPI, f. 17, op. 85, d. 516, ll. 260-61.
81. RGASPI, f. 17, op. 85, d. 518, l. 1.
82. RGASPI, f. 17, op. 85, d. 520, ll. 20-21.
83. RGASPI, f. 17, op. 85, d. 522, ll. 277-78.
84. RGAE, f. 4086, op. 1, d. 95, ll. 15-17.
85. RGAE, f. 4086, op. 1, d. 99, l. 23.
86. RGASPI, f. 17, op. 84, d. 668, ll. 1-2.
87. RGAE, f. 4086, op. 1, d. 159, l. 7.
88. Lars T. Lih, Oleg V. Naumov, and Oleg V. Khlevniuk, eds., *Stalin's Letters to Molotov 1925–1936*, trans. Catherine A. Fitzpatrick (New Haven, Conn.: Yale University Press, 1995), letter 27 (16 September 1926), 127.

89. RGASPI, f. 17, op. 85, d. 516, l. 188.
90. RGASPI, f. 17, op. 85, d. 518, l. 146.
91. See, for instance, information on the Irkutsk organization in RGASPI, f. 17, op. 67, d. 193, l. 1.
92. RGASPI, f. 17, op. 85, d. 523, l. 234.
93. See, for instance, the collection of petitions to the central government after the 1906 revolution compiled by Gregory L. Freeze, *From Supplication to Revolution*. Among the complaints of one civil service employee was that promotion was not based on merit, but rather on brown-nosing, family connections, and the possession of a degree (219).
94. RGASPI, f. 17, op. 85, d. 518, ll. 48-49.
95. RGASPI, f. 17, op. 85, d. 518, l. 47.
96. RGASPI, f. 17, op. 85, d. 524, l. 4.
97. RGASPI, f. 17, op. 85, d. 516, l. 54-57.
98. RGASPI, f. 17, op. 85, d. 516, ll. 75-78.
99. RGASPI, f. 17, op. 85, d. 524, l. 296.
100. RGASPI, f. 17, op. 85, d. 517, l. 81.
101. RGASPI, f. 17, op. 85, d. 517, l. 151.
102. RGASPI, f. 17, op. 85, d. 516, l. 222.
103. RGASPI, f. 17, op. 85, d. 517, l. 20.
104. RGASPI, f. 17, op. 85, d. 523, ll. 235-37.
105. RGASPI, f. 17, op. 85, d. 516, l. 27.
106. RGASPI, f. 17, op. 85, d. 517, l. 119.
107. RGASPI, f. 17, op. 84, d. 646, ll. 220-21.
108. RGASPI, f. 17, op. 85, d. 523, l. 251.
109. RGASPI, f. 17, op. 85, d. 523, l. 196.
110. RGASPI, f. 17, op. 85, d. 517, l. 79.
111. RGASPI, f. 17, op. 85, d. 524, l. 29. In 1918, the Bolshevik government established *Komitety Bednoty* (Committees of the [Village] Poor), or *kombedy*, as local institutions to unify poor peasants in order to advance government policy. During War Communism, the committees' primary tasks were to distribute food and other basic goods and to requisition grain on behalf of the Soviet state to combat chronic food shortages in the cities.
112. RGASPI, f. 17, op. 85, d. 517, l. 180.

Chapter Six

1. On popular perceptions of the polarization of society during the Stalinist 1930s, see Sarah Davies, "Us against Them: Social Identity in Soviet Russia, 1934–41," in *Stalinism: New Directions*, ed. Sheila Fitzpatrick (London: Routledge, 2000), 47-70. Davies focuses on articulations of "'us against them' in the sense of the 'people' (in various guises) against those perceived as powerholders," noting the universality of "this dichotomous image of society" throughout history (48).
2. Mark Galeotti, *The Age of Anxiety: Security and Politics in Soviet and Post-Soviet Russia* (London: Longman Publishers, 1995), 4.

3. Niels Erik Rosenfeldt, "Stalinism as a System of Communication," in *Essays on Revolutionary Culture and Stalinism: Selected Papers from the Third World Congress for Soviet and East European Studies*, ed. John W. Strong (Columbus, Ohio: Slavica, 1990), 148.
4. T. H. Rigby, *Communist Party Membership in the U.S.S.R. 1917–1967* (Princeton, N.J.: Princeton University Press, 1968), 4-5.
5. Sergo Mikoyan, "Stalinism As I Saw It," in *The Stalin Phenomenon*, ed. Alec Nove (New York: St. Martin's Press, 1993), 169.
6. Pitirim Sorokin, *Leaves from a Russian Diary* (Boston: Beacon Press, 1950), 74.
7. Rigby, *Communist Party Membership*, 87.
8. Ibid., 109.
9. Ibid., 74.
10. RGASPI, f. 17, op. 67, d. 152, l. 25.
11. RGASPI, f. 17, op. 67, d. 156, l. 1.
12. RGASPI, f. 17, op. 67, d. 193, l. 1.
13. RGASPI, f. 17, op. 67, d. 106, ll. 2-7.
14. RGASPI, f. 17, op. 67, d. 267, ll. 1-6.
15. RGASPI, f. 17, op. 67, d. 384, ll. 1-3.
16. RGASPI, f. 17, op. 84, d. 647, ll. 21-22.
17. RGASPI, f. 17, op. 84, d. 859, l. 15. The *Krestianskaia gazeta* (Peasants' Gazette) began publication in the wake of the 1905 Revolution and was published by the Communist Party Central Committee in Moscow from 1923 to 1939.
18. Victor Serge, *From Lenin to Stalin* (New York: Pioneer Publishers, 1937), 38-39.
19. RGASPI, f. 17, op. 11, d. 197, l. 65.
20. RGASPI, f. 5, op. 1, d. 1663, l. 28.
21. RGASPI, f. 5, op. 1, d. 1675, l. 3.
22. RGASPI, f. 5, op. 1, d. 1676, l. 1.
23. RGASPI, f. 5, op. 1, d. 1687, l. 2.
24. Mark von Hagen, *Soldiers in the Proletarian Dictatorship: The Red Army and the Soviet Socialist State, 1917–1930* (Ithaca, N.Y.: Cornell University Press, 1990), 96-97.
25. RGASPI, f. 17, op. 67, d. 460, l. 14.
26. von Hagen, *Soldiers in the Proletarian Dictatorship*, 96-97.
27. RGASPI, f. 17, op. 85, d. 514, ll. 312-13.
28. Emma Goldman, *My Disillusionment in Russia*, 22-23.
29. Ibid., 35.
30. RGASPI, f. 17, op. 85, d. 520, l. 155.
31. William G. Rosenberg and Marilyn B. Young, *Transforming Russia and China: Revolutionary Struggle in the Twentieth Century* (New York: Oxford University Press, 1982), 44.
32. von Hagen, *Soldiers in the Proletarian Dictatorship*, 100.
33. RGASPI, f. 5, op. 1, d. 1740, l. 2.4
34. Indeed, "during 1917, struggles within the workplace to control workers were accompanied by the breakdown of worker respect for and deference to owners, managers, technical specialists and foremen . . . even those factory

committees that had assumed managerial functions themselves became targets of workers' wrath" (Lewis H. Siegelbaum, "Defining and Ignoring Labor Discipline in the Early Soviet Period: The Comrades-Disciplinary Courts, 1918–1922," *Slavic Review* 51, no. 4 [winter 1991]: 705-30).

35. Letter from a director of the Textile Glavka of the Simbirsk region to the administration of the Kuznetsko-Gorodishchenskikh Sukonnykh factory, dated 1920, RGAE, f. 3338, op. 1, d. 474, l. 2.

36. RGASPI, f. 17, op. 67, d. 234, ll. 5-16.

37. RGASPI, f. 17, op. 11, d. 306, ll. 1-6.

38. RGASPI, f. 17, op. 85, d. 522, l. 219.

39. Maurice Hindus, *Humanity Uprooted* (New York: J. Cape and H. Smith, 1931), 203.

40. RGASPI, f. 17, op. 85, d. 522, l. 88.

41. RGASPI, f. 17, op. 85, d. 522, l. 129.

42. RGASPI, f. 17, op. 85, d. 524, l. 135.

43. RGASPI, f. 17, op. 85, d. 520, l. 17.

44. RGASPI, f. 17, op. 84, d. 646, ll. 293-94.

45. RGASPI, f. 17, op. 85, d. 521, l. 4.

46. RGASPI, f. 17, op. 67, d. 235, l. 19.

47. Diane Koenker observed that workers complained about some Red factory directors adopting the manner of "the masters" and characterized bad directors as acting as social superiors, treating workers "'as if [they were] creatures of a lower order'" ("Factory Tales: Narratives of Industrial Relations in the Transition to NEP," *Russian Review* 55, no. 3 [July 1996]: 384-411). Jeffrey Rossman noted that a political activist and oppositionist in the textile industry in the 1920s was disaffected partly because of Bolsheviks "appropriating the habits of the old nobility" ("Weaver of Rebellion and Poet of Resistance: Kapitan Klepikov [1880–1933] and Shop-Floor Opposition to Bolshevik Rule," *Jahrbücher für Geschichte Osteuropas* 44, no. 3 [1996]: 374-408).

48. von Hagen, *Soldiers in the Proletarian Dictatorship*, 176-77.

49. RGASPI, f. 78, op. 1, d. 47, l. 89.

50. RGASPI, f. 17, op. 85, d. 520, l. 10.

51. A Red director was a communist worker promoted to factory director.

52. RGASPI, f. 17, op. 85, d. 520, l. 42.

53. RGASPI, f. 17, op. 85, d. 515, l. 165.

54. RGASPI, f. 17, op. 11, d. 72, l. 18.

55. RGASPI, f. 17, op. 85, d. 518, l. 97.

56. RGASPI, f. 17, op. 85, d. 515, l. 207.

57. RCASPI, f. 17, op. 85, d. 522, ll. 67-69.

58. RGASPI, f. 17, op. 11, d. 306, ll. 1-6.

59. RGASPI, f. 17, op. 85, d. 486, l. 7.

60. RGASPI, f. 17, op. 67, d. 106, ll. 2-7.

61. RGASPI, f. 17, op. 85, d. 522, ll. 119-21.

62. RGASPI, f. 17, op. 85, d. 515, l. 101.

63. RGASPI, f. 17, op. 85, d. 523, l. 103.

64. RGASPI, f. 17, op. 11, d. 80, l. 67.

65. RGASPI, f. 17, op. 67, d. 215, ll. 9-10.

66. Socialism in one country, first articulated in the second edition of *Foundations of Leninism* (published after Lenin's death in 1924), was Stalin's idea that, given the defeat of all other communist revolutions in Europe following World War I, the Soviet Union had to build socialism on its own, without outside help. This opposed classical Marxism, which held that socialism had to be established globally, and Leon Trotsky's theory of permanent revolution.

67. RGASPI, f. 17, op. 85, d. 522, ll. 280-81.

68. RGASPI, f. 17, op. 85, d. 522, ll. 114-15.

69. RGASPI, f. 17, op. 84, d. 645, l. 123.

70. John B. Hatch ("The 'Lenin Levy' and the Social Origins of Stalinism: Workers and the Communist Party in Moscow, 1921–1928," *Slavic Review* 48, no. 4 [winter 1989]: 558-77) noted that the Lenin Enrollment and subsequent mass recruitment campaigns only served to worsen party-worker relations by revealing cleavages between the party and its constituents (565); about 25 percent of the newcomers were considered either "disruptive or politically hostile elements and were blamed for introducing sentiments of the so-called backward strata of the working class into the party, including specialist-baiting, anti-intellectual attitudes, egalitarianism, and anti-Semitism" or "politically passive workers and careerists as well as . . . egotistical 'former aktiv, non-party workers,' loudmouths, and know-it-alls who refused to subordinate themselves to party or labor discipline," who had to be molded into "loyal communists" through political "education" and promotion (566-68). Hatch also noted the antagonism caused by the high-handed manner of older party members that the party encouraged, allegedly for the sake of administrative stability (570-71).

71. RGASPI, f. 17, op. 85, d. 514, ll. 135-37.

72. On the etymological roots of the Russian *rab*, and especially skilled workers' resistance to the designation *rabochii* in prerevolutionary times, see Victoria E. Bonnell, ed., *The Russian Worker: Life and Labor under the Tsarist Regime* (Berkeley: University of California Press,1983).

73. RGASPI, f. 17, op. 85, d. 522, ll. 28-30.

74. RGASPI, f. 17, op. 11, d. 342, l. 1 includes statistics on those entering the party in 1922, 43 percent of whom were workers. The report noted that "the majority entering the Party were workers, who had lost touch with the factory bench and occupy one or another office position. . . . [in] economic and provision organs, the militia, the GPU, control, [or] the apparatus of party committees, through which it may be supposed they strive to strengthen their material and administrative standing."

75. Rigby, *Communist Party Membership*, 45.

76. RGASPI, f. 17, op. 85, d. 516, l. 87.

77. RGASPI, f. 17, op. 85, d. 523, ll. 242-45.

78. RGASPI, f. 17, op. 85, d. 517, l. 100.

79. RGASPI, f. 17, op. 85, d. 516, l. 300.

80. RGASPI, f. 17, op. 85, d. 517, l. 273.

81. RGASPI, f. 17, op. 85, d. 521, ll. 218-20.

Chapter Seven

1. See N. S. Simonov, "'Krepit' oboronu strany sovetov' ('Voennaia trevoga' 1927 goda i ee posledstviia)," *Otechestvennaia istoriia*, no. 3 (1996): 155-61. Jeffrey Brooks observed that for the average reader during NEP, the foreign news section was the most popular in the Soviet press ("Public and Private Values in the Soviet Press, 1921–1928," *Slavic Review* 48, no. 1 [spring 1989]: 16-35).

2. K. V. Gusev and V. Z. Drobizhev, eds., *Rabochii klass v upravlenii gosudarstvom (1926–1937 gg.)* (Moscow: Mysl', 1968), 77.

3. Mark von Hagen, "Civil-Military Relations and the Evolution of the Soviet Socialist State," *Slavic Review* 50, no. 2 (summer 1991): 268-76.

4. For a discussion of Stalinists' use of the war scare to gain support among party leaders for using extraordinary measures in procuring grain from the peasantry that heralded the end of NEP, see V. P. Danilov et al., *Kak lomali NEP: Stenogrammy Plenumov TsK VKP(b) 1928–1929 gg.*, vol. 1, *Ob'edinennyi Plenum TsK i TsKK VKP(b) 6-11 Aprelia 1928 g.*, Rossiia XX Vek: Dokumenty, A. N. Iakovlev, gen. ed. (Moscow: Mezhdunarodnyi fond "Demokratiia," 2000), "Aprel'skii Plenum 1928 g.," 7-9. Of course, both the fear of war and the militant character of Bolshevik propaganda, noted by numerous scholars, found its origin in the conditions of war and revolution in which the Soviet state was founded. One contemporary observer noted that "Russia is convinced that sooner or later she is going to be attacked. . . . this conviction has been transmitted, through all the vast apparatus of propaganda at the command of the state, to every individual" (Dorothy Thompson, *The New Russia* [New York: H. Holt and Co., 1928], 169-70).

5. The Russians were not alone in this assumption. Westerners also assumed the inevitability of confrontation between communism and capitalism, even while, like the Soviets, professing a desire for peaceful coexistence. See, for instance, Fabian Vaksman, *Ideological Struggle: A Study in the Principles of Operation of the Soviet Political Mechanism* (Lanham, Md.: University Press of America, 1987), v. A recent study on U.S.-Soviet foreign relations during this period is Norman E. Saul, *Friends or Foes? The United States and Russia, 1921–1941* (Lawrence: University Press of Kansas, 2006), in which the author examines the ambiguous relationship between the two powers leading up to World War II.

6. George F. Kennan, *Russia and the West under Lenin and Stalin* (Markham, Ont.: Penguin Books, 1960), 171. For a comprehensive view of Soviet foreign relations during this period, see also Louis Fischer, *The Soviets in World Affairs: A History of the Relations between the Soviet Union and the Rest of the World 1917–1929*, 2 vols. (1930; reprint, Princeton, N.J.: Princeton University Press, 1951); Anthony Trawick Bouscaren, *Soviet Foreign Policy: A Pattern of Persistence* (New York: Fordham University Press, 1962); and E. H. Carr, *Foundations of a Planned Economy 1926–1929*, vol. 3, pt. 1 (New York: Macmillan, 1976). For an annotated documentary history of Soviet foreign policy, somewhat dated but including the texts of the most important treaties and the various Soviet constitutions, see Donald G. Bishop, ed., *Soviet Foreign*

Relations: Documents and Readings (Syracuse, N.Y.: Syracuse University Press, 1952).

7. Kennan, *Russia and the West*, 204.
8. Ibid., 218.
9. RGASPI, f. 5, op. 1, d. 1675, l. 1.
10. RGASPI, f. 17, op. 85, d. 522, ll. 168-71.
11. RGASPI, f. 5, op. 1, d. 1666, l. 40.
12. RGASPI, f. 17, op. 85, d. 514, ll. 92-97.
13. RGASPI, f. 5, op. 1, d. 1663, l. 18.
14. RGASPI, f. 5, op. 1, d. 1680, l. 21.
15. RGASPI, f. 5, op. 1, d. 1686, l. 17.
16. RGASPI, f. 5, op. 1, d. 1668, l. 1.
17. At a conference in 1994 in Perm on "Totalitariarizm i lichnost'" (*Otechestvannaia istoriia*, no. 2 [1995]: 215-17), it was observed that a totalitarian regime cannot exist without a conception of internal and external "enemies." But the discussant treats these as images, while many supplicants throughout this study described enemies not as abstractions but as real persons or entities, often persons who were known to them and who allegedly had victimized them.
18. RGASPI, f. 17, op. 85, d. 514, ll. 63-65.
19. RGASPI, f. 17, op. 85, d. 514, ll. 125-27.
20. RGASPI, f. 17, op. 85, d. 514, ll. 82-87.
21. RGASPI, f. 17, op. 85, d. 514, ll. 13-18.
22. RGASPI, f. 17, op. 85, d. 514, ll. 204-10.
23. RGASPI, f. 17, op. 85, d. 514, l. 78.
24. Paul Scheffer, *Seven Years in Soviet Russia* (London: Putnam, 1931), 19.
25. RGASPI, f. 17, op. 85, d. 514, l. 304.
26. This mood provided the backdrop for the celebrated Shakhty affair of March 1928, in which mining engineers of the Shakhty region were convicted in a show trial of sabotage. The trial officially signalled the beginning of the war on the intelligentsia. On the Shakhty affair, see, for instance, Kendall E. Bailes, *Technology and Society under Lenin and Stalin: Origins of the Soviet Technical Intelligentsia, 1917–1941* (Princeton, N.J.: Princeton University Press, 1978), chap. 3.
27. RGASPI, f. 17, op. 85, d. 514, ll. 218-21.
28. RGASPI, f. 17, op. 85, d. 522, l. 243.
29. RGASPI, f. 5, op. 1, d. 1663, l. 7.
30. RGASPI, f. 5, op. 1, d. 1673, l. 5.
31. RGASPI, f. 5, op. 1, d. 1698, l. 9.
32. RGASPI, f. 5, op. 1, d. 1684, l. 8.
33. RGASPI, f. 5, op. 1, d. 1724, l. 1.
34. RGASPI, f. 5, op. 1, d. 1749, l. 1.
35. RGASPI, f. 5, op. 1, d. 1736, l. 1.
36. RGASPI, f. 5, op. 1, d. 1663, l. 5.
37. RGASPI, f. 5, op. 1, d. 1714, l. 12.
38. RGASPI, f. 17, op. 85, d. 514, ll. 226-27.
39. RGASPI, f. 5, op. 1, d. 1663, l. 9.

40. RGASPI, f. 17, op. 85, d. 514, l. 115.
41. RGASPI, f. 5, op. 1, d. 1712, l. 1.
42. RGASPI, f. 17, op. 85, d. 514, ll. 165-68.
43. RGASPI, f. 17, op. 85, d. 521, ll. 129-35.
44. RGASPI, f. 17, op. 85, d. 524, ll. 73-75.
45. RGASPI, f. 17, op. 85, d. 524, l. 72.
46. RGASPI, f. 17, op. 85, d. 524, l. 125.
47. Anton Ivanovich Denikin was the main leader of the White Russian Army against the Bolshevik government in southern Russia during the civil war. In 1919 Denikin's forces nearly succeeded in taking Moscow, but with the help of Nestor Makhno's Black (anarchist) Army, the Red Army under the command of Leon Trotsky defeated them. In 1920, after he resigned his command in part for promoting and carrying out virulent anti-Semitic pogroms in the occupied areas under his command, Denikin evacuated Russia via the Crimea.
48. RGASPI, f. 17, op. 85, d. 523, l. 92.
49. Mark Galeotti, *The Age of Anxiety: Security and Politics in Soviet and Post-Soviet Russia* (London: Longman Publishers, 1995), 178.
50. RGASPI, f. 17, op. 85, d. 521, ll. 8, 11-20.
51. RGASPI, f. 17, op. 85, d. 519, l. 148.
52. RGASPI, f. 17, op. 85, d. 515, l. 3.
53. RGASPI, f. 17, op. 85, d. 515, l. 2.
54. RGASPI, f. 17, op. 85, d. 521, l. 26.
55. RGASPI, f. 17, op. 85, d. 516, l. 7.
56. RGASPI, f. 17, op. 85, d. 514, l. 12.

Chapter Eight

1. For a Soviet view on the struggle against former elites, see, for instance, I. Ia. Trifonov, *Likvidatsiia ekspluatatorskikh klassov v SSSR* (Moscow: Politizdat, 1975); on the presence of former nobility, see John Channon, "Tsarist Landowners after the Revolution: Former Pomeshchiki in Rural Russia during NEP," *Soviet Studies* 39 (1987): 575-98; Sof'ia Chuikina, *Dvorianskaia pamiat': "Byvshie" v sovetskom gorode (Leningrad, 1920–30-e gody)* (St. Petersburg: Evropeiskii Universitet v Sankt-Peterburge, 2006); and Matthew Rendle, *Defenders of the Motherland: The Tsarist Elite in Revolutionary Russia* (Oxford: Oxford University Press, 2010); on the history of the nepmen, see Alan Ball, *Russia's Last Capitalists: The Nepmen, 1921–1929* (Berkeley: University of California Press, 1987); and on the bases for disfranchisement of pre- and postrevolutionary elites, see Elise Kimerling Wirtschafter, "Civil Rights and Social Policy in Soviet Russia, 1918–1936," *Russian Review* 41 (1982): 24-46.
2. Lynn Hunt observed that during the French Revolution, "conspiracy was fraternal and hence fratricidal, and the preoccupation with it only grew . . . revolutionaries talked incessantly about unmasking" (*Politics, Culture, and Class in the French Revolution* [Berkeley: University of California Press, 1984],

39). In other words, the very closeness and sameness of potential counterrevolutionaries increased paranoia.

3. On the moral and economic dimensions of popular perceptions of inequality and socioeconomic polarization of society during the 1930s, see Sarah Davies, "Us against Them: Social Identity in Soviet Russia, 1934–41," in *Stalinism: New Directions*, ed. Sheila Fitzpatrick (London and New York: Rutledge, 2000), 56-61 and 61-67, respectively. For the threats that elites—and other marginal elements—posed to Soviet society as a basis of the 1930s purges, see Paul M. Hagenloh, "'Socially Harmful Elements' and the Great Terror," ibid., 286-308. Hagenloh examines how the Terror focused not just on elites but also on marginal elements generally, the purpose being to preserve the organic integrity of Soviet society, *das Volk* (the people; cf. Nazi Germany), as it were. For more on comparisons between interwar German and Soviet history, see the discussion in chapter 10 below.

The related questions of who defined enemies and why they were eliminated is debated but, like the larger question of the underpinnings of Stalinism generally—the focus of the present work—still dominated by top-down explanations. Connected with this is the fact that most of the scholarly discourse on exposing and purging enemies of the state deals with the 1930s and the Great Terror. See, for instance, the recent work by Wendy Z. Goldman, *Inventing the Enemy: Denunciation and Terror in Stalin's Russia* (Cambridge, England: Cambridge University Press, 2011). But note that the letters and appeals referenced in this section were written during the mid 1920s, the height of NEP, preceding both the Terror and Stalin's rise to power. As the editors of *Pis'ma vo vlast'* pointed out, denunciations had to come before repression (7). A recent study on scapegoating in the 1930s criticizing "many scholars' unwarranted obsession with Soviet and Stalinist exceptionalism" is William Chase, "Scapegoating One's Comrades in the USSR, 1934–1937," *Russian History* 38 (2011): 23-41. For more on this problem, see the discussion in chapter 10.

4. See, for instance, Salo W. Baron, *The Russian Jew under Tsars and Soviets* (New York: Macmillan, 1976), 209-10. The author states that "in many areas a NEPman had become synonymous with a Jew, and he was so treated in some of the belle-lettres of the period." In a more recent study of Jews during NEP ("Demonizing Judaism in the Soviet Union during the 1920s," *Slavic Review* 67, no. 1 [spring 2008]: 120-53), Robert Weinberg points out that "Many people tend to view Soviet Jews of the 1920s as victims of an unrelenting and vicious government program to snuff out their religious life and culture. Yet many Soviet Jews championed the communist cause and eagerly participated in the campaign against Judaism" (120). Nevertheless, government efforts to wipe out Judaism as part of the greater anti-religious campaign included both attempts to split the community by portraying Jewish bougeoisie as exploiters of their poor coreligionists and general anti-Semitic propaganda: "Soviet depictions of religious Jews drew upon well-established stereotypical, anti-Jewish motifs such as big noses, thick lips, oversized ears, and greasy, scraggly beards and hair. But they also introduced new and obscure features such as a single eye and a nose in the shape of a fist" (121); "This visualization of Judaism and religious Jews in the Soviet Union during the 1920s drew upon the timeworn religious belief that Jews are in cahoots with the devil and possess inhuman

traits" (123). See also Michael C. Hickey, "Communists vs. Clerics: The Smolensk Choral Synagogue, the Khislavichi Rov Shtibel Synagogue and the NEP Antireligious Campaign," *The NEP Era: Soviet Russia 1921–1928* 2 (2008): 39-59. Recent Russian studies of Jews in the prerevolutionary and Civil War periods include O. V. Budnitskii, *Rossiiskie evrei mezhdu krasnymi i belymi (1917–1920)* (Moscow: ROSSPEN, 2005); and O. V. Budnitskii, O. V. Belova, V. E. Kelner, and V. V. Mochalova, eds., *Mirovoi krizis 1914–1920 i sud'ba vostochnoevropeiskogo evreistva* (Moscow: ROSSPEN, 2005).

5. The conflation of those groups considered to be class enemies is illustrated in an observation made by William Reswick, who worked during the 1920s in the Soviet Union for the Associated Press. Reswick defined the term *lishentsy* as "a newly coined name for Nepmen" (William Reswick, *I Dreamt Revolution* [Chicago: H. Regnery Co., 1952], 166-67). Technically, however, *lishentsy* referred specifically to persons deprived of voting rights and included all manner of class enemies and "former people."

6. RGASPI, f. 5, op. 1, d. 1731, l. 2.

7. RGASPI, f. 17, op. 85, d. 518, ll. 256-64.

8. RGASPI, f. 17, op. 85, d. 520, l. 147. Alexander Kerensky was a Socialist Revolutionary, the only socialist to join the Provisional Government established by the February Revolution in 1917.

9. RGASPI, f. 17, op. 85, d. 514, l. 283.

10. RGASPI, f. 17, op. 85, d. 523, ll. 127-28, 150-51. On Kolchak, see chap. 4 n. 61.

11. This infiltration is also well documented by many historians. See, for instance, T. H. Rigby's observations about early party organization in his *Communist Party Membership in the U.S.S.R. 1917–1967* (Princeton, N.J.: Princeton University Press, 1968).

12. RGASPI, f. 17, op. 11, d. 301, ll. 3-4.

13. RGASPI, f. 17, op. 85, d. 519, l. 159.

14. RGASPI, f. 17, op. 85, d. 522, ll. 35-38.

15. RGASPI, f. 5, op. 1, d. 1671, l. 1.

16. RGASPI, f. 17, op. 84, d. 645, ll. 250-51.

17. RGASPI, f. 17, op. 85, d. 513, l. 258.

18. RGASPI, f. 17, op. 85, d. 518, l. 272.

19. RGASPI, f. 17, op. 67, d. 267, ll. 1-6.

20. RGASPI, f. 17, op. 85, d. 523, l. 164.

21. RGASPI, f. 17, op. 85, d. 524, l. 94.

22. In his study on peasants' early efforts to understand and employ the language of the revolutionary parties, Orlando Figes ("The Russian Revolution of 1917 and Its Language in the Village," *Russian Review* 56 [July 1997]: 323-45) observed that the revolutionary intelligentsia ultimately and ironically were forced to employ peasant language in their propaganda in order to get their message to the peasants.

23. RGASPI, f. 17, op. 85, d. 521, l. 163.

24. Isabel A. Tirado, "The Komsomol and Young Peasants: The Dilemma of Rural Expansion, 1921–1925," *Slavic Review* 52, no. 3 (fall 1993): 460-76.

25. RGASPI, f. 5, op. 1, d. 1716, l. 5.

26. RGASPI, f. 17, op. 85, d. 522, l. 15.

27. On the psychological benefits of Komsomol membership, see, for instance, the memoirs of Victor Kravchenko, *I Chose Freedom: The Personal and Political Life of a Soviet Official* (New York: C. Scribners and Sons, 1946), 38. The Judeo-Christian undertones in communism are obvious, and references to communists and komsomoltsy by themselves and others as a chosen people, ubiquitous.

28. See Tirado, "The Komsomol and Young Peasants."

29. RGASPI, f. 17, op. 85, d. 519, l. 67.

30. RGASPI, f. 17, op. 85, d. 521, l. 155.

31. RGASPI, f. 17, op. 85, d. 517, l. 24.

32. RGASPI, f. 17, op. 85, d. 521, l. 172.

33. RGASPI, f. 17, op. 84, d. 647, ll. 54-57.

34. RGASPI, f. 17, op. 85, d. 514, ll. 170-73.

35. RGASPI, f. 17, op. 11, d. 340, ll. 2-5.

36. RGASPI, f. 17, op. 85, d. 516, l. 118.

37. RGASPI, f. 17, op. 85, d. 523, l. 191.

38. RGASPI, f. 17, op. 11, d. 342, l. 1.

39. RGASPI, f. 17, op. 67, d. 23, ll. 2-3.

40. RGASPI, f. 17, op. 84, d. 646, ll. 192-93.

41. RGASPI, f. 17, op. 84, d. 646, ll. 334-35.

42. RGASPI, f. 17, op. 85, d. 522, l. 287.

43. P. N. Wrangel was one of the outstanding White generals during the civil war. He originated from the Baltic nobility and fought in the Russian Army in the Russo-Japanese War and World War I. After narrowly escaping execution by the Bolsheviks, he joined the White cause, capturing Tsaritsyn (later Stalingrad), and became commander in the Crimea in 1920. He initiated land reform and evacuated 150,000 Whites after the Bolshevik victory in November 1920.

44. RGASPI, f. 17, op. 84, d. 859, l. 20.

45. On the persistence of power structures in the village after the revolution, see, for instance, Orlando Figes, "The Village and Volost Soviet Elections of 1919," *Soviet Studies* 40, no. 1 (January 1988): 21-45; and David L. Hoffman, "Land, Freedom, and Discontent: Russian Peasants of the Central Industrial Region prior to Collectivization," *Europe-Asia Studies* 46 (1994): 637-48.

46. Olga A. Narkiewicz, *The Making of the Soviet State Apparatus*, 64.

47. RGASPI, f. 17, op. 85, d. 516, l. 60.

48. RGASPI, f. 17, op. 85, d. 517, ll. 147-50.

49. RGASPI, f. 17, op. 85, d. 516, ll. 268-69. For a discussion of working-class morality, see Mark D. Steinberg, "Vanguard Workers and the Morality of Class," in *Making Workers Soviet: Power, Class, and Identity*, ed. Lewis H. Siegelbaum and Ronald Grigor Suny (Ithaca, N.Y.: Cornell University Press, 1994), 66-84. See, also, the article by Sarah Davies ("Us against Them: Social Identity in Soviet Russia, 1934–41," in *Stalinism: New Directions*, ed. Sheila Fitzpatrick [London: Routledge, 2000]: 47-70), which focuses on articulations of "'us against them' in the sense of the 'people' (in various guises) against those perceived as power-holders," and notes how "this dichotomous image of society (us being the lowly, them, the elite) is common to many cultures and

stretches back to ancient times" (48). Davies discusses both the moral (56-61) and economic (61-67) dimensions of this dichotomy.

50. Tsar Nicholas II actually had an aunt by that name, Ekaterina Aleksandrovna Bariatinskaia (Iurievskaia), the half-sister of his father, Alexander III, and daughter of Alexander II and his mistress, Ekaterina Dolgorukova. Brought up in France, she lived in Russia after her second marriage during World War I and apparently fled Moscow for Kiev in 1918 during the revolution. It is unclear when she left the Soviet Union, but by 1932 she had settled in England, where she died in 1959, at the age of eighty-one (https://www.geni.com/people/Ekaterina-Aleksandrovna-Baryatinskaya/6000000000632153977).

51. RGASPI, f. 17, op. 85, d. 522, l. 180.

52. RGASPI, f. 17, op. 85, d. 518, l. 192.

53. RGASPI, f. 17, op. 85, d. 514, l. 81. "Denikin, Wrangel, Slashchev" were all leaders of the White Army forces that fought the Bolshevik Red Army during the civil war. Iakov Slashchev was a commander in the army of P. N. Wrangel (see note 43 above).

54. RGASPI, f. 17, op. 85, d. 520, l. 9.

55. According to Sheila Fitzpatrick, during the 1920s schoolteachers were predominantly "non-Marxists and religious believers." Fitzpatrick further observed, however, that "the view of teachers as class enemies had been implanted during the Civil War, when the pre-revolutionary teachers' union had opposed the Bolsheviks" (*Education and Social Mobility in the Soviet Union 1921–1934* [Cambridge, England: Cambridge University Press, 1979], 28-30). Her use of the passive voice here implies that the view of teachers as class enemies was imposed from without, although throughout the work, Fitzpatrick emphasizes the grassroots nature of the cultural revolution in education.

56. RGASPI, f. 17, op. 85, d. 515, l. 28.

57. RGASPI, f. 17, op. 85, d. 522, l. 305.

58. RGASPI, f. 17, op. 85, d. 514, l. 193.

59. RGASPI, f. 17, op. 85, d. 520, l. 45.

60. RGASPI, f. 17, op. 85, d. 515, l. 188.

61. RGASPI, f. 17, op. 85, d. 518, l. 121. Dorothy Atkinson observed that five to six desiatinas "of black soil per (male) soul" were required for subsistence (*The End of the Russian Land Commune, 1905–1930* [Stanford, Calif.: Stanford University Press, 1983], 28).

62. RGASPI, f. 17, op. 85, d. 522, ll. 184-87.

63. V. V. Shul'gin was a Ukrainian landholder and monarchist-nationalist member of the Duma. He fled Russia after October 1917 and actively agitated until late in life against the communist regime. His work *In Three Capitals* (Berlin, 1927) concerned alleged monarchist organizations operating underground in Russia during the 1920s.

64. RGASPI, f. 17, op. 85, d. 522, l. 298.

65. Sergo Mikoyan, "Stalinism As I Saw It," *The Stalin Phenomenon*, ed. Alec Nove (New York: St. Martin's Press, 1992), 159.

66. RGASPI, f. 17, op. 11, d. 234, ll. 17-18.

67. RGASPI, f. 17, op. 84, d. 645, ll. 43-44.

68. RGASPI, f. 17, op. 85, d. 518, ll. 172-79.

69. RGASPI, f. 17, op. 85, d. 522, l. 11.

70. RGASPI, f. 17, op. 85, d. 514, l. 28.
71. RGASPI, f. 17, op. 85, d. 514, l. 98.

Chapter Nine

1. Studies on the precarious position of the intelligentsia following the revolution include Igal Halfin, *From Darkness to Light: Class, Consciousness, and Salvation in Revolutionary Russia* (Pittsburgh, Pa.: University of Pittsburgh Press, 2000), chap. 3, "The 'Intelligentsia': Vicissitudes of the Notion," esp. 193 ff.; and Christopher Read, *Culture and Power in Revolutionary Russia: The Intelligentsia and the Transition from Tsarism to Communism* (London: Macmillan, 1990). Both studies are center-based. Read focuses on the central government's attitude toward the intelligentsia and vice versa, and generally on the development of the intelligentsia during and after the Revolution. His thesis is that the Cultural Revolution was well underway during 1917–27, well before the traditional starting point of the Stalinist Cultural Revolution at the end of the 1920s, as a "surrogate class war" (220).

2. Although supplicants criticized the technical intelligentsia generally for their higher salaries, there were large income disparities within the technical intelligentsia itself both before and after the revolution. While engineers and technical administrators might receive several times the income of skilled workers, technicians such as draftsmen earned only poverty-level wages (Kendall E. Bailes, *Technology and Society under Lenin and Stalin: Origins of the Soviet Technical Intelligentsia, 1917–1941* [Princeton, N.J.: Princeton University Press, 1978], introduction). For more on the subject of specialist-baiting during the early NEP period and the causes of resentment toward specialists, see C. J. Storella, "Soviet Specialist Baiting: The Case of N. A. Dobrosmyslov," *Russian History* 38 (2011): 5-22.

3. John N. Hazard, *The Soviet System of Government*, 5th ed. (Chicago: University of Chicago Press, 1980), 214-15.

4. For a discussion of how the meaning of "intelligentsia" changed with and after the revolution, see Bailes, *Technology and Society under Lenin and Stalin*, introduction. On the technical intelligentsia, see also Nicholas Lampert, *The Technical Intelligentsia and the Soviet State* (New York: Holmes and Meier Publishers, 1979). Notable among Soviet works on the postrevolutionary intelligentsia include those of S. A. Fediukin, *Sovetskaia vlast' i burzhuaznye spetsialisty* (Moscow: Mysl', 1965); and *Velikii oktiabr' i intelligentsiia* (Moscow: Mysl', 1972).

5. George Fischer, "The Intelligentsia and Russia," in *The Transformation of Russian Society: Aspects of Social Change since 1861*, ed. Cyril Black (Cambridge: Harvard University Press, 1960), 262-63. See also Richard Pipes, ed., *The Russian Intelligentsia* (New York: Columbia University Press, 1961); and Elise Kimerling Wirtschafter, *Social Identity in Imperial Russia* (DeKalb: Northern Illinois University Press, 1997), "Middle Groups."

6. Victor Kravchenko, *I Chose Freedom: The Personal and Political Life of a Soviet Official* (New York: C. Scribner's and Sons), 56.

7. See, for instance, Read, *Culture and Power in Revolutionary Russia*, esp. chap. 2, "The Intelligentsia in War and Revolution."
8. Bailes, *Technology and Society under Lenin and Stalin*, 19-24.
9. Fediukin, *Sovetskaia vlast' i burzhuaznye spetsialisty*, 18-21. This observation was echoed by Stephen A. Smith in *Red Petrograd: Revolution in the Factories 1917–1918* (New York: Cambridge University Press, 1983), 233-35.
10. Pitirim A. Sorokin, *Leaves from a Russian Diary, and Thirty Years After* (Boston: Beacon Press, 1950), 225. Sorokin was expelled from Russia by the Bolsheviks, emigrated to the United States in 1922, and founded the department of sociology at Harvard University.
11. N. Valentinov [Vol'skii], *Novaia ekonomicheskaia politika i krizis partii posle smerti Lenina: Gody raboty v VSNKh vo vremia NEP; Vospominaniia* (Stanford, Calif.: Hoover Institution Press, Stanford University, 1971). For a further discussion of the heterogeneous response of the intelligentsia, see Dietrich Beyrau, "Russische Intelligenzija und Revolution," *Historische Zeitschrift* 252 (1991): 559-86.
12. RGASPI, f. 17, op. 84, d. 646, ll. 340-41.
13. Gregory L. Freeze, *From Supplication to Revolution: A Documentary Social History of Imperial Russia* (New York: Oxford University Press, 1988), 210-11, 214-18.
14. William G. Rosenberg and Marilyn B. Young, *Transforming Russia and China: Revolutionary Struggle in the Twentieth Century* (New York: Oxford University Press, 1982), 54-55, quoting an American journalist. Foreigners' attitudes reflected their horror both at the violence of the revolution and the seizure of power by the lower classes. See, for instance, John Maynard Keynes, *A Short View of Russia* (London: L. and Virginia Woolf, 1925), 14.
15. Sorokin, *Leaves from a Russian Diary*, 91. Sorokin described the revolutionary mob as a "wild beast" (31-32, 50) and also as a "monster [which] simply howled aloud the idiotic slogans of the Bolsheviki" (66).
16. Mark von Hagen, *Soldiers in the Proletarian Dictatorship: The Red Army and the Soviet Socialist State, 1917–1930* (Ithaca, N.Y.: Cornell University Press, 1990), 178.
17. Mark von Hagen, "Civil-Military Relations and the Evolution of the Soviet Socialist State," *Slavic Review* 50, no. 2 (summer 1991): 268-76.
18. See, for instance, George A. Burrell, *An American Engineer Looks at Russia* (Boston: The Stratford Co., 1932), 134, 255.
19. Archibald Forman, *From Baltic to Black Sea: Impressions of Soviet Russia To-day* (London: S. Low, Marston, 1932), 267.
20. Dorothy Thompson, *The New Russia* (New York: H. Holt and Co., 1928), 65 66.
21. RGASPI, f. 17, op. 85, d. 521, l. 3.
22. RGASPI, f. 17, op. 85, d. 521, ll. 141-46.
23. RGASPI, f. 17, op. 85, d. 514, ll. 144-45.
24. William Henry Chamberlin, *Soviet Russia: A Living Record and A History* (Boston: Little, Brown, and Co., 1930), 182-83.
25. Alexander Berkman, *The Bolshevik Myth (Diary 1920–1922)* (New York: Boni and Liveright, 1925), 230-31.
26. von Hagen, *Soldiers in the Proletarian Dictatorship*, 1.

27. Theodore Dreiser, *Dreiser Looks at Russia* (New York: H. Liveright, 1928), 110, 116.
28. Edwin Ware Hullinger, *Reforging of Russia* (New York: E. P. Dutton, 1925), 118.
29. T. H. Rigby noted that in the Soviet period, the terms "intelligentsia" and "sluzhashchie" converged in meaning to denote nonmanual workers, while the prerevolutionary intelligentsia were distinct from the tsarist service bureaucracy (*Communist Party Membership in the U.S.S.R. 1917–1967* [Princeton, N.J.: Princeton University Press, 1968], 67). On bridging the cultural gap between the intelligentsia and the masses and official Stalinist rhetoric on this in the 1930s, see Vadim Volkov, "The Concept of *Kul'turnost'*: Notes on the Stalinist Civilizing Process," in *Stalinism*, ed. Fitzpatrick, 210-30. See note 4 above.
30. This, of course, was a criticism that Stalin shared. In July 1927, Stalin wrote to Molotov on the problem of "how [to] fix the conglomerate that we incorrectly call the Chinese Communist Party." Stalin concluded that "a good Marxist-Leninist literature must be created in the Chinese language—fundamental, not made up of 'little leaflets'—and the necessary funds must now be allocated for this, without delay (you can say to Klim [Voroshilov] that this will cost much less than maintaining one hundred of his hemorrhoidal bureaucrat-counterrevolutionaries for half a year)" (Lars T. Lih, Oleg V. Naumov, and Oleg V. Khlevniuk, eds., *Stalin's Letters to Molotov 1925–1936*, Annals of Communism [New Haven, Conn.: Yale University Press, 1995], letter 36 [9 July 1927], 141-42).
31. Sheila Fitzpatrick has noted that one important aspect of cultural revolution at the end of the 1920s was the promotion of a new generation of workers and peasants into the bureaucracy and managerial classes. See, for instance, *Education and Social Mobility in the Soviet Union 1921–1934* (Cambridge, England: Cambridge University Press, 1979); and eadem, "The Russian Revolution and Social Mobility: A Re-examination of the Question of Social Support for the Soviet Regime in the 1920s and 1930s," *Politics and Society* 13, no. 2 (1984): 119-41.
32. RGASPI, f. 17, op. 85, d. 522, ll. 202-9.
33. RGASPI, f. 17, op. 84, d. 645, ll. 362-63.
34. RGASPI, f. 17, op. 84, d. 645, ll. 190-91.
35. Maurice Hindus, *Broken Earth* (New York: International Publishers, 1926), 252.
36. Burrell, *An American Engineer Looks at Russia*, 134. Interestingly, according to Burrell, red directors who had been promoted up from the ranks did not acquire much status: "The worker gains more pay, but not much socially by being promoted to a directorship; only more responsibility, without much additional deference."
37. Allan Monkhouse, *Moscow 1911–1933* (Boston: Little, Brown, and Co., 1934), 191.
38. RGASPI, f. 17, op. 85, d. 516, l. 119.
39. RGASPI, f. 17, op. 85, d. 516, ll. 89-90.
40. See the discussion above on the intelligentsia and revolution.
41. RGASPI, f. 17, op. 84, d. 646, ll. 21, 23.

42. RGASPI, f. 17, op. 85, d. 523, l. 221.
43. RGASPI, f. 17, op. 85, d. 523, l. 223.
44. RGASPI, f. 17, op. 85, d. 516, l. 181.
45. Diane P. Koenker, "Class and Consciousness in a Socialist Society: Workers in the Printing Trades during NEP," in *Russia in the Era of NEP: Explorations in Soviet Society and Culture*, ed. Sheila Fitzpatrick, Alexander Rabinowitch, and Richard Stites (Bloomington: Indiana University Press, 1991), 34-57.
46. RGASPI, f. 17, op. 85, d. 524, l. 55.
47. RGASPI, f. 17, op. 85, d. 516, l. 296.
48. Rossiiskii gosudarstvennyi arkhiv ekonomiki (Russian State Archive of the Economy; hereinafter RGAE), f. 5240, op. 1, d. 4, ll. 3-7.
49. RGASPI, f. 17, op. 85, d. 516, ll. 293-95.
50. Monkhouse, *Moscow 1911–1933*, 142-43.
51. Sorokin, *Leaves from a Russian Diary*, 226-27.
52. RGASPI, f. 17, op. 85, d. 523, l. 200.
53. RGASPI, f. 17, op. 85, d. 524, l. 206.
54. RGASPI, f. 17, op. 85, d. 523, l. 162.
55. RGASPI, f. 17, op. 85, d. 518, l. 180.
56. The connection between anti-communist, anti-intelligentsia, and anti-Semitic sentiment was long recognized by the communists themselves and has been well documented; anti-communist sentiment expressed in anti-Semitic terms was most common in areas of the former Pale of Settlement. Works that explore this topic include *Anti-Semitism in the Soviet Union: Its Roots and Consequences*, 2 vols. (Jerusalem: Hebrew University, 1979–80); and Arkady Vaksberg, *Stalin Against the Jews*, trans. Antonia W. Bouis (New York: Alfred A. Knopf, 1994).
57. RGASPI, f. 17, op. 84, d. 647, ll. 208-9.
58. See, for instance, the appeal of a Jewish communist who was expelled from the party on grounds of being a rabbi and originating from a religious family (RGASPI, f. 17, op. 84, d. 646, ll. 359-60).
59. RGASPI, f. 17, op. 85, d. 516, ll. 179-80.
60. RGASPI, f. 17, op. 85, d. 524, l. 177.
61. RGASPI, f. 17, op. 84, d. 647, ll. 143-49.
62. Igal Halfin studied biographies written for applications to join the party by students, who endeavored to show that their intelligentsia status had not corrupted their communist consciousness ("From Darkness to Light: Student Communist Autobiography During NEP," *Jahrbücher für Geschichte Osteuropas* 45, no. 2 [1997]: 210-36); and idem, "The Construction of the Workers' Intelligentsia" (Ph.D. diss., Columbia University, 1995).
63. RGASPI, f. 17, op. 85, d. 516, l. 197.
64. RGASPI, f. 17, op. 85, d. 523, ll. 165, 181-85.
65. RGASPI, f. 17, op. 85, d. 519, l. 116.
66. RGASPI, f. 17, op. 85, d. 515, l. 37.
67. RGASPI, f. 17, op. 85, d. 515, l. 1.
68. RGASPI, f. 17, op. 85, d. 521, ll. 191-92. Pacifism was historically connected in Russia (as elsewhere) with Christianity in general, and especially with certain sects, such as the Old Believers and evangelical Christians. See, for

instance, Lawrence Klippenstein, "Mennonite Pacifism and State Service in Russia: A Case Study in Church-State Relations, 1789–1936" (Ph.D. diss., University of Minnesota, 1984).

69. RGASPI, f. 17, op. 85, d. 521, ll. 218-20.

70. RGASPI, f. 5, op. 1, d. 1666, l. 10.

71. RGASPI, f. 5, op. 1, d. 1659, l. 1.

72. RGASPI, f. 5, op. 1, d. 1661, l. 1.

73. RGASPI, f. 5, op. 1, d. 1734, l. 5.

74. RGASPI, f. 17, op. 85, d. 521, l. 44.

75. RGASPI, f. 17, op. 85, d. 522, ll. 202-9.

76. In his monograph claiming Bolshevik rhetoric as the primary cause of violent social conflict after the revolution, Igal Halfin ironically appears to echo the appeals of intelligentsia to the center in the 1920s: "My claim . . . will be that the proletariat and the intelligentsia are abstract notions, not empirical entities, and that their ideal unity should be assigned primacy over their historical separateness" (*From Darkness to Light*, 13). Halfin criticizes the tendency of social historians, and Marxists particularly, to categorize subjects into classes, "neglecting to investigate the process by which language produces the subject in the first place" (14). His argument begs the questions surrounding the origins and uses of language explored in this and other studies. Halfin's indictment of Marxism thus minimizes both the agency of average Soviet citizens in the formation of the language used to direct them, and the material bases for class antagonism suggested in letters to the Bolshevik leadership used in this study: a case, perhaps, of an intellectual overstating the importance of ideas and ideology as motive forces in history?

77. RGASPI, f. 17, op. 85, d. 513, ll. 23-32.

78. In her study of popular opinion in the 1930s (*Popular Opinion in Stalin's Russia: Terror, Propaganda and Dissent, 1934–1941* [Cambridge: Cambridge University Press, 1997], ch. 8, "'Us' and 'them': Social identity and the terror"), Sarah Davies noted that people discriminated between "us" and "them" mainly according to the (unequal) distribution of political power, the dichotomy between good and evil, and slaves and masters, and the cleavages between rich and poor; she also observed that "this sense of dichotomy did much to legitimise certain aspects of the terror in the eyes of the ordinary people," whose resentment sometimes turned on the regime itself (126).

Chapter Ten

1. In her explanation of "How I Became a Revisionist," Sheila Fitzpatrick wrote, "With regard to the totalitarian model, I thought the suggestion absurd that any political regime could control a society—not just repress it, but successfully plan its development in a desired direction, anticipating all the consequences of political actions—as the totalitarian model suggested. I also found the totalitarian model tremendously value-laden in a Cold War way, which offended my belief that the historian ought to be nonpartisan. . . . To me it seemed obvious that if you looked only at *Pravda* and Iosif Stalin's *Works* you would form the impression that everything was controlled from the top, for this

was an automatic consequence of the source base. I was also struck by the way that this 'top-down' picture . . . seemed to reproduce the official Soviet picture of total party control and omniscience, just replacing a positive evaluation with a negative one. . . . I [did not] originally have any precise sense of what might be going on at the grassroots; I just thought there had to be something" (from "Revisionism in Retrospect: A Personal View," *Slavic Review* 67, no. 3 [fall 2008]: 683).

It seems that Russian social historians accept the existence of a dialogue between the state and society more readily than Americans. The editors of *Pis'ma vo vlast'* (see introduction n. 39) identified three main reasons for studying letters to the center during the formation of the Soviet Union: identifying changes in popular consciousness, studying social history, and examining "the particular features of the distinctive dialogue between government and society . . . as an element of poltical and administrative relations" (5); they also noted that Bolshevik officials depended on letters to the center for monitoring the public mood and responses to various policies and initiatives (7).

In his preface to *Golos Naroda*, Andrei Sokolov's explanation of his source base suggests that a cultural divide may be keeping Western historians from grasping the connection between popular expressions of opinion and the development of the Soviet state. Westerners are exceedingly individualistic, and assume that state and society are comprised of a simple plurality of autonomous individuals; but from a Russian point of view, as Sokolov says, "each person is not in and of themselves, but an elementary cell of a living and developing social organism" (*Golos Naroda: Pis'ma i otkliki riadovykh sovietskikh grazhdan o sobytiiakh 1918–1932 gg.* [Moscow: Rosspen, 1998], 3). This collective mentality may be the source of what came to be known, and feared, in the West as totalitarianism.

In an extremely thoughtful article, Felix Patrikeeff ("Stalinism, Totalitarian Society and the Politics of 'Perfect Control'," in Shukman, ed., *Redefining Stalinism*, 23-46) locates the origin of Stalinism in wider society; under the subtitle "Bringing the People Back In," he writes: "the Stalinist period . . . must be regarded as at least the second flow; the direct challenge of the masses to the ebb of the New Economic Policy. . . . The masses, quite to the contrary of Deutscher's view, embodied Stalinism and gave life and direction to it" (40). See, also, conclusions n. 7.

2. A recent study that views the origin of Soviet state practices not in Marxist ideology but in modern practices, including state violence, of Western countries, emulated by both the tsarist and Soviet governments, is David Hoffman, *Cultivating the Masses: Modern State Practices and Soviet Socialism, 1914–1939* (Ithaca, N.Y.: Cornell University Press, 2011).

3. Sheila Fitzpatrick noted this limitation in the revisionist model: "The revisionist historians' dichotomy of 'from above/from below" was an advance, though its binary character was also a simplification, and there was some ambiguity about how far down in the society 'below' implied" ("Revisionism in Retrospect," 699).

4. Of course, such comparisons began early on and formed the basis for Cold War research and rhetoric, which spawned the working concept of totalitarianism. Recently, several works both compare Germany and Nazism

with the Soviet Union during Stalinism and explore their interconnected histories. See, for instance, Michael Geyer and Sheila Fitzpatrick, eds., *Beyond Totalitarianism: Stalinism and Nazism Compared* (Cambridge University Press, 2009), an attempt, as the title suggests, to move beyond totalitarianism as an explanatory model for understanding the two regimes; Timothy Snyder, *Bloodlands: Europe between Hitler and Stalin* (New York: Basic Books, 2010); and Michael David-Fox, Peter Holquist, and Alexander Martin, eds., *Fascination and Enmity: Russia and Germany as Entangled Histories, 1914–45* (Pittsburgh, Pa.: University of Pittsburgh Press, 2012).

5. Robert C. Tucker, *Stalin in Power: The Revolution from Above, 1928–1941* (New York: W. W. Norton and Company, 1990), 51-52.

6. A rather colorful and perhaps exaggerated assessment by journalist Simon Sebag Montefiore, in his *Stalin: The Court of the Red Tsar*, quoted in Kevin McDermott, *Stalin: Revolutionary in an Era of War*, European History in Perspective (Palgrave Macmillan, 2006), 11.

7. For instance, Stalin "followed closely" the debate between Trotsky and historian Pokrovsky on the primary forces which formed the tsarist state—economic exploitation of the serfs or hostile encirclement—and he corresponded in 1927 with two students at the Institute of Red Professors who "solicited his view on the controversial question of the historical rise of the Russian autocracy" (Tucker, *Stalin in Power*, 55-56).

8. For the tradition of supplication in Russia and its significance for the Bolsheviks, see the preface and introduction.

9. Hiroaki Kuromiya, *Stalin: Profiles in Power* (Harlow, England: Pearson Longman, 2005), 10.

10. RGASPI, f. 17, op. 85, d. 514, ll. 198-203.

11. Quoted in Kuromiya, *Stalin*, 10. Kuromiya points out that such groveling was not accepted in the revolutionary code of conduct: "Soso twice tendered obsequious petitions for release to the governor of the Caucasus . . . an act tantamount to treason in the eyes of revolutionaries" (ibid.).

12. Tucker, *Stalin in Power*, 7.

13. Quoted in Tucker, *Stalin in Power*, 129.

14. RGASPI, f. 17, op. 85, d. 517, l. 91.

15. The need for party unity was even greater because of the threat to government control and direction brought on by increasing social and economic liberalism of NEP: the two were directly, and consciously, connected, by party leaders (Tucker, *Stalin in Power*, 121). For further discussion of this issue, see chapter 5.

16. A recent study on the origins of state terror under the Bolsheviks is James Ryan, *Lenin's Terror: The Ideological Origins of Early Soviet State Violence* (London: Routledge, 2012), in which the author showed that Lenin "accepted that coercion and violence would be required to transform the country" (184) but hoped at times (of less vulnerability?) for more peaceful resolution of the conflicts inherent to the revolution.

17. Tucker, *Stalin in Power*, 27.

18. Ibid., 28.

19. Marcus C. Levitt and Tatyana Novikov, eds., *Times of Trouble: Violence in Russian Literature and Culture* (Madison: University of Wisconsin Press, 2007).

20. Tucker, *Stalin in Power*, 5.

21. Recent studies on this include Ol'ga Mikhailovna Morozova, *Dva akta dramy: Boevoe proshloe i poslevoennaia povsednevnost' veteranov grazhdanskoe voiny* (Rostov on Don: Isdatel'stvo Iuzhnyi tsentr RAN, 2010); and Sean Guillory, "The Shattered Self of Komsomol Civil War Memoirs," *Slavic Review* 71, no. 3 (fall 2012): 546-65.

22. Kevin McDermott notes the influence of civil war experience, but on party leaders, not the population at large: "War and revolution were inextricably inter-related in Marxist-Leninist theory . . . but for Stalin war became also a central tenet of his *domestic* policies—the idea of an internal 'class war' against ubiquitous 'enemies' seemed to take possession of him by the early 1930s" (emphasis in the original). And further: "Wars, civil wars and the threat of war and social unrest formed a constant leitmotif in the political careers and personal experiences of all top Bolsheviks" (8).

23. For a detailed discussion of the psychological basis of Stalin's search for enemies, see the subchapter "The Need for Enemies," in Tucker, *Stalin in Power*, chap. 7.

24. Kuromiya, *Stalin*, 1.

25. Ibid., 2.

26. Tucker, *Stalin in Power*, 4.

27. Kuromiya, *Stalin*, 3.

28. Sheila Fitzpatrick noted that in the course of her research, she "was also developing the depressing sense that the odds were stacked against the 'good guys,' that is communist intellectuals like Anatolii Lunacharskii and Nadezhda Krupskaia, who tended to recoil from revolutionary violence . . . , and that it was the tough, lower-class, anti-intellectual position that was likely to prevail in any internal party fight. That gave me a different (less benign) idea of what 'worker' might mean in attitudinal terms than was current among labor historians: *Resentiment*, not class solidarity, struck me as the driving emotion of the party's 'proletarian' side" ("Revisionism in Retrospect," 684).

29. In a discussion of revisionist history (see below, note 50), which used social history to bring average people back into the analysis of the Soviet period, J. Arch Getty noted: "Revisionist social history stressed class differences, social support 'from below,' and resentment against privileged, upper-class people. . . . My students from economically disadvantaged backgrounds have little trouble grasping this illiberal, class-conflict part of the picture. Those near the bottom of society always sense class more than those near the top, who may have difficulty understanding or accepting anger down below. Middle-class professors naturally identify with Iosif Stalin's victims, especially the educated ones, more than with his supporters, and think it perverse to write about those willing to trade free speech for cheap food or to accept them as rational actors, however illiberal" ("Comment: Codes and Confessions," *Slavic Review* 67, no. 3 [fall 2008]: 712).

30. Kuromiya, *Stalin*, 6.

31. Ibid., 9.

32. Ibid., 14.
33. Ibid.
34. Interestingly, Stalin, unlike Lenin, also supported at this time "the confiscation of the land and its redistribution among the peasants, an affirmation of peasant revolution" (ibid., 15).
35. Ibid., 21.
36. Ibid., 33.
37. For Hitler, see Rudolph Binion, *Hitler among the Germans* (New York: Elsevier, 1976), especially chapter 5, "Leader and Led"; and for Stalin, see Daniel Rancour-Laferriere, *The Mind of Stalin: A Psychoanalytic Study* (Ann Arbor, Mich.: Ardis, 1988).
38. There is a large body of research on the Komsomol and youth generally during the Soviet period, much of which is cited throughout this study; a recent work on the role of the Komsomol in the "revolution from above" is Matthias Neumann, *The Communist Youth League and the Transformation of the Soviet Union, 1917–1931*, BASEES/Routledge Series on Russian and East European Studies (London: Routledge, 2011).
39. Peter Loewenberg, "The Psychohistorical Origins of the Nazi Youth Cohort," *The American Historical Review* 76, no. 5 (December 1971): 1458.
40. Ibid., 1502.
41. Binion, *Hitler among the Germans*, 118.
42. Ibid., 127.
43. Tucker, *Stalin in Power*, 6.
44. Kuromiya, *Stalin*, ix-x.
45. McDermott, *Stalin*, 10. McDermott added the italics.
46. Kuromiya, *Stalin*, 7.
47. Tucker, *Stalin in Power*, 8-9.
48. Stalin's psychobiographer, Daniel Rancour-LaFerriere, concluded that "[in Stalin's personality] there was also a great sense of personal inferiority. With the help of such unconscious defense mechanisms as projection, overcompensation, denial, and rationalization Stalin dealt with this inferiority and produced a monstrously inflated self-image. Beneath the sadism, power-hunger, and vindictiveness lay a great anxiety concerning potential aggressors" (*The Mind of Stalin*, 118).
49. See, for instance, V. P. Danilov, "The Historical Significance of Alternatives to Stalinism," *Russian Studies in History* 42, no. 4 (spring 2004): 53-69, in which the author's discussion of what brought Stalinism about focuses entirely on the party leadership, while "all the achievements of Soviet society grew out of the powerful socialist momentum generated by the great social revolution of 1917, which preordained the direction and content of economic and cultural construction. The industrialization of the country; universal education; the powerful surge in science, scholarship, and culture; universal health care; and social welfare were embedded not only in the ideas but in the actual practice of the early Soviet years. They became a reality *not thanks to Stalinism but in spite of the obstacles and enormous losses that were directly and unambiguously associated with Stalinism*" (55; emphasis in the original).
50. See the discussion led by Sheila Fitzpatrick in *Slavic Review* 67, no. 3 (fall 2008), 682-723; and the somewhat heated and bitter debate responding to

that discussion in the "Letters" section, *Slavic Review* 68, no. 1 (spring 2009), 219-24.

51. Tucker, *Stalin in Power*, 174.

52. In her comment on the discussion of revisionist history (see note 50), Elena Osokina wrote: "For me there was never a question of whose side to take [in the totalitarian/revisionist debate]. Not only did the 'totalitarian model' of Stalinism that emerged during the Cold War go against common sense . . . but it contradicted my personal life experience under communism . . . Furthermore, the Cold War view of Soviet society under communism somehow hurt my feelings. The idea that Soviet subjects were either brainwashed morons voluntarily going to slaughterhouses or soon-to-be-swallowed rabbits paralyzed by the sight of a boa constrictor made me grin. . . . Each era forms its own stereotypes and phobias, and . . . the phobias of the Cold War generation were not ones I shared. Being a Soviet subject myself, although I did not live under Stalin, I had no doubts that Soviet citizens of the 1930s (after all, my parents belonged to that generation) did not differ much from me or from any other human beings in never forgetting to pursue their personal interests . . . , human beings with personal agendas just like Westerners" ("Comment: Life and Fate of Western Revisionism," *Slavic Review* 67, no. 3 [fall 2008]: 716-17).

53. McDermott, *Stalin*, 4-5.

54. Ibid., 63.

55. This profound reluctance to assign agency among the general population for what occurred under Stalin has recently been addressed: see the article by Lynne Viola, "The Question of the Perpetrator in Soviet History," *Slavic Review* 72, no. 1 (spring 2013): 1-23, and the comments following, by Wendy Z. Goldman, "Twin Pyramids—Perpetrators and Victims," 24-27, and by Peter Fritzsche, "Making Perpetrators," 28-31. Viola begins by noting that "The term [perpetrator] has not generally been used in the historiography of the Stalinist Soviet Union. In part, this omission is based upon a reluctance to go beyond Iosif Stalin in assigning agency or responsibility for the immense crimes of his reign." She goes on to discuss how, "by contrast, historians of Nazi Germany and the Holocaust have discussed this question in great detail, virtually creating . . . a 'separate subdiscipline in the history of the Third Reich'" (1). Later, she notes that "Western historians of the Soviet Union, however, have had greater difficulty moving beyond the paradigm of the totalitarian model" (3), but does not say why she thinks this is so. The rest of her essay attempts to build a picture of the Soviet perpetrator. She ends with the comment: "Perhaps most important, the question of *why* individuals, perhaps Soviet society at large, took part in state repression against officially labeled enemies, mainly innocent people, is arguably the question of questions in our efforts to fathom the mass violence of the Stalin era" (23). Regressing apparently to a totalitarian model, Wendy Goldman argued that "In the Soviet case, the 'enemy' was internal, its identity repeatedly reinvented by the state" (25).

56. McDermott asks, "should scholars seek to historicise the horrors of Stalinism and thus appear to attenuate his personal responsibility and justify the unjustifiable? Or should they routinely condemn the mass murder in the name of humanitarianism and decency?" (ibid., 3). This is a fair expression of

one of the main factors driving the persistent top-down, totalitarian model of Soviet government, and it also fairly suggests the problems with it: first, it is not the job of historians to absolve or condemn, but to explain. As Sheila Fitzpatrick noted, "it was self-evident [to me] that the historian's task was to understand, not to prosecute or bear witness against evil" ("Revisionism in Retrospect," 687). And, second, in answer to McDermott: surely, those who have suffered in the past are better served by the best, most honest explanation possible of why they suffered, based on existing evidence.

Conclusions

1. RGASPI, f. 5, op. 1, d. 1672, l. 4.
2. Stefan Plaggenborg argued that a culture of violence had been sanctioned by the Bolsheviks in 1917 and became endemic to Soviet society, especially among youth ("Gewalt und Militanz in Sowjetrussland 1917–1930," *Jahrbücher für Geschichte Osteuropas* 44, no. 3 [1996]: 431-55). However, while the Bolsheviks legitimized and encouraged violence, the choices for targets of popular violence often ran counter to official party policy—most notably in the case of the intelligentsia in general and specialists in particular. This fact alone recasts the discussion of the origins and causes of violence in Soviet society. In his intellectual history of Bolshevism, Igal Halfin attributes violence under the Communists "directly" to marxism as a "dangerous political doctrine" (*From Darkness to Light: Class, Consciousness, and Salvation in Revolutionary Russia* [Pittsburgh, Pa.: University of Pittsburgh Press, 2000], xi). Halfin's implication, that rhetoric creates classes and thus their revolutionary aspirations, appears not to take people's material circumstances into account.
3. Catherine Merridale noted that the "cultural gulf between the nomenklatura elite [of the party] and the activists on Moscow's factory floors was enormous. At times they hardly seemed to be speaking the same language" (*Moscow Politics and the Rise of Stalin: The Communist Party in the Capital, 1925–32* [New York: St. Martin's Press, 1990], 220). For a discussion of Stalin as an outsider in the Bolshevik leadership and the sources of his (enduring) popularity, see for instance Harold Shukman, "Introduction," in *Redefining Stalinism*, ed. Shukman (London: Frank Cass, 2003), 1-6. An insightful analysis of the sources of Stalin's connection with the people and of Stalinism generally can be found in the biography by Alex de Jonge, *Stalin and the Shaping of the Soviet Union* (New York: Wm. Morrow and Co. Inc., 1986), especially chap. 22, "The Beginnings of Stalinism." Among other factors, de Jonge discusses Stalin's popularity especially among younger party members (illustrated by letters used in this study); Russia's need for a "strong man" (an oft-repeated theme) and how Stalin understood and was able to exploit this; and the contribution of desperate, depressing conditions, especially in the cities, of the 1920s under NEP to Stalin's rise (202-6). Another especially useful analysis echoing these observations can be found in Irina Pavlova, *Mekhanizm vlasti i stroitel'stvo stalinskogo sotsializma* (Novosibirsk: Izd-vo CO RAN, 2001), where, in addition to a discussion on historiography on NEP, the author explores why the Soviets required a "strong man" in the 1920s: 1) a general sense of chaos; 2)

widespread need; 3) the vulnerable international position of the country. These studies show the necessity of contextualization; once included, it becomes easier to address such questions as the origin of the party's self-conceived role from Lenin to Stalin—namely, outside traditional historiographical emphasis on Bolshevik theory, personalities in party leadership, and power dynamics, all of which beg certain questions: why this theory and not that, why the need for a strong man, etc.?

4. Key documents and a detailed discussion of the precise steps taken by party leaders in dismantling NEP are found in V. P. Danilov et al., *Kak lomali NEP: Stenogrammy Plenumov TsK VKP(b) 1928–1929 gg.*, Rossiia XX Vek: Dokumenty, A. N. Iakovlev, gen. ed., 5 vols. (Moscow: Mezhdunarodnyi fond "Demokratiia," 2000).

5. Center-based studies on the reasons why the central party leadership, or Stalin in particular, abandoned NEP are voluminous; see the discussion of traditional historiography on NEP's demise in the introduction to this work. For a useful summary of the issues faced by the party leadership, see also de Jonge, *Stalin and the Shaping of the Soviet Union*, chapter 22, "The Beginnings of Stalinism."

6. This reluctance persists even in so-called revisionist history: in his introduction to a collection of letters spanning the 1930s (Lewis Siegelbaum and Andrei Sokolov, eds., *Stalinism as a Way of Life: A Narrative in Documents*, abridged ed. [New Haven, Conn.: Yale University Press, 2004]), Lewis Siegelbaum discusses the problem of blame and the traditional opposition of the citizen to the party/state prevalent in most history on the Soviet period, but the revisionist approach does not eliminate the opposition of above v. below.

7. Felix Patrikeeff: "The social origins of Stalinism therefore lay not in the 'seeds' of dictatorship and a personality cult, but in a widespread popular desire to break away from this oppressive continuity of the old order, dictated by conventional and *localised* relations of power, coupled with the all too familiar faces of scarcity and deprivation. Stalinism was, in this sense, the emergence and execution of a general will intent on finding solutions to problems (both economic and political) which lay at the core of this paradox. The 'crimes' and 'mistakes' often attributed to Stalinism are, by this definition, nothing more than euphemisms used to explain away the excesses generated in, and by, all spheres of a society bound for an extreme form of self-correction" ("Stalinism, Totalitarian Society and the Politics of 'Perfect Control'," in Shukman, ed., *Redefining Stalinism*, 42; emphasis in the original).

8. William Chase called the NEP economy "semicapitalist" (*Workers, Society, and the Soviet State*, 299).

9. In his essay on the formation of the Komsomol, Matthias Neumann concluded that "the active and significant involvement of the Komsomol in the 'revolution from above' . . . raises the question of whether it was, in a sense, the failure of the first socialist revolution during the years 1917 to 1921, manifested in the implementation of NEP and the creation of a society full of contradictions, which made possible the launch and victory of the second revolution in the period 1928 to 1932. As has been demonstrated, the Komsomol seems to have played a major part in the formation of a social constituency for a revival of the class war. Could, then, the 'revolution from above' have been launched

and have succeeded without this 'evolution from below'?" (Neumann, "Class Ascription and Class Identity," 190).

10. Gregory L. Freeze, *From Supplication to Revolution*, 263.

11. In the French Revolution, Lynn Hunt observed, "[t]he language of ritual and ritualized language served the function of national integration. It expressed the need for social solidarity" (*Politics, Culture, and Class in the French Revolution*, 24). Among leaders in the Russian Revolution, Stalin possessed a keen sensitivity to this need for collective unity which served him well.

12. Michael Reiman, *The Birth of Stalinism: The USSR on the Eve of the Second Revolution*, trans. from German by George Saunders (Bloomington: Indiana University Press, 1987), 120.

13. Gusev, K. V. and V. Z. Drobizhev, eds., *Rabochii klass v upravlenii gosudarstvom, 1926–1937 gg.* (Moscow: Mysl', 1968), 4.

GLOSSARY AND ABBREVIATIONS

Terms

aktiv: militants or activists in or outside the party
apparatchik(i): bureaucrat(s); party functionary
artel: peasants' or workers' cooperative
barin: gentleman; aristocrat; master
batrak: agricultural laborer
bedniak: poor peasant
bezprizornyi(e), bezprizornik(i): homeless child(ren)
byvshie: literally, 'formers'; the old elites
cadres: key party personnel; core of the party
centrosoiuz: central consumer cooperative union
Cheka, G.P.U., O.G.P.U.: successive names for the Soviet secret police
chervonets: currency introduced in the early NEP years
chinovnik: tsarist civil servant
Comintern: Communist International, or Third Socialist International (1919–1943) led by the Soviet Union
commissariat: government ministry
desiatina: old Russian measure equal to about 2.7 acres
detdoma: orphanages; literally, 'children's homes'
gensek: general secretary of the Communist Party
glavki: central economic administration boards
Glavmetall: central administration for the metallurgical industry
Gosplan: state economic planning committee
guberniia: province
gubkom: guberniia-level party committee
gubprodkom: provincial food supply commissariat
gubsek: guberniia party committee secretary
gubsoiuz: guberniia-level consumer cooperative
gubsud: provincial court
intelligentsia: class of persons comprising the intellectual, educated, and cultural elites
khozraschet: cost accounting (industrial self-sufficiency under NEP)
kolkhoz: collective farm
Komintern: Communist International
Komsomol: Communist Youth League
komsomolets(tsy): member(s) of the Communist Youth League

Komvuz: communist university
krai: territory; administrative subdivision of the RSFSR
kulak: better-off peasant; literally, 'fist'
lishenets (lishentsy): person(s) deprived of voting rights in the Soviet period
mir: village commune; also, 'peace' and 'world'
muzhik: peasant
narkomat: commissariat
Narkomfin: People's Commissariat of Finance
Narkompros: People's Commissariat of Enlightenment
Narkomtorg: People's Commissariat of Trade
Narkomtrud: People's Commissariat of Labor
Narkomzem: People's Commissariat of Agriculture
NEP: New Economic Policy (adopted by the Bolshevik government in 1921)
nepmen: those engaged in private trade and industry in the 1920s; also, speculators and moneylenders
NKVD: People's Commissariat of Internal Affairs
nomenklatura: system for matching party members with key positions in the party, state, and other institutions of Soviet society
obkom: oblast-level party committee
oblast': region; administrative subdivision of a union republic
Okhrana: tsarist secret police
okrug: administrative subdivision of a republic, krai, or oblast
okruzhkom: district party committee
Orgburo: Organizational Bureau of the Communist Party
Orgraspred: Organization and Assignment Department of the Communist Party
Politburo: Political Bureau of the Communist Party
prodnalog: tax in kind
prodrazverstka: grain requisition; literally, assessment of produce
rabkor: worker correspondent
Rabkrin: Workers' and Peasants' Inspectorate (government monitoring agency)
rabfak: workers' faculty (department in higher educational institutions preparing under-educated workers and peasants for coursework)
raikom: district-level party committee
raion: district; administrative area within a city, oblast, krai, or republic
RGASPI: Rossiiskii gosudarstvennyi arkhiv sotsial'no-politicheskoi istorii (Russian State Archive of Socio-Political History, the former Central Communist Party Archive, Moscow)
RSFSR: Russian Soviet Federative Socialist Republic
Secretariat: central executive and administrative body of the Communist Party; headed by Stalin (as Gensek, 'general secretary') from April 1922
sel'khoz: village farm
selkor: rural correspondent
seredniak: middle peasant
sluzhashchie: white-collar workers; employees
smychka: alliance (of workers and peasants)
soviet: council of elected representatives
sovkhoz: state farm on which farmers are paid wages

sovnarkhozy: regional economic councils
Sovnarkom: Council of People's Commissars; cabinet
sovznak: early postrevolutionary currency replacing imperial ruble
spetsy: technical specialists
TsIK: Central Executive Committee; until 1937 the highest legislative and administrative authority of the Russian SFSR between sessions of the All-Russian Congress of Soviets
TsK: Communist Party Central Committee
tovarishch: comrade
uezd: district
ukom: uezd-level party committee
verst: old Russian measure of distance equal to .663 miles
Vesenkha (VSNKh): Supreme Council of the National Economy
VKP(b): All-Union Communist Party (Bolshevik)
Vsevobuch: Department of Universal Military Training
volkom: volost-level party committee
volost': territorial subdivision of uezd (district)
vozhd': leader
VUZ(y): higher education institution(s)
vydvizhenets (vydvizhentsy): worker(s) promoted to managerial ranks
vydvizhentsvo: promotion of workers to managerial ranks

Abbreviations

RGASPI (Rossiiskii gosudarstvennyi arkhiv sotsial'no-politicheskoi istorii): Russian State Archive of Socio-Political History
RGAE (Rossiiskii gosudarstvennyi arkhiv ekonomiki): Russian State Archive of the Economy
f.: fond (collection)
op.: opis' (registry)
d.: delo (file)
l., ll.: list, listy (folio, folios)

BIBLIOGRAPHY

Archival Sources

RGASPI

Fond 5	Lenin's Personal Secretariat, 1917–24
Fond 17	Central Committee of the KPSS

RGAE

Fond 3338	Rabkrin (Workers' and Peasants' Inspectorate)
Fond 4086	Glavmetall (Central Administration of Metal Industry)
Fond 5240	Narkomtorg (People's Commissariat of Trade)

Published Works

Ananich, B. V., et al. *Krizis samoderzhaviia v Rossii, 1895–1917* (Crisis of autocracy in Russia, 1895–1917). Leningrad: Nauka, 1984.

Anderson, Barbara. *Internal Migration during Modernization in Late Nineteenth-Century Russia.* Princeton, N.J.: Princeton University Press, 1980.

Anti-Semitism in the Soviet Union: Its Roots and Consequences. 2 vols. Jerusalem: Hebrew University, 1979–80.

Arkhipov, V. A., and L. F. Morozov. *Bor'ba protiv kapitalisticheskikh elementov v promyshlennosti i torgovle, 20-e–nachalo 30-kh godov* (Struggle against capitalist elements in industry and trade, 1920s to the beginning of the 1930s). Moscow: Mysl', 1978.

Atkinson, Dorothy. "The Statistics on the Russian Land Commune, 1905–1917." *Slavic Review* 32, no. 4 (December 1973): 773-87.

———. *The End of the Russian Land Commune, 1905–1930.* Stanford, Calif.: Stanford University Press, 1983.

Aves, Jonathan. *Workers Against Lenin: Labour Protest and the Bolshevik Dictatorship.* London: Tauris Academic Studies, 1996.

Avrich, Paul. *Kronstadt 1921.* Princeton, N.J.: Princeton University Press, 1970.

Badcock, Sarah. "Talking to the People and Shaping Revolution: The Drive for Enlightenment in Revolutionary Russia." *The Russian Review* 65 (October 2006): 617-36.

Bailes, Kendall E. *Technology and Society under Lenin and Stalin: Origins of the Soviet Technical Intelligentsia, 1917–1941*. Princeton, N.J.: Princeton University Press, 1978.

Ball, Alan M. *Russia's Last Capitalists: The Nepmen, 1921–1929*. Berkeley: University of California Press, 1987.

———. *And Now My Soul Is Hardened: Abandoned Children in Soviet Russia, 1918–1930*. Berkeley: University of California Press, 1994.

Barmine, Alexander. *One Who Survived: The Life Story of a Russian under the Soviets*. New York: G. P. Putnam, 1945.

Baron, Salo W. *The Russian Jew under Tsars and Soviets*. New York: Macmillan, 1976.

Berkman, Alexander. *The Bolshevik Myth (Diary 1920–1922)*. New York: Boni and Liveright, 1925.

Beyrau, Dietrich. "Russische Intelligenzija und Revolution" (Russian intelligentsia and revolution). *Historische Zeitschrift* 252 (1991): 559-86.

Binion, Rudolph. *Hitler among the Germans*. New York: Elsevier, 1976.

Bishop, Donald G., ed. *Soviet Foreign Relations: Documents and Readings*. Syracuse, N.Y.: Syracuse University Press, 1952.

Black, Cyril, ed. *The Transformation of Russian Society: Aspects of Social Change since 1861*. Cambridge, Mass.: Harvard University Press, 1960.

Blanka, M. B. "Sovetskii istoricheskii opyt osushchestvleniia NEPa i ego znachenie dlia kubinskoi revoliutsii" (Soviet historical experience of the implementation of NEP and its significance for the Cuban revolution). Diss., Moscow State University, 1981.

Bonnell, Victoria E., ed. *The Russian Worker: Life and Labor under the Tsarist Regime*. Berkeley: University of California Press, 1983.

Bouscaren, Anthony Trawick. *Soviet Foreign Policy: A Pattern of Persistence*. New York: Fordham University Press, 1962.

Brandenburger, David. *National Bolshevism: Stalinist Mass Culture and the Formation of Modern Russian National Identity, 1931–1956*. Cambridge, Mass.: Harvard University Press, 2002.

Brooks, Jeffrey. "Public and Private Values in the Soviet Press, 1921–1928." *Slavic Review* 48, no. 1 (spring 1989): 16-35.

———. *Thank You, Comrade Stalin!: Soviet Public Culture from Revolution to Cold War*. Princeton, N.J.: Princeton University Press, 2000.

Budnitskii, O. V. *Rossiiskie evrei mezhdu krasnymi i belymi (1917–1920)* (Russian Jews between reds and whites [1917–1920]). Moscow: ROSSPEN, 2005.

Budnitskii, O. V., O. V. Belova, V. E. Kelner, and V. V. Mochalova, eds. *Mirovoi krizis 1914–1920 i sud'ba vostochnoevropeiskogo evreistva* (The global crisis of 1914–1920 and the fate of Eastern European Jewry). Moscow: ROSSPEN, 2005.

Burbank, Jane. "Lenin and the Law in Revolutionary Russia." *Slavic Review* 54, no. 1 (spring 1995): 23-44.

Burrell, George A. *An American Engineer Looks at Russia*. Boston: The Stratford Company, 1932.

Bystrova, I. V. "Gosudarstvo i ekonomika v 1920-e gody: Bor'ba idei i real'nost'" (State and economy in the 1920s: Struggle of ideas and reality). *Otechestvennaia istoriia*, no. 3 (1993): 19-34.

Carr, E. H. *A History of Soviet Russia*. 7 vols. New York: Macmillan, 1950–1969.

Carr, E. H., and R. W. Davies. *Foundations of a Planned Economy 1926–1929*. 3 vols. New York: Macmillan, 1969–76.

Chamberlin, William Henry. *Soviet Russia: A Living Record and A History*. Boston: Little, Brown, and Co., 1930.

Channon, John. "Tsarist Landowners after the Revolution: Former Pomeshchiki in Rural Russia during NEP." *Soviet Studies* 39 (1987): 575-98.

Chase, William J. *Workers, Society, and the Soviet State: Labor and Life in Moscow, 1918–1929*. Urbana: University of Illinois Press, 1987.

———. "Scapegoating One's Comrades in the USSR, 1934–1937." *Russian History* 38 (2011): 23-41.

Cheng, Yinghong. *Creating the New Man: From Enlightenment Ideals to Socialist Realities*. Honolulu: University of Hawai'i Press, 2009.

Chuikina, Sof'ia. *Dvorianskaia pamiat': "Byvshie" v sovetskom gorode (Leningrad, 1920–30-e gody)* (Nobleman's memory: "Former people" in the Soviet city [Leningrad, 1920s-30s]). St. Petersburg: Evropeiskii Universitet v Sankt-Peterburge, 2006.

Churchward, L. G. *Soviet Socialism: Social and Political Essays*. London: Routledge and K. Paul, 1987.

Clark, Charles E. "Doloi Negramotnost' [Down with illiteracy]: The Literacy Campaign in the RSFSR 1923–1927." Ph.D. diss., University of Illinois Urbana-Champaign, 1993.

———. *Uprooting Otherness: The Literacy Campaign in NEP-Era Russia*. Selinsgrove, Pa.: Susquehanna University Press, 2000.

Clibbon, Jennifer. "The Soviet Press and Grass-roots Organization: The Rabkor Movement, NEP to the First Five-Year Plan." Ph.D. diss., University of Toronto, 1993.

Cohen, Stephen F. *Bukharin and the Bolshevik Revolution: A Political Biography 1888–1938*. New York: Alfred Knopf, 1973.

———. *Rethinking the Soviet Experience: Politics and History since 1917*. New York: Oxford University Press, 1985.

Conquest, Robert. *The Harvest of Sorrow: Soviet Collectivization and the Terror-Famine*. New York: Oxford University Press, 1986.

Counts, George S. *A Ford Crosses Soviet Russia*. Boston: The Stratford Company, 1930.

Cox, Randi. "'NEP without Nepmen!': Soviet Advertising and the Transition to Socialism." In *Everyday Life in Early Soviet Russia: Taking the Revolution Inside*, edited by Christina Kiaer and Eric Naiman. Bloomington: Indiana University Press, 2006.

"Current Problems of Historical Theory." Roundtable discussion at the Russian Academy of Sciences in 1994. *Russian Studies in History* 35, no. 3 (winter 1996).

Daniels, Robert V. "The Left Opposition as an Alternative to Stalinism." *Slavic Review* 50, no. 2 (summer 1991): 277-85.

Danilov, Alexander A., et al. *The History of Russia: The Twentieth Century*. Translated by Galina Ustinova, translated and edited by Vincent E. Hammond. N.p.: The Heron Press, 1996.

Danilov, V. P. "The Historical Significance of Alternatives to Stalinism." *Russian Studies in History* 42, no. 4 (spring 2004): 53-69.

Danilov, V. P., et al. *Kak lomali NEP: Stenogrammy Plenumov TsK VKP(b) 1928–1929 gg.* (How NEP was destroyed: Stenographic records of the VCP[b] Central Committee plenums [1928–1929]). Rossiia XX Vek: Dokumenty, edited by A. N. Iakovlev. 5 vols. Moscow: Mezhdunarodnyi fond "Demokratiia," 2000.

David-Fox, Michael. *Showcasing the Great Experiment: Cultural Diplomacy and Western Visitors to the Soviet Union, 1921–1941*. Oxford: Oxford University Press, 2012.

David-Fox, Michael, Peter Holquist, and Alexander Martin, eds. *Fascination and Enmity: Russia and Germany as Entangled Histories, 1914–45*. Pittsburgh, Pa.: University of Pittsburgh Press, 2012.

Davies, R. W., ed. *From Tsarism to the New Economic Policy: Continuity and Change in the Economy of the USSR*. Ithaca, N.Y.: Cornell University Press, 1991.

Davies, Sarah. *Popular Opinion in Stalin's Russia: Terror, Propaganda and Dissent, 1934–1941*. Cambridge: Cambridge University Press, 1997.

———. "Us against Them: Social Identity in Soviet Russia, 1934–41." In *Stalinism: New Directions*, edited by Sheila Fitzpatrick. London: Routledge, 2000.

De Jonge, Alex. *Stalin and the Shaping of the Soviet Union*. New York: Wm. Morrow and Co. Inc., 1986.

"Discussion." *Russian Review* 45, no. 4 (October 1986): 357-414.

"Discussion." *Slavic Review* 67, no. 3 (fall 2008): 682-723.

Dmitrenko, V. P. *Torgovaia politika Sovetskogo gosudarstva posle perekhoda k nepu: 1921–1924 gg.* (Trade policy of the Soviet government after the transition to NEP: 1921–1924). Moscow: Nauka, 1971.

Dobb, Maurice. *Russian Economic Development since the Revolution*. London: Routledge and Kegan Paul, 1929.

———. *Soviet Economic Development since 1917*. London: Routledge and Kegan Paul, 1948.

———. *On Economic Theory and Socialism: Collected Papers*. London: Routledge and Kegan Paul, 1955.

———. *Political Economy and Capitalism: Some Essays in Economic Tradition*. New York: International Publishers, 1945; Westport, Conn.: Greenwood Press, 1972.

Dreiser, Theodore. *Dreiser Looks at Russia*. New York: H. Liveright, 1928.

Drobizhev, V. Z., et al. *Rabochii klass Sovetskoi Rossii v pervyi god proletarskoi diktatury: Opyt strukturnogo analiza po materialam professional'noi perepisi 1918 g.* (The working class of Soviet Russia in the first year of the dictatorship of the proletariat: Experience of structural analysis of professional census materials 1918). Moscow: Izd-vo Moskovskogo universiteta, 1975.

Duranty, Walter. *Duranty Reports Russia.* New York: Viking Press, 1934.

———. *I Write as I Please.* New York: Simon and Schuster, 1935.

Efremenko, A. V. "Agronomicheskii aspekt stolypinskoi zemel'noi reformy" (Agronomic aspect of the Stolypin agrarian reforms). *Voprosy istorii*, nos. 11-12 (1996): 3-15.

Ennker, Benno. "Die Anfänge des Leninkultes" (The beginnings of the Lenin cult). *Jahrbücher für Geschichte Osteuropas* 35, no. 4 (1987): 534-55.

———. "Leninkult und mythisches Denken in der sowjetischen Offentlichkeit 1924" (The Lenin cult and mythic thinking in the Soviet public). *Jahrbücher für Geschichte Osteuropas* 44, no. 3 (1996): 431-55.

Fainsod, Merle. *How Russia Is Ruled.* Cambridge, Mass.: Harvard University Press, 1953.

———. *Smolensk under Soviet Rule.* Cambridge: Harvard University Press, 1958.

Fediukin, S. A. *Sovetskaia vlast' i burzhuaznye spetsialisty* (Soviet power and bourgeios specialists). Moscow: Mysl', 1965.

———. *Velikii oktiabr' i intelligentsiia* (Great October [Revolution] and the intelligentsia). Moscow: Mysl', 1972.

Feiler, Arthur. *The Russian Experiment.* New York: Harcourt, Brace and Co., 1930.

Feinstein, C. H., ed. *Socialism, Capitalism and Economic Growth: Essays Presented to Maurice Dobb.* London: Cambridge University Press, 1967.

Ferro, Marc. *The Russian Revolution of February 1917.* Translated by J. L. Richards. Englewood Cliffs, N.J.: Prentice-Hall, 1972.

———. *October 1917: A Social History of the Russian Revolution.* Translated by Norman Stone. London: Routledge and Kegan Paul, 1980.

Figes, Orlando. "The Village and Volost Soviet Elections of 1919." *Soviet Studies* 40, no. 1 (January 1988): 21-45.

———. *Peasant Russia, Civil War: The Volga Countryside in Revolution (1917–1921).* Oxford: Clarendon Press, 1989.

———. "The Russian Revolution of 1917 and Its Language in the Village." *Russian Review* 56 (July 1997): 323-45.

Fischer, George. "The Intelligentsia and Russia." In *The Transformation of Russian Society: Aspects of Social Change since 1861*, edited by Cyril Black. Cambridge, Mass.: Harvard University Press, 1960.

Fischer, Louis. *The Soviets in World Affairs: A History of the Relations Between the Soviet Union and the Rest of the World 1917–1929.* 2 vols. London: Jonathan Cape, 1930; reprint, Princeton, N.J.: Princeton University Press, 1951.

Fischer, Markoosha. *My Lives in Russia.* New York: Harper and Bros., 1944.

Fisher, Harold H. *The Famine in Soviet Russia.* New York: Macmillan Company, 1927.

Fitzpatrick, Sheila, ed. *Cultural Revolution in Russia, 1928–1931.* Bloomington: Indiana University Press, 1978.

Fitzpatrick, Sheila. *Education and Social Mobility in the Soviet Union 1921–1934*. Cambridge: Cambridge University Press, 1979.

———. "The Russian Revolution and Social Mobility: A Re-examination of the Question of Social Support for the Soviet Regime in the 1920s and 1930s." *Politics and Society* 13, no. 2 (1984): 119-42.

———. "The Problem of Class Identity in NEP Society." In *Russia in the Era of NEP*, edited by Sheila Fitzpatrick, Alexander Rabinowitch, and Richard Stites. Bloomington: Indiana University Press, 1991.

———. "Ascribing Class: The Construction of Social Identity in Soviet Russia." *Journal of Modern History* 65, no. 4 (December 1993): 745-70.

———. *Stalin's Peasants: Resistance and Survival in the Russian Village after Collectivization*. New York: Oxford University Press, 1994.

———. "Supplicants and Citizens: Public Letter-Writing in Soviet Russia in the 1930s." *Slavic Review* 55, no. 1 (spring 1996): 78-105.

———, ed. "Petitions and Denunciations in Russia from Muscovy to the Stalin Era." *Russian History* 24, nos. 1-2 (spring/summer 1997).

———, ed. *Stalinism: New Directions*. London: Rutledge, 2000.

———. *Tear Off the Masks!: Identity and Imposture in Twentieth-Century Russia*. Princeton, N.J.: Princeton University Press, 2005.

———. "Foreigners Observed: Moscow Visitors in the 1930s under the Gaze of Their Soviet Guides." *Russian History/Histoire Russe* 35, nos. 1-2 (spring-summer 2008): 215-34.

———. "Revisionism in Retrospect: A Personal View." *Slavic Review* 67, no. 3 (fall 2008).

Fitzpatrick, Sheila, Alexander Rabinowitch, and Richard Stites, eds. *Russia in the Era of NEP: Explorations in Soviet Society and Culture*. Bloomington: Indiana University Press, 1991.

Forman, Archibald. *From Baltic to Black Sea: Impressions of Soviet Russia To-day*. London: S. Low, Marston, 1932.

Fox, Michael S. "Political Culture, Purges, and Proletarianization at the Institute of Red Professors, 1921–1929." *Russian Review* 52, no. 1 (January 1993): 20-42.

Freeze, Gregory L. "The Soslovie (Estate) Paradigm and Russian Social History." *American Historical Review* 91, no. 1 (February 1986): 11-36.

———. *From Supplication to Revolution: A Documentary Social History of Imperial Russia*. New York: Oxford University Press, 1988.

———, ed. *Russia: A History*. Oxford University Press, 1997.

Friedgut, Theodore H. *Iuzovka and Revolution: Life and Work in Russia's Donbass, 1869–1924*. 2 vols. Princeton, N.J.: Princeton University Press, 1989.

Fritzsche, Peter. "Making Perpetrators." *Slavic Review* 72, no. 1 (spring 2013): 28-31.

Furet, François, and Mona Ozouf, eds. *A Critical Dictionary of the French Revolution*. Translated by Arthur Goldhammer. Cambridge, Mass.: Belknap Press/Harvard University Press, 1989 (1988).

Gaida, F. A. "Fevral' 1917 goda: Revoliutsiia, vlast', burzhuaziia" (February 1917: Revolution, power, bourgeoisie). *Voprosy istorii*, no. 3 (1996): 31-45.

Galeotti, Mark. *The Age of Anxiety: Security and Politics in Soviet and Post-Soviet Russia*. London: Longman Publishers, 1995.

Gerson, Lennard D. *The Secret Police in Lenin's Russia*. Philadelphia, Pa.: Temple University Press, 1976.

Getty, J. Arch. *Origins of the Great Purges: The Soviet Communist Party Reconsidered, 1933–1938*. Cambridge: Cambridge University Press, 1985.

———. "The Politics of Stalinism." In *The Stalin Phenomenon*, edited by Alec Nove. New York: St. Martin's Press, 1993.

———. "Comment: Codes and Confessions." *Slavic Review* 67, no. 3 (fall 2008).

Getzler, Israel. *Kronstadt 1917–1921: The Fate of a Soviet Democracy*. New York: Cambridge University Press, 1983.

Geyer, Michael, and Sheila Fitzpatrick, eds. *Beyond Totalitarianism: Stalinism and Nazism Compared*. Cambridge University Press, 2009.

Gill, Graeme. "The Soviet Mechanism of Power and the Fall of the Soviet Union." In *Mechanisms of Power in the Soviet Union*, edited by Niels Erik Rosenfeldt, Bent Jensen, and Erik Kulavig. New York: St. Martin's Press, 2000.

Gimpel'son, E. G. "NEP: Byla li vozmozhnost' 'vyzhit'?" (NEP: Was it possible to survive?). In *NEP v kontekste istoricheskogo razvitie Rossii XX veka* (NEP in the context of the historical development of twentieth-century Russia), edited by Andrei Sokolov. Moscow: Russian Academy of Sciences, Institute of Russian History, 2001.

Ginzburg, A. M., ed. *Chastnyi kapital v narodnom khoziaistve SSSR* (Private capital in the economy of the USSR). Material of the commission of VSNKh SSSR. Moscow: Promizdat, 1927.

Gleason, Abbott, Peter Kenez, and Richard Stites, eds. *Bolshevik Culture: Experiment and Order in the Russian Revolution*. Bloomington: Indiana University Press, 1985.

Goland, Iu. *Krizisy, razrushivshie NEP/Valiutnoe regulirovanie v period NEPa* (Crises, destruction of NEP/Exchange regulation in the period of NEP). Moscow: Fond ekonomicheskoe knigi "Nachala," 1998.

Golder, Frank Alfred, and Lincoln Hutchinson. *On the Trail of the Russian Famine*. Stanford, Calif.: Stanford University Press, 1927.

Goldman, Emma. *My Disillusionment in Russia*. Garden City, N.Y.: Doubleday, Page and Co., 1923.

Goldman, Wendy Z. *Women, the State, and Revolution: Soviet Family Policy and Social Life, 1917–1936*. Cambridge: Cambridge University Press, 1993.

———. *Inventing the Enemy: Denunciation and Terror in Stalin's Russia*. Cambridge, England: Cambridge University Press, 2011.

———. "Twin Pyramids—Perpetrators and Victims." *Slavic Review* 72, no. 1 (spring 2013): 24-27.

Gorham, Michael S. "Tongue-Tied Writers: The Rabsel'kor Movement and the Voice of the 'New Intelligentsia' in Early Soviet Russia." *Russian Review* 55, no. 3 (July 1996): 412-29.

Gorsuch, Anne E. "NEP Be Damned! Young Militants in the 1920s and the Culture of Civil War." *Russian Review* 56, no. 4 (October 1997): 564-80.

Gorzka, Gabriele. "Proletarian Culture in Practice: Worker's Clubs, 1917–1921." In *Essays on Revolutionary Culture and Stalinism: Selected Papers from the Third World Congress for Soviet and East European Studies*, edited by John W. Strong. Columbus, Ohio: Slavica Publishers, 1990.

Greenwall, H. J. *Mirrors of Moscow*. London: G. G. Harrap, 1929.

Guelfat, Isaac. *Economic Thought in the Soviet Union: Concepts and Aspects*. Liège: C.I.R.I.E.C., 1969.

Guillory, Sean. "The Shattered Self of Komsomol Civil War Memoirs." *Slavic Review* 71, no. 3 (fall 2012): 546-65.

Gusev, A. V. "Levokommunisticheskaia oppozitsiia v SSSR v kontse 20-x godov" (Left-communist opposition in the USSR at the end of the 1920s). *Otechestvennaia istoriia*, no. 1 (1996): 85-103.

Gusev, K. V., and V. Z. Drobizhev, eds. *Rabochii klass v upravlenii gosudarstvom (1926–1937 gg.)* (The working class in control of the state [1926–1937]). Moscow: Mysl', 1968.

Hagenloh, Paul M. "'Socially Harmful Elements' and the Great Terror." In *Stalinism: New Directions*, edited by Sheila Fitzpatrick. London: Routledge, 2000.

Haimson, Leopold. "The Problem of Social Stability in Urban Russia, 1905–1917 (Part One)." *Slavic Review* 23, no. 4 (December 1964): 619-42.

———. "The Problem of Social Stability in Urban Russia, 1905–1917 (Part Two)." *Slavic Review* 24, no. 1 (March 1965): 1-22.

———. "The Problem of Social Identities in Early Twentieth-Century Russia." *Slavic Review* 47, no. 1 (spring 1988): 1-20.

Halfin, Igal. "The Construction of the Workers' Intelligentsia: 'Proletarianism' of Soviet Universities in the 1920s." Ph.D. diss., Columbia University, 1995.

———. "From Darkness to Light: Student Communist Autobiography during NEP." *Jahrbücher für Geschichte Osteuropas* 45, no. 2 (1997): 210-36.

———. *From Darkness to Light: Class, Consciousness, and Salvation in Revolutionary Russia*. Pittsburgh, Pa.: University of Pittsburgh Press, 2000.

Harry, Elizabeth. "Petitioners and Their Discontents: The Lost Generation of the 1920s." *The NEP Era: Soviet Russia 1921–1928* 2 (2008): 61-80.

Hatch, John B. "The 'Lenin Levy' and the Social Origins of Stalinism: Workers and the Communist Party in Moscow, 1921–1928." *Slavic Review* 48, no. 4 (winter 1989): 558-77.

———. "Labor Conflict in Moscow, 1921–1925." In *Russia in the Era of NEP: Explorations in Soviet Society and Culture*, edited by Sheila Fitzpatrick, Alexander Rabinowitch, and Richard Stites. Bloomington: Indiana University Press, 1991.

Hazard, John N. *The Soviet System of Government*. 5th ed. Chicago: University of Chicago Press, 1980.

Hickey, Michael C. "Communists vs. Clerics: The Smolensk Choral Synagogue, the Khislavichi Rov Shtibel Synagogue and the NEP Antireligious Campaign." *The NEP Era: Soviet Russia 1921–1928* 2 (2008): 39-59.

Hicks, Jeremy. "From Conduits to Commanders: Shifting Views of Worker Correspondents." *Revolutionary Russia* 19, no. 2 (December 2006): 131-49.

———. "Worker Correspondents: Between Journalism and Literature." *The Russian Review* 66 (October 2007): 568-85.

Hilton, Majorie L. *Selling to the Masses: Retailing in Russia, 1880–1930*. Pitt Series in Russian and East European Studies. Pittsburgh, Pa.: University of Pittsburgh Press, 2012.

Hindus, Maurice. *Broken Earth*. New York: International Publishers, 1926.

———. *Humanity Uprooted*. New York: J. Cape and H. Smith, 1931.

Hoffman, David. "Land, Freedom, and Discontent: Russian Peasants of the Central Industrial Region prior to Collectivisation." *Europe-Asia Studies* 46, no. 4 (1994): 637-48.

———. "History and Literary Criticism." *Russian Review* 55, no. 3 (July 1996): vii-viii.

———. *Cultivating the Masses: Modern State Practices and Soviet Socialism, 1914–1939*. Ithaca, N.Y.: Cornell University Press, 2011.

Hosking, Geoffrey. *The First Socialist Society: A History of the Soviet Union from Within*. Enlarged ed. Cambridge, Mass.: Harvard University Press, 1990.

Hullinger, Edwin Ware. *The Reforging of Russia*. New York: E. P. Dutton and Co., 1925.

Hunt, Lynn. *Politics, Culture, and Class in the French Revolution*. Berkeley: University of California Press, 1984.

Husband, William B. "The New Economic Policy (NEP) and the Revolutionary Experiment, 1921 1929." In *Russia: A History*, edited by Gregory Freeze. Oxford University Press, 1997.

Isaev, I. A. "Kollektivnoe bessoznatel'noe i predstavlenie o zakonnosti v revolutsii" (Collective unconscious and the view on th elegality of the revolution). Paper presented at a conference in 1994, "Revolutsiia i chelovek: Sotsial'no-psikhologicheskii aspekt" (Revolution and the individual: Social-psychological aspect). *Otechestvennaia istoriia*, no. 4 (1995): 211-18.

Jones, Gareth Steadman. *Languages of Class: Studies in English Working-Class History 1832–1982*. Cambridge: Cambridge University Press, 1983.

Karlgren, Anton. *Bolshevist Russia*. London: G. Allen and Unwin, 1927.

Katsenelinboigen, Aron. *Studies in Soviet Economic Planning*. White Plains, N.Y.: M. E. Sharpe, 1978.

Keep, John. "The Agrarian Revolution of 1917–1918 in Soviet Historiography." *Russian Review* 36, no. 4 (October 1977): 405-23.

Kennan, George F. *Russia and the West under Lenin and Stalin*. Markham, Ontario: Penguin Books, 1960.

Kerblay, Basile. "The Peasant." *Survey* 64 (July 1967).

Keynes, John Maynard. *A Short View of Russia*. London: L. and Virginia Woolf, 1925.

Khromov, S. S., et al. *Istoriia sovetskogo rabochego klassa v shesti tomakh* (History of the Soviet working class in six volumes). Moscow: Nauka, 1984–88.

Kiaer, Christina, and Eric Naiman, eds. *Everyday Life in Early Soviet Russia: Taking the Revolution Inside*. Bloomington: Indiana University Press, 2006.

Kimerling Wirtschafter, Elise. "Civil Rights and Social Policy in Soviet Russia, 1918–1936." *Russian Review* 41, no. 1 (January 1982): 24-46.

———. *Social Identity in Imperial Russia*. DeKalb: Northern Illinois University Press, 1997.

Klippenstein, Lawrence. "Mennonite Pacifism and State Service in Russia: A Case Study in Church-State Relations, 1789–1936." Ph.D. diss., University of Minnesota, 1984.

Koenker, Diane P. "Urbanization and Deurbanization in the Russian Revolution and Civil War." In *Party, State, and Society in the Russian Civil War: Explorations in Social History*, edited by Diane P. Koenker, William G. Rosenberg, and Ronald G. Suny. Bloomington: Indiana University Press, 1989.

———. "Class and Consciousness in a Socialist Society: Workers in the Printing Trades during NEP." In *Russia in the Era of NEP: Explorations in Soviet Society and Culture*, edited by Sheila Fitzpatrick, Alexander Rabinowitch, and Richard Stites. Bloomington: Indiana University Press, 1991.

———. "Factory Tales: Narratives of Industrial Relations in the Transition to NEP." *Russian Review* 55, no. 3 (July 1996): 384-411.

Koenker, Diane P., William G. Rosenberg, and Ronald G. Suny, eds. *Party, State, and Society in the Russian Civil War: Explorations in Social History*. Bloomington: Indiana University Press, 1989.

Kolonitskii, Boris I. "Antiburzhuaznaia propaganda i 'antiburzhuiskoe' soznanie." *Otechestvennaia istoriia*, no. 1 (1994): 17-27. Translated by Kurt S. Schultz, "Antibourgeois Propaganda and Anti-'Burzhui' Consciousness in 1917." *Russian Review* 53, no. 2 (April 1994): 183-96.

Konecny, Peter. "Chaos on Campus: The 1924 Student Proverka in Leningrad." *Europe-Asia Studies* 46, no. 4 (1994): 617-35.

Korol'kov, O. P. "Sovremennaia sovetskaia istoriografiia ekonomicheskikh problem NEPa" (Current Soviet historiography on the economic problems of NEP). Diss., Moscow Academy of Social Sciences, 1990.

Kravchenko, Victor. *I Chose Freedom: The Personal and Political Life of a Soviet Official*. New York: C. Scribner's and Sons, 1946.

Krest'ianskoe Vosstanie v Tambovskoi Gubernii v 1919–1921 gg. "Antonovshchina": Dokumenty (Peasant revolt in Tambov gubernia 1919–1921 "Antonov mutiny": Documents). Tambov, 1994.

Kulikova, G. B. "NEP i problema vovlechenie mass v deiatel'nost' gosudarstva" (NEP and the problem of the involvement of the masses in the activities of the state). In *NEP v kontekste istoricheskogo razvitie Rossii XX veka* (NEP in the context of the historical development of twentieth-century Russia), edited by Andrei Sokolov. Moscow: Russian Academy of Sciences, Institute of Russian History, 2001.

Kuriianov, A. I. "Istoricheskaia antropologiia v Rossii: Problemy stanovleniia" (Historical anthropology in Russia: Problems of formation). *Otechestvennaia istoriia*, no. 4 (1996): 86-99.

Kuromiya, Hiroaki. *Stalin's Industrial Revolution: Politics and Workers, 1928–1932*. Cambridge: Cambridge University Press, 1988.

———. *Stalin: Profiles in Power*. Harlow, England: Pearson Longman, 2005.

Lampert, Nicholas. *The Technical Intelligentsia and the Soviet State*. New York: Holmes and Meier Publishers, 1979.

Landis, Erik C. *Bandits and Partisans: The Antonov Movement in the Russian Civil War*. Pitt Series in Russian and East European Studies. Pittsburgh, Pa.: University of Pittsburgh Press, 2008.

Lebin, B. D., and M. N. Perfil'ev. *Kadry apparata upravleniia v SSSR: Sotsiologicheskie problemy podbora i rasstanovki* (Personnel of the management apparatus of the USSR: Sociological problems of selection and placement). Leningrad: Izd-vo Akademii nauk, 1970.

Leizerovich, E. E. "Kolonizatsiia i razvitie Kazakhstana i Srednei Azii v xix-xx vekakh: Dinamika natsional'nostei, transformatsiia khoziaistva, perspektivy regionov" (Colonization and development of Kazakhstan and Central Asia in the nineteenth-twentieth centuries: Dymanics of nationality, economic transformation, regional perspectives). In *Rossiia i Vostok: Problemy vzaimodeistviia*. Moscow, 1993.

Lenoe, Matthew. "NEP Newspapers and the Origins of Soviet Information Rationing." *The Russian Review* 62 (October 2003): 614-36.

"Letters." *Slavic Review* 68, no. 1 (spring 2009): 219-24.

Levitt, Marcus C., and Tatyana Novikov, eds. *Times of Trouble: Violence in Russian Literature and Culture*. Madison: University of Wisconsin Press, 2007.

Lewin, Moshe. *Russian Peasants and Soviet Power: A Study of Collectivization*. Translated from French by Irene Nove and John Biggart, preface by Alec Nove. London: Allen and Unwin, 1968.

———. *Political Undercurrents in Soviet Economic Debates: From Bukharin to the Modern Reformers*. Princeton, N.J.: Princeton University Press, 1974.

———. *The Making of the Soviet System: Essays in the Social History of Interwar Russia*. New York: Pantheon Books, 1985.

Lih, Lars T. "Political Testament of Lenin and Bukharin and the Meaning of NEP." *Slavic Review* 50, no. 2 (summer 1991): 241-52.

———. "The Mystery of the ABC." *Slavic Review* 56, no. 1 (spring 1997): 50-72.

———. "Bukharin's 'Illusion': War Communism and the Meaning of NEP." *Russian History/Histoire Russe* 27, no. 4 (winter 2000): 417-59.

Lih, Lars T. "Perestroika's Revival of NEP: A Contemporary Chronicle 1985–1990." *The NEP Era: Soviet Russia 1921–1928* 3 (2009): 1-35.

Lih, Lars T., Oleg V. Naumov, and Oleg V. Khlevniuk, eds. *Stalin's Letters to Molotov 1925–1936*. New Haven, Conn.: Yale University Press, 1995.

Litvin, Alter, and John Keep, eds. *Stalinism: Russian and Western Views at the Turn of the Millennium*. London: Routledge, 2005.

Livshin, A. Ia., and I. B. Orlov, comps. *Pis'ma vo vlast', 1917–1927: Zaiavleniia, zhaloby, donosy, pis'ma v gosudarstvennye struktury i bolshevistskim vozhdiam* (Letters to power, 1917–1927: Statements, appeals, denunciations, letters to state agencies and Bolshevik leaders). Moscow: ROSSPEN, 1998.

Loewenberg, Peter. "The Psychohistorical Origins of the Nazi Youth Cohort." *The American Historical Review* 76, no. 5 (December 1971).

Maklakov, V. "The Agrarian Problem in Russia Before the Revolution." *Russian Review* 9, no. 1 (January 1950): 3-15.

Malia, Martin. *The Soviet Tragedy: A History of Socialism in Russia, 1917–1991*. New York: Macmillan, The Free Press, 1994.

Mandel, David. *The Petrograd Workers and the Fall of the Old Regime: From the February Revolution to the July Days, 1917*. New York: St. Martin's Press, 1983.

Marot, John Eric. "Alexander Bogdanov, Vpered, and the Role of the Intellectual in the Workers' Movement." *Russian Review* 49, no. 3 (July 1990): 241-64.

Maynard, John. *Russia in Flux: Before October*. London: V. Gollancz, 1946.

McCauley, Martin. *The Soviet Union 1917–1991*. 2d ed. London: Longman, 1993.

McClellan, Woodford. *Russia: A History of the Soviet Period*. Englewood Cliffs, N.J.: Prentice-Hall, 1986.

McDermott, Kevin. *Stalin: Revolutionary in an Era of War*. European History in Perspective. Palgrave Macmillan, 2006.

Melancon, Michael. "The Ninth Circle: The Lena Goldfield Workers and the Massacre of 4 April 1912." *Slavic Review* 53, no. 3 (fall 1994): 766-95.

"'Mentalitet i agrarnoe razvitie Rossii v xix-xx vekakh': Mezhdunarodnaia konferentsiia v Moskve" (Mentalité and agricultural development of Russia in the nineteenth-twentieth centuries: International conference in Moscow). *Otechestvennaia istoriia*, no. 1 (1996): 195-204.

Merridale, Catherine. *Moscow Politics and the Rise of Stalin: The Communist Party in the Capital, 1925–32*. New York: St. Martin's Press, 1990.

Mikoyan, Sergo. "Stalinism As I Saw It." In *The Stalin Phenomenon*, edited by Alec Nove. New York: St. Martin's Press, 1993.

Mironov, Boris. "The Russian Peasant Commune after the Reforms of the 1860s." Translated by Gregory Freeze and Carol S. Leonard. *Slavic Review* 44, no. 3 (fall 1985): 438-67.

———. "The Myth of a Systemic Crisis in Russia after the Great Reforms of the 1860s–1870s." *Russian Studies in History* 47, no. 4 (spring 2009): 40-52.

Mishakov, V. P. "Razoblachenie fal'sifikatsii 'ostforshungom' leninskikh printsipov ekonomicheskoi politiki perekhodnogo perioda" (Exposure of the falsification of "Ostforschung" of leninist principles of economic policy in transition). Kand. diss., Moscow State University, 1971.

Mommsen-Reindl, Margareta. *Hilf mir, mein Recht zu finden: Russische Bittschriften von Iwan dem Schrechlichen bis Gorbatschow* (Help me to find justice: Russian petitions from Ivan the Terrible to Gorbachev). Frankfurt a. M.: Propylaen, 1987.

Monkhouse, Allan. *Moscow 1911–1933.* Boston: Little, Brown, and Co., 1934.

Morozova, Ol'ga Mikhailovna. *Dva akta dramy: Boevoe proshloe i poslevoennaia povsednevnost' veteranov grazhdanskoe voiny* (Two-act drama: Combat past and everyday postwar life of civil war veterans). Rostov on Don: Isdatel'stvo Iuzhnyi tsentr RAN, 2010.

Murphy, Kevin. *Revolution and Counterrevolution: Class Struggle in a Moscow Metal Factory*. 2005. Chicago: Haymarket Books, 2007.

Narkiewicz, Olga A. *The Making of the Soviet State Apparatus.* Manchester, England: Manchester University Press, 1970.

Neizvestnaia Rossiia: XX Vek (Unknown Russia: Twentieth century). 3 vols. Moscow: Istoricheskoe Nasledie, 1992.

Neumann, Matthias. "Class Ascription and Class Identity: *Komsomol'tsy* and the Policy of Class during Nep." *Revolutionary Russia* 19, no. 2 (December 2006): 175-96.

———. *The Communist Youth League and the Transformation of the Soviet Union, 1917–1931.* BASEES/Routledge Series on Russian and East European Studies. London: Routledge, 2011.

Nove, Alec. *An Economic History of the U.S.S.R.* 2[d] ed. London: Penguin Books, 1989.

———, ed. *The Stalin Phenomenon.* New York: St. Martin's Press, 1993.

Osokina, Elena. "Comment: Life and Fate of Western Revisionism." *Slavic Review* 67, no. 3 (fall 2008): 716-17.

Patrikeeff, Felix. "Stalinism, Totalitarian Society and the Politics of 'Perfect Control.'" In *Redefining Stalinism*, edited by Harold Shukman. London: Frank Cass, 2003.

Pavlova, Irina. "The Strength and Weakness of Stalin's Power." In *Mechanisms of Power in the Soviet Union*, edited by Niels Erik Rosenfeldt, Bent Jensen, and Erik Kulavig. New York: St. Martin's Press, 2000.

———. *Mekhanizm vlasti i stroitel'stvo stalinskogo sotsializma* (Mechanism of power and the building of Stalinist socialism). Novosibirsk: Izd-vo CO RAN, 2001.

Pethybridge, Roger. *One Step Backwards, Two Steps Forward: Soviet Society and Politics in the New Economic Policy.* Oxford: Clarendon Press, 1990.

Phillips, Laura L. "Message in a Bottle: Working-Class Culture and the Struggle for Revolutionary Legitimacy, 1900–1929." *Russian Review* 56, no. 1 (January 1997): 25-43.

Pierce, Richard. *Russian Central Asia, 1867–1917: A Century of Colonial Rule.* Berkeley: University of California Press, 1960.

Pinnow, Kenneth M. *Lost to the Collective: Suicide and the Promise of Soviet Socialism, 1921–1929.* Ithaca, N.Y.: Cornell University Press, 2010.

Pipes, Richard. *The Russian Revolution*. New York: Alfred A. Knopf, 1990.
———. *Russia under the Bolshevik Regime*. New York: Alfred A. Knopf, 1993.
———, ed. *The Russian Intelligentsia*. New York: Columbia University Press, 1961.
Plaggenborg, Stefan. "Gewalt und Militanz in Sowjetrussland 1917–1930" (Violence and Militancy in Soviet Russia 1917–1930). *Jahrbücher für Geschichte Osteuropas* 44, no. 3 (1996): 431-55.
Pogorelskin, Alexis. "Guest Editor's Introduction: The Politics of NEP and the Politics of Its Historiography." *Russian History/Histoire Russe* 27, no. 4 (winter 2000): 377-79.
Pokrovskii, N. N., and E. K. Pomodanovskaia, eds. *Sibirskoi istochnikovedenie i arkheografiia* (Siberian chronology and archaeology). Novosibirsk: Izd-vo Nauka, 1980.
Pushkarev, L. N. "Chto takoe mentalitet?" (What is mentalité?). *Otechestvennaia istoriia*, no. 3 (1995): 158-66.
Rabinowitch, Alexander. "The Evolution of Local Soviets in Petrograd, November 1917–June 1918: The Case of the First City District Soviet." *Slavic Review* 46, no. 1 (spring 1987): 20-37.
Radkey, Oliver. *The Agrarian Foes of Bolshevism: Promise and Default of the Russian Socialist Revolutionaries February to October 1917*. New York: Columbia University Press, 1958.
Rancour-Laferriere, Daniel. *The Mind of Stalin: A Psychoanalytic Study*. Ann Arbor, Mich.: Ardis, 1988.
Read, Christopher. *Culture and Power in Revolutionary Russia: The Intelligentsia and the Transition from Tsarism to Communism*. London: Macmillan, 1990.
Rees, E. A. *State Control in Soviet Russia: The Rise and Fall of the Workers' and Peasants' Inspectorate, 1920–34*. New York: St. Martin's Press, 1987.
Reiman, Michael. *The Birth of Stalinism: The USSR on the Eve of the Second Revolution*. Translated from German by George Saunders. Bloomington: Indiana University Press, 1987.
Rendle, Matthew. *Defenders of the Motherland: The Tsarist Elite in Revolutionary Russia*. Oxford: Oxford University Press, 2010.
Reswick, William. *I Dreamt Revolution*. Chicago: H. Regnery Co., 1952.
"Revolutsiia i chelovek: Sotsial'no-psikhologicheskii aspekt" (revolution and the individual: Social-psychological aspect). *Otechestvennaia istoriia*, no. 4 (1995): 211-18.
Rigby, T. H. *Communist Party Membership in the U.S.S.R. 1917–1967*. Princeton, N.J.: Princeton University Press, 1968.
Ro'i, Yaacov, ed. *Jews and Jewish Life in Russia and the Soviet Union*. Portland, Ore.: Frank Cass, 1995.
Robinson, Geroid T. *Rural Russia under the Old Regime: A History of the Landlord-Peasant World and a Prologue to the Peasant Revolution of 1917*. New York: Macmillan, 1949.
Rosenberg, William G., and Marilyn B. Young. *Transforming Russia and China: Revolutionary Struggle in the Twentieth Century*. New York: Oxford University Press, 1982.

Rosenfeldt, Niels Erik. "Stalinism as a System of Communication." In *Essays on Revolutionary Culture and Stalinism: Selected Papers from the Third World Congress for Soviet and East European Studies*, edited by John W. Strong. Columbus, Ohio: Slavica, 1990.

Rosenfeldt, Niels Erik, Bent Jensen, and Erik Kulavig, eds. *Mechanisms of Power in the Soviet Union*. New York: St. Martin's Press, 2000.

Rossman, Jeffrey J. "Weaver of Rebellion and Poet of Resistance: Kapitan Klepikov (1880–1933) and Shop-Floor Opposition to Bolshevik Rule." *Jahrbücher für Geschichte Osteuropas* 44, no. 3 (1996): 374-408.

Ryan, James. *Lenin's Terror: The Ideological Origins of Early Soviet State Violence*. London: Routledge, 2012.

Saul, Norman E. *Friends or Foes? The United States and Russia, 1921–1941*. Lawrence: University Press of Kansas, 2006.

Schapiro, Leonard B. *The Communist Party of the Soviet Union*. London: Eyre and Spottiswoode, 1960.

———. *The Government and Politics of the Soviet Union*. New York: Random House, 1965.

———. *The Origin of the Communist Autocracy: Political Opposition in the Soviet State, First Phase, 1917–1922*. New York: Praeger, 1965.

Scheffer, Paul. *Seven Years in Soviet Russia*. London: Putnam, 1931.

Selunskaia, V. M., ed. *Izmeneniia sotsial'noi struktury sovetskogo obshchestva: Oktiabr' 1917–1920* (Changes to the social structure of Soviet society: October 1917–1920). Moscow: Mysl', 1976.

Serge, Victor. *From Lenin to Stalin*. New York: Pioneer Publishers, 1937.

Service, Robert. *The Bolshevik Party in Revolution: A Study in Organisational Change 1917–1923*. London: Macmillan, 1979.

———. "Stalinism and the Soviet State Order." In *Redefining Stalinism*, edited by Harold Shukman. London: Frank Cass, 2003.

Shanin, Teodor. *The Awkward Class: Political Sociology of Peasantry in a Developing Society, Russia 1910–1925*. Oxford: Clarendon Press, 1972.

Shukman, Harold, ed. *Redefining Stalinism*. London: Frank Cass, 2003.

Shul'gin, V. V. *In Three Capitals*. Berlin, 1927.

Shustov, K. B. "Zhaloby i prosheniia kak istochnik po istorii politicheskogo soznaniia krest'ian zapadnoi Sibiri vtoroi poloviny xix v." (Appeals and petitions as a source for the history of political consciousness of peasants of western Siberia in the second half of the nineteenth century). In *Sibirskoi istochnikovedenie i arkheografiia* (Siberian chronology and archaeology), edited by N. N. Pokrovskii and E. K. Pomodanovskaia. Novosibirsk: Izd-vo Nauka, 1980.

Siegelbaum, Lewis H. "Defining and Ignoring Labor Discipline in the Early Soviet Period: The Comrades-Disciplinary Courts, 1918–1922." *Slavic Review* 51, no. 4 (winter 1992): 705-30.

———. *Soviet State and Society between Revolutions, 1918–1929*. Cambridge: Cambridge University Press, 1992.

Siegelbaum, Lewis H., and Ronald G. Suny, eds. *Making Workers Soviet: Power, Class, and Identity*. Ithaca, N.Y.: Cornell University Press, 1994.

Siegelbaum, Lewis, and Andrei Sokolov, eds. *Stalinism as a Way of Life: A Narrative in Documents*. Abridged ed. New Haven, Conn.: Yale University Press, 2004.

Simonov, N. S. " 'Krepit' oboronu strany sovetov' ('Voennaia trevoga' 1927 goda i ee posledstviia)." *Otechestvennaia istoriia*, no. 3 (1996): 155-61.

Simonova, M. S. "Pereselencheskii vopros v agrarnoi politike samoderzhaviia v kontse xix-nachale xx v." (The resettlement question in the agrarian policy of autocracy in the late nineteenth and early twentieth centuries). In *Ezhehgodnik po agrarnoi istorii vostochnoi Evropy 1965 g.* (Yearbook of agrarian history of Eastern Europe for 1965). Moscow, 1970.

Skliarov, L. F. *Pereselenie i zemleustroistvo v Sibiri v gody Stolypinskoi agrarnoi reformy* (Resettlement and planning in Siberia in the years of the Stolypin agrarian reforms). Leningrad, 1962.

Smith, Scott B. *Captives of Revolution: The Socialist Revolutionaries and the Bolshevik Dictatorship, 1918–1923*. Pitt Series in Russian and East European Studies. Pittsburgh, Pa.: University of Pittsburgh Press, 2011.

Smith, Stephen A. *Red Petrograd: Revolution in the Factories 1917–1918*. New York: Cambridge University Press, 1983.

Snyder, Timothy. *Bloodlands: Europe between Hitler and Stalin*. New York: Basic Books, 2010.

Sokolov, Andrei K., ed. *Golos naroda: Pis'ma i otkliki riadovykh sovetskihk grazhdan o sobytiiakh 1918–1932 gg.* (Voice of the people: Letters and responses of ordinary Soviet citizens to events of 1918–1932). Moscow: ROSSPEN, 1998.

———. "Istoricheskoe znachenie NEPa" (Historical significance of NEP). In *NEP v kontekste istoricheskogo razvitie Rossii XX veka* (NEP in the context of the historical development of twentieth-century Russia), edited by Andrei Sokolov. Moscow: Russian Academy of Sciences, Institute of Russian History, 2001.

———. *NEP v kontekste istoricheskogo razvitie Rossii XX veka* (NEP in the context of the historical development of twentieth-century Russia). Moscow: Russian Academy of Sciences, Institute of Russian History, 2001.

Sominskii, M. *Antisemitizm i Antisemity* (Anti-Semitism and anti-Semites). Jerusalem: Leksikon, 1991.

Sorokin, Pitirim A. *Leaves from a Russian Diary, and Thirty Years After*. Boston: Beacon Press, 1950.

Steinberg, Mark D. "Vanguard Workers and the Morality of Class." In *Making Workers Soviet: Power, Class, and Identity*, edited by Lewis H. Siegelbaum and Ronald Grigor Suny. Ithaca, N.Y.: Cornell University Press, 1994.

———. "Stories and Voices: History and Theory." *Russian Review* 55, no. 3 (July 1996): 347-54.

Stern, Ludmila. *Western Intellectuals and the Soviet Union, 1920–1940: From Red Square to the Left Bank*. BASEES/Routledge Series on Russian and East European Studies, no. 31 New York: Routledge, 2007.

Stites, Richard. *Revolutionary Dreams: Utopian Vision and Experimental Life in the Russian Revolution*. New York: Oxford University Press, 1989.

Stolee, Margaret K. "Homeless Children in the USSR, 1917–1957." *Soviet Studies* 40, no. 1 (January 1988): 64-83.

Storella, C. J. "Soviet Specialist Baiting: The Case of N. A. Dobrosmyslov." *Russian History* 38 (2011): 5-22.

Strong, John W., ed. *Essays on Revolutionary Culture and Stalinism: Selected Papers from the Third World Congress for Soviet and East European Studies*. Columbus, Ohio: Slavica Publishers, 1990.

Tchernavin, Vladimir V. *I Speak for the Silent*. Boston: Hale, Cushman and Flint, 1935.

Teague, Elizabeth. *Solidarity and the Soviet Worker: The Impact of the Polish Events of 1980 on Soviet Internal Politics*. New York: Croom Helm/Methuen Publishers, 1988.

Thompson, Dorothy. *The New Russia*. New York: H. Holt and Co., 1928.

Tikhonov, B. V. *Pereseleniia v Rossii vo vtoroi polovine xix v.: Po materialam perepisi 1897 g. i pasportnoi statistike* (Resettlement in Russia in the second half of the nineteenth century: On the basis of census materials of 1897 and passport statistics). Moscow: Nauka, 1978.

Tirado, Isabel A. "The Komsomol and Young Peasants: The Dilemma of Rural Expansion, 1921–1925." *Slavic Review* 52, no. 3 (fall 1993): 460-76.

Tokmakoff, George. "Stolypin's Agrarian Reform: An Appraisal." *Russian Review* 30, no. 2 (April 1971): 124-38.

"Totalitariarizm i lichnost'" (Totalitarianism and personality). *Otechestvannaia istoriia*, no. 2 (1995): 215-17.

Treadgold, Donald. *The Great Siberian Migration: Government and Peasant in Resettlement from Emancipation to the First World War*. Princeton, N.J.: Princeton University Press, 1957.

Trifonov, I. Ia. *Klassy i klassovaia bor'ba v SSSR v nachale nepa* (Classes and class struggle in the USSR at the beginning of NEP). Vol. 2, *Podgotovka ekonomicheskogo nastupleniia na novuiu burzhuaziiu* (Preparing the economic offensive against the new bourgeoisie). Leningrad: Izd-vo Leningradskogo universiteta, 1969.

———. *Likvidatsiia ekspluatatorskikh klassov v SSSR* (Liquidation of the exploiting classes in the USSR). Moscow: Politizdat, 1975.

Tucker, Robert. *Stalin in Power: The Revolution from Above, 1928–1941*. New York: W. W. Norton and Company, 1990.

———. "Soviet History in the 1920s." *Slavic Review* 50, no. 2 (summer 1991): 239-40.

. "Foreword." In *Mechanisms of Power in the Soviet Union*, edited by Niels Erik Rosenfeldt, Bent Jensen, and Erik Kulavig. New York: St. Martin's Press, 2000.

Tumarkin, Nina. *Lenin Lives! The Lenin Cult in Soviet Russia*. Cambridge, Mass.: Harvard University Press, 1983.

———. "The Myth of Lenin during the Civil War Years." In *Bolshevik Culture: Experiment and Order in the Russian Revolution*, edited by Abbott Gleason, Peter Kenez, and Richard Stites. Bloomington: Indiana University Press, 1985.

Vakar, Nicholas. *The Taproot of Soviet Society*. New York: Harper, 1962.

Vaksberg, Arkady. *Stalin against the Jews*. Translated by Antonia W. Bouis. New York: Alfred A. Knopf, 1994.

Vaksman, Fabian. *Ideological Struggle: A Study in the Principles of Operation of the Soviet Political Mechanism*. Lanham, Md.: University Press of America, 1987.

Valentinov (Vol'skii), N. *Novaia ekonomicheskaia politika i krizis partii posle smerti Lenina: Gody raboty v VSNKh vo vremia NEP; vospominaniia* (The New Economic Policy and the crisis of the party after the death of Lenin: Years working in the Supreme Economic Council at the time of NEP; Memoirs). Stanford, Calif.: Hoover Institution Press, Stanford University, 1971.

Van Ree, Eric. "Stalin's Organic Theory of the Party." *Russian Review* 52, no. 1 (January 1993): 43-57.

Velikanova, O. V. "Obraz Lenina v massovom soznanii" (Lenin's image in the mass consciousness). *Otechestvennaia istoriia*, no. 2 (1994): 177-85.

Verner, Andrew. "Discursive Strategies in the 1905 Revolution: Peasant Petitions from Vladimir Province." *Russian Review* 54, no. 1 (January 1995): 65-90.

Vinogradoff, Eugene D. "The Russian Peasantry and the Elections to the Fourth Duma: Estate Political Consciousness and Class Political Consciousness." Ph.D. diss., Columbia University, 1974.

Viola, Lynn. *The Best Sons of the Fatherland: Workers in the Vanguard of Soviet Collectivization*. New York: Oxford University Press, 1987.

———. "The Question of the Perpetrator in Soviet History." *Slavic Review* 72, no. 1 (spring 2013): 1-23.

Volkov, Vadim. "The Concept of *Kulturnost'*: Notes on the Stalinist Civilizing Process." In *Stalinism: New Directions*, edited by Sheila Fitzpatrick. London: Rutledge, 2000.

Von Hagen, Mark. *Soldiers in the Proletarian Dictatorship: The Red Army and the Soviet Socialist State, 1917–1930*. Ithaca, N.Y.: Cornell University Press, 1990.

———. "Civil-Military Relations and the Evolution of the Soviet Socialist State." *Slavic Review* 50, no. 2 (summer 1991): 268-76.

Voslensky, Michael. *Nomenklatura: The Soviet Ruling Class*. Translated by Eric Mosbacher. Garden City, N.Y.: Doubleday, 1984.

Wallace, Sir Donald Mackenzie. *Russia on the Eve of War and Revolution*. Edited by Cyril Black. New York: Vintage Books, 1961.

Ward, Chris. *Stalin's Russia*. 2d ed. 1993. Reprint, New York: Oxford University Publishing, 1999.

Weinberg, Robert. "Demonizing Judaism in the Soviet Union during the 1920s." *Slavic Review* 67, no. 1 (spring 2008): 120-53.

Weiner, Douglas. "Razmychka? Urban Unemployment and Peasant In-Migration as Sources of Social Conflict." In *Russia in the Era of NEP: Explorations in Soviet Society and Culture*, edited by Sheila Fitzpatrick, Alexander Rabinowitch, and Richard Stites. Bloomington: Indiana University Press, 1991.

Weissman, Benjamin M. *Herbert Hoover and Famine Relief to Soviet Russia, 1921–1923*. Stanford, Calif.: Hoover Institution Press, 1974.

White, Elizabeth. *The Socialist Alternative to Bolshevik Russia: The Socialist Revolutionary Party, 1921–1939*. BASEES/Routledge Series on Russian and East European Studies, no. 68. London: Routledge, 2011.

Yaney, George L. *The Urge to Mobilize: Agrarian Reform in Russia, 1861–1930*. Urbana: University of Illinois Press, 1982.

———. "Some Suggestions regarding the Study of Russian Peasant Society prior to Collectivization." *Russian Review* 44, no. 1 (January 1985): 27-34.

Zubkova, E. Iu., and A. I. Kupriianov. "Mental'noe izmerenie istorii: Poiski metoda" (The mental dimension of history: Search for a method). *Voprosy istorii*, no. 7 (1995): 153-60.

INDEX

MINNESOTA MEDITERRANEAN AND EAST EUROPEAN MONOGRAPHS

Theofanis G. Stavrou, general editor

1. *Kosovo: Legacy of a Medieval Battle*
   edited by Wayne S. Vucinich and Thomas A. Emmert

2. *Inside the Cyprus Miracle: The Labours of an Embattled Mini-Economy*
   by Demetrios Christodoulou

3. *Modern Greek Word Formation*
   by Olga Eleftheriades

4. *Prelude to the Great Reforms: Avraam Sergeevich Norov and Imperial Russia*
   by Peter R. Weisensel

5. *Blocking the Sun: The Cyprus Conflict*
   by John L. Scherer

6. *Britain and the International Status of Cyprus, 1955–59*
   by Evanthis Hatzivassiliou

7. *A Missionary for History: Essays in Honor of Simon Dubnov*
   edited by Kristi Groberg and Avraham Greenbaum

8. *Cyprus 1957–1963: From Colonial Conflict to Constitutional Crisis: The Key Role of the Municipal Issue*
   by Diana Weston Markides

9. *The Gates of Hell: The Great Sobor of the Russian Orthodox Church, 1917–1918*
   by James W. Cunningham, edited by Keith and Grace Dyrud

10. *Russian-Ottoman Relations in the Levant: The Dashkov Archive*
    by Theophilus C. Prousis

11. *The Cyprus Question, 1878–1960: The Constitutional Aspect*
    by Evanthis Hatzivassiliou

12. *Lessons Unlearned: Thucydides and Venizelos on Propaganda and the Struggle for Power*
    by Evie Holmberg

13. *Church and State in Late Imperial Russia: Critics of the Synodal System of Church Government (1861–1914)*
    by John Basil

14. *War and Cultural Heritage: Cyprus after the 1974 Turkish Invasion*
    by Michael Jansen

15. *Cyprus: A Contemporary Problem in Historical Perspective*
by Van Coufoudakis

16. *Fettered Independence: Cyprus, 1878–1964*
by Stella Soulioti

17. *International Aggression and Violations of Human Rights: The Case of Turkey in Cyprus*
by Van Coufoudakis

18. *The International Decorative Arts Exposition in St. Petersburg, 1908*
by Ann T. Walton

19. *Russia's Dissident Old Believers, 1650–1950*
edited by Georg B. Michels and Robert L. Nichols

20. *Partition through Foreign Aggression: The Case of Turkey in Cyprus*
by William Mallinson

21. *Mysteries from the History of Ancient Music*
by Evgeny V. Gertsman

22. *Permanent Revolution: A Study of the Early Soviet State*
by Elizabeth A. Harry